Informal Logic

Informal Logic is an introductory guidebook to the basic principles of constructing sound arguments and criticizing bad ones. Non-technical in approach, it is based on 186 examples, which Douglas Walton, a leading authority in the field of informal logic, discusses and evaluates in clear, illustrative detail. Walton explains how errors, fallacies, and other key failures of argument occur. He shows how correct uses of argument are based on sound strategies for reasoned persuasion and critical responses. Among the many subjects covered are: forms of valid argument, defeasible arguments, relevance, appeals to emotion, personal attack, straw man argument, jumping to a conclusion, uses and abuses of expert opinion, problems in drawing conclusions from polls and statistics, loaded terms, equivocation, arguments from analogy, and techniques of posing, replying to, and criticizing questions.

This edition takes into account many new developments in the field of argumentation study that have occurred since 1989, many created by the author. Drawing on these developments, Walton includes and analyzes thirty-six new topical examples and also brings in recent work on argumentation schemes.

Ideally suited for use in courses in informal logic and introduction to philosophy, this book will also be valuable to students of pragmatics, rhetoric, and speech communication.

Douglas Walton is Distinguished Research Fellow of CRRAR (Centre for Research in Reasoning, Argumentation and Rhetoric) at the University of Windsor, and Assumption University Chair in Argumentation Studies (University of Windsor). The author of more than thirty books, he has received major research grants from the Social Sciences and Humanities Research Council of Canada and the Isaak Walton Killam Memorial Foundation. He was awarded the ISSA Prize by the International Society for the Study of Argumentation for his contributions to research on fallacies, argumentation, and informal logic, among many honors he has received for his achievements.

Informal Logic

A PRAGMATIC APPROACH

Second Edition

Douglas Walton
University of Winnipeg

CAMBRIDGE
UNIVERSITY PRESS

CAMBRIDGE UNIVERSITY PRESS
Cambridge, New York, Melbourne, Madrid, Cape Town,
Singapore, São Paulo, Delhi, Mexico City

Cambridge University Press
32 Avenue of the Americas, New York, NY 10013-2473, USA

www.cambridge.org
Information on this title: www.cambridge.org/9780521713801

First published 1989
Second edition published 2008
9th printing 2012

A catalog record for this publication is available from the British Library.

Library of Congress Cataloging in Publication Data

Walton, Douglas N.
Informal logic : a pragmatic approach / Douglas Walton. – 2nd ed.
    p.   cm.
Includes bibliographical references and index.
ISBN 978-0-521-88617-8 (hardback) – ISBN 978-0-521-71380-1 (pbk.)
1. Logic. 2. Reasoning. I. Title.
BC177.W324   2008
168–dc22   2007042373

ISBN 978-0-521-88617-8 Hardback
ISBN 978-0-521-71380-1 Paperback

For Karen, with love.

Contents

Preface

The purpose of this handbook is to furnish the reader with the basic methods of critical analysis of arguments, as they occur in natural language in the real marketplace of persuasion on controversial issues in politics, law, science, and all aspects of daily life. This is very much a practical (applied) subject, because each individual argument is, to some extent, unique. The technique of applying the general guidelines of criticism for each type of argumentation scheme to each individual case requires practical skills of good judgment and judicious interpretation in identifying the argument, and sorting out the main thread of the argument from the discourse it is contained in. These are pragmatic skills requiring prior identification of the type of dialogue in which an argument occurs.

Logical semantics is an important subject in its own right. It is the construction of consistent and complete theories based on semantical constants and the use of variables. Chapter 5 is about semantics, but the remaining eight chapters are mainly about the pragmatics of argumentation. For the most part, applying critical rules of good argument to argumentative discourse on controversial issues in natural language is an essentially pragmatic endeavor. It is a job requiring many of the traditional skills associated with the humanities: empathy, a critical perspective, careful attention to language, the ability to deal with vagueness and ambiguity, balanced recognition of the stronger and weaker points of an argument that is less than perfectly good or perfectly bad, a careful look at the evidence behind a claim, the skill of identifying conclusions, sorting out the main line of argument from a mass of verbiage, and the critical acumen needed to question claims based on expert knowledge in specialized claims or arguments.

A basic requirement of critical argumentation is that any argument that a critic attempts to evaluate must be set out and sympathetically appreciated in the context of dialogue in which the argument occurs. This means that we must sometimes contend with lengthy and complex arguments, and we must sometimes probe in depth into the unstated parts of an argument, into the arguer's position and commitments as indicated by the evidence of the text, and into the question that the argument was supposed to answer. This requirement means that if a criticism is to be made of an argument, or if the argument is to be called weak, erroneous, or even fallacious, substantial justification for the reasonableness of the criticism must be given in the form of documented evidence from the actual wording and context of the given argument. This dialectical type of approach to the study of arguments means that the question-answer context of an argument is crucially important to bring out in all reasoned criticism and analysis of arguments. Thus every argument is conceived along the lines of a challenge-response model of interactive dialogue, where two people "reason together." Some of the most important types of contexts of argumentation will be profiles of sequences of question-answer dialogue on disputed subjects. Thus generally the theory of informal logic must be based on the concept of question-reply dialogue as a form of interaction between two participants, each representing one side of an argument, on a disputed question.

As Erik Krabbe (1985) has indicated, the concept of critical argument analysis as a dialogue logic deserves to be the cornerstone of the emerging theories of argumentation now the subject of so much interest. In recent times, the attention to the classical logic of propositions and its extensions has begun to shift, through the need for a practical approach to the study of arguments, towards a pragmatic conception of reasonable dialogue as a normative structure for argument. This shift has been signalled by the appearance of many new practically oriented textbooks but also by scholarly work in this emerging field. Two new important journals have recently begun publication – *Informal Logic* and *Argumentation* – and the Association for Informal Logic and Critical Thinking, as well as the International Society for the Study of Argumentation, have been founded. On June 26–28, 1978, the First International Symposium on Informal Logic was held at the University of Windsor. In more recent years, the development of argumentation systems has become an increasingly important research topic in computing, especially in the area of artificial intelligence. The first international conference on computational models of argument (COMMA) was held in the Department of Computer Science at the University of Liverpool in September 2006. Topics studied included systems for learning through argument, tools for supporting argumentation, dialogue-based argument systems, and computational properties of argumentation (Dunne and Bench-Capon 2006). These trends point to a welcome shift towards the practical in logic, accompanied by a growing use of argumentation theory in computing, and a resurgence of interest in the study of argumentation generally.

At this point in the history of the subject, it is timely to raise the terminological question of whether it should still be called 'informal logic' or something else, such as 'argumentation'. It is good that the term 'logic' should be retained, but it is a problem that for the purposes of computing, an exact science, any useful system of analyzing and evaluating arguments needs to be at least partly formal. Standardized forms of argument that represent common species of arguments encountered in everyday conversational argumentation need to have a precise, partly formal structure. However, these forms of argument also have a pragmatic factor. As a result, the practice is arising in artificial intelligence of calling these forms of argument semi-formal. Verheij (2003, 172) has described them as "semi-formal rules of inference" or "semi-formal argument templates". What is happening now could be described as a movement from informal logic to semi-formal logic. By these lights, a more suitable title for this book might be *Semi-formal Logic*, but the title *Informal Logic* has been retained (but with the new subtitle, *A Pragmatic Approach*), to preserve continuity with the first edition.

Whatever happens in the next few years in the theory of argumentation study, it is clear that a new approach to logic and argument study has already begun to be taught in logic classes around the world, and has been taken up not only in philosophy but in fields like computing, linguistics, and speech communication. While that new logic is based on new theoretical foundations, including abstract structures of formal dialogues and pragmatic structures of discourse analysis, at the same time it is a subject that has moved much closer to many of the traditional aims of the humanities through a more practical approach to the study of particular arguments in natural language.

Acknowledgments

The work in the first edition was supported by a Killam Research Fellowship, a Fellowship from the Netherlands Institute for Advanced Studies in the Humanities and Social Sciences, and a research grant from the Social Sciences and Humanities Research Council of Canada. The techniques used were much refined and improved by discussions with Frans van Eemeren and Rob Grootendorst during workshops and discussions at the University of Amsterdam, and also by many discussions with Erik Krabbe during a five-month period of joint research on a related project at NIAS in 1987–1988.

Another important stimulus in writing the first edition was the International Conference on Argumentation in Amsterdam in June 1986. Among other colleagues whose papers, conversations, or correspondences were particularly helpful in shaping ideas in the present work, I would like to thank Francisca Snoeck Henkemans, Tjark Kruiger, Johan Kaufmann, John Woods, Bob Binkley, Jim Mackenzie, William Mann, Henry W. Johnstone, Jr., Dick Epstein, Max Cresswell, Michael Wreen, Christoph Lumer, Tony Blair, John Haugland, Ralph Johnson, Michael Schmitt, Trudy Govier, John Biro, Ed Damer, Maurice Finocchiaro, Alan Brinton, and Michel Meyer. Terry Moore, the editor of the first edition, suggested writing a second edition. I respected his judgment and enjoyed his company. I miss Terry, and after he died in 2004, I kept his advice in mind, and it was what led to my writing the second edition.

There were some influences on my thinking about the subjects in the second edition of this book that should be acknowledged. A discussion forum that shaped my views on some pragmatic aspects of relevance was the conference Relevance in Argumentation, held in June 1991, at McMaster University. Among the participants with whom I discussed the problem of relevance at the conference, I would especially like to thank Frans van Eemeren and Rob Grootendorst again, as well as Scott Jacobs and Sally Jackson, Chris Tindale, John Woods, Tony Blair, Jim Freeman, David Hitchcock, and Erik Krabbe. For support in the form of a Research Grant in 1994–1997, and another one in 1999, I would like to thank the

Social Sciences and Humanities Research Council of Canada. I would also like to thank the Canada–U.S. Fulbright Foundation for a Senior Fulbright Fellowship in 1999, and the Department of Communication Studies of Northwestern University for hosting me as Visiting Professor during that period. While I was at Northwestern, discussions with Jean Goodwin and Michael Leff were instrumental in refining many of my views on relevance, and other pragmatic features of argumentation.

I learned a lot about new developments in computing that turned out to be central to my changing views on argumentation theory at the Symposium on Argument and Computation at Bonskeid House in Perthshire, Scotland, in June and July 2000. I would especially like to thank Tim Norman and Chris Reed for organizing the conference, and for what they taught me during the tutorials and discussions at the conference. The following conference participants also deserve thanks for informing me about the state of the art of AI and clarifying many questions related to defeasible reasoning: Trevor Bench-Capon, Daniela Carbogim, Jim Crosswhite, Aspassia Daskalopulu, John Fox, Jim Freeman, Janne Maaike Gerlofs, Michael Gilbert, Rod Girle, Floriana Grasso, Leo Groarke, Corin Gurr, David Hitchcock, Hanns Hohmann, Erik Krabbe, Peter McBurney, Henry Prakken, Theodore Scaltsas, Simone Stumpf, and Bart Verheij.

Finally, I would like to give special thanks to Tom Gordon, Henry Prakken, Chris Reed, and Bart Verheij, for many discussions over the period of 1997–2007 that helped to sharpen my grasp of how crucial questions should be used as tools for analyzing and evaluating argumentation. My thanks as well to Rita Campbell for creating the index, and to Anahid Melikian for help with proofreading.

Informal Logic

1

Argument as reasoned dialogue

The goal of this book is to help the reader use critical methods to impartially and reasonably evaluate the strengths and weaknesses of arguments. The many examples of arguments studied in this text are familiar, yet controversial specimens from such sources as political debates, legal arguments, international disputes on foreign policy, scientific controversies, consumer decision-making questions, ethical problems, and health issues. Any argument, including contexts of lively debate, conflict of opinion, reasoned persuasion, questioning, criticism or cross-examination, can be usefully analyzed by the methods that follow.

It is to be emphasized that the methods of this undertaking are essentially practical. They come as much or more under the topic of what is properly called logical pragmatics, as opposed to (semantical) logical theory. Logical theory traditionally has tended to emphasize semantic relationships, that is, relationships between sets of true or false propositions (the subject-matter of chapter 5 in this text). Logical pragmatics has to do with the use of these propositions by an arguer to carry out a goal of dialogue in reasoning with a second participant in the dialogue. One common and important type of goal is to successfully convince or persuade another arguer with whom the first arguer is engaged in reasoned dialogue. In logical theory, an argument is a set of propositions, nothing more or less. And all that matters is the truth or falsehood of these propositions. The wider context of dialogue is not taken into account. In logical pragmatics, an argument is a claim which, according to appropriate procedures of reasonable dialogue, should be relevant to proving or establishing the arguer's conclusion at issue.

Logical semantics then, is centrally concerned with the propositions that make up an argument. Logical pragmatics is concerned with the reasoned use of those propositions in dialogue to carry out a goal, for example, to build or refute a case to support one's side of a contentious issue in a context of dialogue. It is concerned with what is done with those propositions in a context of dialogue, what use is made of them, to convince another arguer. Logical pragmatics is a practical discipline, an applied art.

1

The distinction between semantics and pragmatics can be picturesquely illustrated by considering the following dialogue (Levinson 1983, p. 292):

Example 1.0

A: I have a fourteen-year-old son.
B: Well that's all right.
A: I also have a dog.
B: Oh I'm sorry.

Looked at in isolation from a context, this conversation seems bizarre, but looked at in the context of a conversation about apartment rental, we can see that it is comprehensible immediately. Once we know that B is the supervisor of an apartment complex and that A is looking for an apartment to rent, the dialogue seems natural and no longer bizarre. We know that while children are typically allowed in apartments, allowing a tenant to keep a dog in the apartment may be a problem. From the pragmatic point of view, made evident by filling in the wider context of the dialogue, we can see that B's last move in the dialogue was perfectly appropriate. The participants in the conversation know that they are apartment supervisor and potential tenant, so of course the dialogue makes sense to them.

A typical problem of logical pragmatics is that in a given argument, various important factors of the context of dialogue can be unclear, vague, ambiguous, and generally problematic to pin down. Or they may simply not be known, as in the case of the dialogue above. It may not be clear what the real issue is supposed to be. It may not even be clear what the argument is. Before an argument, or what looks like an argument, can be evaluated as strong or weak, good or bad, it may be a non-trivial job to pin down just what the argument is, or may be taken to be. Much of the work of logical pragmatics is in this preliminary phase of clearing up or clarifying exactly what the argument may reasonably be taken to be.

Of course, it is well known that applying any theory to real, complex objects as they occur in ordinary experience and issues is a project that has certain problems unique to this type of practical endeavor. And so it is with practical logic. Each raw, given argument must be approached with care, and the best use made of the evidence that is given, if it is to be reasonably evaluated. From the pragmatic point of view, any particular argument should be seen as being advanced in the context of a particular dialogue setting. Sensitivity to the special features of different contexts of dialogue is a requirement for the reasoned analysis of an argument.

2

1.1 TYPES OF ARGUMENTATIVE DIALOGUE

Dialogue is a sequence of exchanges of messages or speech acts between two (or more) participants. Typically however, dialogue is an exchange of questions and replies between two parties. Every dialogue has a goal, and requires co-operation between the participants to fulfill the goal. This means that each participant has an obligation to work towards fulfilling his own goal in the dialogue, and also an obligation to co-operate with the other participant's fulfillment of his goal. The basic reason why any argument can be criticized as a bad argument always comes down to a failure to meet one of these basic obligations.

One context of dialogue is the *personal quarrel*, characterized by aggressive personal attack, heightened appeal to emotions, and the desire to win the argument at all costs. The quarrel is characterized by bitter recriminations, a loss of balanced perspective, and afterwards, most often regret for excessive personal attacks that were not meant or deserved. The quarrel is no friend of logic, and frequently represents argument at its worst. The goal of the quarrel is for each arguer to attack or "hit" one's opponent at all costs, using any means, whether reasonable, fair, or not. Thus the quarrel is characterized by the fallacious *ad hominem* attack (attack against the person, rather than the argument), and by emotional arguments that would not be judged relevant by more reasonable standards of argument. The quarrel is classified as an eristic type of dialogue (from the Greek word *eris*, meaning a fight or adversarial confrontation), in which each party tries to attack and defeat the other.

The quarrel represents the lowest level of argument. Reasonable standards of good argument should be designed to prevent argument from deteriorating into the personal quarrel. Most of the logical lessons to be drawn from the quarrel turn out to be pathological. The quarrel too often represents the bad argument, the heated argument, the medium of fallacies, vicious attacks and one-sided criticisms that should be avoided or discouraged by reasonable dialogue. When an argument descends to the level of the quarrel, it is usually in deep trouble.

Another context of dialogue is the (*forensic*) *debate*. The forensic debate is more regulated than the quarrel. In a debate there are judges or referees who determine, perhaps by voting, which side had the better argument. The debate is regulated by rules of procedure that determine when each arguer may speak, and how long each may speak. In some cases, a debate may be judged by an audience who may take a vote at the conclusion of the debate, the majority of voters determining who won the debate.

3

The forensic debate is more congenial to logical reasoning than the personal quarrel is, because the outcome is decided by a third party who is not subject to the personal attacks that may be contained in the arguments. Also, some debates are controlled by rules that disallow the more severe forms of personal attack and other aggressive or fallacious tactics. The rules of the forensic debate are often very permissive, however, and may allow all kinds of fallacious arguments. Sometimes very damaging personal allegations are allowed in questions, and the answerer may be hard-pressed to respond to extremely aggressive questions while trying to answer. Such fallacious moves may not only be tolerated, but even praised as good tactics of debating.

Clearly, the debate is a step above the personal quarrel, from the point of view of logic.[1] However, the basic purpose of the forensic debate is to win a verbal victory against your opponent, by impressing the audience (or referee) of the debate. This means that fallacious arguments and personal attacks are a good idea, if they help you to win the argument. In other words, a successful argument, in the context of a debate, is not necessarily a reasonable argument from the standpoint of logic. It may be good strategy to *appear* to have a reasonable argument, but really having a reasonable argument is not the main thing. The main thing is to win the debate. Consequently, the standards of good forensic debate do not necessarily or reliably represent good standards of reasonable argument.

A third context of argument is that of *persuasion dialogue*,[2] also sometimes called *critical discussion*. In this type of dialogue, there are two participants, each of whom has a thesis (conclusion) to prove. The main method of persuasion dialogue is for each participant to prove his own thesis by the rules of inference from the concessions of the other participant.[3] If you and I are engaged in persuasion dialogue, my goal is to persuade you of my thesis. And hence my obligation should be to prove that thesis from premises that you accept or are committed to. Your obligation is to prove your thesis from premises that I accept or am committed to (figure 1.1).[4]

The goal of persuasion dialogue (critical discussion) is to persuade the other party of your thesis (conclusion, point of view), and the method

---

1 For more on the quarrel and debate as models of argument, see Walton (1998a).
2 See Walton (1984), Walton and Krabbe (1995) and Prakken (2006). The notion of reasonable dialogue as a regulated structure of logical reasoning was systematically analyzed by Lorenzen (1986) and Hamblin (1970).
3 Theoretical models of this type of dialogue in reasoned argument are outlined in Hintikka (1981) and Barth and Krabbe (1982).
4 See Krabbe (1985).

Figure 1.1. Obligations of persuasion dialogue (critical discussion).

is to prove your thesis.[5] However, two kinds of proof may be involved. *Internal proof* by a participant means proof by inferring a proposition from the other participant's concessions in the dialogue. This is the primary method of persuasion dialogue. Persuasion dialogue can also be facilitated by the bringing in of external scientific evidence. *External proof* entails the introduction of "new facts" into the argument by appealing to scientific evidence or expert opinion of a third party or group of expert sources.[6] Guidelines for the use of external proof in persuasion dialogue are studied in chapters 7 and 8. Once a proposition is advanced by one participant on the basis of external proof, and accepted by the other participant, it can then be appealed to as a premise suitable for an internal proof.

Although the primary obligation of a participant in persuasion dialogue is to prove his thesis from the other participant's concessions, a secondary obligation to co-operate with the other participant's attempts to prove his thesis also exists. This obligation requires giving helpful and honest replies to the other participant's questions, in order to allow him to extract commitments from you in dialogue that can then be used as premises in his arguments.[7] Argument in persuasion dialogue is based on the concessions of the other party, and a participant is free to concede any proposition he cares to.

In another type of dialogue, called the *inquiry*, premises can only be propositions that are known to be true, that have been established as reliable knowledge to the satisfaction of all parties to the inquiry. An example of an inquiry would be the kind of official investigation conducted in the

---

5 The concept of a critical discussion is outlined in van Eemeren and Grootendorst (1984).

6 Van Eemeren and Grootendorst (1984, p. 167) refer to an intersubjective testing procedure in dialogue as a method whereby the participants agree on how they will determine what is acceptable as evidence in an argument.

7 This idea was modeled precisely in the formal structure of persuasion dialogue presented in Prakken (2006).

case of an air crash disaster. The Warren Commission Report on the death of John F. Kennedy, which attempted to determine the known facts relevant to the assassination, and thereby produce a proof of an established conclusion, was an inquiry that many have been skeptical about. However, the intent of an inquiry is to remove such doubt by conclusively proving some designated proposition.

By contrast, a persuasion dialogue might typically be on an issue like "Is socialism the best form of government?" where the goal is not conclusive proof of one side or the other of the issue, but an evaluation of the persuasiveness of the arguments on both sides.[8] Such arguments can reveal important convictions and reasons for personal commitments on an issue, even if the goal is not to establish conclusive proof based on premises known to be true.

The basic goal of the inquiry is increment of knowledge, and therefore the inquiry is an essentially *cumulative* type of dialogue, meaning that retraction of commitment is not anticipated. The inquiry too is based on an initial position, but the position here is a certain degree of lack of knowledge which needs to be overcome. Thus the inquiry seeks out *proof*, or the establishment of as much certainty as can be obtained by the given evidence. Evidential priority is the key feature of the inquiry, for the inquiry is strongly directed towards deriving conclusions from premises that can be well established on solid evidence. This contrasts with persuasion dialogue, where the best one can hope for is plausible commitment to an opinion based on reasoned (but not conclusive) evidence.

In the inquiry, the participants are supposed to be neutral investigators of an objective truth, to the extent that is possible. The inquiry is a cooperative rather than an adversarial context of dialogue.[9] Logical proof is important in the inquiry, but the method may vary with the subject-matter or area of the inquiry. Inquiry most often purports to be "scientific" and "factual" in its methods and standards.

In *negotiation dialogue*, the primary goal is self-interest, and the method is to bargain. Bargaining makes no pretensions to be an objective inquiry into the truth of a matter. Indeed, negotiation, in contrast to persuasion dialogue, need not involve commitment to the truth of propositions, or

---

8 This function of dialogue that reveals concealed commitments is brought out in the analysis of Walton (1984, ch. 5).
9 Reasonable evaluation of any argument always involves the given data of a text of discourse to be analyzed. Common but unstated presumptions of the arguer and the evaluator also play a role in the evaluation.

conviction that ideals are based on strong arguments. In negotiation, opinions about what is true, or convictions about what is believable, are not centrally at stake, and may even be contravened by a good negotiator. The concessions in bargaining are not commitments in the same sense as in persuasion dialogue, but trade-offs that can be sacrificed for gains elsewhere. The position now becomes a bargaining position. Logical proof is not important in negotiation dialogue, for this type of dialogue is completely adversarial.[10] This type of dialogue is frankly based on personal gain, and makes no pretense of being neutral or objective, or of being an inquiry into truth. Coalitions may be made with partners, but the objective is always self-interest in "making a good deal."

The negotiation type of dialogue is called the *interest-based conflict* by Moore (1986, p. 74) who describes it as "competitive cooperation" where "the disputants are collaborating to compete for the same set of goods or benefits" in conditions of "perceived or actual scarcity." In this situation, gains for one participant may mean losses for another. The dialogue is a kind of trading of concessions to the satisfaction of both participants.

Some cases of argumentative discourse combine two or more of these different types of dialogue. For example, a divorce dispute may begin as a competition to see which party is to obtain custody of the children. However, if the dialogue turns to a consideration of the issue of which party is best suited to look after the children, the dialogue may cease to be an interest-based bargaining dialogue, and become a persuasion dialogue. This particular shift in the context of dialogue could be highly constructive and beneficial. It may betoken a shift from the individual interests of the husband and wife to a wider consideration of what is best for everyone, including the children. Often a shift from the negotiation model to the persuasion model is a good step.

Although the persuasion, inquiry, and negotiation types of dialogue are among the most basic types for the purpose of studying the fundamental kinds of reasoned criticism in argumentation, there are three other basic types of dialogue that need to be taken into account. One is the *information-seeking* type of dialogue, where one party has the goal of finding information that the other party is believed to possess. Another is the *action-seeking* type of dialogue recognized by Mann (1988) where the goal of one party is to bring it about that the other party carries out a specific

10 The exception occurs in the kind of case where there is a shift from negotiation to persuasion dialogue. In this case giving reasons to convincingly support a claim can help the negotiation dialogue move forward.

Table 1.1 *Types of dialogue*

Type of dialogue	Initial situation	Participant's goal	Goal of dialogue
Persuasion	Conflict of opinions	Persuade other party	Resolve or clarify issue
Inquiry	Need to have proof	Find and verify evidence	Prove (disprove) hypothesis
Negotiation	Conflict of interests	Get what you most want	Reasonable settlement both can live with
Information-seeking	Need information	Acquire or give information	Exchange information
Deliberation	Dilemma or practical choice	Co-ordinate goals and actions	Decide best available course of action
Eristic	Personal conflict	Verbally hit out at opponent	Reveal deeper basis of conflict

course of action. Yet another type is the *educational* dialogue where one party (the teacher) has the goal of imparting knowledge to the other party (the student). Each of these models of dialogue has a different initial situation, and different rules of procedure for arriving at the goal from the initial situation.

The properties of the six basic types of dialogue are summarized in table 1.1 (Walton 2006, p. 183). From the point of view of critical argumentation taken in this book, persuasion dialogue (critical discussion) is the single most important type of dialogue. It represents an ideal, or normative model of reasoned dialogue, because it has normative rules that, taken together, set a standard of how rational argument used to persuade should take place. However, it is important to be able to recognize the other types of dialogue indicated above, because significant errors and misunderstandings may occur when there is a dialogue shift (dialectical shift) from one type of dialogue to another. If such a shift goes unnoticed, it can lead to misinterpretations, errors, and fallacies of argumentation.

1.2 COMPONENTS OF ARGUMENTATIVE DIALOGUE

Any sequence of argumentative dialogue can be broken down into three stages.[11] In the *opening stage*, the type of dialogue should be specified. At

11 There are four stages of dialogue in the account of van Eemeren and Grootendorst (1984). They divide what is called the opening stage into two stages called the confrontation stage

this stage, the participants should agree to engage in a specific type of dialogue, or at least indicate their willingness to take part in a certain type of dialogue. All good dialogue has procedural rules, and the rules of the dialogue should be as clear as possible to the participants, as part of the opening stage of the dialogue. In some cases, these rules are explicitly stated or codified, e.g., in a criminal trial. In conversation, these rules are usually matters of custom and politeness which set normal expectations of dialogue conduct (rules of Gricean[12] implicature). Nevertheless, the rules can be explicitly stated, and agreed to by the participants, where it is useful and necessary, at the opening stage.

There are four kinds of dialogue rules. The *locution rules* state the kind of speech acts or locutions that are allowed. For example, typically in persuasion dialogue, questions and assertions are permissible locutions. The *dialogue rules* specify turn-taking, and other questions of when participants are allowed or required to advance locutions. The *commitment rules* specify how each type of locution leads to commitments on the part of a participant. For example, an assertion of a proposition by a participant is immediately followed by the inserting of this proposition into his store of commitments. Finally, the *strategic (win-loss) rules* determine what sequence of locutions constitutes fulfillment of the goal of the dialogue.

All dialogue arises from a problem, difference of opinion, or question to be resolved that has two sides. The two sides constitute the *issue* of the dialogue. The *opening stage* is the stage where the issue of the dialogue must be announced, agreed upon, or clarified, so that the goal of each participant in the dialogue is clearly agreed upon. At this stage, both parties agree to use the methods of argumentation appropriate for this type of dialogue, and to follow the rules for using these methods.

The *argumentation stage* is the middle stage, where each side puts forward its arguments to defend its view, and also puts forward criticisms and objections to the other party's view. During this stage, the obligation of each party in contributing to or fulfilling the goal of the dialogue must be carried out by the appropriate methods. A participant has an obligation to make a serious effort to fulfill his own goal in the dialogue. He also has an obligation to allow the other party to fulfill his obligation. These obligations imply certain dialogue rules. For example, they require that

and the opening stage. We have recognized only three stages to emphasize that a dialogue always has a start point, an end point, and a sequence of argumentation between.
12 Grice (1975).

participants take turns in an orderly fashion, to give the other party a reasonable opportunity to reply to a question or make a point.

The *closing stage* of a dialogue is the point where the goal of the dialogue has been fulfilled, or where the participants agree that the dialogue can end. There are proper ways of closing a dialogue, and this has implications for rules of how a good dialogue should be conducted. A participant should not try to opt out illicitly just because things do not seem to be going his way. And in general, participants must continue to carry on with a dialogue, following the rules, until the dialogue is properly closed.

These general requirements of the four stages of dialogue imply other rules that are applicable to specific problems encountered in the remaining chapters of this book. *Relevance rules* require that a participant not wander too far off the point (the goal of dialogue), or he can be challenged. *Co-operativeness rules* require that a respondent answer questions co-operatively and accept commitments if they reflect his position accurately. *Informativeness rules* require that a participant tailor his arguments to what his respondent knows or does not know. A participant should provide enough information to convince his respondent, but not provide more information than is required or useful for that purpose.

Section 1.3 illustrates how these rules specifically apply to the type of dialogue called persuasion dialogue. Section 1.4 itemizes some negative rules or prohibitions that indicate some important types of faults or failures of persuasion dialogue. Section 1.5 gives an introductory survey of some of the most important of these failures that are especially significant to watch out for in argumentation, because they can be used as systematic, clever tactics of deception to cheat and trick you.

1.3 PERSUASION DIALOGUE (CRITICAL DISCUSSION)

As illustrated in figure 1.1, each participant in a persuasion dialogue is supposed to use arguments exclusively composed of premises that are commitments of the other participant. This obligation is an important feature of persuasion dialogue. It is an important kind of failure of an argument that it is not based on such premises, but on propositions that the party whom it is intended to persuade does not accept. Certain important fallacies, as will be shown below, violate this requirement. Generally, a persuasion dialogue can be successful only if both of the parties base their arguments on each other's commitments. They must try to persuade each other using the strongest and most probing arguments possible, to reveal both the weaknesses and strengths of their opponent's arguments

10

and those of their own arguments as well. They must ask critical questions that respond to or rebut the arguments of the opposed side. They should not try to avoid either of these obligations.

A persuasion dialogue can be of two basic types. In an asymmetrical persuasion dialogue, the type of obligation of the one participant is different from that of the other. In the symmetrical persuasion dialogue, both participants have the same types of obligations. Example 1.1 is an instance of an asymmetrical persuasion dialogue.

Example 1.1   asymmetrical

Karl is a committed believer in God who is trying to convince Erik that God exists. Erik is not convinced by Karl's arguments and raises many doubts. Erik is not an atheist, but calls himself an agnostic.

In this case, the obligations of Karl and Erik are of different types. Karl has taken upon himself to try to prove to Erik the positive thesis that God exists. Erik is a doubter (agnostic). He is not trying to prove the negative thesis that God does not exist. His obligation is only to raise questions which reflect his doubts about the acceptability of Karl's arguments.

By contrast, example 1.2 is a case of a symmetrical persuasion dialogue.

definiting   Black or

Example 1.2   Symmetrical.   white.

Mary is a committed atheist who is arguing that God does not exist. Barbara is a believer in God, and she is trying to convince Mary that God does exist. Each person is trying to refute the thesis of the other.

In example 1.2, both Mary and Barbara have the same type of obligation, namely to prove her thesis. We could say that both have a positive burden of proof, whereas in example 1.1, only Karl had a positive burden of proving his thesis. Erik had only the negative burden of throwing doubts on Karl's proof.[13] A symmetrical persuasion dialogue is sometimes called a dispute, as contrasted with a dissent, the shorter term for an asymmetrical persuasion dialogue.

In a persuasion dialogue, the basic goal is to prove a thesis in order to resolve an issue. Hence the primary obligation in a persuasion dialogue is a *burden of proof*, meaning that the participant with an obligation to prove

---

13 See Walton (1988) for a conceptual outline of burden of proof.

has the "burden" (or obligation) to carry out this task. In the symmetrical persuasion dialogue (or dispute), both parties have a burden of proof.[14]

In a case like example 1.2, a dispute, we also say that the obligations of the two participants are *strongly opposed*, meaning that one is obliged to prove a thesis which is the opposite (negation) of the thesis which the other is obliged to prove. However, in a case like example 1.1, a dissent, we say that the obligations of the two participants are *weakly opposed*, meaning that one is obliged to resist, question, or not accept the attempts to prove the thesis of the other, but he is not obliged to prove the opposite of the other's thesis. In such a case, we say that the one participant has a burden of proof, but the other does not. The other player has a lighter burden – it is only a burden of raising questions.

The following example is a case of a symmetrical persuasion dialogue which shows strong opposition of the participants.

Example 1.3

Bob: Tipping is good because it rewards excellence of service. If excellence is rewarded, it leads to better effort, and to better work. Therefore, tipping should be maintained as a practice.

Helen: If a person is doing a good job, they should get regular pay which reflects the worth of the work. A worker should not have to depend on the whims of their clients to get an appropriate salary. Therefore, tipping should not be maintained as a practice.

Bob's conclusion (prefaced by the word 'therefore') is the opposite of Helen's conclusion (prefaced by the same conclusion indicator word). This textual evidence indicates that the persuasion dialogue in example 1.3 is symmetrical.

One important component of persuasion dialogue is the arguer's position.[15] Let us imagine that the dialogue in example 1.3 is carried further, and that through the course of the argument, it becomes evident that each of the two participants has certain distinctive commitments. Bob is committed to tipping as an acceptable practice because it is a free-market economy exchange. Helen is against tipping because leaving such decisions to the vicissitudes of the free-market economy is not necessarily fair or equitable, in her view. She favors government regulation to assure every

---

14 How the concept of burden of proof is important to the theory of argument is well established in Rescher (1976).
15 Walton (1985a).

working person a steady income based on the comparable worth of his or her job. Thus each has revealed a position, defined by those commitments which they have incurred in their questions and replies.

Once we have followed through the whole course of the argument, we get a picture of which propositions each arguer is committed to. According to the conception of argument modeled in Hamblin (1970), the most fundamental aspect of argument as persuasion dialogue is that each participant in the dialogue must have a set of commitments called a commitment-store. Physically speaking, a commitment-set can be visualized as a set of statements written out in a list on a blackboard. Or it could be visualized as a set of propositions recorded in the memory of a computer. The point is, in any event, that a commitment-store must be a definite set of propositions. It can be an empty set, unless the thesis of each participant must be counted as an initial, given commitment of that participant.

What Hamblin calls a commitment-set of a player we here call, collectively, the position of that participant in persuasion dialogue. Hamblin thinks of the commitment-set as being visible to all the participants. However, it does not necessarily need to be visible to all or any players at all or any times. All that is required is that it be a definite set of propositions. The idea is that as the game of dialogue proceeds, propositions are added to, or deleted from the commitment-sets of each of the players, according to the rules of the dialogue. As shown by Walton and Krabbe (1995), sometimes participants will have to retract a commitment, for example, if they are shown that it is inconsistent with their other commitments.

The goal of a persuasion dialogue sets the burden of proof. But it is important to recognize that there can be differing standards of strictness for meeting this requirement. The most strict standard is set for the *deductively valid argument*, which requires that it be logically impossible for the conclusion to be false while the premises are true. Suppose that Helen were to argue as follows, in the dialogue on tipping.

Example 1.4   deductively

Every person who does a good job should get regular pay that reflects the value of their work.

Alice is a person who does a good job.

Therefore, Alice should get regular pay that reflects the value of her work.

This argument is deductively valid, meaning that if the premises are true, then the conclusion *must* be true. There is no weaseling out of the conclusion, if you accept the premises. In other words, it is logically impossible for the conclusion to be false and the premises true.

But suppose Helen had argued as follows.

Example 1.5 ⌐ *Strong*

Most people who do a good job should get regular pay that reflects the value of their work.

Alice is a person who does a good job.

Therefore, Alice should get regular pay that reflects the value of her work.

In this case, the argument is not deductively valid. It might be that the premises are true. Yet even so, the conclusion could possibly be false. But the argument is *inductively strong*, in the sense that if the premises are true, then it is probable that the conclusion is true. Clearly, inductive strength is a less strict requirement for an argument to be successful than deductive validity.

In a third type of argument, called *plausible argument*, the requirement for success is even less strict than that of the inductively strong argument.

Example 1.6 ⌐ *weaker*   It is possible true.

It is widely accepted that people who do a good job should get regular pay that reflects the value of their work.

Alice is a person who does a good job.

Therefore, Alice should get regular pay that reflects the value of her work.

This type of argument is intrinsically weaker. In a plausible argument, if the premises are plausibly true, then the conclusion is as plausibly true as the least plausible premise.[16] This does not mean that it is impossible or even improbable for the conclusion to be false, given that the premises are true. It only means that the conclusion is at least as plausible as the premises. This means that if an arguer is committed to the premises, as part of his position, then he should be no less strongly committed to the conclusion. In other words, if he rejects the conclusion while he is committed to acceptance of the premises, then the burden of proof is placed upon him, by example 1.6 in this case, to show why he does not accept the conclusion as plausible.

16 Rescher (1976, p. 15).

The function of plausible argument is to shift the burden of proof. Many of the types of argument criticisms we will subsequently study are good criticisms to the extent that they successfully serve to shift the burden of proof onto an opponent's side of the argument in persuasion dialogue.

1.4 NEGATIVE RULES OF PERSUASION DIALOGUE

The positive rules of persuasion dialogue provide a *normative model* of good persuasion dialogue, a kind of ideal of dialogue against which particular cases of argumentation can be judged. These positive rules also imply *negative rules* that state prohibitions. Violating these prohibitions can result in errors, faults, and shortcomings, of various kinds, in argumentation.

Certain characteristic types of faults or errors in argumentation have traditionally been classified under the heading of *informal fallacies*, systematically deceptive strategies of argumentation based on an underlying, systematic error of reasoned dialogue. Unfortunately however, the traditional category of informal fallacy has been stretched too widely in traditional accounts, including not only arguments that are weak or incomplete, but even instances of argument that are basically correct and reasonable as mechanisms of argument in persuasion dialogue.

Some violations of negative rules of dialogue are better classified as *blunders* rather than fallacies because they are moves in dialogue that are not systematic or clever deceptions in proving a point, but are simply errors or lapses that damage or weaken the case of their proponent rather than defeating his opponent in the dialogue. Other arguments are incomplete because they do not respond adequately to the critical questions of the participant they were designed to persuade. Such arguments are not "fallacies." They are better classified as weak or incomplete instances of argumentation.

To claim that an argument commits a fallacy is a strong form of criticism implying that the argument has committed a serious logical error, and even more strongly implying that the argument is based on an underlying flaw or misconception of reasoning, and can therefore be refuted. However, we will see that many valuable criticisms of argument that do not completely refute the argument still make an important point of criticism. And indeed to interpret them so strongly would imply an unwarranted dogmatism (itself an error).

A criticism always invites a reply, but a good, well-argued criticism in dialogue also shifts the burden of proof onto the proponent of the argument criticized. However, in order for it to be a reasonable criticism which does call for a reply, there is an obligation on the critic to give reasons for his criticism. We will see, in each chapter, how each type of criticism needs to be documented and backed up, and that many important kinds of fault and error in argumentation consist of failures to answer critical questions.

Those kinds of arguments now called informal fallacies in logic texts are historically descended from what Aristotle called *sophistici elenchi*, meaning sophistical refutations.[17] A sophistical refutation of an argument is a refutation that plausibly appears to be a successful refutation, but is not. The term 'sophistical' refers to a certain trickery or illusion that conceals a logical incorrectness. Both the use of the term *sophistici elenchi* and its descendant "fallacies" have engendered the unfortunate misconception that all kinds of arguments coming under the traditional categories of "fallacies" are inherently bad or worthless, and that all such arguments should, by the standards of logic, be thoroughly refuted in every instance. As explained by Tindale (2007), the fallacies are more complex and deserving of much fuller analyses than the traditional textbook treatments have suggested. The old approach was to simply assign each fallacy a label and automatically declare an argument fallacious if it seemed as if that label could be attached to it. Recent research has indicated that many of the fallacies are instances of reasonable forms of argument, and therefore such forms of argument cannot be automatically dismissed without examining each case in detail (Tindale 2007). The newer approach requires that each argument to be evaluated as fallacious or not needs to be considered in relation not only to the form of the argument, but also in relation to the context of dialogue in which it is embedded.

In section 5, some major informal fallacies (to be studied in subsequent chapters) will be introduced. It will also be indicated how some of these famous fallacies are associated with violations of specific negative rules.

Negative Rules of Persuasion Dialogue

Opening Stage
1. Unlicensed shifts from one type of dialogue to another are not allowed.

Confrontation Stage
1. Unlicensed attempts to change the agenda are not allowed.
2. Refusal to agree to a specific agenda of dialogue prohibits continuing to the argumentation stage.

17 See Hamblin (1970).

16

Argumentation Stage

1. Not making a serious effort to fulfill an obligation is bad strategy. Notable here are failures to meet a burden of proof or to defend a commitment when challenged.
2. Trying to shift your burden of proof to the other party, or otherwise alter the burden of proof illicitly, is not allowed.
3. Purporting to carry out an internal proof by using premises that are not commitments of the other party is not allowed.
4. Appealing to external sources of proof without backing up your argument properly can be subject to objection.
5. Failures of relevance can include providing the wrong thesis, wandering away from the point to be proved, or answering the wrong question in a dialogue.
6. Failure to ask questions that are appropriate for a given stage of dialogue should be prohibited, along with asking questions that are inappropriate.
7. Failure to reply appropriately to questions should not be allowed, including replies that are unduly evasive.
8. Failure to define, clarify, or justify the meaning or definition of a significant term used in an argument, in accordance with standards of precision appropriate to the discussion, is a violation, if the use of this term is challenged by another participant.

Closing Stage

1. A participant must not try to force closure of a dialogue until it is properly closed, either by mutual agreement or by fulfillment of the goal of the dialogue.

These rules are not complete, and it requires judgment to apply them to specific contexts of argumentative discourse. In general however, for every fallacy or blunder in a context of dialogue, there is some rule for the conduct of the discussion that has been broken or tampered with. How strictly the rules are formulated or enforced depends on the specific context of dialogue. For example, rules of relevance may be much more strictly formulated and enforced in a court of law than in a philosophical discussion.

The rules above, however, give the reader the flavor of a persuasion dialogue as a coherent and regulated form of activity. The basic purpose of a persuasion dialogue (critical discussion) is to allow each participant a chance to express his opinions on an issue and to prove them if he can.

17

Such a dialogue should be a free exchange of points of view where probing questions are freely asked and relevant answers are freely given. Each side should have a fair opportunity to express his point of view and to challenge the other's point of view.

However, there are other kinds of dialogue, such as negotiation, for example, where rules may be different in certain respects from those of the persuasion dialogue. Hence dialectical shifts can influence our judgment on whether a certain speech act is "fallacious" or not.

1.5 SOME MAJOR INFORMAL FALLACIES

Several important kinds of errors or deceptive tactics of argumentation are especially significant and have traditionally been labeled as (major) *informal fallacies*. Before proceeding to study these fallacies in depth in each chapter, the reader should be briefly introduced to them.

The *fallacy of many questions* (*complex questions*) occurs where a question is posed in an overly aggressive manner, presupposing commitment to prior answers to questions not yet asked. The strategy of this deception is to try to trap or confuse the answerer into incurring damaging commitments that can be used to defeat him. The classic case is the question, "Have you stopped abusing your spouse?" No matter which way the respondent answers, he (or she) is in trouble. For any direct answer already presumes that the answerer has acknowledged having a spouse whom she (he) has abused in the past. These overly aggressive questioning tactics violate rules 2 and 6 of the argumentation stage, as shown in chapter 2.

The *fallacy of ignoratio elenchi*, also often called the *fallacy of irrelevant conclusion* or the *fallacy of ignoring the issue*, occurs where an argument is directed towards proving the wrong, or an irrelevant conclusion. Such an argument may be valid, but the problem is that it has strayed from the point (failure of relevance; see rule 5). For example, an attorney prosecuting a defendant for murder in a criminal trial may argue successfully that murder is a horrible crime. However, this line of argument may be an emotionally compelling, but misleading distraction if the conclusion the attorney is supposed to be proving is that this particular defendant is guilty of the crime of murder. The fallacy of irrelevance in argumentation most often is a failure of a participant in persuasion dialogue to fulfill his primary obligation to prove his thesis which is supposed to be at issue in the dialogue. When an arguer strays too far from his obligation to stick to the issue of contention, he can (and in many instances) should be challenged on grounds of irrelevance.

18

Several of the fallacies have to do with appeals to emotions like pity, fear, and enthusiasm. Emotions can be distracting in argumentation, and hence these emotional fallacies are often categorized as fallacies of relevance. Emotions can also be used to try to force premature closure of an argument, violating the negative rule for the closing stage.

The fallacy of the *argumentum ad baculum* (appeal to force) is said to be committed by an appeal to force or the threat of force (intimidation) to gain acceptance of a conclusion without giving proper or adequate argument for it. The *argumentum ad misericordiam* is the appeal to pity, and the *argumentum ad populum* is the appeal to the emotions, enthusiasms, or popular feelings of a group audience. Both of these uses of emotional appeals in argument are said to be fallacies where they are used to gain acceptance to a conclusion without fulfilling the obligation of supporting the conclusion by providing strong and relevant evidence to meet a burden of proof. The emotional appeal is used as a cover-up to disguise the lack of solid evidence for a contention when a fallacy of one of these types is perpetrated.

However, the use of emotion in argument is not intrinsically wrong or fallacious in itself. Only the misuse of an emotional appeal should be criticized as fallacious. Plenty of examples of emotional appeals in argumentation are examined in chapter 4. The task of argument analysis is to judge when a given emotional appeal can rightly be criticized, in a particular case, as an irrelevant or fallacious deception or distraction in the argument.

Personal attack in argumentation is always dangerous, and often leads to heightened emotions and bitter quarrels instead of reasoned discussion of an issue. The fallacy of the *argumentum ad hominem* is said to be committed when one person criticizes an argument by attacking the arguer personally instead of considering his argument on its real merits. In some cases, questions of personal conduct and character are relevant to consideration of an argument. But the *ad hominem* fallacy arises when they are not. The following two examples of uses of the argumentum *ad hominem* are quoted in Christopher Cerf and Victor Navasky, *The Experts Speak*.

Example 1.7

"The so-called theories of Einstein are merely the ravings of a mind polluted with liberal, democratic nonsense which is utterly unacceptable to German men of science."[18]

18 Dr. Walter Gross, the Third Reich's official exponent of "Nordic Science," quoted in the *American Mercury*, March 1940, p. 339, as cited in Christopher Cerf and Victor Navasky, *The Experts Speak* (New York; Pantheon, 1984), p. 300.

Example 1.8

"The theory of a relativistic universe is the hostile work of the agents of fascism. It is the revolting propaganda of a moribund, counter-revolutionary ideology."[19]

What is relevant in judging the scientific validity of the theory of relativity is scientific evidence. The personal, moral, or political beliefs of the discoverers or exponents of the theory are not relevant, in the context of a serious, scientific investigation or corroboration of the theory. Hence the use of personal attack in examples 1.7 and 1.8 above is a fallacious type of *argumentum ad hominem*.

Often the *ad hominem* fallacy arises from an illicit dialectical shift from one type of dialogue to another. In examples 1.7 and 1.8, the shift is from a scientific inquiry to a persuasion dialogue concerning political beliefs and personal convictions.

Another type of fallacy is the *argumentum ad verecundiam*, or "appeal to modesty," the misuse of expert opinion or authority-based sources to try to suppress someone's opinion in argument by suggesting that they should not dare to oppose the word of an authority on an issue. Appeal to expert opinion is, in itself, a legitimate form of argumentation, but one that can be employed wrongly, leading to violations of argumentation rule 4.

Some fallacies have to do with induction and statistical reasoning. A case in point is the infamous *post hoc, ergo propter hoc* fallacy of wrongly basing a causal conclusion on a weak statistical correlation between two events. For example, although there may be a genuine statistical correlation between the stork population and the (human) birth rate in Northern Europe, it could be an error to conclude that there is a causal connection between these two things. Citing of statistical sources of evidence can result in violations of argumentation rule 4, studied in chapter 8.

Other fallacies have to do with the use of natural language in argumentation. These problems arise because of the vagueness and ambiguity of terms and phrases in natural language. Vagueness and ambiguity are not inherently bad in themselves, but problems and confusions can arise because of disagreements and misunderstandings about the definitions of controversial words or phrases in an argument. Chapter 9 outlines several important types of fallacies that relate to the meanings of terms in natural language. These fallacies relate to rule 8 of the argumentation stage.

19 *Astronomical Journal of the Soviet Union*, quoted in *The American Mercury*, March 1940, p. 339, cited in ibid.

Among the remaining fallacies to be pointed out, six are noteworthy here as common errors in argumentation which will be subject to analysis in the remaining chapters of this book.

1. The fallacy of the *argumentum ad ignorantiam* (argument from ignorance) could be illustrated by the argument that ghosts must exist because nobody has ever been able to prove that ghosts do not exist. This type of argument illustrates the danger of arguing from ignorance, and shows that failure to disprove a proposition does not necessarily prove it. This fallacy is discussed in section 2.5.

2. The fallacy of equivocation turns on the confusion between two different meanings of a term in the same argument, where there is a contextual shift. Consider the argument, 'All elephants are animals, and Henri is an elephant, and Henri is a small elephant; therefore Henri is a small animal.' The problem here is that the relative term 'small' shifts its meaning when applied to elephants (relatively large animals), as opposed to when it is applied to animals generally. This fallacy is discussed in section 9.3.

3. The straw man fallacy occurs where an arguer's position is misrepresented, by being misquoted, exaggerated, or otherwise distorted, and then this incorrect version is used to attack his argument and try to refute it. For example, an environmentalist may have put forward a reasonable argument for reducing air pollution by using less fossil fuel, and her opponent may then go on the attack by saying, "Your argument is absurd because you want to eliminate private corporations from manufacturing." If the environmentalist never made any claim of this sort, her opponent is guilty of committing the straw man fallacy.

4. The fallacy of arguing in a circle (also called *petitio principii* or begging the question), is when the conclusion to be proved by an arguer is already presupposed by his premises. For example, suppose that Bob, an atheist, asks Leo to prove that God is benevolent, and Leo argues: "God has all the virtues, and benevolence is a virtue; therefore God is benevolent." Bob could object, in this case, that Leo is assuming the very conclusion he is supposed to prove. For Bob doubts whether God has any of the virtues (including benevolence), or even whether God exists at all. Hence Leo's argument begs the question it is supposed to prove. This argument is discussed in section 2.7.

5. The slippery slope fallacy occurs where a proposal is criticized, without sufficient evidence, on the grounds that it will lead, by an inevitable sequence of closely linked consequences, to an end result that is

21

catastrophic. For example, a proposal to permit legalized abortion in some cases might be criticized by arguing that such a step would lead to loss of respect for human life, which would eventually lead to concentration camps to eliminate people who are not useful to the economy. This type of argument, studied in chapter 9, section 9.7, proceeds by presuming that there is an inevitable sequence of steps leading down a slippery slope, once you take that first step of accepting a proposal at issue.

6. The fallacy of composition argues unreasonably from attributes of some parts of a whole, or members of a collection, to attributes of the whole, or collection itself. For example, it might be an error to conclude that a certain hockey team will do well and win a series because each of the players is individually excellent. The players may be good, but if they can't work well together, the team may do poorly. The fallacy of division is the opposite kind of questionable argumentation. For example, to argue that a certain university is noted for excellent scholarship, and conclude that therefore, Professor Slacker, who is on the faculty at that university, must be noted for his excellent scholarship, would be an instance of this fallacy. Composition and division are treated in section 5.7.

The above list of fallacies is by no means complete, but it gives the reader an introductory idea of the classic types of errors of reasoning that are the main focus of concern in informal logic.

1.6 THE STRAW MAN FALLACY

As indicated in the previous section, the straw man fallacy is committed by an arguer when he misrepresents his opponent's position in order to refute it more easily by making it seem implausible, or weaker than it really is, and then argues against this set-up version. The straw man fallacy can involve exaggeration or misquotation, as well as other forms of distortion of an opponent's position. Consider the following dialogue (Freeman 1988, p. 88) in which one party attacks the prior argument of another.

Example 1.9

C: It would be a good idea to ban advertising beer and wine on radio and television. These ads encourage teenagers to drink, often with disastrous consequences.

A: You cannot get people to give up drinking; they've been doing it for thousands of years.

Assuming that the concerned citizen did not maintain that people should give up drinking, the alcohol industry representative has committed the straw man fallacy by arguing against this position that he attributes to her. To analyze the fallacy more deeply, Freeman (1988, p. 88) contrasts the following pair of propositions, asking which is the easier to refute.

A: It would be a good idea to ban advertising beer and wine on radio and television (the concerned citizen's original conclusion).

B: It would be a good idea to get people to stop drinking (the alcohol industry representative's portrayal of that conclusion).

B is much easier to refute than A. Thus the alcohol industry representative improperly represented the concerned citizen's position in a way easy to refute, and then proceeded to attack it.

The straw man fallacy has three essential components. The first is that there is a pair of arguers taking part in a dialogue. The second component is that each is arguing with the other. The third is that each is advocating a position opposed to that of the other party. This third component is important to emphasize, because the determination and evaluation of the straw man fallacy in a given case depends on the arguers' commitments in the dialogue. An arguer's position is defined as his commitments at any given point in a dialogue where a particular argument has been put forward. This point is an important one about fallacies, from a theoretical point of view. Whether an argument is fallacious sometimes turns on what the arguer's commitments are at some point in a dialogue.

In some cases, misquotation and wrenching from context are parts of the method used to distort an arguer's position to make it more susceptible to refutation. In such cases an arguer's actual words may have been changed in order to misrepresent his position. In other cases, the respondent may have been quoted accurately, but what he said is placed in a context different from the original one.

The following example concerns media reporting of then Vice-President Al Gore that led to the widely circulated story that he claimed to have invented the Internet. The numerous attacks on Gore on the basis that he claimed to have invented the Internet originally arose from an interview with Wolf Blitzer on CNN's *Late Edition* program on March 9, 1999.[20]

20 Http://www.cnn.com/ALLPOLITICS/stories/1999/03/09/president.2000/transcript. gore/index.html

Blitzer asked Gore what distinguished him from a challenger for the presidential nomination. Gore's reply is quoted below.

Example 1.10

> During my service in the United States Congress, I took the initiative in creating the Internet. I took the initiative in moving forward a whole range of initiatives that have proven to be important to our country's economic growth and environmental protection, improvements in our educational system.

Gore's claim to have "taken the initiative" is vague and ambiguous. If you look at what he said, there is little evidence that he claimed to have invented the Internet. A more accurate and sympathetic interpretation of what he said is that he was claiming to be responsible for helping to create the environment in a way that fostered the development of the Internet. Yet the unsympathetic and inaccurate version of Gore's claim was often used by commentators, including his political opponents, to try to distort his political views to make them appear to be unrealistic. Such misrepresentations made Gore appear ridiculous, someone who exaggerates his claims and brags about them, i.e., a politician who should not be taken seriously. These examples show how the straw man fallacy is an extremely powerful and deceptive argumentation tactic in the political arena.

1.7 ARGUMENT FROM CONSEQUENCES

There is a common form of argument called argument from consequences, where one party in a dialogue says to another, "This action would not be good, because it could have bad consequences." For example, suppose you are thinking of playing the last round of golf, but you see some dark clouds on the horizon and there's some rumbles that suggest thunder. Your caddie says to you, "I would recommend against playing this last round, because if we get caught in a thunderstorm, we could be struck by lightning." This form of argument, called argument from negative consequences, cites foreseeable negative consequences of a proposed action as the premise. The conclusion is a statement claiming that the action is not recommended. Argument from consequences can also be used in a positive way, where a policy or course of action is supported by citing the positive consequences of carrying it out.

Argument from consequences is often used in economic and political deliberations where two parties (or groups) disagree on what is the

24

best course of action to pursue. For example, in the dialogue on tipping described in section 1.3, Bob might use the following argument.

Example 1.11

If the practice of tipping were discontinued, unemployment would result.

Unemployment is a bad thing.

Therefore it would not be a good idea to discontinue the practice of tipping.

In this instance, Bob has used an argument from negative consequences. By citing negative consequences of the policy of discontinuing tipping, Bob has argued against this policy as a good course of action.

In reply, Helen might use the following negative form of argument from consequences to counter Bob's previous argument.

Example 1.12

If the practice of tipping were discontinued, service providers would increase self-esteem.

Increasing self-esteem is a good thing.

Therefore the practice of tipping should be discontinued.

In this use of argument from consequences, Helen cited positive consequences of discontinuing tipping as a reason for supporting that policy or course of action as being a good idea. This example is about the negative action of discontinuing tipping. Nevertheless it is an example of positive argument from consequences because Helen is claiming that increasing self-esteem is a good thing, and she is using this allegedly positive outcome as a reason to support her conclusion that the practice of tipping should be discontinued.

As these examples show, positive argument from consequences is often pitted against negative argument from consequences in argumentation in deliberation about what should be done in a given situation.

Example 1.13

In March 1995 voters in the province of Quebec were having town hall meetings deliberating on whether to have a referendum giving them a choice to leave Canada, and form a separate country, or stay as a province in Canada. Some argued that the economic consequences of separation from Canada would be highly negative for Quebec. Others argued that having a single French-speaking country separate from English-speaking Canada would have positive consequences for French culture in Quebec.

In political deliberations in such cases, trying to conjecture what might or might not happen in the future tends to be a highly conjectural matter, because many complex and rapidly changing factors are involved. In such cases, positive argument from consequences may need to be balanced against negative argument from consequences. Typically, neither argument is conclusive by itself, although each may carry some weight in the deliberations on one side or the other.

Argumentation schemes are forms of inference from premises to a conclusion of the kind used in arguments used in dialogues in which each party is trying to get the other to come to accept his or her conclusion. Typically they represent arguments of a kind that provide reasons for or against a plausible hypothesis that is being considered under conditions of uncertainty and lack of knowledge. Schemes are useful for identifying, analyzing and evaluating arguments. The tool used for evaluation is the set of appropriate critical questions matching each scheme.

The following two argumentation schemes for argument from consequences were given in Walton (1996, p. 75).

Argumentation Scheme for Argument from Positive Consequences
Premise: If *A* is brought about, good consequences will plausibly occur.
Conclusion: *A* should be brought about.

The scheme for argument from negative consequences takes the following form.

Argumentation Scheme for Argument from Negative Consequences
Premise: If *A* is brought about, bad consequences will plausibly occur.
Conclusion: *A* should not be brought about.

In the framework for evaluating both forms of argument presented in Walton (1996, pp. 76–77), the following three critical questions are appropriate.

CQ1. How strong is the probability or plausibility that these cited consequences will (may, might, must) occur?

26

CQ2. What evidence, if any, supported the claim that these consequences will (may, might, must) occur if A is brought about?

CQ3. Are there consequences of the opposite value that ought to be taken into account?

The argument has a presumptive status, once the positive or negative consequences are cited as reasons to support the proposed course of action. The argument is cast into doubt if there is a failure to answer any of these critical questions adequately, once they have been asked. So conceived, argument from consequences can be strong in some cases, weak in others. It can be weak if it fails to answer appropriate critical questions that have been or might be asked in a dialogue.

Although argument from consequences is very often a reasonable kind of argument, in some instances it can be fallacious. Consider the following example.

Example 1.14

The United States had justice on its side in waging the Mexican war of 1848. To question this is unpatriotic, and would give comfort to our enemies by promoting the cause of defeatism.

This example was taken to have committed the fallacy of arguing from consequences, according to a logic textbook (Rescher 1964, p. 82). It is interesting to ask why it was so taken. First, we need to know that the claim might be true that questioning whether the United States had justice on its side in this instance might give comfort to enemies by promoting the cause of defeatism. In one way, because this claim might be true, the argument seems to be a good one. But in another way, the argument is faulty because the real issue in the case is which country had justice on its side in the Mexican war of 1848. To answer this question, we need to look at evidence of who started the war, what the dispute was all about, who may have broken a treaty, and so forth. The question at issue in the dialogue is a historical one, or perhaps an ethical one, which needs to be decided or discussed by looking at the facts of the case. Claiming that even to question that the United States had justice on its side would have negative consequences by promoting the cause of defeatism is an argument that is not really relevant in discussing this historical issue. True, it may be a practical reason for arguing that one should not raise this question, perhaps in the context of a present war where questions of morale are a matter of public urgency, but it is not a relevant reason for arguing that the United States had justice on its side, or did not. Thus the reason that the argument is rightly judged to be fallacious is one of relevance. The argument from negative consequences may be reasonable, if looked at purely as an argumentation scheme that cites negative consequences as prudential evidence against a course of action. The problem is that it is not a relevant argument in relation to the issue that is supposedly being discussed. We could even say that the prudential argument is being used to shut down the possibility of continuing the historical argument on grounds of negative consequences. In effect, it is being used to shut down that argument and prohibit historical reasons from being put forward.

The structure of the argument can be shown using an automated tool called *Araucaria* (Reed and Rowe 2002) that can be used to aid an argument analyst in constructing a diagram representing the structure of the argument.[21] Using this tool to draw the argument diagram, the structure of the Mexican war argument can be analyzed as shown in figure 1.2. The conclusion is statement A, and the rest of the statements in the text boxes represent premises of the argument. Notice that the two premises at the lower right of figure 1.2 are linked together, showing that they go together in support of conclusion A. The remaining argument has only a single premise, B. Note that the premise D appears in a darkened box, indicating that it is an implicit premise that was not stated in the text of the argument, but is needed to support the conclusion adequately. Note also that the argumentation scheme (argument from consequences) that links premises C and D to conclusion A has been represented in the diagram.[22] Notice that when we move from the conclusion A to the premise B, and also when we move from A to the argument made up from premises C and D, there has been a perceptible shift. Instead of simply offering reasons that support the acceptance of A, both sets of premises offer reasons why we should not question A. This type of shift should raise a red flag, because

---

21 *Araucaria* uses a simple point-and-click interface, which may be then saved in a portable format called AML, or Argument Markup Language (Reed and Rowe 2006). The user inserts the example to be analyzed as a text document, then draws arrows from each premise to each conclusion it supports, thus producing an argument diagram connecting all the premises and conclusions.

22 The scheme is added to the diagram by pulling down a list of schemes from the toolbar and selecting the appropriate scheme from the list. In this instance the scheme is that for argument from negative consequences.

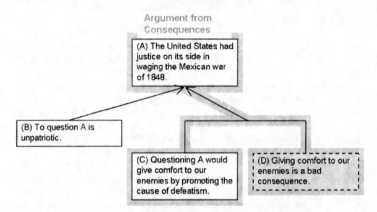

Figure 1.2. Argument diagram of the Mexican war argument.

it makes a move to shut down critical questions that might be posed in questioning A. Also, we need to look more closely at the argument from C and D to A. It is an argument from consequences in which both premises might be true.

In this interesting case there has been what is called a dialectical shift from an original persuasion dialogue about an issue to a practical deliberation concerning consequences of actions, and the negative impact of these actions. The fallacy is subtle, however, because the argument from consequences used in the case fits the argumentation scheme for negative argument from consequences, and when looked at from this perspective is an inherently reasonable argument. We also have to look at the argument from the perspective of the original dialogue that was supposedly under way in the case. To see that the argument should be judged to be fallacious from this perspective, one has to be aware that there has been a dialectical shift. There has been a concealed shift from one type of dialogue to another, in this case a shift from a persuasion dialogue to a deliberation. It is the shift that makes the argument fallacious, on the grounds that the negative argument from consequences, although it may be quite reasonable within the perspective of the deliberation dialogue, is not relevant as an argument situated in the context of the persuasion dialogue about which country had justice on its side.

Another example can be used to show how the use of argument from negative consequences can be not only complex and controversial, but politically divisive as well.

Example 1.15

In a book, *The Enemy at Home*, right-wing critic Dinesh D'Sousa used argument from negative consequences to blame recent terrorist attacks by Islamic fundamentalists on left-wing politicians, celebrities, and activists. He named more than a hundred people as part of a "domestic insurgency" working in tandem with Osama bin Laden to defeat Bush. He claimed not to be accusing these people of being terrorists themselves, or of actively working to promote their interests, or spreading defeatism. He did claim, however, that they are responsible for causing the hatred of the terrorists by their attempts to promote their decadent moral values and impose them on the rest of the world. D'Sousa denounced America as having sunk into decadent moral values, and as having become perceived, especially by religious fundamentalists, as the worst civilization in this respect. Examples of actions he cited include widespread use of intoxicants, gambling, and fornication.[23] He argued that the attempts to promote gender equality in the developing world, to cite another example, can be seen as promoting values considered disgusting and deviant by traditional cultures.

D'Sousa cited many consequences of left-wing views and activities to promote these views by activists, intellectuals, and celebrities. He portrayed the outcomes of these efforts as being negative, and as causing harm to not only their exponents but to everyone living in America. The example is therefore similar in certain respects to the use of argument from negative consequences in the Mexican war example. Based on this comparison, can we conclude that the argument in the domestic insurgency example is a fallacious instance of argumentation from negative consequences? We return to this question after explaining how fallacies of relevance are based on an underlying dialectical structure.

In example 1.15 there is a dialectical shift from a discussion about ethical values to a citing of alleged negative consequences of the expression and promotion of these values by certain parties. However, the argument in this particular instance is more subtle and indirect than that of the Mexican war example. D'Sousa did argue at length that the political activism of the persons and groups cited had bad negative consequences. He did not argue that these people have no right to express their views or to promote them politically, however. Like the case of the Mexican war example, it was argued that the bad consequences involve loss of life. In the Mexican war example, loss of morale in war was cited as the bad outcome – giving comfort to our enemies. In the domestic insurgency example, the

23 Jerry Adler, 'America's Most Wanted,' review of *The Enemy at Home*, *Newsweek*, February. 5, 2007, p. 46.

consequences cited are even worse. The argument equates the bad consequences with loss of life in terrorist attacks, and even appears to partially lay blame for these attacks on the parties cited. Thus there is a dialectical shift from a discussion of the political views in question to a deliberation dialogue about the allegedly bad consequences of these views. The secondary dialogue even takes the form of laying guilt for these bad consequences on the parties who are alleged to have contributed to them, even if unknowingly.

The argumentation in this case is much more complex than the one in the Mexican war example, because it was put forward in a whole book, and because of its politically divisive nature. Those on the right will like the argument in the book, while those on the left will be strongly inclined to disagree with its argument. But it would be an error to leap too quickly to one side or the other. To properly evaluate the argument, one would have to examine the specific claims made in the individual cases cited, and the arguments offered to back up these claims. There is no space for that here. Still, it is interesting to cite the example to show how argumentation from negative consequences is used in a subtle way in everyday conversational arguments of the most common kind, for example, in political rhetoric. Such cases verge on the fallacious, because of the shift concealed within the sequence of argumentation, and can certainly be highly deceptive. It would be erroneous, however, to declare them fallacious in a wholesale fashion, and each case needs to be judged on its merits or demerits, taking the dialectical shift into account.

Argument from consequences is such a common and fundamental form of argument in everyday conversational interactions that we tend not to be aware that we're using it all the time. It is often implicit in other arguments. For instance, let's reconsider example 1.9. In this case, the concerned citizen argued that it would be a good idea to ban advertising beer and wine on radio and television because these ads encourage teenagers to drink, often with disastrous consequences. Clearly the argument used in this case is an instance of negative argument from consequences. As shown in figure 1.3, the argument from consequences shown on the right side of the diagram is made up of the two premises at the bottom and the conclusion which appears at the top. The shaded line around this argument, along with the label 'Argument from Consequences' at the top, shows how the scheme for argument from consequences applies to this part of the argument.[24] We

---

24 It is shown in Walton and Reed (2005) how argumentation schemes can be used in conjunction with argument diagrams, to identify implicit premises (and conclusions) in

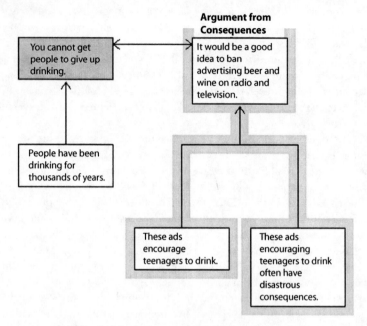

Argument from Consequences

You cannot get people to give up drinking.

It would be a good idea to ban advertising beer and wine on radio and television.

People have been drinking for thousands of years.

These ads encourage teenagers to drink.

These ads encouraging teenagers to drink often have disastrous consequences.

Figure 1.3. Argument diagram for example 1.9.

see how argument from negative consequences links the two premises on the right to the conclusion that it would be a good idea to ban advertising beer and wine on radio and television. At the top of the diagram, we see that the proposition 'You cannot get people to give up drinking' is joined by a double-headed arrow to the conclusion of the argument shown in the box to the right of it. The double-headed arrow represents refutation, a relation in which one proposition is opposed to another. For example, the proposition 'Snow is white' is opposed to the proposition 'Snow is not white' because the one proposition is the negation of the other. In *Araucaria*, a refutation is always displayed in a darkened box joined by a double-headed arrow to the proposition it is taken to refute. The diagram in Figure 1.3 shows how the proposition 'You cannot get people to give up drinking' is used as a refutation of the conclusion. As shown in figure 1.3, a reason is given to support the proposition that you cannot get people to

arguments. This capability is extremely useful as a tool for analyzing cases where a straw man fallacy has been alleged.

32

give up drinking, namely the proposition that people have been drinking for thousands of years. This part of the argument seems in itself to be fairly reasonable, and if you look at the argument from consequences on the right side of the diagram, that argument also seems to be fairly reasonable. How then did we arrive at the conclusion that this argument commits the straw man fallacy?

We know from our understanding of the dialogue in example 1.9 that the alcohol industry representative wants to make us believe the concerned citizen advocates total abstinence. That was our basis for classifying the argument in this case as an instance of the straw man fallacy, but we need to ask how could we prove this allegation? Where is the evidence? The evidence is found in the observation that the alcohol industry representative's statement, 'You cannot get people to give up drinking,' when placed in the dialogue as his response to the prior move by the concerned citizen, is clearly meant to be a refutation move in the dialogue. When we reconstruct the context of the dialogue from the text of example 1.9, we can see that the alcohol industry representative is implying that the reason why the concerned citizen is claiming that it would be a good idea to ban advertising beer and wine on radio and television is that he is trying to get people to give up drinking. Of course, this could be one common reason why many people might advocate banning advertising beer and wine on radio and television. We know this, and therefore it is easy for us to make the transition to the claim that the ordinary citizen is arguing this way because he is trying to get people to give up drinking. Is this inference really warranted? It may not be. There is no specific textual evidence given by what the concerned citizen says in the example that requires him to be committed to the proposition that it is a good idea for people to give up drinking. Here is where the straw man fallacy comes in. The alcohol industry representative has attributed a position to the concerned citizen that he is not really committed to, or that he certainly does not need to be committed to, given the evidence of what we know about his viewpoint and previous commitments in the dialogue.

What we have seen both in considering the straw man fallacy and the fallacy of argument from consequences is that the fallacy does not reside exclusively in the inference from the premises to the conclusion of the given argument. In other words the fallacy does not reside in the form of argument, the argumentation scheme itself. To analyze the fallacy, you have to see how this scheme is used in a context of dialogue. Once the context of dialogue in which the argument is situated is examined carefully, it may

33

be shown that the argument is not relevant, or that it is used in a tricky way that conceals a mistaken attribution of an arguer's commitment in the dialogue. This lesson is an important one in relation to studying fallacies throughout the rest of this book. While studying the form of an argument is vitally important, it is also necessary to study how the argument was used in a given context of dialogue before a proper determination of whether a fallacy has been committed can be made.

1.8 THE CRITICAL PERSPECTIVE

Essentially, reasonable dialogue should be open, and should encourage the asking of probing questions on all relevant aspects of a controversial issue. The adversarial cut and thrust of pointed criticisms and forceful rebuttals is not in itself bad or fallacious. In fact, this adversarial interplay which pits one argument against another is, within limits, an essential aspect of revealing and enlightening argumentation. The rules of reasonable dialogue should not be so tight that they exclude room for free argumentation.

Reasonable argument characteristically does have an adversarial aspect, because an arguer is trying to persuade or win over an audience or another arguer. When this adversarial aspect of the argument becomes too aggressive or personal, an argument tends to become less reasonable and more bellicose. Yet the adversarial nature of argument is not in itself bad or contrary to reason. For in argument on a controversial issue, the strength of an argument should be judged on how well it has fared in free discussion against countervailing arguments. In scientific inquiries, the test of an argument is whether it can be falsified by contrary empirical evidence. In disputation on controversial issues, where reasoned conviction is the best outcome one can hope for, the test of an argument is whether it can be refuted by contrary arguments in reasonable dialogue. Thus the adversarial aspect of reasonable dialogue is, or at least can be, an important part of what makes the dialogue reasonable. The adversarial aspect of a dispute is not necessarily, in itself, a bad thing.

The problem with the debate and the quarrel as models of argument is that personal victory at any cost becomes the goal, even if impartial standards of logical reasoning may have to be waived or contravened. Yet dialogue can be reasonable only to the extent that the goal of building a stronger case than the opposition's is carried out within a structure that is binding on both parties. Otherwise the argument has a strong tendency to diverge from the path of dialogue where the sequence moves towards

34

revealing the deeper positions of the participants on the issue to be discussed. A one-sided diatribe is worthless and unrevealing.

Hence the importance of impartial criticism. An important skill is to be able to recognize those types of critical points where reasonable dialogue becomes less than reasonable or is diverted away from a better line of argument. In fact, being able to recognize these critical points in an argument, and deal with them by asking the right critical questions, are the key skills of informal logic as a discipline.

The major informal fallacies listed in section 1.5 above represent the most important types of deceptive attacking strategy of argumentative dialogue that can be used effectively to press forward against an opponent and prevail in the dialogue, even where the argument used for this purpose is weak or faulty. They are like the different tricks and tactic that can be used in wrestling to trip a stronger opponent and cause him to fall, or even to lose the match. In examining examples of the straw man fallacy and the example of fallacious argument from consequences, it was shown that it may not be just the argument form (argumentation scheme) of the given argument that needs to be considered. It may also be important to study how the argument was used in a context of dialogue. We need to recall the negative rules of persuasion dialogue in section 1.4. Rule 5 stated that failures of relevance can include proving the wrong thesis or wandering away from the point to be proved. This failure occurred in the argument in the Mexican war example because there was a dialectical shift to a different type of dialogue. The rule for the closing stage stated that a participant must not try to force premature closure of a dialogue until it is properly closed. This problem also occurs in the same example because the dialectical shift involved prevents the respondent from asking appropriate critical questions. It is also easy to see that in cases of the straw man fallacy the main problem is the violation of rule 3, which requires that an argument in a persuasion dialogue should be based on the commitments of the other party. Although logical semantics is important in evaluating arguments in a case where a fallacy might have been committed, logical pragmatics is often equally important in pinning down important factors of the context of dialogue.

The types of tactic associated with the traditional informal fallacies are not always used illicitly (violations of rules of fair dialogue). They can, in some cases, be used fairly to support legitimate objectives of reasoned dialogue. This lesson will emerge in the subsequent chapters, in the case of each and every one of these fallacies. Moreover, in other cases, argument moves which have the same argumentation scheme as one of those identified with a major fallacy turn out to be arguments that are not "fallacious," but only weak, or lacking in essential support. These arguments need to be criticized, but they do not always need to be rejected as "fallacious." Often the proponent of the argument can respond to critical questioning by filling in the gaps in this argument. In this type of case, both participants in the argument can benefit by reasoning together. The fallacies are important types of argument strategy to become familiar with because they represent powerful methods of attack in argumentation that can be used for deceptive as well as legitimate purposes. In many cases, however, there is much to be said about arguments that are neither perfectly bad (fallacious) nor perfectly good.

In arguments on controversial subjects the job of the reasonable critic is not necessarily to show that an argument he criticizes is fallacious, logically inconsistent, or based on worthless evidence that can be rejected completely. Most often, such strong refutation is simply not appropriate. More often, the job of the critic is to show that an argument is open to reasonable doubt or lacks needed support, and is therefore open to questioning. This weaker form of criticism is very often enough to reserve or withdraw the commitment of the audience to whom the argument is directed. By showing gaps in an argument that can be questioned, the critic can show that the argument is open to reasonable criticism. That in itself may be a very valuable job, and the critic may have no need to do more to have achieved a worthwhile objective. By shifting the burden of proof, a criticism may be enough to make an audience withdraw its commitment to an argument. In arguments on controversial subjects, this form of criticism is often enough to successfully and reasonably persuade an audience to change its point of view on an issue.

When we criticize arguments, we are often involved in the argument, taking one side of it against the other. Hence the ever-present danger in argument on controversial issues that really matter to us is the loss of a proper critical perspective. This does not mean that one side of an argument is always as good as the other. It does mean that the reasonable critic must make enough of an effort to probe both positions, both sides of the argument, in order to evaluate criticisms and replies in a sensitive and intelligent way. The fault of blind dogmatism, of only seeing one side of the argument as a position worth investigating, is among the most severe impediments or handicaps in reasonable dialogue. By learning the argumentation schemes and critical questions that come under the headings of

36

the different kinds of fallacies and errors studied in subsequent chapters, the reader can learn how to criticize an opposed point of view, even while appreciating its merits. Through the application of these guidelines, arguments can be evaluated on their real merits or faults, not just because we agree or disagree with their conclusions, or because they appear to be congenial with one's own personal position on an issue.

2

Questions and answers in dialogue

Normally in reasonable dialogue one is obliged to try to give a direct answer to a question, if one knows the answer, and if the question is reasonable and appropriate. If one does not know the direct answer, or for some reason cannot give it, then one is obliged to be as informative as possible. The reason behind this normal expectation is that our usual and reasonable presumption in many contexts is that a question is a sincere request for information where the questioner expects, or at least hopes, that the answerer may have this information and be able to give it. Therefore, if the answerer does not give a direct answer, his reply may be perceived as unhelpful or evasive.

Because of these normal expectations in reasonable dialogue, the most general purpose of a question is a request for information. Here, information refers to a set of propositions. So posing a question is a request to the answerer to supply a set of propositions.

There are several different types of questions each of which has a different format for requesting propositions.[1] A *whether-question* poses a set of alternatives, and requests the answerer to select one. For example, the whether-question "Was she wearing the grey slacks or the red dress or blue jeans?" requests the answerer to pick one proposition from the disjunction. An example of a direct answer would be: "She was wearing the red dress." A *yes-no* question allows only two alternatives, the affirmative or the negative answer, and is therefore a simple, two-option type of whether-question. A *why-question* asks for a set of propositions that provide premises in a reasonable argument for the proposition queried.[2]

A *direct answer* to a question supplies exactly the information requested by the question. An *indirect answer* supplies only part of that information. A *reply* to a question is a response to the question that may not be a direct or

---

1 Harrah (1984, p. 716) lists eleven different types of questions recognized by most theorists in the logic of questions.
2 See Aqvist (1965) and Belnap and Steel (1976) for formalized treatments of these types of questions.

indirect answer.[3] Sometimes, a reasonable reply is to question the question itself. But as we noted above, the normal expectation is that the helpful answerer will give an answer.

However, this normal and reasonable expectation is not true of all questions. Some questions are not sincere requests for information. They are aggressively posed questions with harmful presuppositions that may discredit an answerer if he attempts to give a direct answer. For this reason, some tricky questions are deliberately mischievous, and where an answerer fails to give a direct answer, his reply should not necessarily be open to criticism as evasive or irrelevant. For to give a direct answer in such a case would be to fall into the questioner's trap. Therefore, some questions ought to reasonably be answered by posing another question in reply.

It requires good judgment to know whether a question is reasonable in a specific context, or whether a failure to give a direct answer should justifiably be criticized as an evasion or irrelevance. In this chapter, we will study several factors that need to be considered in reasonably evaluating a sequence of questions and answers in dialogue.

2.1 PRESUPPOSITIONS OF QUESTIONS

A *presupposition* of a question is a proposition that is presumed to be acceptable to the respondent when the question is asked, so that the respondent becomes committed to the proposition when he gives any direct answer. In general, a question may have several presuppositions. A presupposition is itself a proposition, and this means that the asking of a question contains within it positive information in the form of a proposition. Consequently, asking questions may be a form of asserting propositions in dialogue. Therefore, asking questions can be a form of arguing, and thereby influence the subsequent course of an argument in reasonable dialogue.

What is most important about presuppositions of questions, for our purposes, is that the answerer who gives a direct answer to a question automatically becomes committed to all the presuppositions of the question.[4] Therefore, the asking of questions can strongly affect the answerer's position, his set of commitments in a dialogue. The question itself can be argumentative.

---

3 Harrah (1984, p. 715) notes that most theorists acknowledge the distinction between a reply and an answer.
4 We will define 'presupposition' towards the end of this chapter.

Certain types of questions have traditionally been thought fallacious because they are packed with presuppositions that trap the answerer no matter how he responds. The most famous example is the classical spouse abuse question.[5]

Example 2.0

Have you stopped abusing your spouse?

The main objectionable feature of this trick question is that whichever way you answer, 'yes' or 'no,' you become committed to having abused your spouse at some time or other. Of course, the ordinary non–spouse-abuser therefore answers the question only by being trapped into conceding a proposition that she or he is not really committed to. The question is a coercive trick to trap him or her into admitting something prejudicial. Hence example 2.0 is considered the classical case of the *fallacy of many questions*, sometimes called the *fallacy of complex question*.

Other questions similar to 2.0 are not hard to find. They all have the same objectionable feature.

Example 2.1

Have you always been a liar, or are you just starting now?

Example 2.2

Did you make profitable investments from the money you obtained through your unethical use of government funds?

In each case, the question contains a damaging presupposition. Whichever way the answerer replies, he concedes something incriminating. Whether he answers 'yes' or 'no' to question 2.1, the answerer commits himself to

---

5 The fallacy of many questions was recognized as a sophistical tactic by the ancient Greek writers on logic. According to Diogenes Laertius (*Lives of Eminent Philosophers*, VII.187), Eubulides posed the fallacy of the horns in the form of a logical inference: if you never lost something, you have it still; but you never lost horns; therefore you have horns. This same fallacy was also expressed in ancient times using an example comparable to the spouse abuse question of the modern logic textbooks. According to Diogenes Laertius (*Lives*, II.135), Alexinus of Elis, a member of the Eristic School of Eubulides, was said to have asked another philosopher whether he had stopped beating his father. The other philosopher was said to have answered: "I was not beating him and have not stopped."

being a liar. Once having conceded this proposition, he is not likely to have much credibility in any further exchanges in the dialogue.

Or consider question 2.2. A subsequent context of dialogue might run as follows.

Example 2.3

White: Did you make profitable investments from the money you obtained through your unethical use of government funds?

Black: No.

White: So, you admit you made unethical use of government funds. I demand your resignation at once. Don't you know that unethical use of government funds is adequate reason for your dismissal?

Here the questioner concludes by following up his attack with another loaded question.

The basic problem, which in these cases arises from the 'yes-no' format of the questions, is that the question does not allow a third option, or escape-clause. Of course, the best way to reply to such a question may be to object to the question itself – to question the question – if that type of reply is allowed. One might reject the presupposition, or at least answer the question by questioning the presupposition. Why each of the first two questions above is thought to be especially fallacious is that their yes-no format calls for a simple yes or no answer. In a yes-no question, there are only two direct answers 'yes' or 'no.' Therefore, it is fair to say that if you fail to give a direct answer to 2.0, 2.1, or 2.2, it may not necessarily mean that you are evading the question unfairly, or failing to give a relevant answer. With some questions, the most reasonable response may not be to give a direct answer, because the question itself is not fairly framed, so that the answerer can assert his own position.

One might think that all questions that have presuppositions are fallacious, but many questions that have significant presuppositions can be reasonable and legitimate.

Example 2.4

Is the man in the last row wearing the red hat a member of the psychology class?

This question has many presuppositions. It presupposes that there is a man in the last row, that he is wearing something, that he is wearing a hat, that the hat is red, and so forth. This question may be no problem to answer, and there may be no question of its being fallacious. It is also a yes-no question with multiple presuppositions, but in most contexts, there would be no good reason to regard it as a trap question or as a fallacy of many questions.

The difference between the harmless question in example 2.4 and the previous three fallacious questions lies in the nature of their presuppositions. In the last case, the presuppositions seem harmless or innocent, but in the case of the first three questions, the presuppositions are propositions that most participants in argument would not want to go on record as being commitments of theirs. We could call these presuppositions *unwelcome commitments* and questions that contain them *loaded questions*. Whether a question is loaded depends on the position of the answerer. If the answerer clearly would not want to be committed to a presupposition of a particular question, then the question may be described as loaded with respect to the position of that answerer.

For the average answerer, in most contexts of reasonable dialogue, 2.0, 2.1, and 2.2 could fairly be described as loaded questions. Consider yourself. Would you want to or should you have to admit to spouse-beating activities? If not, then 2.0 would be a loaded question if addressed to you. Scarcely anyone would want to admit, in answer to 2.1, that he is a liar or has been, for that admission would tend to discredit him in any further argument, and undermine the possibility of reasonable dialogue. Finally, in answer to 2.2, anyone innocent of the allegation of unethical use of government funds would not be likely to want to commit himself to conceding having used such funds to make a profit. It is possible that he might wish to so commit himself, but the context suggests the profile of an average (innocent) answerer for whom such a commitment would not be welcome or appropriate. Hence 2.0, 2.1, and 2.2 would normally be regarded (with reason) as loaded questions.

2.2 COMPLEX QUESTIONS

We have seen that not all questions that have presuppositions are fallacious. Indeed, every question has some presupposition. Even a question like 'Is 2 a number?' has the presuppositions that there are numbers, and that 2 is the sort of thing that can be a number. Even the most innocent question has presuppositions, but they may not be a problem, or an indication that the question that contains them is in any way suspicious or fallacious.

Another lesson to observe is that there are complex questions that may not be fallacious or problematic. Despite the tradition of calling "complex question" a fallacy, there is nothing intrinsically wrong with asking complex questions. In many cases, asking a complex question is necessary in order to communicate in a dialogue successfully.

Example 2.5

Did you pick up your shirt and put it in the laundry?

Example 2.6

Will you open the door if Kevin forgets his key?

Example 2.7

Suppose two people are trying to fix a photocopier machine, and they have a conversation of the following kind.

Laura: How do you fix a paper jam that happens when that red light at level one goes on?

Trevor: I can't quite figure out what the instructions are telling me to do. If I lift the top part of the machine, push the yellow release catch, empty the paper in the roller, and then click the release catch back into place, would that clear this kind of jam, provided I turn the power off, and make sure not to stick my fingers in where the roller engages with the teeth?

Each of these questions is semantically complex. Example 2.5 is a conjunctive question, and 2.6 is a conditional question.[6] In example 2.7, since Laura and Trevor need to deal with complex matters relating to ordered procedures for maintaining a complex machine, they need to ask each other complex questions. If they had to break every complex question down into simple, single questions, it would make the kind of dialogue required in this case difficult, or perhaps even impossible to conduct in language each could follow.

In most contexts, none of the questions in these examples should reasonably be called a loaded question or a fallacious question. In other words, there is nothing inherently wrong with a question that has complex (multiple) presuppositions. Yet in other cases, complex questions are not only terribly confusing and misleading, they are used as aggressive attack strategies that make an appropriate response difficult.

6 A careful study of problems of multiple questions is given in Hintikka (1976, ch. 6).

To realize how enormously complex a question can be in an argument, it may be well to reflect on the following sample of dialogue from the Oral Question Period of Hansard.[7] Mr. Chrétien's question is unusually complex for the Question Period, a type of dialogue where questions are supposed to be short, and not "arguments."

Example 2.8

Hon. Jean Chrétien (Saint-Maurice): Mr. Speaker, my question is directed to the Right Hon. Prime Minister.

According to a story published in the press today, the Minister of Regional Industrial Expansion owns a company; he has a 50 per cent interest in a company that manufactures shoes, and since he is responsible for the Anti-dumping Tribunal and for setting quotas on footwear, and the president of the company said that the company was having problems because of imports, did the Right Hon. Prime Minister take the necessary precautions when appointing the Minister of Industry, Trade and Commerce or the Minister of Regional Industrial Expansion by asking him certain pertinent questions, and did the Minister inform the Prime Minister of the potential conflict of interest that existed at the time, and if the Prime Minister was aware of the situation, how could the Member in question become the Minister of a department where he must make daily decisions that may affect the financial position of a company in which he has a 50 per cent interest?

Right Hon. Brian Mulroney (Prime Minister): I am surprised and surprised [*sic*] at the Hon. Member for asking such a question. However, I can assure him that all legal requirements were met before anyone was appointed, including the Minister in question. The Hon. Member is no doubt aware that from time to time, Canadian citizens, including Members of this House who have worked in the business world, have been faced with certain problems, and I must say I have received every assurance that all legal requirements had been met, and I am confident that the Hon. Member in question has the integrity and competence required to perform his duties as Minister.

Mr. Chrétien's question has so many presuppositions that it could be very difficult for any respondent to keep track of them. And his question is also quite aggressive. It poses an allegation of conflict of interest against a Minister of the Government. Nonetheless, for all that, the question does not seem to be a basically unreasonable one for Mr. Chrétien to ask. Although Mr. Mulroney rejects the implication of the question that there may be some possibility of conflict of interest in this case, he does not

7 *Canada: House of Commons Debates (Hansard)*, vol. 126, November 16, 1984, p. 297).

appear to reject the question as inherently objectionable or inappropriate on grounds of its structure.

The rules of order for debate in the House of Commons in Canada require that a question should not be a "speech," and should not be of an unreasonable length. Perhaps then the Speaker of the House should have intervened, and barred Mr. Chrétien's long question. However, in response to such an objection, Mr. Chrétien could possibly argue that all the matters in the question are connected, and that therefore, in this case, the length of the question is not unreasonable. It is accepted that not every restriction on questions asked in rules of debate can be applied in every case.

Even though Mr. Chrétien's question illustrates how remarkably complex a question can actually be, and that such complexity could be awkward and confusing for a respondent, it does not follow that a question should always be judged fallacious or erroneous on grounds of its complexity alone. It is the loaded nature of Mr. Chrétien's question that combines with its multiplicity to make it difficult for a respondent to sort the whole question out. Thus although there do seem to be presuppositions of the question that are not acceptable to the respondent, it would not seem right to conclude that the question is fallacious because of its complexity. Admittedly, the question is remarkably complex, but that in itself does not seem deeply objectionable, at least to the extent that we would conclude that it is a fallacious question for that reason.

While it may be true that there could be practical limits on the length of a question, even so it seems that a fairly unusual degree of complexity of presuppositions is tolerable. If this is so, it suggests that complexity of questions as such – within reasonable limits – is not inherently fallacious.

Moreover, to ban all complex questions from reasonable dialogue as a general policy would seem to be an extremely dubious proposal. To altogether forbid the asking of conjunctive, disjunctive, or conditional questions would be to impoverish a questioner's ability to ask many kinds of important and legitimate questions. Such an impoverishment would surely have to be balanced by a strong argument for believing that semantically complex questions are inherently misleading or fallacious. This approach seems misdirected, for semantically complex questions only seem to be fallacious when several other factors combine to make them problematic, as in the spouse-beating question.

Complex questions can pose a problem, however, if the answerer wants to respond to each part of the question separately. A good strategy is to ask for the questions to be divided, for it may be that the answer to the one question need not foreclose an answer to the other.

Example 2.9

Do you support fair hiring practices and job quotas for racial minorities?

This question is addressed in the yes–no form, and consequently poses a problem for the answerer who may want to reply 'yes' to one part and 'no' to the other. A best strategy is to ask that the two questions be posed separately, or at any rate to answer them singly.

Another problem, however, is that dividing the question is not always allowed in every context. It is a common practice in legislatures and congresses to tack a controversial bill onto a larger piece of proposed legislation that is favored by the opposition. Then the opposition can only veto the controversial bill they may not like, at the cost of also rejecting the more significant piece of legislation they would like to see passed.[8] This is essentially the same sort of problem as that posed by side effects in medical treatment. In that case it is Nature who lets you have the beneficial effects of treatment at the cost of the negative side effects.

Fortunately, in many contexts of reasonable dialogue, it is not only permissible but quite reasonable to ask to have a question divided into smaller questions. The important thing is to be aware of this possibility, and to demand it where the question reasonably requires dividing.

2.3 HAVE YOU STOPPED ABUSING YOUR SPOUSE?

We have now seen that some questions are complex questions and some questions are loaded questions. Moreover, asking a complex question need not necessarily be fallacious, and asking a loaded question need not be, in itself, fallacious either, even though it is a good idea to be very careful in attempting to answer a loaded question. Sometimes it is better not to answer it, but to question its presuppositions. Now we will see more precisely why example 2.0, the spouse abuse question can be problematic. The problem arises because it is a question that is both complex and loaded at the same time, and this combination is used in a coercive fashion against a respondent.

8 See examples 2.16 and 2.17 below.

The spouse abuse question is a complex question. It could be broken down into two parts by the respondent who is innocent of spouse abuse, and then each part can be answered separately.

No, I have never abused my spouse in the past.
No, I am not abusing my spouse now.

This response by dividing would defeat the questioner's fallacious attack. And we should observe that the spouse abuse question is loaded, presuming of course that the answerer is not committed to the practice of spouse abuse and does not want to personally acknowledge it.

But there is also a third aspect to the fallaciousness of the spouse abuse question. Since it is posed in the format of a yes–no question, it is disguised as a type of question that should be completely harmless. Normally, a yes–no question is *safe*, meaning that its presupposition is trivially true. For example, the yes–no question 'Is snow white?' has as its presupposition the trivial truth 'Snow is white or Snow is not white.' Nobody could reasonably deny that presupposition, and therefore the question is harmless. It has no significant presupposition that could lead an answerer to reasonably consider it to be a loaded question. Normally, yes–no questions are perfectly safe. However, the spouse-beating question only appears to be safe, insofar as it is posed in the format of a yes–no question. In fact, either way you answer, 'yes' or 'no,' you are automatically committed to an extremely prejudicial proposition. Figure 2.1 illustrates the problem. The problematic aspect is that the spouse-beating question is devised to force the answerer to accept the presupposition no matter which way the question is answered. And because the question is of the yes–no format, the answerer is directed exclusively to the two alternatives 'yes' or 'no.'

To sum up then, the spouse abuse question is a problematic instance of a complex question because it combines three elements in the one question: (1) it is a complex question, (2) it is a loaded question, and (3) it is a yes–no question. The answerer is impaled on the horns of an unfair choice. If he has stopped, that means that he used to do it, but if he hasn't stopped, that means he is still doing it. Either way, he loses.

The spouse abuse question is not necessarily problematic or objectionable in every context of dialogue, however. Suppose a defendant in a trial had previously admitted her spouse abuse activities. In that case, if the prosecuting attorney were to ask, "Have you stopped abusing your spouse?," the question could be perfectly appropriate and reasonable, and the respondent might have no objection to answering it. Hence it is misleading to call the spouse abuse question a fallacy, or to call it the *fallacy*

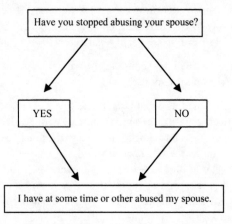

Figure 2.1. The spouse abuse question.

of many questions. For this type of question is not always erroneous or wrong. Yet this type of question certainly can pose an important problem in dialogue.

The underlying problem with the spouse abuse question, when it is a problem, is that the question does not fit into a reasonable order of questioning and answering in the context of dialogue. To see why, you must compare the context of the asking of the question with a profile of reasonable question-answer sequence for that context. Then it can be seen whether or not the question asked violates that reasonable order of dialogue. The spouse abuse question, to be a reasonable question, presupposes that the respondent has already given or is committed to affirmative answers to two prior questions asked in the following order: (1) Do you have a spouse? (2) Have you ever abused your spouse? If these two questions have not been asked and answered first, then the spouse abuse question violates the order of reasonable dialogue, but it is not only the prior context of dialogue that is involved. The spouse abuse question also invites a subsequent attack by the questioner, once any direct answer to the question is given. Figure 2.2 shows a profile of dialogue against which the reasonableness of the spouse abuse question can be evaluated. The profile of dialogue clearly shows the strategy of the asker of the spouse abuse question. By packing the two prior questions into the spouse abuse question, the strategy is to build in affirmative answers to these questions without giving the respondent an opportunity to deny positive concessions.

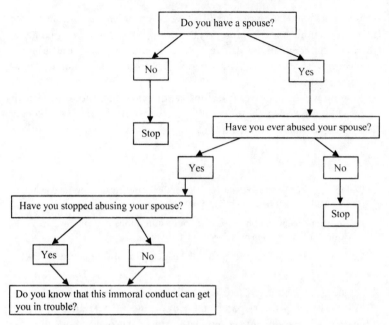

Figure 2.2. Profile of dialogue for the spouse abuse question.

A similar strategy is left open for the sequence of dialogue after the posing of the spouse abuse question. The questioner can follow up with even more incriminating questions like the bottom one in the profile. Or, to cite another possible line of dialogue, he could follow up with a circumstantial personal attack by posing the following type of question: "How can you reconcile your immoral conduct with your own personal standards of morality?" If the respondent falls into his trap, the questioner can follow up by repeating the same strategy over and over until the respondent's side of the argument is completely destroyed.

We can see then how the spouse abuse type of question is coercive. By not giving the respondent a fair chance to answer one question at a time, the questioner can push ahead, leaping over unanswered questions to defeat the respondent's case. In short, the real complexity of the spouse-beating type of question is not just the semantic complexity of its presupposition. A pragmatic complexity pertaining to the order of a sequence of questions and answers in the context of dialogue is also involved.

The purpose of questioning in dialogue may be to extract commitments from a respondent that can later be used as concessions to persuade the respondent, but a question should allow a respondent reasonable choice in expressing his honest opinion. The spouse abuse question attempts to force a respondent into a damaging concession, and move the dialogue prematurely to closure. For this reason, it violates the requirements of good dialogue.[9]

Judging when an answer is reasonable, therefore, depends on the prior judgment of whether the question itself is reasonable. In the following example, the reply is condemned as evasive, but is this criticism justified?

Example 2.10

Q: How long are you prepared to condemn this company to continued failure by your stubborn failure to change your disastrous policies?

A: I do not accept for one moment your assumptions that my policies are disastrous or that my behavior has been stubborn.

Q: You haven't answered the question! That's typical of your evasive tactics.

The questioner's strategy here is to follow up a loaded, aggressive question by criticizing the respondent for evasiveness (irrelevance of reply). However, the respondent has replied correctly by questioning the presuppositions of the question. Of course normally, a respondent has an obligation to give a direct answer to a question if that is possible, and can be done without unreasonable difficulties. In example 2.10, however, a direct answer would trap the respondent unfairly. Hence the "evasive" reply is reasonable.

2.4 DISJUNCTIVE QUESTIONS

When evaluating realistic samples of dialogue, one naturally tends to concentrate on criticizing the answers when looking for fallacies. Even questions, though they often seem harmless enough, may commit fallacies or be open to criticism. Therefore, in evaluating dialogues, one should begin by examining the questions that were asked. First, we should ask: what type of question is it? A yes-no question is supposed to be safe, but as we have seen, many a yes-no question is loaded and complex in its presuppositions. Such questions are not safe.

---

9 It may be interesting to keep the lessons of how to manage aggressive questions in mind when coming to the sportsman's rejoinder case in section 6.2, which has the form of a question.

Another type of question is the *whether-question* that poses a number of alternatives. One fallacy to be on guard against with whether-questions is where the range of reasonable alternatives is not fairly represented. This type of question is said to commit the *black and white fallacy*, where the question poses an exclusive disjunction that is overly restrictive in representing the various reasonable possibilities that should be allowed in a direct answer. It is classically illustrated by the following question.

Example 2.11

Is a zebra black or white?

The problem with this question is that one should be allowed to answer truly that a zebra is both black and white. Yet insofar as the question is posed or taken as an exclusive disjunction, it does not allow for the answer 'Both.' In other words, the presupposition of the question is that a zebra is either black or white but not both. Presuming that this presupposition is false, the question may rightly be regarded as objectionable because it does not permit an answerer to give the right answer or at least a direct answer that he feels is reasonable.

Examples of this type of question are not hard to find.

Example 2.12

Are you a pacifist or a warmonger?

Example 2.13

(Book title) *The Abolitionists: Reformers or Fanatics?*

These disjunctive questions can be objected to when they are overly restrictive, and therefore do not permit an answerer reasonable latitude in giving a direct answer. Once again, the best answer may be to rebut the presupposition by posing another question as your reply. While normally it may be reasonable to require a direct answer, with questions like these, such a requirement is overly restrictive.

Another interesting example is the following question, printed in large letters heading up an ad for a ballpoint pen in *Newsweek* (April 24, 1995, p. 57).

51

Example 2.14

Is the Paper Mate *Dynagrip* a great pen because it's so comfortable or because it writes really smoothly?

In this case, the question contains the presupposition that the Dynagrip is a great pen. And then this presupposition, taken as an accepted or proven fact, is backed up by giving the disjunctive proposition 'The Dynagrip is so comfortable or it writes really smoothly' as a sort of explanation or justification. The idea is that the reader of the ad can choose one or the other of the alternatives in the disjunction, but that is the only choice allowed by the structure of the question. So the reader has no choice but to accept the proposition, 'The Dynagrip is a great pen.' Whichever alternative he accepts in the disjunction, both of which are highly positive reasons for buying the Dynagrip, he must accept the presupposition. So the question in the example above is a loaded question that incorporates a disjunctive feature as part of its strategy and structure. The question in this example illustrates how people often try to frame the issue of a discussion as a dichotomy, so that it appears that the respondent should be concerned with working out which one of the alternatives should be chosen, instead of thinking about other possible alternatives. Using the form of posing an issue is often a way of trying to put pressure on a respondent to go in a particular direction.

In principle, there is nothing wrong with asking a disjunctive (either-or) type of complex question. So what exactly is wrong with either-or questions when they are objectionable? The basic problem with objectionable disjunctive questions is the same root problem characteristic of the spouse abuse question. Such a question, when it is objectionable, violates the reasonable order of question-asking and answering in dialogue. Consider a question like the following example.

Example 2.15

Should we allow the government to take total control of health care or must we allow physicians to be completely free of government regulation?

The problem here is the presumption by the questioner that a reasonable respondent must accept one or the other of the posed alternatives. However, this presumption is highly implausible, and would need to be established by a prior question, or sequence of questions and answers, before the question in example 2.15 could be established as reasonable.

While there is nothing intrinsically wrong with complex questions, they can get us into difficulties in certain kinds of cases, where splitting up the question is important in light of a respondent's commitments in the dialogue.

Example 2.16

A new health care bill transferring responsibility for health care funding from the federal to the state governments has been put forward in the Legislative Assembly for a vote. A Democrat, Representative Munson, would very much like to vote against this bill. However, attached to the bill is a rider – a piece of legislation that would retain a strong form of affirmative action as policy for the Federal Government. Representative Munson is in a pickle. Which way should he vote? If he votes against the health care bill, he also has to vote against affirmative action. But in order to vote for the proposal strengthening affirmative action, he would also have to vote for the health care bill (which he is against).

Because of the way voting on bills is structured, Representative Munson does not have the choice of doing what he really wants to do, which is to vote for the one bill and against the other. So he must make up his mind on the basis of his priorities which of the two policies is most important for him to support, by voting one way or the other. No matter which way he votes, however, he goes against his commitments on one proposition or the other. So here, the complex nature of the question is a problem.

This problem of having to vote on a complex bill that may have several propositions in it is common to all legislatures, parliaments, and congresses that allow amendments to be "tacked onto" bills. However, most parliaments require that such an amendment be relevant, or "germane" to the bill being considered. However, the U.S. Senate allows for non-germane amendments to be added onto a bill. What this means, according to Froman (1967, p. 132), is that anything can be added to a bill to be voted on, whether it is relevant to the bill or not.

Example 2.17

What this means, in effect, is that any matter, whether it has been previously introduced or not, whether it has been referred to committee or not, and whether it is germane to the pending business or not (except general appropriation bills) may be introduced as an amendment. This was, in fact, the manner in which the 1960 Civil Rights Bill was brought to the floor in the Senate. Senator Lyndon B. Johnson, then majority leader, in motioning up

53

an obscure bill to aid a school district in Missouri that was federally impacted, announced that the bill would be open to civil rights amendments.

The problem of having to vote on complex propositions is not unique to the U.S. Senate, but the most dramatic cases of having to vote on complex legislation, where the voter's commitments are sharply divided on different issues, occur there, because there is no requirement of relevance on amendments.

In some cases of very aggressive use of disjunctive questions, the strategy of dichotomizing the question in a way that makes it impossible to answer directly without having to commit to something you don't agree with is even more transparent.

Example 2.18

Is snow black, or are you one of those crazy people who think it's white?

Here, the questioner has tried to pre-empt the expected answer by portraying it within the question as an option that has already been ruled out as "crazy." The reasonable order of questioning would be to first inquire whether or not snow is black, and if the answer is "Snow is white" then to go on and criticize that answer. Thus the solution to this kind of problem is to break the complex question down into smaller questions and then restructure the dialogue so that each is asked separately, and in the right order.

Another type of question is the *why-question*, which may demand an explanation for something, or a reason for accepting some proposition. One important kind of why-question in reasonable dialogue is the request for grounds for accepting a proposition that is subject to question or controversy.

Example 2.19

Why is pacifism morally wrong?

Quite often the context of this sort of why-question is a dispute, where the answerer has adopted or is committed to a certain position. The question can be a challenge for the answerer to provide premises that imply the proposition queried, where that proposition is a significant part of the answerer's position. In example 2.19, the context of the disputation could be that the answerer is defending a position that is opposed to pacificism, and the questioner is challenging him to supply grounds for his acceptance of the proposition that pacifism is morally wrong.

The problem with why-questions is knowing how direct an answer must be to qualify as relevant. A direct answer to a why-question like example 2.19 may be defined as a set of propositions that implies the presupposition of the question by valid arguments according to the rules of valid argument appropriate to the dialogue. However, sometimes an answerer in a controversial dispute needs room to argue. He may not be able to prove the queried proposition directly, but may need to obtain the concession of other propositions from the questioner as additional premises in order to work towards proving his conclusion. How much room to argue should a questioner reasonably allow the answerer of a why-question? Once again, judgment is needed to evaluate whether an answer is relevant if it seems to be heading in the right direction. One must not be too quick to condemn an answer as irrelevant if it does not immediately give the required proof in one step.

To sum up then, there are several different kinds of questions, including yes–no questions, whether-questions, and why-questions. The first step in the analysis of any dialogue is to identify the type of question involved. The second step is to identify and state the presuppositions of the question. The third step is to ask whether the presupposition of the question is complex. The fourth step is to evaluate whether the presupposition of the question is loaded. If the answer to steps three and four is 'yes,' then the fifth step is to ask whether the question is an instance of the fallacy of many questions. Having evaluated the question, it is now appropriate to turn to an evaluation of the answer.

The sixth step in the analysis of dialogue is to evaluate whether the answer is a direct answer. If not, then the seventh step is to ask whether the answer is reasonably relevant. However, this seventh step must always be judged relative to the appropriateness and reasonableness of the question. If the question is fallacious or overly aggressive, then the fact that a direct answer was not given may be no good grounds for criticizing the answer as irrelevant or evasive. Whether the answer is to be judged as relevant or not must be evaluated in relation to the fairness of the question in the context of the objectives and rules of reasonable procedure of the dialogue.

In the analysis of any argument, questions or answers to questions (assertions) should never be answered in isolation from each other. In other words, every argument is really a dialogue, and should be evaluated as such. Every argument has two sides.

It is the obligation of an answerer in reasonable dialogue to give an informative and relevant direct answer to a reasonable question if he can. If an answerer truly does not know whether the proposition queried is true or false, he should have the option, in reasonable dialogue, of replying 'I don't know' or 'No commitment one way or the other.' In other words, the ignorant answerer should be able to admit his ignorance. For, as Socrates reminded us, the beginning of wisdom is to admit your ignorance if you really don't know the answer to a question. Hence any structure of dialogue that does not allow an answerer the 'No commitment' option, in replying to questions, would not be tolerant of wisdom.

The idea that an answerer should concede that he doesn't know the answer, if he really doesn't, is reflected in a traditional fallacy called the *ad ignorantiam* fallacy.

Example 2.20

Elliot: How do you know that ghosts don't exist?

Zelda: Well, nobody has ever proved that ghosts do exist, have they?

Here, Elliot asks Zelda to give justification for her commitment to the proposition that ghosts do not exist. Zelda answers by shifting the burden of proof back onto Elliot to prove that ghosts do exist. However, this reply is said to commit the fallacy of arguing from ignorance (*argumentum ad ignorantiam*): just because a proposition has never been proved true, that does not mean that it is false.[10]

For example, Fermat's last theorem in mathematics had never been proved true at the time of the publication of the first edition of this book (1989).[11] Fermat wrote out the theorem in notes in 1637, and wrote that he has a marvelous proof of it, but that the margin was too narrow to contain it. Over the years, there have been many failed attempts, but no mathematician was able to prove Fermat's last theorem until 1994, when Andrew Wiles and Richard Taylor worked out a proof based on methods developed by other mathematicians. However, prior to 1994, it was still an open question whether it can be proved that Fermat's last theorem is unprovable. All that was known then is that it might be unprovable,

---

10 See Woods and Walton (1978).
11 Fermat's last theorem states that it is impossible to separate any power higher than the second into two like powers.

but there was hope that it might be just very difficult to prove it. Thus the question whether a proposition has been proved is separate from the question of whether that proposition can be proved or not. It might be the case that it has not been proved because it can't be proved, but then again it might not. That may remain to be shown. You can't argue from ignorance.

The *ad ignorantiam* argument can be defined as an argument of one of the following two forms.

(I1) Proposition A is not known to be true, therefore A is false.

(I2) Proposition A is not known to be false, therefore A is true.

As an instance of (I2), we might cite the following example.

Example 2.21

Some philosophers have tried to disprove the existence of God, but they have always failed.

Therefore, we can conclude with certainty that God exists.

The problem with example 2.21 is similar to the previous examples of arguing from ignorance. It might be that nobody has ever disproved the existence of God, but it does not follow that it is impossible to prove it. That is a separate question which remains to be shown. Hence both (I1) and (I2) are rightly regarded as forms of argument that are not generally valid.

The next point we must recognize, however, is that arguments having the form of *ad ignorantiam* are not always unreasonable. Consider the following case.

Example 2.22

Mr. X has never been found guilty of breaches of security, or of any connections with the KGB, even though the Security Service has checked his record.

Therefore, Mr. X is not a KGB spy.

This argument has the form of *ad ignorantiam* inference, but is it a fallacy? Well, if the Security Service has checked Mr. X out very thoroughly, and there is absolutely no grounds for doubting Mr. X, and he has an excellent record of service and loyalty, then there is at least some basis for the plausible presumption that Mr. X is not a KGB spy. Of course, we can probably never know such a thing for sure. So to conclusively assert that "beyond doubt" Mr. X cannot be a KGB spy could easily be an overly strong conclusion to draw, and could therefore be an unjustified argument from ignorance. Nonetheless, if the search was very thorough, it could be reasonable to draw the conclusion that Mr. X should be plausibly presumed not to be a spy, until we find evidence to suggest otherwise. Hence the *ad ignorantiam* argument is not always fallacious, and it is misleading to call it a fallacy. What this case suggests is that the *ad ignorantiam* is a form of plausible reasoning that can be a reasonable, albeit weak, form of plausible argument, depending on the context. In this case, the context is how thorough the Security Service search was.

If the conclusion of the argument is phrased in strong terms – for example, using the term 'definitely' or 'conclusively' – then that is a sign that the argument could be fallacious. If the conclusion is phrased as a plausible presumption however, and the context of dialogue supports it, then these are signs that the argument from ignorance may be reasonable (non-fallacious).

For example, we saw that in the case of a mathematical proposition, if it has never been proven, it would be a fallacious *ad ignorantiam* argument to conclude that it cannot be proven. For proving that it has not been proven yet and proving that it cannot be proven are two different things. However, if many clever mathematicians have tried to prove the propositions by all the most powerful methods and never succeeded, then that may be plausible grounds for concluding that the best way to proceed is to presume that the proposition is false. The suggested course of action would then be to concentrate on trying to prove that it is false, rather than carrying on trying to prove that it is true.

In short then, as a weak (plausible) form of argument, an *ad ignorantiam* argument can sometimes be non-fallacious. It depends on the context. The argument from ignorance can become weak or erroneous where it is taken as a stronger form of argument than the evidence warrants. In effect, this means that arguing from ignorance may not always be fallacious in every case, in reasonable dialogue. Although, as we saw before, (I1) and (I2) are not generally valid forms of argument, in some cases arguments having those forms can be reasonable. Consider (I2) for example. Sometimes even though a proposition is not known to be false, it may be reasonable to presume that it is true.

Example 2.23

I do not know that this rifle is unloaded. Therefore, it is reasonable to presume that it is loaded.

In this case, the argument from ignorance could be reasonable. Even though I may have no good evidence to indicate whether or not in fact the rifle is loaded, it may be reasonable to conclude that I should commit myself to the proposition that it is loaded, at least until I find out one way or the other. That is, sometimes it is reasonable to presume commitment, even though you don't know the answer to a question.

The reason for the reasonableness of example 2.23 has to do with the normal context of the argument. In normal circumstances, safety when handling dangerous weapons is a high priority. Therefore, the burden of proof is always to assume that the weapon may be loaded. In this context, if you have not checked the firing chamber, it is best to assume that there may be a round in it. We make this presumption because accidentally discharging a loaded rifle is very dangerous. Hence our standards of safety need to be very high.

However, notice that in another context, if I do not know whether the rifle is loaded, it may be better to operate on the presumption that it is not loaded. If a soldier is under attack by a dangerous, hostile enemy, then he may be well advised to check to be sure that his rifle is loaded. If he cannot be sure, it may be best for him to presume that it is not loaded, and check to make sure. In this context, example 2.23 would not be a plausible argument.

The burden of proof varies from one context of dialogue to another. So it is the context of dialogue that can make an *ad ignorantiam* argument plausible or implausible in a given case. It is important, however, to recognize that when an argument from ignorance is a reasonable argument, it is a weak form of argument that depends on the context of dialogue. To treat it as a strong form of argument, as a deductively valid argument that leads to a conclusion beyond doubt, is a presumption that can easily lead to error and confusion.

Care is needed with an argument from ignorance to take each case individually, because sometimes these arguments are not unreasonable. Certainly (I1) and (I2) could be fallacious in many cases if they are taken to be deductively valid arguments of the following form, taking (I2) as the example: proposition A is not known to be false, therefore it must follow that A is known to be true, but if (I2) is taken in a weaker form, it can be reasonable in some cases: proposition A is not known to be false, therefore it is reasonable to commit myself to the presumption that A is true.

Whether an *ad ignorantiam* argument is reasonable or not often depends on the burden of proof as indicated by the context of dialogue. For example, the criminal law presumes that a person is not guilty if he has not been shown to be guilty. This is an *ad ignorantiam* form of argument, but it can be reasonable in the context of the rules of argument in the criminal law. In the criminal law, there is a burden of proof on the prosecution to prove that the defendant is guilty beyond reasonable doubt. This is a very high burden of proof, because it is very difficult to prove anything beyond all reasonable doubt. The reason the standard is set so high is because of the necessity to build in safeguards against the possibility that an innocent person could be ruled guilty in a criminal trial. This outcome is thought to be more significant than the possibility that some guilty persons could go free. Hence the burden of proof is asymmetrical.

Similarly with example 2.23. Where there is a serious potential danger to be guarded against, the burden of proof may be adjusted to minimize the possibility of realizing that dangerous outcome. It is in such cases that the *ad ignorantiam* can be a plausible form of argument.

In reasonable dialogue there is very often a reasonable presumption of burden of proof. If I am heavily committed to one side of a dispute and my position indicates a strong presumption that I accept a certain proposition, then it is fair for my questioner to presuppose that proposition in his questions, and to directly ask me about my acceptance of that proposition and expect a direct answer. My position obliges me to defend and acknowledge propositions that I have accepted and should reasonably accept as part of that position. This means that in reasonable dialogue, if I am asked 'Why A?' where A is in fact a thesis I have advocated, I may not be allowed to shift the burden of proof back to my questioner with the *ad ignorantiam* reply 'Why not-A?' In other words, if asked 'Why do you accept A?' I should not always be allowed to bounce the ball back to your court and reply 'Why don't you accept A?' Before making that move in reply, I may be reasonably required to, first, give some reason or argument for positively accepting A. Otherwise, the argument could go back and forth forever with no real dialogue or constructive interaction taking place at all. For example, the believer and the atheist could ask back and forth forever, 'Why don't you believe in the existence of God?' *versus* 'Why do you believe in the existence of God?' This procedure would not advance the argument at all. To get anywhere, each side must assume a reasonable burden of proof. In dialogue, this means that each side must sincerely try to justify his adopted position, and to incur commitment when queried, if one's position truly requires that commitment.

Just as questions can be loaded, in some cases *ad ignorantiam* arguments can also be stacked against the one to whom the argument is directed.

Example 2.24

No person who is reasonably intelligent and well informed could doubt that there has never been any serious and well-established evidence for extra-sensory perception. Therefore extra-sensory perception does not exist.

The premise of example 2.24 is loaded with the presupposition that anyone who could accept the evidence for extra-sensory perception (ESP) would be unintelligent or not a well-informed person. For anyone who might not be committed to the premise would, according to the premise, have to fall into one or more of these categories. This creates pressure against anyone who might question the premise. For by conceding that he falls into one of these categories, he might weaken his own credibility to continue with the argument.

The best reply for the one against whom example 2.24 is directed is to ask what putative evidence has been alleged for ESP and why has it been shown to be so dubious. Of course it should also be pointed out that too hastily arriving at the conclusion to reject ESP on the basis of ignorance could be a dogmatic and premature dismissal of an argument.

In short, one must always try to avoid the error of hastily making overly firm conclusions on the basis of ignorance. That is called dogmatic reasoning, and it is the worst mistake in reasonable dialogue. One must always be aware that there could be reasonable arguments on the other side of an issue as well as on your own side. On the other hand, in moral and political controversies for example, we may often have to make commitments even without knowing for sure that we are right, or completely justified in accepting a proposition. Consequently, it is often reasonable to make commitments on the basis of what seems plausible on the best arguments you have, as you see the issue. Without a willingness to incur commitments, even with due caution and hesitation, no argument on a controversial issue would ever get anywhere. Sometimes you must try your best to answer a question honestly and sincerely, even if you do not know the answer, if the question is reasonable and relevant to an issue on which you have taken a stand in dialogue.

2.6 REPLYING TO A QUESTION WITH A QUESTION

If a questioner asks a loaded question, the burden of proof ought to be on him to prove the presuppositions of the question. However, argument is often like a game of tennis in the respect that failure to return the ball strongly enough at the next move may result in a loss of the exchange, or even a loss of the game. For when a question is posed aggressively, it often does shift the burden of proof onto the respondent to justify his position. If he fails to do this strongly enough, the accusations in the question may appear to be conceded and confirmed.

What the respondent ought to do in such a case is to require that the questioner give evidence for the assumptions made in the question, or if he cannot, to retract them. This approach makes it clear that the burden of proof should be on the questioner to support his allegations.

Richard Whately (1846, p. 114) warned that if the victim of an unsupported accusation takes upon himself the burden of trying to prove his innocence, instead of defying the questioner to prove his charge, he may appear to concede his own guilt. It is a case of "Qui s'excuse, s'accuse." Whately (1846, p. 113) compared it with the case of a body of troops, strong enough to hold a fort, who sally forth into the open field and are defeated. In other words, if you have the presumption on your side, to concentrate on trying to defend your own case could be a serious error. For you might be overlooking one of your strongest arguments, namely the burden of proof. In short, sometimes the policy of questioning the question is both reasonable and strategically sound in dialogue.

Generally speaking, the strategy of aggressive questioning is to pack so much loaded information into the presupposition of a loaded question that the answerer would be severely implicated and condemned by any attempt to give a straight answer. If he fails to give a straight 'yes' or 'no' answer then the questioner can accuse him of being evasive and failing to answer the question. No matter which way the answerer proceeds, he could be in trouble. If he answers the question directly, he becomes committed to some proposition that can then be used against him. If he attempts to divide up the question and separately question its presuppositions, he may appear to be failing to honestly answer the question. Such a loaded question is trickily aggressive – its purpose is to deflect the burden of proof onto the answerer and, if possible, aggressively attack the answerer's position by the mere act of asking a "harmless" question.

Generally, the best strategy for the answerer of such a question is to try to deflect the burden of proof back onto the questioner while trying not to appear too evasive. Then of course, the best strategy for the questioner is to accuse the answerer of being irrelevant, or failing to answer the question. In either case, whether a question or reply is to be judged as reasonable or not may depend very much on a prior evaluation of the burden of proof.

Although in many cases it is reasonable to reply to a question by questioning the question itself, such a strategy can become an abuse of reasonable dialogue if carried too far. For in general, there is an obligation to answer a question, if possible, in reasonable dialogue. However, there may be many good reasons for not answering a question. These may include the following reasons. The question may be unduly aggressive or argumentative. The question may lack clarity, and be misleading or ambiguous. The question may repeat a previous question. The respondent may not know the answer, or for various legitimate reasons, may not be able to give it, even if he knows it. If the question is addressed to the respondent as an expert, it may be outside the respondent's field of expertise. Thus if a respondent gives any one of these or other good reasons for not answering a question, his obligation to answer it can be removed, or excused by the questioner. The burden on a respondent then is either to answer a question or give some justifiable reason why he cannot or will not answer it. It follows that not every reply to a question with another question is a reasonable or non-objectionable reply.

In some cases using a question to reply to a question can be an evasive attempt to shift the burden of proof back onto the questioner. The following dialogue arose through the practice of using for-profit hospitals to treat teenagers with drug or alcohol dependence problems. It was alleged that some of these teenagers were not being properly supervised, and a controversy had arisen about whether any proper treatment was being given in these institutions.

Example 2.25

Parent: Why weren't you looking after my child properly?

Hospital Director: How can we look after thirty-six when you can't take care of one?

In this case, the Hospital Director was evading answering the question by shifting the burden of proof back onto the parent with another question. The strategy in this case was to avoid answering the question while at the same time appearing to give a reasonable reply, but is the reply reasonable?

The question appears to be a reasonable one to ask in the given context of dialogue, but the reply is an effective tactic to divert the questioner and audience from the real issue, because of its emotional impact on the parent. For the parent is probably deeply disturbed about the problems he or she has had with the teenager, and may feel partly responsible or guilty.

Hence it would be difficult for the parent not to be distracted by this clever reply. However, in this case, the use of the question to reply to the question is an objectionable tactic used to try to shift the burden of proof and avoid the obligation to answer the question. Because there is generally an obligation to answer a question, a reply that is irrelevant or evasive can, in many cases, be criticized as an objectionable move in reasonable dialogue. So to avoid answering a question is not always an acceptable type of response.

So when is the tactic of replying to a question with a question allowable in reasonable dialogue? The most general answer relates to burden of proof in dialogue. If the context of dialogue and the respondent's commitments and assertions in dialogue make it clear that he should be obliged to justify or explain a specific proposition, then there is a burden on the respondent to answer a question that asks for such justification or explanation. If he fails to answer the question without giving a good reason for this failure, his reply may be judged irrelevant or unduly evasive. But if the question is unduly aggressive, or is packed with presuppositions the respondent does not accept, this could be an excellent and fully justifiable reason for questioning the question.

Questions of burden of proof are decided in a specific case by looking at the context of dialogue and determining, in accord with the outline of dialogue given in chapter 1, what the issue really is, and what each participant in the argument should be trying to prove.

2.7 BEGGING THE QUESTION

In a persuasion dialogue, the goal of each participant is to prove his conclusion from premises that are accepted as commitments by the other participant. However, if a premise has not already been explicitly accepted by a respondent, it must at least be a proposition that he could possibly accept, consistently with his own obligation to prove his conclusion. Otherwise the argument using this premise as a basis could not be useful for the purpose of persuading the respondent to accept its conclusion. This type of inadequate or useless attempt at proof is a violation, error, or shortcoming in a persuasion dialogue, because such an argument stands no chance of fulfilling its proponent's obligation to prove his conclusion in the discussion.

The following example is a case in point. Suppose that Bob and Leo are engaged in a critical discussion, and Bob is a skeptic who doubts the existence of God. Leo is a religious believer who has taken on the burden of proving to Bob that God exists. At some point in the dialogue, Bob asks Leo to prove that God is benevolent. Leo advances the following argument in reply.

Example 2.26

God has all the virtues.

Benevolence is a virtue.

Therefore, God is benevolent.

What would Bob's likely response be? The answer is that since Bob is a committed skeptic, he has every right to object that Leo's argument begs the question. Bob might reply: "Well, of course, if you accept both premises of your argument, Leo, then you have to accept the conclusion of this valid argument. Since I don't accept the conclusion, how can you reasonably expect me to accept the first premise? Consistently with my point of view as a skeptic about the whole enterprise of religion, I not only doubt whether it is correct to say that God has any of the virtues, I even doubt that God exists as an entity that can have virtues." Given Bob's obligation to question the existence of God, he can hardly go around accepting statements like "God has all the virtues," without virtually conceding the whole issue by making his own position inconsistent.

In this sort of situation, Leo's argument could be criticized by saying that it begs the question. For Leo's argument only "begs for" Bob's acceptance of the proposition (question) to be proved, instead of doing the proper job of proving it by deducing it from premises that Leo has a chance of proving in his persuasion dialogue with Bob. An argument that begs the question is also often said to commit the fallacy of arguing in a circle. In this case, there appears to be no way that Leo could prove the premise 'God has all the virtues,' without already presupposing that 'God is benevolent' as a prior assumption (given that it is accepted that benevolence is a virtue). We could say then that Leo's argument "chases its own tail" or goes in a circle.

The following example, called the clock and gun case (Walton 1984, p. 16), illustrates circular reasoning of a kind where the fallacy of arguing in a circle is involved.

Example 2.27

An efficiency expert visiting a factory was told that the workers knew when to return to work because a gun was fired at exactly one o'clock by a man standing on the roof. When asked how he knew it was one o'clock, the man on the roof said that he verified the time by looking across the street to the clock on the store. The efficiency expert went to the store, and asked the owner how often he checked his clock. He replied: "Never. It's always dead right by the one o'clock gun."

The problem posed by circularity in this case is that the reliability of each method of telling the time relies on the other only, so both could be wrong, even though they agree. If the clock runs slow, and becomes more and more inaccurate over the passage of time, for example, neither party will be aware of the error in telling the time.

Circular sequences of questions and answers are not always fallacious instances of begging the question in all contexts of dialogue. Suppose I ask you, "Why does Bruno like Betty?," and you reply, "Because Betty likes Bruno." This sequence is circular, but it need not be fallacious as an explanation of human behavior. It could be that both Betty and Bruno are the kind of people who respond to affection. They like others because others like them. Thus their behavior as a mutual admiration society is an instance of a circular, feedback process between Betty and Bruno. Explaining this behavior by pointing out its circular structure is not fallacious, or an erroneous case of begging the question.

What is needed to make the reasoning in the clock and the gun case non-fallacious is some third, independent means of telling the time. For example, suppose the store owner were to check the time listed on his television weather channel, a highly reliable source. In such a case, there is still a circle in the reasoning (between the clock criterion and the gun criterion), but the circular reasoning is no longer fallacious. The reason is that the store owner has an independent criterion that is not dependent solely on the firing of the gun, for showing that his setting of the clock is correct.

Whether circular reasoning is fallacious or not depends on the context of dialogue in which the circular argumentation was used. Begging the question is a fault in persuasion dialogue because a circular argument is useless for the purpose of persuading someone to accept a conclusion on the basis of premises that they are, or can become committed to. An argument that begs the question is doomed from the outset as a persuasive proof. An argument that begs the question does not count as a useful move to facilitate an inquiry either. In an inquiry, the premises must be known or better established than the conclusion to be proved. Otherwise the inquiry makes no progress.

2.8 QUESTIONS IN POLLS

It is easy for beginning students of logic to think that being concerned with the formulation of questions is a trivial matter. However, all polls used to collect statistical data on matters of the utmost importance in a democracy are based on the asking of questions. Such polls are often manipulated and the results are misrepresented by powerful groups promoting a social agenda. We often suspect that such use of statistics in polling may be subtly trying to manipulate us by using numbers to distort the truth. We could just be skeptical about all statistics, but we need polls based on good statistics to talk realistically about social problems. Hence it is very important to think critically about how to formulate a question used in a poll, and about how to draw a reasonable conclusion about the statistical find in the poll. Polls are based on what is called sampling, the drawing of an inference about a larger population by collecting evidence about the properties of the smaller subset of that population. Sampling works by extrapolating from the properties of the smaller set by statistical reasoning to the larger set. How sampling works as a procedure will be described more fully in section 8.2.

The most problematic aspect of the sampling inference drawn in a poll is the phrasing of the question. The question is phrased in words that are not defined, but that have a meaning to the respondents. The problem of question wording effect is that an apparently small or insignificant variation in the words chosen to appear in a question can have an (unpredictably) large effect on the statistical outcome of the poll. One question wording effect relates to the positive or negative connotations of words chosen in a question. What may superficially appear to be the same, or an equivalent word, may have different connotations for respondents. Hence an apparently slight rewording of a question may result in a dramatic difference in a poll outcome.

You might think that public support for welfare would be equivalent, or roughly the same as public support for the poor, but a national survey in 1985 showed that only 19 per cent of people said that too little was being spent on "welfare," while 63 per cent said that too little was being spent on "assistance to the poor" (Moore 1992, p. 344). The difference of 44 percentage points is a statistically significant one in the outcomes of the two polls, even though they both appeared to be asking pretty much the same question. The researcher conjectured that the word "welfare" has negative connotations of welfare fraud for many respondents, while the term "assistance to the poor" has positive connotations of providing better conditions and "care of the people" (Moore 1992, p. 344). Because of this variance of connotations of words chosen, the variance in poll outcomes was huge.

Howard Schuman and Stanley Presser did an experiment in 1940 to study the question wording effect of changing 'forbid' to 'allow' when the question of whether the United States should forbid speeches against democracy was put to a sample of respondents. For a detailed account of their research on wording of questions in polling, see Schuman and Presser (1981). The two questions in this particular experiment were the following.

(Q1) Should the United States forbid public speeches against democracy?
(Q2) Should the United States allow public speeches against democracy?

Forty-six per cent of respondents said 'no' to (Q1), but only 25 per cent said 'yes' to (Q2), according to the account of this experiment given in Moore (1992, p. 334). This impressive difference of 21 percentage points was produced just by a change in a single word. Schuman and Presser also tested the forbid/allow substitution in the question of whether the government should forbid the showing of X-rated movies, but the outcome here was a difference in only four percentage points in the responses of the two groups polled. The lack of consistency between this outcome and the previous one Moore describes (p. 335) as "dismaying."

The structure of the question used in a poll is of a kind that is meant to narrow down the range of responses to definite outcomes that can be counted up in a numerical outcome. This structure may not only introduce a bias by encouraging the respondent in one direction as opposed to another, it may also impose a definiteness on an issue that is not really appropriate, or consistent with what the respondent really thinks about the issue. The sampling procedure used to get the poll result may generate an outcome that is highly misleading. The outcome of the poll may impute a definiteness that is not really there.

One solution to this problem frequently suggested is the use of open as opposed to closed questions, as indicated by the following examples.

Closed question: Do you think the government is doing a good job of dealing with inflation, or not?

Open question: What kind of job do you think the government is doing in dealing with inflation?

The open question is preferable to the closed question, because it leaves open a range of permissible responses, instead of narrowing the responses down to two, as in the closed (yes-no) question. But the practical problem is that, given the nature of polling as a quantitative, statistical undertaking, there is a need to get the questionnaire in a form whereby it can be tabulated numerically by counting up the answers. This limitation means that in practice, the open question, of the type above for example, has to be reduced to some sort of closed or multiple choice question, with only definite answers allowed of a kind leading to results that can be counted. So the open question ultimately has to become a closed question of some sort. For example, the open question above might become the following multiple choice question.

Multiple choice question: What kind of job do you think the government is doing in dealing with inflation: (a) good, (b) fair, (c) poor?

Putting in a fourth opinion, 'None of the above' is possible, but may not make for a very exciting outcome.

If given a yes-no question, or another type of multiple choice question that admits of only a small list of choices as answers, many people, as noted above, will opt for one choice or the other, even though they don't know the answer to the question. The results of such a poll could be quite consistent, in the sense that subsequent polls putting the same question would get the same statistical result. Payne (1951, p. 17) states the problem succinctly:

With straight faces we might start our interviews among the general public by asking, Which do you prefer, dichotomous or open questions? We might be surprised at the proportion of people who would soberly express a choice. Their selections obviously would not be meaningful in the desired sense. Yet it would be incorrect to assume that their answers were entirely meaningless or haphazard. People might vaguely think that they understood us but not know the first term might choose the second in high proportions. And in passing, we might forecast that repeated experiments with the same question would probably give closely duplicating results. Stability of replies is no test of a meaningful question. The more meaningless a question is, the more likely it is to produce consistent percentages when repeated.

Would it be a good guide to rational deliberation on a question if we used the results of a poll based on this type of question? No, it would not, because the poll is not telling us correctly what the opinion of those polled really is, although citing the results of such a poll in an argument could sound impressive.

When the results of a poll are given with an exact numerical figure representing the "margin of error", many people think that this number represents how accurate the poll has been in correctly ascertaining the opinion of the population group. In other words, the figure is taken to refer to the probability that the poll might be wrong in drawing the conclusion that a group of people believe a particular opinion. But that is not what the figure represents at all. The figure represents the probability that when the same poll is run with another sample group of respondents, it will come up with the same statistical results. So in other words, the margin of error is the probability that the poll has not picked out the respondents by a sample that is adequate. The figure says nothing at all about whether the poll is really accurate in the sense that its conclusion represents the real opinions stated. So even if this figure is very high, as Payne points out, showing that the poll agrees with the results of repeated trials, it could still be that the poll is biased, or for other reasons, does not give a true picture of what the respondents think.

Polls inflate and dramatize people's real opinions by forcing a respondent to make up his or her mind, frequently by asking a yes–no question, on an issue where the respondent may not have arrived at a decision. This speeding up of the decision process to get a definite answer is described by Crossen (1994, p. 106):

It is a poller's business to press for an opinion whether people have one or not. "Don't knows" are worthless to pollers, whose product is opinion, not ignorance. That is why so many polls do not even offer a "don't know" alternative. If someone volunteers a "don't know" (and studies have shown many people will guess an answer rather than volunteer their ignorance) the interviewers are often told to push or probe. In choices among candidates, those who say they are undecided might be asked how they "lean." The result is that people seem more decided about issues and candidates than they are.

Public opinion polls are generally good at predicting the outcome of an election, because when a person votes, he or she also has to make up his or her mind, and vote one way or the other (although polls have been wrong, as in the 1992 general election in Britain, where they wrongly predicted a Labour victory). On an issue requiring deliberation, where people have not made up their minds, or on a question that the respondents know little about, a public opinion can be misleading, suggesting a definite opinion on one side or the other of an issue where none exists. According to Wheeler (1990, p. 196) pollsters are "instinctively hostile to the idea of people without opinions," and so they will go to great lengths to force people to state a preference. Also in reporting the results of a poll, the people who were undecided may not be reported as part of the sample.

2.9 ADVOCACY AND PUSH POLLING

Those who conduct polls and surveys are aware that question wording will affect the outcome of a poll. In what is called *advocacy research* (Best 2001, p. 47), an advocate paying for his own survey shapes the wording of the question in order to encourage people to respond in a way that will yield an outcome showing widespread public support for the position advocated. An example is the following poll question, shaped to encourage a positive response.

Example 2.28

Do you favor cracking down against illegal gun sales?

According to Best (2001, p. 47), a gun control advocate putting this question would know that most people oppose illegal acts and that questions of this kind routinely find that more than three-quarters of Americans favor gun control.

Use of slanted questions in political opinion polls to make a candidate look good or bad has become so common that it has even been given a name, according to Kesterton (1995, p. A24):

Push polling: A deceptive political telephone tactic that aims to sway, rather than survey, the opinions of voters. For example, people in Colorado last year were asked: "Please tell me if you would be more likely or less likely to vote for Roy Romer if you knew that Governor Romer appoints a parole board which has granted early release to an average of four convicted felons per day every day since Romer took office."

The fact that push polling has become a recognized technique of argumentation for political and public relations purposes indicates that asking critical questions about the question wording of a poll is by no means purely an academic exercise.

Anyone who is using push polling to influence public opinion is likely, as part of the tactic, to try to deflect critical questions about the structure and wording of the question actually used to obtain the poll results. Typically, media reports do not include this information. Because it is typically not possible to get answers to critical questions about methods used in polling from media reports, or from an arguer who has used a poll to support

71

his claim, it is vital to ask who did the polling, and whether they are a reliable organization. Even reputable polling organizations have been known to make serious mistakes. Even worse, there is growing concern that reputable polling agencies can have an active agenda to advocate the particular view or interests of a group that stands to gain or lose by the poll outcome (Best 2001, p. 48).

Example 2.29

Advocates word questions so as to encourage people to respond in the desired way. For example, surveys by gun control advocates may ask: "Do you favor cracking down against illegal gun sales?" Most people can be counted on to oppose illegal acts, and such questions routinely find that (according to the gun control activists' interpretations of the results) more than three-quarters of Americans favor gun control. On the other hand, the National Rifle Association opposes gun control, and it sponsors surveys that word questions very differently, such as: "Would you favor or oppose a law giving police the power to decide who may or may not own a firearm?" (Quoted from Best 2001, p. 48)

In making public policy decisions in a democracy, it is very tempting for advocacy groups to use polling as an instrument to influence opinion. Because of its use of statistical sampling methods, polling appears to many to be a purely objective kind of inductive inference that is only "reporting the facts." However, in many cases, this appearance of objectivity is an illusion.

Precisely because statistical polls do so heavily influence government and political deliberations in a democracy, advocacy groups have now undertaken to use statistics to get more funding for causes they advocate by showing a problem is much worse than anyone thought. Inflated figures on poverty, abuse of women by domestic partners, and other issues where advocacy groups have made exaggerated claims based on polls, have been the subject of much critical scrutiny in recent years. At one point, *Time* reported that four million women are assaulted by a domestic partner every year. *Newsweek* reported that two million women are beaten by husbands, ex-husbands, and boyfriends every year. Both figures were based on polls, but subsequent polls contradicted these large numbers, raising many doubts about the questions asked and words used in these suspect polls (Adler 1994, p. 57). Advocacy groups see questioning of these statistics as an unjustified attack on their goals, using the argument: "If they can save even one woman from being battered, they don't see the harm" (Crossen 1994). This use of argumentation from consequences is, in effect a justification of the use of biased polling techniques to influence public opinion for political purposes.

Advocates for political and social causes on both sides, right and left, define the terms used in polling questions in ways that reflect their own views. A famous example is the definition of the term 'poverty' as used in polling questions (Best 2001, p. 52). Political liberals define the term in such a way as to raise the poverty line, whereas conservatives tend to adopt a meaning of the term that sets the poverty line low. When these choices of how to measure poverty are kept hidden from those to whom the outcome of the poll is publicized, the outcome of the poll can be highly distorted. Activists, reporters, government officials, and private organizations can not only propose solutions to social problems, they can define the problem itself, by using biased polls. We will return to such dangers of inductive and statistical reasoning in chapter 8.

2.10 QUESTION-ANSWER RULES IN DIALOGUE

We have examined several different types of question, each of which has a different type of direct answer. The direct answer to a yes–no question is 'yes' or 'no'. The direct answer to a why-question is to produce a set of propositions that implies the proposition queried. The direct answer to a whether-question is to produce a proposition that represents one of the alternatives posed by the question. No matter what type of question you are confronted with, the important thing to remember is that every question has presuppositions. In effect then, questions are not harmless, because presuppositions are propositions. If you answer a question directly, you then become committed to these propositions, and this means that by answering a question, you make positive assertions, whether you realize it or not.

Despite the fact that there are different types of questions, the concept of a presupposition of a question may be generally defined as follows. A *presupposition of a question* is a proposition that anyone who gives a direct answer to the question thereby automatically becomes committed to. Although as we have seen, questions have many presuppositions, generally there is one important or main presupposition of any question. Or, in the case of complex questions, there may be two or more main presuppositions. For example, the spouse-beating question presupposes that the answerer has a spouse, and that the answerer has beaten this spouse at some time in the past.

Generally speaking, the important presupposition of most questions is fairly clear. In a yes-no question, the important presupposition is normally that either the yes-answer is true or that the no-answer is true. For example, the important presupposition of 'Is snow white?' is the disjunction: either snow is white or snow is not white. In a why-question, the important presupposition is that the proposition queried is true. For example, the important presupposition of 'Why is chlorine heavier than air?' is the proposition that chlorine is heavier than air. In a whether-question, the important presupposition is that at least one of the alternatives is true.

However, great care and judgment are needed in determining the important presuppositions of some tricky or objectionable questions. For example, the spouse abuse question looks like a harmless yes-no question, but it is not. In fact, its important presupposition is that the answerer has engaged in the past practice of spousal abuse.

By now we understand why questions are not harmless and why questions can in fact be arguments in some cases. Normally, we would say that a logical error is a wrong argument of some sort, where an argument is defined as a positive claim made by a set of propositions advanced. Questions, however, are not propositions. So how can questions exhibit faults of logic? The answer is that questions have presuppositions, and therefore a question can advance a set of propositions in just the following way. A question calls for or requires an answer, but when the answerer gives a direct reply, as requested, he then automatically becomes committed to certain propositions. And that is why questions can influence the course of an argument most decisively.

When exactly does a question become objectionable? We have seen that questioning becomes especially dangerous and objectionable when it becomes too aggressive. We saw in example 2.10 how a highly aggressive question can be a form of attack. The problem with answering this type of overly aggressive question is that if the answerer gives a direct answer, as required by the question, he is undone and discredited. Clearly, he would be naive and ill-advised to reply that he is now prepared for the next ten days to condemn his company to continued failure because of his stubborn failure to change his disastrous policies. Yet that would be a direct answer, and that is the sort of direct answer that the question requires. So this type of question violates a reasonable order of questioning and answering in dialogue, and does not give the respondent a fair chance to express a direct reply.

Now notice that, on the other hand, an aggressive question requires a direct answer, and, if the answerer does not give a direct answer, then the questioner can accuse him of being evasive (committing an error of irrelevance). In example 2.10 we saw that the questioner can accuse an answerer of not having answered the question, where the answerer has only tried to rebut an unwelcome presupposition of the question. In political debate, such an accusation could easily make the answerer look guilty and evasive. So the problem is that the answerer must answer, but what fair and reasonable rules of dialogue should regulate when and how an answerer must answer?

If a person does not know the answer to a question, and he is forced to answer the question 'yes' or 'no,' then the rule of dialogue that requires this direct answer, in effect, commits a form of *ad ignorantiam* fallacy. In effect, the answerer is unwisely forced to argue from his own ignorance. Therefore, in reasonable dialogue we do not want to have question-answering rules and conventions that are so strict that the *ad ignorantiam* error is built right into the rules. Such a conception of dialogue would not represent reasonable dialogue, unless the participants were omniscient.

Now a question becomes especially objectionable when it is overly aggressive, but when is a question overly aggressive? A question is overly aggressive when it attempts to force the answerer by an unreasonable sequence of questioning in dialogue, to accept propositions that are pre-suppositions of the question that are unwelcome to the answerer. By *unwelcome*, we mean propositions that the answerer is not committed to, propositions that he should not become committed to because they are prejudicial to his side of the argument. Hence a question is objectionable if it attempts to pre-empt the answerer's acceptance of the unwelcome proposition by presupposing that the answerer already accepts it, or has accepted it.

This is the problem with begging the question. It is an attempt to push an argument on a respondent where a premise (or premises) could only be accepted by that respondent at the cost of prejudicing or destroying his own point of view in the issue of the dialogue.

But there is a dilemma in trying to deal fairly with these aggressive types of tactic in a persuasion dialogue. For if we were to always allow an answerer the 'No commitment' option to any question, then the answerer could always frivolously play the skeptic, if he wished, and say 'No commitment' in answer to every question. Then the dialogue could go nowhere, and a truculent participant in dialogue could prevent his companion from proving anything or getting anywhere in his questioning. An answerer could be as evasive as he wished, with no penalty. And that would not be conducive to reasonable dialogue either.

The solution to this dilemma is to require in reasonable dialogue that an answerer's answer should co-operatively reflect what he honestly and truly thinks, if he has a definite opinion or commitment on the question. If he has no firm commitment on the matter, he should reply 'No commitment,' but if he is truly committed to a proposition, then his answer should reflect that commitment. This way of regulating question-answer procedures is the best way to assure the progress of reasonable dialogue on an issue. Such rules are matters of politeness and helpful collaboration that are essential to the progress and success of a critical discussion.

For example, if I were to ask you the question, 'Why is 3 an even number?,' you would rightly feel that the question is objectionable. Why? Well, if you are a normally intelligent arguer, the proposition that 3 is an even number will not be acceptable to you. You would not, and should not, accept that proposition as a commitment. However, if you give a direct answer to the question, you are automatically forced to accept that commitment, like it or not. For you as answerer then, the question is too aggressive. Your best reply is to reject the presupposition instead of directly answering the question. You should reply: '3 is not an even number.' If the question was, 'Why is 3 an odd number?' then you would, or should have no similar objection to it. If you accept that 3 is an odd number, then the question is not a problem for you. It is no longer overly aggressive or objectionable.

In short, where a question is overly aggressive, the answerer must attack the question itself. He must question the question by querying its presuppositions. In some cases, he must firmly reject an important presupposition of a question if that presupposition is very damaging to his own side of the argument. When the question is overly aggressive, the answerer must be somewhat aggressive too, though in a reasonable way. The answerer must bounce the ball back into the questioner's court, and shift the burden of proof back onto the questioner to justify the presuppositions alleged by the question.

What it means then to say that a question is fallacious is to say that the question is objectionable to the answerer because the question is constructed to pre-empt the answerer into forcibly accepting a proposition that he should not accept.[12] This problem is compounded if the question is also semantically complex. A semantically complex question is one that contains a connective, 'and,' 'or,' or 'if-then' in its presupposition. Once again, the answerer must question the question by requesting that

---

12 Ruth Manor concludes that a question that is an act of presupposing a proposition not previously accepted by an answerer can be wrong in dialogue where it denies the answerer the chance to react to the presupposition by questioning it. See Manor (1981, p. 13).

the propositions in the presupposition be separated into units that he can reasonably deal with.

What it means to say that a question is objectionable is that the question is open to reasonable criticism or objection by the answerer. The answerer should sometimes be allowed to query or criticize a question in some cases. Where the question is overly aggressive, then reasonable dialogue requires that an answerer be given the option of questioning the question.

The problems and errors of question-asking encountered in this chapter show that an answerer should not always be forced to give a direct answer to every question, in reasonable dialogue. The argument from ignorance has the same lesson. Sometimes the best answer to a question is 'No commitment' or 'I don't know.' Yet on the other hand, an answerer should not be allowed to duck every question, or he would never have to make any commitments, and reasonable dialogue would not be well served. The solution to this problem is to be sought in the requirement that each party in reasonable dialogue has the burden of proving his own thesis and defending his own position on the issue. If questioned to prove, clarify, or defend a proposition that he is clearly committed to, an answerer should directly respond. If the question presupposes propositions that he may not be committed to, an answerer should have a right to question the question.

In general, the basic rule of burden of proof in reasonable dialogue is: he who asserts must prove.[13] Someone who has previously asserted a proposition as part of his position should be accounted as answerable to that proposition unless he retracts it, or removes his commitment to it subsequently. Once I am committed to a proposition A, I should not be freely allowed to say 'No reply' if I am asked again about it. I may not know in fact whether or not A is true, but if I am committed to A, then I should be guided by that commitment in subsequent dialogue.

If a question is loaded, it makes an assertion, or at least creates an assertion for the respondent who must answer it. Therefore, it can be reasonable to place a burden of proof on the asker of the loaded question to justify his presupposition. And therefore, it is reasonable for the respondent of such a question to challenge the question by asking the questioner to meet the burden of proof he took on by asking the question.

13 See Walton (1987).

3

Criticisms of irrelevance

One of the most common criticisms made in argument is the reply "That's beside the point!" or "That's irrelevant." However, relevance is such a broad term that the criticism of being irrelevant could refer to many different kinds of failure or shortcoming in an argument. The study of relevance in argument begins by clarifying and classifying these different types of alleged failure that can prompt the criticism that a breach of relevance has been committed.

The primary basis of allegations of irrelevance stems from an important basic feature of all reasonable dialogue. Every argument presupposes a context of dialogue in which there is an issue, or perhaps several issues, being discussed. An *issue* means there is a proposition or question of controversy under discussion. Typically, an issue in dialogue suggests that there are two sides to the discussion. In other words, there is a certain specific proposition being discussed, and one participant in the dialogue is committed to that proposition being true while the other participant is committed to its being false. Of course, dialogues are not always this clear or simple, but when they are of this form, the type of dialogue may be called a *dispute* (or *disputation*). A dispute is a dialogue where one side affirms a certain proposition, and the other side affirms the opposite (negation) of that proposition.

This means that it is a characteristic feature of reasonable dialogue that each participant in an argument should have a particular proposition assigned to him or designated by him that represents his *thesis*, or conclusion to be proven. The two theses of the two participants in the argument define the issue of the argument, and the issue is the primary factor in fairly enabling us to evaluate claims concerning what is or is not relevant to the issue of a particular argument.

Of course, one main problem in the practical job of evaluating realistic argumentation is that arguers may not even be clear on what they are arguing about. Allegations of irrelevance cannot fairly be settled if the issue of the argument was never stated or understood in the first place.

An argument ostensibly about one issue may really be about another. A husband and wife may be arguing about who should take the garbage out this morning, but the real issue may be that one of them came home late the night before with no explanation. So sometimes arguers are not clear about what they are arguing about. But if their dialogue is to be reasonable, they should be clear about this, or at least be able to clarify it. Only then can allegations of irrelevance be reasonably adjudicated and settled.

3.1 ALLEGATIONS OF IRRELEVANCE

The traditional fallacy of *ignoratio elenchi* (ignoring the issue, sometimes also called irrelevant conclusion) is said to be committed when an argument fails to prove the conclusion (thesis) it is supposed to prove, and instead, is directed towards proving some irrelevant conclusion. The following is a traditional case.

Example 3.0

A particular proposal for housing legislation is under consideration. A senator rises to speak in favor of the bill. However, his whole argument is directed to the conclusion that all people should have decent housing.

The reason why this example is said to be a case of the fallacious *ignoratio elenchi* is that the senator should be proving that this particular bill is worth voting for because it will improve the housing situation. However, instead he argues for the proposition that all people should have decent housing, a proposition that is not the real issue of the dispute and one that virtually any party to the dispute would agree to anyway. Thus his argument misses the point, and may therefore be criticized as irrelevant.

From one point of view, the criticism of irrelevance here amounts to the claim that the senator's argument is not valid. In other words, the senator has really argued as follows.

[Premise]	All people should have decent housing.
[Conclusion]	This particular proposal will improve the housing situation.

The proposition marked 'conclusion' is the proposition that the senator should prove, according to the procedures for dialogue of this legislative assembly. But the information the senator actually puts forward, marked 'premise', is not sufficient to establish the required conclusion by valid argument. From this point of view, the charge of irrelevance basically amounts to the criticism that the senator's argument is simply not valid, when directed to its proper conclusion. From another point of view, you could say that the mistake is that the senator got his own argument wrong. He misidentified his own conclusion. Or perhaps better, he attempted to mislead his audience into taking a proposition for the conclusion that is, in reality, not the correct conclusion to be argued for.

Another interesting observation about example 3.0 is that the senator is being criticized not so much for what he did, as what he didn't do. Probably all of us accept the premise 'All people should have decent housing.' However, what remains to be shown is how the particular proposal at issue will provide decent housing in the present circumstances. Because the senator's argument failed to establish that missing premise, it is a very weak argument indeed.

Notice however that the senator's argument could possibly be improved if he could go on to show why the particular proposal at issue could provide decent housing in the present circumstances. Then the premise 'All people should have decent housing' would not be irrelevant, because it would be an essential part of a valid argument for the right conclusion. In other words, while the senator's argument above (example 3.0) is open to criticism or questioning for what it lacks, it is not necessarily a fallacious argument if by "fallacious" we mean hopelessly bad or illogical, or so bad that it cannot be repaired by continuing with it. For example, the senator's argument might be even worse, or more irrelevant, if his only premise was something like 'All people deserve dignity and freedom.' This premise doesn't seem to have anything to do at all with the proper conclusion he is supposed to prove. At least the former premise was more closely connected to that conclusion, even if it did not prove it. So while irrelevance should rightly be open to criticism in reasonable dialogue, to call irrelevance a fallacy in every case is an exaggeration.

The force of the criticism that the senator's argument is an *ignoratio elenchi* depends on the presumption that the senator has finished his argument, and that is all he has to say on the subject. For it might be that if he were to say more, he would show why his premise is connected to the conclusion, and therefore why his argument is relevant. The question of how final the criticism of irrelevance should be taken to be, therefore, depends on whether the dialogue can be continued. In the present case, perhaps it couldn't be, but in many cases, it can be. Therefore it is often wiser to treat the *ignoratio elenchi* allegation as a criticism, one that could be replied to, rather than as a fallacy, or conclusive refutation that wholly destroys the worth of the argument against which it is directed.

The point here is that in the midst of dialogue, it may be hard to see where another participant's argument appears to be headed. If so, you can always ask: "Is that proposition relevant?" And in some cases the arguer may reasonably reply: "Yes, it will turn out to be relevant once I get to that point in my argument. Hang on for a bit and I'll show you why." This reply is sometimes a reasonable one, especially if the required chain of argumentation is long and complex. Hence one has to be careful that a serious criticism of irrelevance is not premature. Sometimes a criticism of irrelevance is best treated more like a request for more information.

The term *ignoratio elenchi*, from Aristotle, literally means "ignorance of refutation." The origin of this term derives from the Greek tradition that contestive argument is like a game of dialogue where each participant has a thesis or conclusion to be proven. The argument is contestive, i.e., a dispute, if the thesis of the one participant in the dialogue is opposed to the thesis of the other. Therefore, the point of the game is for each player to refute the thesis of the other. Any argument that seems to refute the thesis of the other, but really does not, could be seen as a case of ignorance of refutation. In other words, the arguer only thought his argument refuted his opponent's thesis, but in reality he was ignorant of the fact that it did not.

To go back to example 3.0 as an illustration, the following propositions form the issue to be contested.

(S1) This bill will improve the housing situation.
(S2) This bill will not improve the housing situation.

The senator's argument is supposed to refute (S2) by establishing his own conclusion to be proved, (S1). However, the whole problem was that his given premise failed to prove (S1). So Aristotle would say his argument was an *ignoratio elenchi* because it fails to refute (S2). It merely refutes the proposition 'Not all people should have decent housing' at best. And that is not the proposition at issue, to be refuted in this particular game of dialogue. In other words, there is only ignorance of refutation instead of genuine refutation of the thesis at issue.

Aristotle's conception of *ignoratio elenchi* represents the basic idea of the criticism of irrelevance in reasonable dialogue. However, his conception is a very broad one. The basic purpose of all argument in reasonable dialogue is to prove one's conclusion or thesis that is set as the proposition to be established by the argument. And any argument that fails in this objective could therefore be fairly said to be open to criticism or improving. So virtually any of the traditional fallacies or shortcomings of arguments could potentially fall under the classification of *ignoratio elenchi*. In fact, we will see that many of the appeals to emotion are said to be fallacies, in large part, because they are weak arguments of the *ignoratio elenchi* type. For example, the abusive and circumstantial *ad hominem* fallacies could be classified, in large part, as arguments that are open to criticism because they fail to prove or refute successfully the conclusions they are supposed to prove or refute in reasonable dialogue.

In short, the criticism of irrelevance is a broad category of criticism in evaluating arguments, and there are several more specific criticisms of particular kinds of irrelevance that can usefully be identified. We now turn to studying these more particular categories. The basic fallacy of irrelevance is simply the misidentification of the proper conclusion to be proven in reasonable dialogue.

3.2 GLOBAL IRRELEVANCE

A reasonable dialogue is a sequence of questions and answers where each participant has a thesis or conclusion to be proved. Over the whole sequence of the dialogue, a proposition may be said to be *globally irrelevant* if it occurs at some stage of the dialogue but fails to be relevant to the ultimate conclusion to be proven by the party who advanced that proposition in the dialogue. As we have seen, one main problem with adjudicating allegations of global irrelevance is that in some arguments, the participants have not made it clear exactly what each of their ultimate conclusions is supposed to be.

In some contexts however, the objective of the dialogue does make it clear what the thesis of each arguer is supposed to be. For example, in a criminal trial in a court of law, the prosecuting attorney is supposed to prove that the defendant is guilty of an alleged offence. The defence attorney is supposed to refute the prosecuting attorney's argument by showing that it does not prove that the defendant is guilty. In other words, the burden of proof is on the prosecution to prove guilt, beyond reasonable doubt. The defence only has to show that there can be reasonable doubt. That is, the defence only has to show that the opposing argument is weak, or at any rate, not strong enough to convict the defendant.

This type of argument is not exactly a classical dispute, where one arguer has to prove one proposition and the other has to prove the opposite proposition, but it is like a dispute, because the conclusions of the two parties are opposed to each other. Yet the defence attorney does not have to prove positively that his client did not commit the crime. He only has to prove the weaker conclusion that the prosecutor's arguments do not show that the defendant committed the crime. Here, the conclusions to be proved are asymmetrical. The defence attorney does not need a strong refutation of the prosecuting attorney's thesis, i.e., to show that it is false. He only needs a weak refutation of the prosecuting attorney's thesis, i.e., to show that it is subject to reasonable doubt.[1]

In short, the criminal trial is not a *symmetrical dispute*, where one arguer has to prove a proposition A and the other arguer has to prove the negation, not-A. It is a kind of asymmetrical dispute where the burden of proof is stronger on one side than on the other. In fact, the burden of proof is (positively) on one side only. The other side needs only to defend by weakly refuting the first side's argument. Let us call this kind of asymmetrical dispute a *weakly opposed dispute* or *asymmetrical dispute*. In a weakly opposed dispute, one party must positively prove his thesis, the other need only show that the first party's proof does not succeed. He is not required to show that the first party's thesis is false, but only that it is open to doubt or reasonable challenge. The criminal trial is an asymmetrical dispute, but many civil cases in law are symmetrical disputes where the burden of proof is evenly weighted.

Whether a trial is an asymmetrical dispute or a symmetrical dispute then, the thesis to be proved by each attorney is clearly defined at the outset by the procedural rules of dialogue for that particular type of case. If an attorney's argument seems to wander, the other attorney or the judge can question the relevance of a line of argument to the thesis to be proved by that attorney. Such a question is a criticism of global irrelevance. The judge may query, "Can you show the court why this line of argument is relevant to your case?"

---

1 It is very important not to confuse weak and strong refutation. In fact, the following form of this confusion is exactly the *ad ignorantiam* fallacy: an arguer purports to have strongly refuted a proposition at issue when in fact he has given evidence to support it that is, at best, a weak refutation of the proposition. In other words, just because a proposition is subject to reasonable doubt, it doesn't necessarily follow that the proposition is shown to be false. So to argue is to commit the *ad ignorantiam* fallacy.

Example 3.1

The prosecuting attorney in a criminal trial is supposed to prove that the defendant is guilty of murder. However, the prosecuting attorney argues at length that murder is a horrible crime. He holds up the victim's bloody shirt for the jury to see. He expostulates at length on the horror of this crime and all crimes of murder.

As the prosecuting attorney's argument goes on and on, the court may begin to wonder if he is ever going to get around to arguing that this particular defendant is guilty of the admittedly horrible crime of murder. As it becomes reasonable to question whether such an argument is forthcoming, it is appropriate to question the relevance of the attorney's line of argument. If the attorney finishes his argument without really coming around to the question of the guilt of this particular defendant, then he may fairly be accused of committing a classical *ignoratio elenchi*. For he has failed to prove what he was supposed to prove by his argument. In short, the reasonable suspicion may be that he has tried to get the jury to accept the idea that the issue of the trial is whether murder is a horrible crime. Of course, that conclusion is not a basis for conviction. So a criticism of *ignoratio elenchi* has a sharply defined edge in law because the thesis to be proved by each participant in the dialogue is defined by procedural rules.

What is worth noticing here however, is that until the case is finally concluded, an allegation of global irrelevance is not a conclusive refutation of an argument. Suppose in the midst of the argument, the prosecuting attorney is spending a lot of time arguing that murder is a horrible crime, and then suppose that the attorney brought in evidence to show that the defendant had exhibited traumatic behavior just after the time the crime was alleged to have taken place. The attorney might then be about to argue that this unusual behavior is consistent with someone committing a horrible crime. If so, the premise 'Murder is a horrible crime' might legitimately have a role to play in the attorney's global network of argumentation as he builds a case for his conclusion that the defendant is guilty of murder.

So one has to be careful here. An allegation of global irrelevance cannot be finally or conclusively deemed justifiable until the dialogue is terminated. Otherwise, it is best treated as a challenge, or weak refutation at best, and not as a clearly established fallacy.

In reasonable dialogue, criticisms of irrelevance should be treated as fundamentally global in nature, but very often such criticisms are meant to be taken in a local way. We have already seen, for example, that failure to give a direct answer to a question is often labelled as a kind of irrelevance. However, the irrelevance here is primarily local, for the reply may be criticized because it is not thought to be a direct enough answer to one particular question at some point in a dialogue. So one important type of criticism of relevance is that of question-answer relevance.

3.3 QUESTION-ANSWER RELEVANCE

In some cases, a criticism of irrelevance relates to a specific question-answer pairing during a sequence of dialogue. The criticism "That's irrelevant" in such a case means that the respondent's reply was not an answer to the specific question asked. This type of criticism is not one of global relevance. Rather it is a local irrelevance concerning the relation between a reply and a specific question asked at some particular point in the sequence of dialogue. Also, this type of criticism is not one that, strictly speaking, concerns a relationship between assertions or propositions.[2] Instead, the relationship is one between a question and a reply to that question. We could call this type of relevance *question-answer* relevance, because the failure occurs where the reply does not answer the question. Or, at any rate, the reply is not a direct enough answer to the question to satisfy the critic who cites it as irrelevant.

In the following example, a reporter asks a specific question, and a university dean gives an answer that appears to be relevant.

Example 3.2

Reporter: I am concerned about affirmative action programs, and would like to ask how many of the proposed faculty cuts at the university are women's positions.

Dean: Only one position in the women's studies department will be cut. But that is balanced by the new proposal for the women's studies chair, which will mean adding a new position to women's studies.

Reporter: My question wasn't about women's studies. There are a number of faculties that are cutting positions, including arts, science, and engineering. I want to know how many of those faculty members who are women will be cut.

2 Epstein (1979, p. 156). See Sperber and Wilson (1986) on some other kinds of relevance.

Note that in this case, the problematic question and reply were topically related – both were about women faculty members whose positions are being cut. And they were globally related on the same general issue. Yet even so, the reporter's criticism that the respondent did not answer her question could and would be described as a criticism that the reply was not relevant to her question. As she put it, her question was not about women's studies. So, we might say, the reply *about* women's studies was not strictly relevant, meaning that it did not address the specific question asked.

There is an unfortunate tendency in ordinary conversation, and even in logic textbooks, to use "irrelevance" as a kind of catch-all criticism for any sort of failure of argument or weak argument. An instance of this sort in a logic text is cited below. The following dialogue quoted from the British *Press Reports* was cited as an instance of diversion from the point at issue by L. Susan Stebbing (1939, p. 196). Sir Charles Craven was the director of Vickers-Armstrong Ltd., an armaments firm.

Example 3.3

When Sir Charles Craven was being questioned by Sir Philip Gibbs yesterday, he said Messrs. Vickers' trade was not particularly dangerous.

Sir Philip: You do not think that your wares are any more dangerous or obnoxious than boxes of chocolates or sugar candy? – No, or novels.

Sir Philip: You don't think it is more dangerous to export these fancy goods to foreign countries than, say, children's crackers?

Sir Charles: Well, I nearly lost an eye with a Christmas cracker, but never with a gun.

According to Stebbing's evaluation of this case, Sir Charles' reply to Sir Philip's second question is an irrelevant response because the issue of the dialogue is supposed to be armaments (p. 196). It is difficult to believe that these replies were intended to be serious. There is an obvious diversion from the point under the guise of a contemptuous joke. At least, I think it must have been meant for a joke, although it is certainly a poor one.

Stebbing goes on to object that armaments, unlike firecrackers, are made "solely for the purpose of killing and wounding people and destroying buildings." Her objection is that it is armaments that are being discussed, not firecrackers.

Stebbing is certainly justified in criticizing Sir Charles' reply as weak, unconvincing, and even morally reprehensible, but is she justified in criticizing it as *irrelevant*? To answer this question, note that it was Sir Philip, in his question, not Sir Charles, in his reply, who first introduced the topic of firecrackers into the dialogue. Therefore, if the topic of firecrackers is irrelevant, it is Sir Philip's question that is irrelevant, not Sir Charles' reply. Sir Charles' reference to the topic of firecrackers, in his reply, is locally relevant to the subject matter of Sir Philip's question that preceded it.

This particular example reveals two special features of relevance in dialogue that are interesting to note. First, it suggests that a question can be relevant or irrelevant. This is interesting because we encounter criticisms of irrelevance, at the local level especially, where a reply to a question is said to be evasive or irrelevant. Can questions themselves be irrelevant? It seems possible that they can be. For example, if you and I are discussing the sale of a building near the university, and I unexpectedly inject the question "When was Albert Einstein born?" into the dialogue, you may well ask me why my question is relevant. Or in some cases, you might even criticize my question as irrelevant to the discussion. Therefore, it seems that questions, as well as answers, can be criticized as irrelevant to a discussion.

Second, example 3.3 illustrates how there can be a conflict in some cases between relevance at the local level and relevance at the global level. Stebbing criticized Sir Charles' reply on the grounds that the topic of the discussion is armaments, not firecrackers. However, even granting that this claim is true at the global level, it nevertheless remains that Sir Charles' reply on the subject of firecrackers and armaments is relevant, at the local level, to Sir Philip's question.

So there seems to be a conflict in the evaluation of this case. Which is more important – relevance at the global level or relevance at the local level? Stebbing seems to think the former more important, but this contention does not seem very plausible. For the following principle seems generally reasonable: if a questioner introduces a new subject matter into a discussion in a question, then the respondent should be allowed to incorporate that subject matter into his reply as well, without necessarily being reasonably criticized for irrelevance.

Another case will illustrate a kind of reply where a question is criticized as irrelevant. Curiously however, in this particular case, the respondent is trying to avoid answering the question. His evasive reply, however, adopts the highly aggressive tactic of trying to claim that the question is irrelevant.

This discussion was an interview by Barbara Frum on the CBC television program, *The Journal*, on September 26, 1986. The subject of the interview was the declaration of a No Crime Day by the City of Detroit, a city that had been plagued by a high crime rate, and in particular, a high murder rate. The persons being interviewed were the mayor of Detroit and an athlete who had proposed the idea of the No Crime Day, a public appeal to keep the City of Detroit free of violent crime for one day. A reconstruction of the interview is given below.

Example 3.4

Mrs. Frum: The murder rate this year so far is over three hundred people murdered in Detroit. More people were murdered last month in Detroit than in the whole year in Toronto so far. Do you feel that this represents a failure or problem, from your point of view as mayor?

Mayor: You are asking me questions about this high murder rate in Detroit. That is not the question. Other cities like New York also have high rates. The topic is No Crime Day. This murder rate question is not relevant.

Mrs. Frum: Well, yes it really is relevant. [She then goes on to ask another question of the other person.]

The first thing to notice about this case is that the mayor's reply is simply false. Mrs. Frum is quite justified in replying that the question of the murder rate in Detroit is relevant to the topic of No Crime Day. For murder is certainly a type of crime, and a very important type of crime, to be sure.

The Mayor may see the topic of the murder rate as "irrelevant" because it poses a political liability for his political standing as mayor, but Mrs. Frum certainly sees it as part of the topic. Of course, we do not know whether Mrs. Frum and the mayor agreed to any fixed agenda or topic prior to the interview. Even if they did agree that No Crime Day was to be the subject of the interview, murder is clearly related to crime, and to No Crime Day as a topic.

3.4 SETTING AN AGENDA FOR A DISCUSSION

One way of keeping the issues of a controversy within manageable proportions is to restrict the set of admissible topics to what is directly relevant to a specific issue. In the following example, a meeting of the library committee has been scheduled, and the only item on the agenda is the issue of whether library hours should be extended on Sundays. The library is open for eight hours on Sundays, and the Student Association has made a proposal to extend the Sunday library hours to ten. During the meeting, the following exchange takes place.

Harry: Not only should the library remain open longer so that students can have a place to study, but student tuition fees should be lowered as well.

Pam: Hold on, Harry. The topic of this meeting is the proposal for the extension of library hours. What does the topic of tuition fees have to do with it? I don't see the relevance of that issue.

Harry: Well, if students didn't have to pay so much tuition, they could afford better lodging, and therefore better facilities to study at home. I mean it's all connected because many factors are responsible for not providing students with adequate facilities for studying. Therefore my point is relevant.

Is Harry's point relevant? No doubt it can be related to the issue of extended library hours, the issue that was specified as the topic to be discussed on the agenda of this meeting. The issue for changing tuition fees was not on the agenda of this meeting, although it may well be an issue for other meetings held in the university throughout the year. So, although Harry has responded to Pam's criticism by establishing a connection between the issues, we need to ask whether the connection is a legitimate one, of a sort to require the meeting to include the discussion of tuition fees.

In an interesting way, the problem in example 3.4, the murder rate in Detroit example, is the opposite side of the same problem that was noted in example 3.5, the case of the discussion of library closing hours. There, Harry is trying to maintain that tuition fees were relevant to the topic, whereas their relevance was too marginal to the discussion to sustain his case for relevance. In example 3.4, by contrast, the mayor is claiming that the murder rate is not relevant, whereas in fact the two topics at issue are so closely related that his disclaimer cannot be sustained.

If a group of students and faculty were having an informal discussion, it might be quite reasonable to include arguments on tuition fees in with arguments on library hours. In some ways, the two issues could be connected. If a meeting is called on the topic of a specific proposal to extend library hours, the issue is defined very narrowly on purpose, and it may be quite reasonable to restrict discussion to issues directly relevant to the proposal being discussed. Thus although Harry has made a connection between the two topics, it is not a strong enough connection to adequately reply to Pam's objection that the topic of fee decreases is not relevant.

Not all discussions have a specific agenda set as boundaries of the discussion. Where irrelevance can be a serious problem, an agenda can be useful. An *agenda* may be defined as a specific set of issues (propositions) to be discussed, often in a specific order.

What is or is not reasonably relevant to a discussion, however, may be highly controversial in some cases. To fairly rule on such criticisms of irrelevance, we have to look carefully at the agenda set for discussion by the participants. We need to ask how specific the precise issue under discussion is supposed to be. If the issue is a specific proposal, other controversial issues may reasonably be excluded from a particular meeting or discussion if they are only tangentially relevant, and cannot therefore be adequately dealt with in the context of another issue that needs to be resolved.

Hence a criticism of irrelevance is a procedural point of order in a regulated dialogue. Such a point of order questions the relevance of an argument to the question at issue. Where the issue is precisely and clearly delimited at the outset, as agreed by the participants in the discussion prior to the beginning of dialogue, then such a point of order can and should be reasonably restrictive.

How strictly relevance of arguments should be controlled by a chairman or moderator of a discussion, however, varies with the context of dialogue, and specific agreements made or accepted by the participants. In a stockholders' meeting to decide whether to declare a dividend, for example, any discussion not directly related to the agenda may be cut off peremptorily. The urgency of the decision may require strict standards of relevance, and the stockholders may want these standards enforced. Thus the question of tolerance of irrelevance in a discussion may be a question of judgment relative to the goals of the discussion and the narrowness of the agenda.

There is an inherent practical problem in ruling on questions of relevance in a specific context of dialogue. This is essentially because it may be impossible for a moderator or other participants in a discussion to see where a particular arguer may be leading us in his arguments. This, of course, is because an argument in dialogue is made up of a series of links at the local level that are uncompleted as a chain until the argument has been concluded. In mid-stream, it may be difficult to see where an argument may be leading us. In retrospect, once the argument is completed, it may be much easier to judge relevance. A moderator or referee of a discussion may have to try to judge relevance during the actual debate. Therefore, in the midst of a discussion, judgments of relevance may have to be based on reasoned trust, a willingness to co-operate, or on the reassurance of a speaker that his line of argument will turn out to be relevant.

However, even in the midst of a discussion, a move in dialogue can be judged irrelevant if it is not an appropriate response to the previous move by the other participant. Thus if you ask me a question, and I respond with another question that does not reply to, or even address the first question, my response may rightly be judged as irrelevant.

Many of the problems of irrelevance studied so far pertain to the argumentation stage of a dialogue, but irrelevance can even be a problem at the opening stage of a discussion. A practical problem is that participants in a discussion may actually have differing preconceptions of what the issue of a case should be. In a case described by Moore (1986), a social service organization planned to build a health clinic for low-income patients in a certain residential neighborhood. A group of neighbors opposed the location of the project in their neighborhood. The neighbors defined the issue of the discussion as whether the clinic should be located in their area. According to Moore (p. 173), the issue for the social service organization was how the project of setting up the clinic can be carried out: "They want to discuss how a building can be leased and what resistance they will encounter in locating their facility." If each group in this case were asked to define the issue of the dispute, one group would give a quite different answer from the other.

In this case, the discussion appears to be a dispute, but in fact each party is prepared to discuss a different issue. Hence if they were to begin to engage in the process of argument, in fact they would be arguing at cross-purposes. In this case, the thesis of the one party is partially opposed to the thesis of the other. For if the building cannot be located in the neighborhood, then of course the project of building the clinic there cannot be carried out. So there certainly is some opposition, and some room for dispute.

However, there can be a serious problem nonetheless, for if each party defines the issue differently, then it may be difficult or impossible for the dialogue to lead to any resolution of the controversy. For arguments supporting one side of the alleged issue may be rightly perceived by the other side to be irrelevant to the issue as they define it. Lacking any basic agreement on global relevance, both parties may well be led into sequences of questions and replies that lead only to objections and criticisms of irrelevance that cannot possibly be resolved to the satisfaction of both sides. So in fact this kind of misunderstanding about the issue of a dispute can undermine reasoned dialogue and lead to a failure of resolution of the controversy.

Thus there are many very real practical difficulties in ruling on relevance in a particular dispute. The agenda may only seem to be defined, while the disputants may in fact misunderstand how the issue is defined. Or the participants may even strenuously disagree on how the issue should be defined. In union-management disputes, for example, negotiations may be deadlocked because the disputing parties cannot even agree on what should be on the agenda. Here, difficulties of setting standards to define relevance can be extreme, even prior to the main stages of entering into argumentation. Even if the issue has been clearly defined, and all participants have agreed to the agenda, practical difficulties of preventing very aggressive arguers from going off track into emotional appeals, personal attacks, and other digressions, may require a skilled moderator with sensitive judgment. To define relevance is one thing, to interpret it fairly in a particular discussion is something else.

3.5 RED HERRING VERSUS WRONG CONCLUSION

In section 1.8, we examined an example of an argument said to commit the fallacy of irrelevant conclusion, which was said to occur when an argument is directed towards proving the wrong, or an irrelevant conclusion. As noted, such an argument may be valid, but if it has strayed from the point and not proved the conclusion that was supposed to be proved, it is useless as an argument, and may be highly misleading. The example we chose to illustrate this fallacy was the case where an attorney prosecuting a defendant for murder in a criminal trial argues that murder is a horrible crime. This argument could be a misleading distraction given that the prosecutor is supposed to be proving that the defendant is guilty of having committed the crime of murder. In such a case, the prosecutor is proving the wrong conclusion, and thereby committing the fallacy of irrelevant conclusion. The fallacy could be called the fallacy of wrong conclusion, because the prosecutor's conclusion is different from the conclusion that is supposed to be proved by his argument in the trial. Moreover, the real conclusion he proves, the proposition that murder is a horrible crime, is not useful for establishing the conclusion he is supposed to prove. Presumably, nobody disagrees that murder is a horrible crime, and whether it is or not, it is hard to see how that fact would be of any use as a premise that would help establish the conclusion that the defendant is guilty of the crime of murder. Why would the prosecutor use such a strategy at all, since it would appear to be so unconvincing to the jury?

One possibility is that the prosecutor hopes to establish a link in the jury's mind between these two propositions. Once the jury starts to dwell on the proposition that murder is a horrible crime, they might somehow begin to associate the committing of this crime with the defendant. Perhaps, for example, the defendant looks like a scary person who might be capable of committing such a horrible crime. The jury might put two and two together, and draw the inference that he has the capability of committing such a crime, suggesting that he did commit the crime.

There is also another possibility that suggests a different strategy. It could be that the prosecutor is trying to distract the jury by introducing a diversion. To modify the example a bit however, let's assume that the attorney also goes on to describe at length how horrible a crime murder is by talking about how the victim suffered in other cases where an innocent victim was cruelly murdered. Here the attorney is straying away from the issue even further by going into the gory details of other crimes. The tactic here is one of distraction and diversion. By leading the path of argumentation away from the specific case of the murder committed by the defendant, the attorney is wandering off the point and trying to divert the jury by using an emotional appeal that may be prejudicial by connecting the accused with the horrors of the crime of murder. So modified, the example presents a problem. Is the fallacy of irrelevance committed, one of arguing to the wrong conclusion, or is it one of creating a distraction that has not led to any specific wrong conclusion but has diverted the audience away from the real conclusion to be proven? In short, there are two theories about the fallacy committed in this case. Is it the fallacy of wrong conclusion, or is it the fallacy of diverting the audience away from the real conclusion to be proved, perhaps even without arriving at any specific wrong conclusion at all?

There are other examples of arguments that do not seem to fit the wrong conclusion model, but where a fallacy of relevance appears to have been committed. In these examples, the arguer wanders off the point, and may even be trying to divert the audience with an emotional appeal. However, it may not be clear what he is trying to prove, and he may not be trying to prove any specific conclusion, but merely distract the audience by wandering off in a different direction. The common name for this use of strategic diversion is the red herring fallacy. There are many cases in which the red herring fallacy does not consist in an argument to the wrong conclusion, but is merely an attempt at distraction that leads off to a different issue or even on a distracting trail to nowhere. Here is an example of such a red herring fallacy taken from a logic textbook (Hurley 2003, p. 132).

Example 3.6

Professor Conway complains of inadequate parking on our campus, but did you know that last year Conway carried on a torrid love affair with a member of the English department? The two used to meet every day for clandestine sex in the copier room. Apparently they didn't realize how much you can see through that fogged glass window. Even the students got an eyeful. Enough said about Conway.

Bringing in the exciting account of the torrid love affair is meant to arouse the interest of the audience and distract them. It doesn't really lead to any specific conclusion about the parking issue, or even about anything else. It could perhaps be just an attempt to pass on some exciting gossip about Professor Conway. Some might say the argument is an *ad hominem* attack that attempts to discredit Conway. There is little evidence, however, to show that the arguer is trying to argue that Conway's previous argument about inadequate parking should not be seen as plausible because Conway has a bad ethical character and therefore should not be trusted to speak the truth on this issue. Certainly however, the argument is prejudicial against Conway by alleging that he did something that most of us would disapprove of, or would think inappropriate conduct in a public place in an educational institution. The more significant strategy in this colorful allegation against Conway is that it distracts the audience from considering the reasons that can be given for or against Conway's position on the parking issue. The argument is a red herring meant to distract the audience by leading it off to a different issue that bears no real relevance to the parking issue.

What these examples suggest is that there are two different kinds of fallacy of relevance. One could be called the wrong conclusion fallacy while the other could be called the red herring fallacy. Both can be subsumed under the general category of what is called misdirected argumentation, or argument directed other than along a path of argumentation leading towards the conclusion to be proved. Sometimes the path leads to the wrong conclusion, one other than the one that is supposed to be proved, and the fallacy of wrong conclusion has been committed. Sometimes the path leads away from the conclusion to be proved, but not to any specific alternative conclusion. Here the fallacy of red herring has been committed.

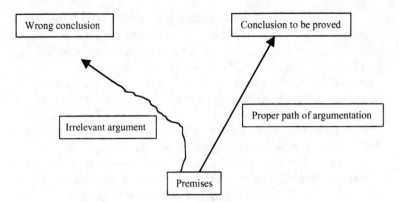

Figure 3.1. The structure of fallacies of irrelevance.

The difference between these two fallacies, as well as the common structure that they share, can be brought out by considering figure 3.1 (Walton 2004, p. 76).

The Structure of Fallacies of Irrelevance

In a given example where failure of relevance is a concern, suppose the line of argumentation initially looks as if it is moving toward the designated conclusion to be proved, but then strays off in a different direction, as shown in Figure 3.1. This pattern would indicate that the fallacy committed is one of red herring. However, consider a different kind of case where the wavy line on the left definitely arrives at the wrong conclusion, a conclusion other than the one that is supposed to be proved. In this kind of case the proper diagnosis would be that the fallacy of wrong conclusion has been committed.

This analysis of the structure of argumentation where there is a suspected fallacy of relevance helps us to distinguish, at least in theory, between the wrong conclusion fallacy and the red herring fallacy. However, if we look at real examples, there still remains a problem of how to classify these examples by looking at the evidence given in the text of discourse of the example. The problem is that even when an argument strays off in a different direction, attempting to use a strategy of diversion by introducing some emotional issue, the argument may still arrive at a conclusion other than the one that is supposed to be proved. In example 3.1, to cite a case in point, the attorney may indeed be proving the conclusion that murder is a horrible crime. This finding may make it seem to us as though the fallacy of irrelevance in the case should be classified as that of wrong conclusion, whereas really the problem is that the attorney is trying to distract the jury by bringing in all kinds of emotional details about the horribleness of murder as a crime. So the argumentation in this example should best be classified as falling under both the wrong conclusion fallacy and the red herring fallacy.

Looking at other cases, however, a distinction between the two kinds of fallacy needs to be made. What appears to be wrong in the Conway case (example 3.6) is not that the arguer is trying to establish any particular wrong conclusion. His strategy is merely to distract the audience by taking them off in a different interesting and colorful direction. In other cases however, the strategy is not that the arguer is trying to distract the audience from the issue. The problem is merely that the arguer jumps to a conclusion other than the one that is supposed to be proved. For example, we might cite a case paraphrased from Whately (1826, p. 141).

Example 3.7

> Instead of proving that a man does not have the right to educate his children in the way he thinks best, you show that the way in which he educates his children is not really the best.

In this case, it would appear that the arguer has simply made the mistake of arguing for some proposition other than the one he is supposed to prove. There is no evidence that this move is being used as a tactic of distraction to divert the attention of the audience away from the real issue. The really important factor to be aware of is that the argument simply leads to a wrong conclusion.

Given that the argument in the horrible crime of murder case could be taken to commit either of these fallacies, the problem is how we can devise specific criteria to enable the argument evaluator to distinguish between these two fallacies in specific cases. It could well be that the argument in that case commits both of these fallacies, but even so we still need some method for determining in a given case whether it is the one fallacy that is committed or the other, or both. The clue to the solution to this problem is the observation that the best kind of evidence for the red herring fallacy is that which indicates that the arguer is using the tactic of strategic diversion of the kind represented in figure 3.1.

The way to solve the problem is to assume that we as critical argument evaluators have the ability to recognize a strategic diversion when we see one at work. A strategic diversion is a line of argumentation that not only goes away from the conclusion that is supposed to be proved and leads in a different direction, but does so in a colorful way that is meant as a strategy to distract the audience to a different issue. In other words, to distinguish between these two fallacies of relevance, we need to do more than just identify the premises and conclusions of the argument in a given case as propositions. We need also to recognize the strategy of the arguer and be able to analyze a specific case by identifying such a strategy as one of inserting a distraction that moves away from the original conclusion to be proved.

Based on these observations, the following criteria for identifying cases where the red herring fallacy has been committed can be proposed.

Criteria for Identifying Cases of the Red Herring Fallacy

1. The argument wanders off in a different direction from the path of reasoning needed to support the conclusion to be proved.
2. The interlude in the strategic diversion is a distracting interval meant to capture the attention of the audience and move it away from the issue, but that carries little or no weight as relevant evidence to prove the conclusion that is supposed to be proved.
3. There is no particular proposition the argument arrives at that can be specified as the wrong conclusion, a specific proposition that is different from the conclusion to be proved that looks enough like it to appear to be identical to it.

The following criteria for identifying cases of the wrong conclusion fallacy can now be stated.

Criteria for Identifying Cases of the Wrong Conclusion Fallacy

1. The argument actually presented has a conclusion that is different from the one that is supposed to be proved.
2. The actual conclusion looks similar enough to the real conclusion to be proved so that the arguer and/or audience could mistake the one for the other.
3. There is lack of sufficient evidence to prove the existence of a strategic diversion used to try to distract the audience.

4. The fault seems like an error that has been committed, as opposed to being a strategic maneuver of distraction used by the arguer.

Applying these two sets of criteria to real cases assumes that we can determine in a particular case whether there is sufficient evidence to prove the existence of a strategic diversion. It also assumes that we can define what a strategic diversion is.

The existence of a strategic diversion in a given case cannot be proved or disproved merely by examining the premises and conclusion of the argument in that case. [Instead, the evidence needed pertains to the structure of the dialogue in the case.] One has to look at the sequence of argumentation in light of what needs to be proved in the dialogue as a whole and examine the argumentation by both sides to see what strategies they are using. This aspect of the dialogue is often called strategic maneuvering (van Eemeren and Houtlosser 2006). As noted in the horrible crime of murder case above, there will be some examples where there is evidence that both fallacies have been committed. What we need to do in a case like this is to separate the two fallacies out, to show that there is evidence for one, but also evidence of the other. This will mean that while there may be no need to consider evidence of strategic diversion as far as the committing of the wrong conclusion fallacy is concerned, the other fallacy can also be committed independently if there is evidence of strategic diversion.

Some comments on how much evidence is needed when applying these criteria will also prove useful. The first comment concerns how much evidence of strategic diversion is needed. It is not helpful to try to quantify a degree or amount of such evidence required. All one can say is that there has to be definite textual evidence of the kind indicated in the examples classified as red herring. Even if it is possible that the argumentation in the case could be part of a strategic diversion tactic, it is not justified to classify the fallacy as one of red herring unless definite textual evidence of the diversion strategy is given. The second comment concerns how much evidence of wrong conclusion is needed. First, what the actual conclusion of the argument is needs to be shown. Second, it has to be shown that the conclusion that is supposed to be proved is different from this proposition. This too is a dialectical matter that cannot be exclusively proved from the premises and the conclusion actually put forward by the arguer. We need to determine what conclusion was supposed to be proved in the case, and this means that we have to determine what the original issue was.

These observations show that both fallacies are at least partly dialectical in nature.

3.6 VARIETIES OF CRITICISMS OF IRRELEVANCE

Consider the following example.

Example 3.8

Your friend Margie says that Taster's Choice coffee tastes better than Folgers. Apparently she is ignoring the fact that Taster's Choice is made by Nestle, and Nestle is the company that manufactured that terrible baby formula for third world countries. Thousands of babies died when the dry milk formula was mixed with contaminated water. Obviously your friend is mistaken.

The problem with the argumentation in this example is that it confuses two distinct arguments with different conclusions. One is the argument that it wouldn't be a good idea to buy Taster's Choice coffee because it is made by Nestle, a company that manufactured another product whose use led to bad consequences. This may be a good argument, or it may not be. It probably seems like a pretty good argument to those who believe in buying products on an ethical basis, for example, by giving preference to products that support the environment, or do not harm the environment. On the other hand, just because Nestle made one bad product, it doesn't necessarily follow that Taster's Choice coffee is a bad product. This argument could be seen as a kind of practical argument about what to buy, based on the consequences of buying a certain product. A lot of people might take it to be a fairly reasonable argument. But there is also another argument in this example, with a different conclusion. The conclusion of this argument is the statement that Taster's Choice coffee tastes better than Folgers.

The two arguments can be compared by examining figure 3.2. In the argument on the left, two premises go together to support a conclusion. Actually the argument for the conclusion on the left is more complicated than shown in figure 3.2, but the point is that at least an argument is given that offers some evidence to support its conclusion, and it could be taken to be a plausible argument. The problem is more with the line of argument shown on the right.

Notice that no evidence at all is given by the argumentation in example 3.8 to support the conclusion that Taster's Choice coffee tastes better

Figure 3.2. Comparison of the two conclusions in example 3.8.

than Folgers. The whole line of argumentation is taken up with arguing against buying Taster's Choice coffee on the grounds that its manufacturer has made another product whose use led to bad consequences. Example 3.8 represents a classical case of *ignoratio elenchi* of the wrong conclusion type. The basic error is to present an argument for a proposition that is different from the real conclusion to be proved. But this case is a special type of *ignoratio elenchi* that works because the argument supporting the proposition selected as the apparent conclusion could look convincing, whereas no evidence is given at all to support the real conclusion that the arguer announced at the beginning.

In other instances the conclusion of an argument is misconstrued because it is overlooked that the conclusion is complex, and a simpler proposition is substituted instead.

Example 3.9

Alfred and Boris are arguing about gun control on a panel discussion. Alfred is an expert on gun control in Alabama. As his part in the discussion, he has agreed to give evidence to support his contention that if gun control is not introduced in Alabama, there will be much greater incidence of violent crime. However, during the course of his argument, Alfred stresses that the majority of people in Alabama have been strongly against gun control by stricter licensing laws for firearms. Alfred concludes that gun control will not be introduced in Alabama.

If the above example is a fair description of Alfred's argument, then it is open to a criticism of *ignoratio elenchi*. For Alfred was supposed to prove the conditional proposition: if gun control is not introduced in Alabama, there will be much greater incidence of violent crime. However, instead Alfred has directed his argument to proving the antecedent of that conditional as his conclusion, but proving that the antecedent is true does not prove that the whole conditional is true. In short, his argument is not valid when directed to its proper conclusion. It is a classical *ignoratio elenchi*. This type of argument that confuses simple and complex propositions is a common form of fallacy of irrelevant conclusion.

Sometimes the premises of an argument can be criticized as irrelevant, rather than the conclusion. In such a case the conclusion may be fairly clear, and some of the premises relevant, but then the arguer goes "off the track" and brings in irrelevant premises. On one occasion, Senator Paul Martin rose to defend his home town of Windsor, Ontario, against a passage in Arthur Hailey's novel about the U.S. auto industry, *Wheels*. Hailey had written about "grimy Windsor" just across the border from Detroit, "matching in ugliness the worst of its U.S. senior partner." Martin's response reads as follows.

Example 3.10

When I read this I was incensed. . . . Those of us who live there know that [Windsor] is not a grimy city. It is a city that has one of the best flower parks in Canada. It is a city of fine schools, hard-working and tolerant people.

To begin with, Senator Martin's argument makes a reasonable point. The fact that Windsor has a flower park does serve as reasonable evidence to rebut the thesis that Windsor is an ugly city. At that point, as Johnson and Blair (1983, p. 87) point out, Martin has changed the subject: "Fine schools and hard-working, tolerant people are no doubt an asset, but they have nothing to do with whether a city is fair or ugly." Accordingly, Johnson and Blair criticize Senator Martin's argument as a *red herring* or irrelevant shift in argument.

The novelty here is that some of the premises in the argument are perceived as irrelevant, rather than the conclusion. The first premise about the flower park was relevant to the conclusion that Windsor is not an ugly city, but the next premises, citing the fine schools and the hard-working citizens, are not relevant. So the problem is not that Senator Martin has selected the wrong conclusion. Rather, he has gone "off the track" and started bringing in irrelevant premises.

However, we can see that this example does follow the pattern of the *ignoratio elenchi* failure of relevance if we realize that the premises and the conclusion of a reasonable argument must be connected or linked to each other. So you could say that by introducing premises that are irrelevant to the proper conclusion, an arguer is, in effect shifting to a different conclusion. Senator Martin was sticking to the proper conclusion when he talked about the flower parks. But when he went on to introduce the premises concerning hard-working and tolerant citizens he was, in effect, giving an argument that, if reasonable, could only prove some other conclusion, i.e., that Windsor is a city that has nice, upstanding citizens. So whether you focus on the premises or the conclusion, the problem is the same. The right sort of relationship between the given premises and the proper conclusion is lacking.

While *ignoratio elenchi* is the fallacy of getting the wrong conclusion or thesis in reasonable argument, sometimes the focus is more on specific premises used or needed in getting to that conclusion. But the basic problem of *ignoratio elenchi* is that the link or relation required between the premises and conclusion in reasonable argument is lacking. Therefore, we say that the arguer has strayed off the track of the argument and committed a red herring move, which opens his argument to a criticism of irrelevance.

3.7 SUMMARY

In every reasonable dialogue, in theory each participant should have a clearly designated thesis or conclusion which he is obliged to argue for as his part in the argument. This means that he is under a burden of proof to establish this particular conclusion. Hence if there is justifiable reason to think he may be straying off the course of fulfilling this burden of proof, his argument is open to a charge of *ignoratio elenchi* (irrelevance).

This irrelevance may be global or local. Global relevance concerns the over-all direction and trend of a participant's arguments as they move towards establishing his thesis in a long and possibly complex chain or network of linked arguments. Once the dialogue is concluded, it is much easier to make judgments or evaluations of global relevance. Local relevance concerns the specific relationships of particular propositions that occur at single stages of an argument. Local relevance may pertain to the relationship between a question and answer in a dialogue. Or it may pertain to the relationship between a pair of propositions in an argument.

Within both local and global relevance, there are two basic ways a premise may be said to be relevant to a conclusion. First there is subject-matter relatedness. Here we need to ask whether the premise is connected to the conclusion by sharing some common subject matters of the topics of the argument. Second, there is *probative relevance*, meaning relevance in the sense of playing some part in proving or disproving the thesis at issue. Here we need to ask whether the premise plays some role in counting towards or against the conclusion at issue.[3]

There are two separate types of relevance to check for. A premise could be subject matter related to a conclusion without playing any part in proving or disproving the conclusion in the argument. For example, "Bob has red hair" and "Bob is guilty of aiding a criminal" are subject matter–related because both share the common topic "Bob." But it may be that "Bob has red hair" does not play any part in proving or disproving the contention that Bob is guilty of aiding a criminal, in the argument under discussion. On the other hand, the proposition "Bob was seen selling weapons to Harry, a known criminal" may be relevant to the proposition "Bob is guilty of aiding a criminal" in both types of relevance in an argument.

We could sum up by generalizing that there are four different types or dimensions of relevance to be considered.

Global relevance	Local relevance
Subject matter relevance	Probative relevance

The proving-or-disproving (probative) kind of relevance was also called *pertinence* in the Middle Ages. According to the medieval logician William of Sherwood – see Walton (1982, p. 63) – a statement that is *pertinent* is one that either follows from what precedes or is logically repugnant to what precedes. What William presumably meant here is that relevance should be judged in relation to the previous statements that an arguer is committed to in the course of dialogue. This would be a partly global conception

---

3 According to Govier (1985, p. 101), a statement A is relevant to a statement B "if A either counts towards establishing B as true, or counts against establishing B as true." According to Wright and Tohinaka (1984, p. 197), first you should ask whether a premise "has a bearing on the topic by dealing with a related matter," and second, "[d]oes the premise lend some support to the conclusion?"

of relevance.[4] And what makes a proposition probatively relevant is its relationship, either one of following logically from or one of being inconsistent with the previous set of commitments. At any rate, the notion of proving-or-disproving relevance has been recognized in the older traditions of teaching logic.

In addition to the above general categories of relevance and irrelevance, the examples we have studied suggest several specific ways in which the *ignoratio elenchi* can be committed in practice. We have distinguished several different specific kinds of criticism of irrelevance that can be brought against an argument.

1. Drawing the wrong conclusion from one's own argument is the basic type of *ignoratio elenchi* fallacy.
2. Sometimes *ignoratio elenchi* means failure to refute your opponent's thesis in a dispute. In a dispute, there are two arguers and the thesis of one is the opposite of the thesis of the other. One variant of the *ignoratio elenchi* (called misconception of refutation by Aristotle) occurs where the argument of one disputant fails to refute, or to provide reasonable evidence against the thesis of the other disputant.
3. A third type of *ignoratio elenchi* occurs where the whole issue is changed by introducing a distracting parallel that may not be relevant. Suppose in a criminal trial the defence attorney proposes that the real issue is discrimination, because the defendant belongs to an ethnic minority. Care may be needed if that is not the real issue at all, but if the jury gets so excited over the issue of discrimination, they may lose sight of the real issue.
4. One extreme form of irrelevance is failure of subject-matter overlap. If some propositions introduced in an argument are so irrelevant that they do not even share any common subject matters with the proposition to be established, then the relevance of these propositions may reasonably be challenged.
5. One particular type of *ignoratio elenchi* occurs where an arguer exaggerates the conclusion his opponent is supposed to prove.
6. Sometimes the conclusion of an argument is mistaken because it is overlooked that the conclusion is a complex proposition. For

---

4 The conception is partly global because a proposition only has to be locally related to the previous propositions in the argument, not the propositions that may occur in subsequent dialogue.

example, a conditional proposition may be incorrectly treated as a simple proposition.

7. Sometimes the focus of a charge of irrelevance falls more onto the premises than the conclusion. In this type of case, the arguer may build a good case up to a point, and then introduce additional premises that go "off the track."

Each of these seven types of criticism of irrelevance has a common, root idea. This is that every reasonable dialogue should be about an issue or controversy. That is, each arguer must have a side, a thesis or conclusion to be proved as his job in the argument. When he tends to stray away from this job, his argument can become open to a charge of irrelevance.

It is most important to remember, however, that charges of irrelevance can sometimes be successfully replied to by someone who defends his argument. Until a dialogue is finally concluded, an arguer may be able to vindicate his argument as relevant, once he has filled in more steps. Therefore, most often, irrelevance is best treated as a criticism that can, in some instances, be replied to, rather than as a fallacy or knock-down refutation of an argument. Thus a criticism of irrelevance that occurs in the middle of an ongoing argument is often best treated as a procedural point of order requesting an arguer to show why his contention is relevant to the issue under dispute. Such a request, if reasonable, must be replied to if the arguer wants to avoid the failure of his argument in reasonable dialogue on grounds of irrelevance.

Relevance in argumentation presupposes that an agenda has been set prior to the actual stage of engaging in the dispute itself. Practically speaking, however, this precondition may not be met, or interpreted correctly or unanimously by all parties to the dispute at the confrontation stage. Another practical problem is that even if the agenda is set, and relevance is theoretically well defined, there may remain room in the context of a particular discussion whether a point really is relevant enough to merit extended time for discussion. Ruling in a particular case may require the good judgment of a mediator who can sensitively interpret the goals of the dialogue, the urgency of the debate, the relative importance of the main concerns which should be aired in the debate, and the standards of strictness of relevance best suited to the context of dialogue.

Many of the fallacies studied in the subsequent chapters are specific types of failure of relevance in argumentation that are powerful tricks for distracting an opponent.

105

4

Appeals to emotion

Argumentation that takes place in the conversational marketplace of every-day persuasive appeals is heavily interlaced with emotional overtones and suggestions. Successful advertising, for example, seems for the most part to consist of well-orchestrated appeals to emotions, and it is quite plausible to suggest that many political debates and controversies are decided as much on the basis of emotional appeals and loyalties as on purely dispassionate reasoning.

Personal attack is often so successful as an argument tactic because of its hot appeal to personal emotions, as chapter 6 will indicate. However, here we turn to several other types of argument that have traditionally been regarded as problematic or fallacious because they use the pull of certain basic emotions. We will mainly be concerned with the emotions of pity, fear, and group solidarity.

Popular rhetoric is argument designed to persuade a specific target audience or readership. The objective is to build a personal bond with this audience, to establish a personal link between the arguer and the recipient of his message. The successful building of this emotional relationship invites the person to whom the argument is directed to trust the person who addresses him, to give him loyalty and to suspend the queries and criticisms characteristic of argument and reasonable dialogue. Personal rhetoric is therefore more directed to the instincts than to calculative reason. The emotional appeal is directed to the person's unthinking reactions, and so attempts to bypass the critical questioning and logical assessment normally characteristic of reasonable dialogue. Too often, such appeals are tactics that violate rule 1 of the negative rules of persuasion dialogue set out in chapter 1. That is, they are attempts to get away with a failure to make any serious effort to fulfill the obligation to meet a burden of proof in argument.

Traditionally, appeals to emotion in argument have been distrusted, and even labelled categorically as logical fallacies. There is a common tendency to contrast "impartial reason" with "the passions" and to distrust the latter in reasoned argument. This tendency is often affirmed in logic texts where

106

appeals to emotion have been treated as inherently illogical, and subject to strong censure.[1]

However, some decisions to act on an emotional reaction, like fear, can turn out to be sound and justified conclusions which have survival value. Moreover, many arguments on controversial issues, for example, in politics and religion, may quite rightly be based on passionate conviction. Especially where morals and values are involved, ignoring our "decent instincts" may be to overlook some of the best reasons for adopting a certain position. And it is a given of democratic politics in free countries that political loyalty based on instincts or appeal to deep emotional wellsprings of conviction may be a legitimate and important part of election speeches and political dialogue. Lincoln's speeches were deeply emotional, but that should not lead us to conclude that they must be inherently fallacious or illogical. Far from it! Because they do appeal to our deep instincts on what is right, their arguments are judged more compelling and important.

Hence it is not always easy to sort out when emotional appeals in argument should be properly subject to criticism on logical grounds. Practical decisions to act are often rightly made on the basis of personal experience, which may manifest itself in emotions or a gut feeling about the best way to proceed. There is nothing wrong with this, and in many cases practical skill and experience may be the best guides. A technical expert who gives you advice on how to solve a problem, based on his instinctive feeling about the best course of action, may be giving you the best advice (external proof) you could get.

One problem with emotional appeals is that they tend to be inherently weak but plausible arguments, and if stronger and more objective arguments are also available, the problem is not to overlook them and be seduced by the more attractive pull of personal emotions and interests. Hence emotional appeals can induce a failure to ask the right questions, or mask a failure to back up an argument properly (negative rules 6 and 4 in section 1.4). Appeals to emotions are powerful distractions that can be used to cover any of the failures described by the negative rules of persuasion dialogue.

4.1 ARGUMENTUM *AD POPULUM*   *essay.*

The *ad populum* (to the people) fallacy is traditionally characterized as the use of appeal to mass enthusiasms or popular sentiments in order

---

1 See Hamblin (1970) and Walton (1987).

to win assent for the conclusion of an argument not supported by good evidence. One can easily appreciate the effectiveness of this sort of strategy in argument. Most of us like to think that our views are in line with popular trends, and any feeling that we are left out or left behind the accepted styles or leading opinions of the day would not be welcome. Any arguer who is in the business of public persuasion would not get very far if he were ignorant of the popular beliefs and accepted views of his target audience.

A type of persuasive argument often cited as a case of *ad populum* appeal can be illustrated by the following example, describing a commercial advertisement.

Example 4.0

A television commercial for life insurance portrays a scene of a happy, handsome-looking family having a picnic on a river bank. They are fishing in the river, and generally having a nice time together. The commercial message is a series of slogans about happy family life, including phrases like "peace of mind today" and "security for the future." The insurance company is described as a place where the family and the insurance agent can "work things out together." No mention is made of the types of policies available, the interest rates paid on these policies, or other specifics for anyone interested in shopping for the best insurance coverage at reasonable rates.

The reason why commercial messages of this sort are often cited as instances of the *ad populum* fallacy is not hard to appreciate. Clearly the scene portrayed in the commercial is carefully produced to appeal winningly to popular sentiment. The insurance agent is portrayed as a fatherly man whom one would be inclined to trust, but in its preoccupation with this appeal, the commercial message has failed to give us any useful information about the relative merits of the policies of his particular company. The folksy appeal of the commercial hits the heartstrings of its target audience, but does not spend any time providing information about the relevant aspects of insurance policies that should properly play a role in a reasonable person's decision to take out a policy from this company.

What is most likely to seem fallacious or open to criticism about this sort of commercial message is what it lacks. The appeal to sentiment need not necessarily, in itself, be a bad thing, but the fact that it is a substitute for genuinely useful information makes the appeal to sentiment open to criticism. Our criticism may be then that the appeal to sentiment in the portrayal of the happy family scene is really irrelevant, or only marginally relevant to the real issue that the commercial message should address. Is the insurance coverage by this company a good buy that offers advantages over the competition? The whole commercial seems to be a systematic evasion of the issue. In other words, the *ad populum* here seems to be a failure of relevance (negative argumentation rule 5 of section 1.4).

If the insurance company were to be addressed with this criticism, how do you think they might reply? They might well respond that they are in the business of selling insurance, and to do that they must be competitive. They must draw attention to their product. They evidently have come to the conclusion that the best way to do this is to present a commercial that has popular appeal. Perhaps they might say that if their commercial simply gave the facts and figures about their interest rates and coverage benefits, the public would be bored by that information, and their competitors would do better business by presenting more lively commercials. After all, the time to discuss facts, figures, and rates, they might say, is when you talk personally with your customer. Hence, they might argue, in a commercial message on television, the popular appeal type of approach is not irrelevant and not fallacious.

What is one to say to this type of reply? First, one should acknowledge that the reply is based on two sound points about allegations of emotional fallacies.

The first point is that there is nothing wrong per se with an appeal to popular sentiment.[2] Sometimes we do make decisions to trust people based on our instincts, and that is not necessarily bad in every case, even though it is wise to be careful whom you trust. No business in a mass market can be successful unless its products are popular. There is nothing wrong in trying to appeal to a popular audience or constituency, and in fact, sometimes it can be commendable and reasonable. So we should concede that the insurance company is not necessarily being fallacious, or even wrong in any other way, by trying to be competitive through drawing popular attention to their product.

The second point is that if the insurance company is only trying to direct attention to their product and their company, they may not even be trying to present an objective argument – premises and conclusion containing information about their policies – in their commercial message. Instead of fulfilling a burden of proof, perhaps all the commercial is really trying to say is: "Trust us. We are a large, reliable company with values that you share. Next time you are shopping for insurance, consider us." Notice

2 See the discussion of this point in Walton (1987).

109

that if this is their message, it is not even clear that it is an argument which is designed to persuade the viewer of the benefits of this company's insurance policies. Instead, it is a subjective appeal to the customer to accept this insurance company as trustworthy and reliable. If this is right, then it is not so clear that the insurance company's appeal to emotion is irrelevant. It depends on what the purpose of the commercial is, or should be, as a type of argumentation.

The problem here is that the insurance company's message seemed to be fallacious because the appeal to popular sentiment is an irrelevant argument. If the insurance company's possible replies to this objection are acceptable, perhaps they were not trying to argue for the benefits of their policies at all. In short, if there is no burden of objective proof, there may be no fallacy of irrelevance. Or at any rate, it may be not so easy or straightforward to pin down exactly what the alleged fallacy consists in.

The replies open to the defender of a popular appeal like that in example 4.0 can contain some reasonable points. Nevertheless, the bottom line is that many of us may justifiably feel that there has been an evasion in this type of popular appeal. True, the insurance company's message may have to include emotional popular appeals in order to be competitive, but surely it should also include some relevant facts about insurance for the intelligent consumer. Instead of appealing to the lowest common denominator, the message should contain useful information. Anyone who feels that the value of this company's insurance to the consumer is the real issue, has the basis of a criticism of irrelevance. Even if the fallacy is not just the use of an emotional appeal in itself, still, one might reply, the fallacy could be the evasion of a burden of proof where there should be some objective argument given about the value of this company's product.

The issue comes down to the question of whether there ought to be a reasonable burden of proof on the insurance company to supply information in their commercials over and above emotional appeals. If so, an *ad populum* criticism is justified. If not, then this criticism could be defended against with some justification.

So far, what can be open to criticism in an *ad populum* argument is that the popular emotional appeal can be a tactic to disguise a failure to address what should be the real issue of an argument. Such criticisms need to be evaluated with care, because there can still be room at the confrontation stage of argument to determine what the real issue should be. What is the proper agenda of a television commercial? Is it to persuade the viewer to buy a product on its merits, or is it only a vehicle to draw attention to the product, to give "brand name recognition"? The viewer who uncritically accepts the commercial message for something it is not could be failing to ask the right questions, and ignoring better sources of evidence which would enable him to arrive at an informed decision. This failure may not be so much a fallacy as simply a bad blunder.

4.2 THE ARGUMENT FROM POPULARITY

One of the most common types of argument cited as an instance of the *ad populum* fallacy is the political speech of the cracker barrel or down home type. For example, suppose a political candidate who has a Ph.D. in economics is addressing a group of local farmers in a rural riding. This politician has a "hobby farm" to supplement his income as a consultant and university professor. Part of his speech runs as follows.

Example 4.1

The other day when I was out working in the fields, seeing the sun glinting on the wheat, I reflected on how hard it has become for the farm producer to make a living. We farmers are the food suppliers of the nation, and we've got to stand solidly on the side of freedom against the collectivists and other parasites that are ripping us off with higher taxes and restrictive marketing regulations. We good citizens, the producers who work the land to feed the nation, must stand together to fight for our rights and the interests of the middle majority of productive contributors to our standard of living in this great country.

It is easy to spot the phony aspect of this argument, and no doubt its intended audience would perceive it as well. The speaker is not really a full-time working farmer, but he tries to pose as one in order to appeal to a sympathetic feeling of group solidarity in his audience. What then is the fallacy?

Well, of course, one criticism is that the speaker is just not a real farmer, so his appeal is really based on a false posture, a kind of hypocrisy or lie. We feel that he may be talking down to his audience, because of his phony posture and heavy-handed attempts to enlist sympathy. However, these faults are not necessarily fallacies, or even incorrect arguments. It may be simply that the man's attempt at persuasive rhetoric is clumsy and unconvincing. It's not that an appeal to group solidarity need always be intrinsically wrong or fallacious, it's just that this man's attempt at it is a bad attempt to make this type of appeal. What may be wrong is not so much fallacious argument as simply bad speechmaking, which is not necessarily a failure of logic as much as a failure to communicate with this specific audience.

Of course, the argument could be a failure of relevance. But perhaps there was no set thesis or conclusion for the speech on this particular occasion, so that is not the problem. What could be wrong, alternatively, is that the speaker has tried too hard to zero in on the position of this particular audience by appealing to their pride and interests too exclusively and transparently, even to the point of trying to pass himself off, somewhat weakly, as a farmer himself. Just as the *ad hominem* argument was an argument that, as we saw, appealed to the personal position of the party on the other side of the argument, so the *ad populum* is targeted to the position of the specific group to whom the argument is directed in persuasion. Instead of advancing objective premises that any reasonable person should accept, the *ad populum* argument uses premises that may be weak but that have strong rhetorical appeal to the sentiments of group solidarity of one particular audience. Surely such a selectively subjective appeal is open to the charge of being fallacious. But is it? We will see in chapter 6 that the *ad hominem* argument, despite its being an argument directed to a particular arguer's position, is not always fallacious in every case. The same could be said here.

In a democratic country, any stance or argument taken by a politician will only be successful in the political forum of debate if it positively appeals to a broad majority of constituents. Hence popular appeal to a majority, or to a particular audience of constituents, is surely not an absolutely wrong objective in a politician's argument. We saw that in persuasion dialogue (critical discussion), arguments are properly directed to the position of the other participant in the argument. In political debate, if a politician wants to convince an audience of his stance on an issue, he had better use propositions as premises that this particular audience is committed to, or can be made to accept. In democratic countries, political debate is essentially an adversarial arena, and the successful politician must carefully address his argument to the audience he wants to convince to support his position. There is nothing wrong with this partisan element in all democratic political argumentation, in itself. It only becomes fallacious, or at least open to criticism, where it is subject to particular abuses or excesses. So what are these particular errors connected with the *ad populum* appeal?

One basic argument that is implicit in many an *ad populum* appeal is that generally speaking, popular belief does not establish the truth of a matter.

In other words, the two basic inference forms below are not, in general, deductively valid.

(P1)   Everybody accepts that A is true.
Therefore, A is true.
(P2)   Nobody accepts that A is true.
Therefore, A is false.

We could call (P1) and (P2) the basic forms of the argument from popularity. Then an argument could be criticized as a weak argument from popularity if it treats either (P1) or (P2) as being deductively valid forms of argument, or as being stronger arguments than the evidence merits. In other words, if all the arguer has to offer as premises for his conclusion that A is true (or false) is the evidence that a lot of people accept A as true (or that nobody accepts A as true), then his argument is likely to be a weak one. Certainly it is not, in general, deductively valid. If he treats the argument as a strong one, or even as a valid one, he commits a significant misjudgment, and his argument should be open to reasonable criticism.

However, we must be careful here. Although (P1) and (P2) are not deductively valid as forms of argument, they can represent weaker forms of argument that can reasonably shift the burden of proof in dialogue. If I propose to argue for a proposition that virtually everyone rejects as false or wildly implausible, then the burden of proof imposed against me should be much stronger than if I propose to argue for a conclusion that virtually everyone accepts as highly plausible, or even certainly true.

Similarly, (P1) and (P2) can be weak arguments in some cases that nevertheless have some plausibility value in directing a person towards a particular line of action in a situation where objective knowledge of the facts is lacking, yet a practical decision must be made. For example, if I am late for my train and I do not know where the train platform is located, I may be guided by seeing everybody else in the area heading towards a tunnel. Suppose I ask someone to direct me to the platform and he replies, "Everyone is heading for the platform. They are all going through that tunnel." Now this person could be wrong, or he could be misleading me, but unless I have reason to think that this is so, it is reasonable to act on the presumption that he is probably (or plausibly) right, and giving me good advice. Hence (P1) and (P2) are weak, but sometimes reasonable types of argumentation. So *ad populum* arguments are not inherently wrong, but they are weak kinds of argumentation which can easily go wrong in various ways.

Thus the traditional *ad populum* fallacy is most often a combination of two main kinds of errors in argument. One is the fault of irrelevance. The other is the misuse of the argument from popularity, a weak argument that may be over-estimated, or taken as more compelling than it should be. The two errors are often combined, because a weak argument may divert our attention from more relevant considerations, or mask the fact that these other arguments are lacking, and have not been considered.

4.3 PROBLEMS WITH APPEALS TO POPULARITY

Operating on the basis of a consensus of what the majority want, or what the majority do, is a common way of deciding how to act. There is nothing inherently wrong with it as a kind of argument to decide how to act personally, but there are often specific problems with how this type of argument from popularity may be used to try to persuade someone to act in a similar fashion.

Politicians often try to persuade people to follow their policies because, they claim, that is what the majority of citizens now want. But do they? Polls may be appealed to, but public opinion can be fickle, and change fast. It may be better political wisdom to look deeper, and explore the reasons for a particular policy, or even to stick to an unpopular conclusion. For what is now popular has a way of becoming unpopular when circumstances change.

Often arguments from popularity contain an appeal to what is currently accepted as a custom or standard of behavior in a group the arguer wants to identify with or cite as an authoritative source of norms. But too often there is an element of "peer pressure" implicit in these arguments.

Example 4.2

Mother: I thought you would say 'Thank you' for all the work I put into planning your birthday party.

Daughter: Mom, people just don't talk that way any more, these days.

No doubt the daughter feels that she has had the last word on the issue, but if her claim is true that the people she associates with do not have the sensitivity or good manners to say 'Thanks' when thanks are due, it may simply be a reflection of their lack of good values or immaturity. So identification with the group should not be the final word. The question remains whether the group values or standards can be justified.

If some practice is accepted as a custom or standard by a dominant or popular group, it may take a strong argument to go against this establishment of cited precedents. There are always exceptions to customs, and there may be opposing groups who have a different custom. Often, the argument comes down to whose group is more trendy or progressive, in line with currently accepted views. Claims of whose group is more dominant at any particular time may be hard to support with real evidence, and even if evidence is given, there remains the question of whether the group practice cited can be justified as a good or reasonable standard of behavior.

In some cases the argument from popularity is mixed with a kind of weak appeal to authority. The argument is that everybody who is knowledgeable, civilized, enlightened, etc., is doing it, therefore you should be doing it too.

Example 4.3

If we vote to return the death penalty in Canada, we, along with a few states, will be the only jurisdictions in the western world with a death penalty. Not one country in Europe has a death penalty. New Zealand doesn't have it. Australia doesn't have it. It is on the books in Belgium, but they haven't had an execution since 1945. It is abolished in all other western countries. We will be joining countries like Iran and Turkey that are not models of democratic civilization or human rights.[3]

By arguing that all civilized countries ban capital punishment, and suggesting that countries with capital punishment may be less civilized, this argument uses the bandwagon strategy to try to create a presumption against capital punishment. However, even if the arguer's statistics are right that most western countries do not have capital punishment, it may be questioned whether these countries can be the only countries that are models of democratic civilization and human rights. But even if this argument were to be conceded, the possibility exists that these countries might change their policies if strong arguments for capital punishment in the present context of law enforcement were brought forward by the advocates of such a policy. If these various countries do not have capital punishment, then they must have reasons for this policy, or at any rate, arguments can be given for or against these policies. The important thing then is to examine

3 This example is based on an argument the author heard in a televised interview with a politician on the CBC program *This Week in Parliament*, February 28, 1987.

115

these arguments rather than simply assume that these countries must be right because they are models of democratic civilization. Thus although the appeal to popularity in this example does contain a certain appeal to the expertise of those countries who are allegedly models of democratic civilization, this is a weak argument at best.

Yet another distinct type of problem with popular appeal can occur where a speaker tries to subvert or shut down reasonable dialogue by closing the audience's reception to any possible contrary viewpoint. This can occur where an arguer tries to appeal to bonds to unite him and his audience in a common cause and exclude outsiders from the mutual interest group. The outsiders are portrayed as potential enemies whom we must not listen to or allow into consideration. It is as though the argument gives the message that what is important is group solidarity, so any possibly contrary point of view in dialogue must be excluded at the outset, or paid no attention.

An example of this type of popular appeal rhetoric is provided by Bailey (1983, p. 134), who quotes a speech of Walter Reuther in 1957 on the topic of racketeering in trade unions.

Example 4.4

I think we can all agree that the overwhelming majority of the leadership of the American movement is composed of decent, honest, dedicated people who have made a great contribution involving great personal sacrifice, helping to build a decent American labor movement. . . . We happen to believe that leadership in the American movement is a sacred trust. We happen to believe that this is no place for people who want to use the labor movement to make a fast buck.

A reasonable observation about this speech is that it attempts to put its conclusion beyond questioning by portraying it as a fact to which everyone must agree. In effect then, the listener is left no room for further argument. The *ad populum* message cuts off reasonable dialogue. The "we" who accept the movement are included. The "people who want to . . . make a fast buck" are excluded. In other words, either you join the labor movement position or you are an offending outsider who is immoral and against the movement. Those are your choices. As Bailey (1983, p. 135) comments, this type of *ad populum* tactic is the "rhetoric of belonging." If you don't belong, then your word is worthless, and your point of view is of no account.

What is objectionable in this type of *ad populum* appeal is not only that the argument is weak in the way the previous types of *ad populum* arguments we noted are. But the added twist is the attempt to thwart or seal off argument and reasonable dialogue, and dogmatically enforce one's own position. The tactic open to criticism here is the unreasonable exclusion of further argument. It is a problem of premature closure of dialogue which violates the rule for the closing stage, the last rule of negative rules of persuasion dialogue given in chapter 1, section 1.4.

4.4 THREATENING APPEALS TO FORCE

The *ad baculum* fallacy is traditionally said to be the resort to force or the threat of force to make someone accept the conclusion of an argument. *Ad baculum* literally means "to the stick, or club." The kinds of examples often given of this type of fallacy cite the use of strong-arm methods and goon squads.

Example 4.5

According to R. Grunberger, author of *A Social History of the Third Reich*, published in Britain, the Nazis used to send the following notice to German readers who let their subscriptions lapse: "Our paper certainly deserves the support of every German. We shall continue to forward copies of it to you, and hope that you will not want to expose yourself to unfortunate consequences in the case of cancellation." (*Parade*, May 9, 1971)[4]

One can easily see why this sort of threat or appeal to force is contrary to the aims and methods of reasonable dialogue. In reasonable dialogue, an arguer should have the freedom to make up his own mind whether or not to accept a conclusion, based on the argument given for it, or the arguments that can be given against it. The threat of force no longer leaves these options open to reason, and tries to forcefully close off the possibilities of free dialogue. Force seems contrary to the aims of reason.

On the other hand though, an appeal to force, in some instances, can be not altogether unreasonable. For example, there are laws in some countries that impose severe penalties for conviction for drunk driving. Although such a law does seem to constitute an appeal to force or to the threat of forceful intervention, it could be argued that the law is not unreasonable. It could be argued that such a law is both fair and necessary, and that appeal to this type of law in arguing against drunk driving in public service messages

---

4 Example 4.5 first came to the author's attention in Irving M. Copi's text, *Introduction to Logic*, where it was cited as an instance of the *ad baculum* fallacy.

is not fallacious. Certainly it is not clear why reminding the public of this law in order to discourage drunk driving should be regarded as a fallacious argument.

Let us go back to example 4.5. What is fallacious about the argument represented there that is not fallacious in the drunken driving case? One suggestion is that example 4.5 describes an ugly, menacing threat that would terrorize its recipient, unlike the other case, where only a warning is conveyed, not a threat. But what is the difference between a threat and a warning? If the penalty for drunken driving is a two-year sentence in jail or on a work detail, that may be extremely threatening if directed to most of us. Generally, whether something is a threat or a warning may depend on how it is taken, and that seems variable, and hard to predict in many cases. Granted, warning someone of danger, or dangerous consequences, may not be fallacious at all, but in both cases above there does seem to be a threat of the use of force, as well as a warning.

Perhaps we are inclined to see a significant difference between the two cases because we think that one penalty is reasonable whereas the other is not. Most of us probably think that a good case can be made for having severe penalties for drunken driving, but we feel that everyone should have the freedom to make up their own minds what newspaper to read. Using the threat of force to compel someone to read one particular newspaper is just not fair or reasonable. However, this distinction is a matter of opinion. In non-democratic countries, readers are not given a choice. There are only official news sources, and foreign media are forcefully excluded by law. Does this mean that an *ad baculum* argument could be fallacious in the United States but non-fallacious in one of these non-democratic countries? Such a conclusion is not acceptable. The distinction between an argument that is fallacious and one that is non-fallacious must rest on more than just opinions on what is reasonable, or opinions on what laws are fair. We conclude that it is not easy to tell exactly what the significant difference is between these two cases of appeal to force. What makes one possibly legitimate while the other is not?

Perhaps the key difference is that we feel that the penalty for drunken driving is, or can be based on reasonable arguments that could, at least to some extent, be challenged or backed up by reasonable dialogue. However, the context of example 4.5 suggests that if one were to try to reason with the Nazi newspaper vendors you would expect to get beaten up, or perhaps put in a concentration camp. In the other case, even though a law against drunken driving is enforced, one could expect to be given reasons why this law is thought to be reasonable if one were to question or challenge the fairness of the law. In short then, the Nazi notice is essentially a non-rational type of intimidation because no argument why one should reasonably subscribe to this newspaper is given, and no challenge or questioning of any such argument would be tolerated. At least, so one may reasonably presume from the context of example 4.5. Hence the problem here is similar to the one type of *ad populum* argument we considered (example 4.4) where the illicit tactic was the attempt to prematurely close off reasonable dialogue. In the drunken driving case, the law also is forceful, but at least leaves open the reasonable consideration of the basis or reasoning behind this law. You may have to follow the law, but you are allowed to question or discuss its reasonableness without fear of force.

These two examples indicate that appeals to force need to be examined carefully, for not all appeals to force are fallacious. One must be prepared to state clearly why a particular appeal to force is to be criticized as an instance of an *ad baculum* error or fault in argument.

We must also be careful to draw a distinction between arguments using a threat and fear appeal arguments that do not specifically make a threat, because many logic textbooks classify both types of argument under the heading of *ad baculum*. Advertisers often place ads in the media that are based on fear appeal arguments. For example, the Canadian government agency Health Canada has often used televised ad messages targeted to teens to try to get them to stop smoking, citing the dangers of smoking and portraying the deadly consequences of nicotine addiction in a dramatic way. For example, an ad might show someone smoking and then later dying painfully of lung cancer. In one ad, scary music accompanies a scene in which second-hand smoke drifts into an infant's crib. A widely shown Canadian ad against drunk driving showed a scene where some teens are getting in a car after the driver has been drinking at a party. The ad then shows the vehicle crashing, and one of the passengers, a young girl, is taken off in an ambulance. In the final scene of the ad, the driver of the car has to tell the girl's parents that she is dead. No threat was made in the argument in the ad to the viewers to carry out some negative action against them if they drink while driving. The ad did not mention legal penalties of drinking and driving, or threaten to bring about any such penalties should the viewers engage in this practice. Hence arguments of this sort, while they should definitely be classified as fear appeal arguments, should not be classified as arguments using force or the threat of force. We need to make a clear distinction between threat appeal arguments and fear appeal arguments where no threat was made in order to support the argument.

Fear appeal arguments like the ones cited can often be quite reasonable. Certainly if we want to support any argument that might help reduce drinking and driving, smoking, or other dangerous activities that can be prevented, we should not declare that the fear appeal arguments in these ads are inherently fallacious. Many fear appeal arguments, when judged in context, appear to be reasonable, even though they represent a fallible kind of argumentation that can be deceptive because of their emotional impact.

We saw that the *ad baculum* fallacy has been described as the threat of force, but one must be careful in some cases to distinguish between a threat and a warning. Suppose Lois is a newspaper reporter investigating a possible case of criminal conspiracy. A person she is interviewing makes the following remarks.

Example 4.6

I would be very careful if I were you. Pursuing this story further could be very dangerous. Recently someone else who was investigating these same people was run over by a bulldozer after his family had been threatened.

Now if these remarks are taken as a threat, it could be quite reasonable to propose that they might constitute an instance of an erroneous *ad baculum* argument that should be subject to criticism. Much depends on who the speaker is, what the reporter knows about him, and the tone of voice he uses to convey these remarks. It could be that the speaker is sincerely concerned about the safety of the reporter and is trying, perhaps even at risk to himself, to warn her of the danger in her present course of action. If so, his remarks could best be interpreted as a warning, and not as a threat at all. Perhaps they were not meant as a threat, and should not reasonably be so taken. If that is the right interpretation, then a criticism that the speaker has committed a fallacious *ad baculum* would be unwarranted and incorrect. Here, it depends on what type of speech act is involved in the dialogue, to determine whether the speech act is that of a threat or a warning.

Fear and threat appeal arguments have specific argumentation schemes. According to the analysis presented in Walton (2000, p. 143), the argument from fear appeal has a structure that can be modeled in a dialogue format. The dialogue has a proponent P and an respondent R. The dialogue is a deliberation structure in which the goal of P is to try to get R to carry out a particular action A. One means for P to get R to carry out A is a danger, D, that represents a bad consequence from R's point of view. In

120

a fear appeal argument, D is taken to represent something that is taken to be particularly fearful for R. Defined in this dialogue format, the fear appeal argument can be classified as a species of argument that has three distinctive premises.

Scheme for the Fear Appeal Argument

Premise 1: If you (the respondent) do not bring about A, then D will occur.

Premise 2: D is a very bad outcome, from your (the respondent's) point of view.

Premise 3: D is such a bad outcome that it is likely to evoke fear in you (the respondent).

Conclusion: Therefore, you (the respondent) should bring about A.

The fear appeal argument is based on the presence of the speech act of warning. A warning can be expressed in the form of a conditional statement, where S and D are states of affairs (things that can be brought about by an agent), and where the pronoun 'I' represents the proponent, and the pronoun 'you' represents the respondent.

> If you bring about (fail to bring about) S, then something very bad from your point of view, D, will come about.

The presence of this conditional statement as part of an argument indicates that the argument is based on the speech act of warning. We must now proceed to clarify the distinction between a warning and a threat.

The fear appeal argument is not based on a threat. As noted above, a government anti-smoking ad that graphically portrays the horrible consequences of smoking, like getting lung cancer or dying of chronic lung disease, is a fear appeal argument. But it is not a threat appeal argument provided that it is not making a threat to the viewers by telling them, for example, that the government will give them lung cancer or chronic lung disease if they fail to quit smoking. True, the ad may be threatening to the viewers. It may make them afraid about their continued health. It is supposed to do that, but it is not making a threat to them, in a very specific meaning of the expression 'making a threat.'

The other type of *ad baculum* argument, typically called appeal to force or threat, lies in the additional premise in which the speaker makes a threat to the hearer. When the proponent makes a threat to the respondent, he is not only telling the respondent that the bad state of affairs D will happen, unless she brings about A. He is making a commitment to her that he will make it happen if she does not bring about A. To express the scheme for the appeal to threat type of argument, the following additional premise needs to be added to the scheme for the fear appeal argument: I (the proponent) will undertake to see to it that D will occur if you (the respondent) fail to bring about A. This fourth premise adds a personal factor to the effect that the proponent is declaring that she will bring about the event D, unless the respondent takes the right (indicated) action with respect to A. In this connection, the notion of a credible threat is important. A threat is credible where the proponent is in a position to carry out the bad event in question, and where the respondent is aware that the proponent is in this position, and is aware that the proponent is ready and willing to carry it out. In short, a credible threat is one where it really looks to the respondent that the proponent is both willing and able to bring D about.

According to the definition, making a threat is a speech act in a dialogue exchange. The proponent of the threat warns the respondent that something that is very bad for the respondent (like loss of life) will or may happen to him. The proponent also indicates to the respondent that she (the proponent) will see to it that this bad event occurs, unless the proponent complies by carrying out (or omitting to carry out) some designated action. In the speech act of making a threat, the speaker declares the intention of carrying out a designated action not wanted by the hearer, unless the hearer carries out another designated action (Nicoloff 1989). Speech acts of making a threat are often used as means of persuasion based on argumentation from positive or negative consequences. For the speech act to truly be a threat (or the making of a threat, more precisely), the proponent must actually convey his commitment to carrying out the bad outcome (bad, from the respondent's point of view). Otherwise, the speech act is not that of a threat, but only that of warning. In the analysis of Walton (2000, pp. 113–114), three essential conditions for the speech act of making a threat are set out. The preparatory condition states that the respondent believes that the proponent can bring about the bad outcome in question. The sincerity condition states that the respondent wants to avoid the bad outcome. The essential condition states that the proponent is making a commitment to bring about the bad outcome if the respondent does not comply.

The essential condition for the threat type *ad baculum* argument requires that a special premise must be present. This premise is the making of a threat, a statement of the following form made by the proponent.

I will see to it that D comes about, unless you bring about S.

This expression of commitment by the proponent, characteristic of the speech act of making a threat, is an essential characteristic of the appeal to threat type of *ad baculum* argument. If the proponent only makes a warning to the respondent in a case, but not a threat, the argument should be classified under the category of fear appeal but not under the category of threat appeal. The statement above, expressing the essential requirement of the making of a threat, is the criterion that separates the appeal to threat type of *ad baculum* argument from the fear appeal type.

Commonly there may be a fairly reasonable presumption that an argument contains a threat, but there is little unequivocal evidence of a threat that can be clearly documented. Most threats are veiled because a frank threat could result in legal or other recriminations. Thus even when it is reasonably clear that a threat has been made, citing irrefutable evidence of this may be problematic.

Example 4.7

Oral Roberts, the fundamentalist preacher, cited a deadline from God that he must raise eight million dollars in one year, by March 31, or die. Reverend Roberts retired to his Prayer Tower to fast and pray for the money. The evangelist said on his national television program that his life would end at the end of March if the money was not raised by then: "I'm going to be in and out of the Prayer Tower until victory comes or God calls me home." (Associated Press, 'Roberts Ransom Assured,' *Winnipeg Free Press*, March 22, 1987, p. 1)

Now does this plea for funds contain a threat or not? Most of us would be inclined to interpret Reverend Roberts' statements to contain a kind of threat. No doubt he might deny that this is so, claiming that the outcome is in God's hands. On the other hand, Reverend Roberts' argument takes the classic form of a threatening argument: 'Either do this or something bad will happen.' But is this his argument? The question of whether he has committed an *ad baculum* fallacy rests on this question of interpretation of Roberts' speech act.

Thus once again it is good to stress that while finding the specific form of inference or argumentation scheme that an argument fits in a given case is an important task in analyzing and evaluating the argument, it is not the whole job. The argument also has to be situated pragmatically into its context of dialogue. An important aspect of analyzing *ad baculum* arguments is to carefully assemble the evidence in the case to see whether a threat was made. Only then can we have the evidence we need to reasonably classify the argument as a threat appeal argument, in contrast to other kinds of argument such as a fear appeal argument. This problem is not overwhelming, however, when it comes to evaluating arguments that we think might be fallacious, because we often need to make a conditional evaluation depending on how the argument should be interpreted in the context of dialogue in a given case. Many arguments in natural language discourse are ambiguous, vague, and in many instances are even meant to be deceptive and confusing. When analyzing such arguments we need to make a hypothesis concerning how to interpret the argument based on the textual evidence and the context of dialogue in the given case. If an argumentation scheme can be fitted to the argument in a given case based on an interpretation of it, we can then analyze and evaluate the argument in light of the requirements of the scheme.

4.5 FURTHER *AD BACULUM* PROBLEMS

One kind of problem the *ad baculum* shares with other emotional appeals is that it may not be clear that a decision arrived at on the basis of emotion or instinct is really an argument. The suspicion may be that the decision was based on fear, self-interest, self-preservation, or instinct rather than on evidence at all.

Animal behavior is often described in terms of instincts. In many cases, it also seems natural to describe the action as a kind of reasoning process ascribed to the animal whereby one emotion overcomes another.

Example 4.8

A bird being photographed by a naturalist photographer alights at the mouth of its burrow in the bed of a creek with a minnow to feed its chicks. Afraid of the photographer's camera light, the mother bird backs away, and flies off. Returning several minutes later, it approaches a chick and gives it the fish. The commentator describes the situation by saying that the mother bird's maternal instinct overcame its fear of the camera light.

Could the bird be engaging in a kind of practical (goal-driven) reasoning based on its instincts and perceptions of a situation? If so, then many an emotional appeal may be based on a kind of argument or reasoning, rather than being a replacement of reason by emotion. Much depends on what we are prepared to call "reasoning" in this type of situation.

In the same way, the prisoner who "confesses" under threats, or under the fear of force, may not be illogical, or have thrown argument to the winds and embraced emotions. He may simply be responding to a different kind of argument, or basing his decision on a kind of practical reasoning that puts survival over telling the truth, at least for the moment. So there are questions here about *ad baculum* as a kind of argument.[5] It may involve a kind of argument or reasoning that we are not familiar with in traditional logic, and that is difficult to interpret because of its emotional and instinctive nature. But whether it is reasoning or not, it is a powerful tactic used in argument, and a common way of arriving at a course of action.

The lesson is that the *ad baculum* appeal is used as a tactic in argument to unduly influence an opponent in dialogue. What is important is to try to see how it is being used as a strategy of argumentation that may violate one or more of the negative rules of persuasion dialogue. The types of problem that can be identified with *ad baculum* appeals are often similar in nature to the varieties of *ad populum* problems. Sometimes the appeal to fear or to the threat of force is used as an emotional distraction that is irrelevant to the real issue. Therefore, in approaching an *ad baculum* appeal discourse, it is important to try to identify the conclusion that is supposed to be proved. And therefore, identifying the argument containing the *ad baculum* appeal can be important.

We may have a case where there is a threat, but the threat may not necessarily be used as an argument, or part of an argument to persuade somebody to do something or influence them with regard to a conclusion at issue. The person who admittedly made the threat may argue – in some cases with reason – that there was no connection between the threat and the conclusion at issue.

Example 4.9

Ed Brutus, gangland figure, is accused of using threats to force Shakey Trembler, owner of a chain of pizza outlets, to make him a partner in the pizza business. Mr. Brutus acknowledges that he had threatened to use physical violence against Mr. Trembler. However, he argues that his threat was a response to Mr. Trembler's failure to pay back a loan.

Could Mr. Brutus have a reasonable argument to defend himself against a charge of using threats to illegally force Mr. Trembler to enter into a business contract with him? Each case must be decided on its own merits, but here we should allow that it could be possible that Mr. Brutus' threat was not intended to force Mr. Trembler to make him a partner.

What this shows is that just because a threat has been made, it doesn't necessarily follow that an *ad baculum* fallacy can be declared or claimed to

5 See also Walton (1987).

be committed in relation to a specific argument or case at issue. There may be a threat, but the threat may not be related in the right way to the conclusion advanced by an arguer for us to claim with justification that an *ad baculum* fallacy has been committed. If an allegation of *ad baculum* fallacy has been made, but there is a failure of relevance between the threat issued by an arguer and the conclusion of his specific argument in a particular case, then the *ad baculum* allegation itself is a failure of rule 5 of the negative rules of persuasion dialogue listed in section 1.4. Or other violations of these rules could be involved as well, in differing cases of the *ad baculum* fallacy. Intimidation has been used as a tactic not only to divert an argument, or to try to prevent the argument from getting started, but even to prevent the procedure of dialogue from getting under way.

Example 4.10

According to a *Newsweek* report (Fred Coleman, 'A Threat of Proletarian Justice,' December 22, 1986, p. 38), the trial of the terrorist group Direct Action was delayed in the French courts because of jury intimidation. The defendant threatened the jury with the "rigors of proletarian justice," on the first day of his trial, by asking: "I would like to know how long security measures will continue to be applied to the jurors." Direct Action claimed responsibility for many recent terrorist attacks in France, and police suspected that the recent murder of a French auto executive was intended to frighten this jury. Evidently, the intimidation tactics were successful, for the trial had to be indefinitely delayed because so many jurors failed to appear in court.

In this case, the question asked by the defendant does not explicitly state that the jurors will be harmed. Semantically speaking, his question is one about security measures. However, the jury members would take this question as a serious threat. And indeed, they evidently would have good reason to take it that way, in view of what is known or suspected about the activities of the Direct Action group.

In this case, the question can be seen as a breach of procedures of reasonable dialogue, because the defendant has used it as a tactic to convey an emotional message which will have the effect of subverting or closing off the process of dialogue to be undertaken. Here, when the defendant asks his threatening question, it may not be too clear that he is in fact arguing. Nor may it be clear exactly what his argument or statement amounts to, because the threat is implied rather than explicitly articulated. Even so, it is clear that he is blocking off dialogue by his move. And therefore, it is a move that is inimical to reasoned dialogue. Therefore, from a point of view of dialogue as due process in the legal system, the threat offered in the question should be regarded as objectionable and open to criticism, as it relates to the argument to be undertaken in the trial.

The conclusion of the dispute should come from the dialogue leading the jury to hand down a verdict ensuing from the trial. The *ad baculum* maneuver, in this instance, short-circuits that process of dialogue, and thereby prevents the conclusion from being arrived at on the basis of the evidence available. Instead, the issue has come to be left undecided for fear of the safety of the jury.

Where it is difficult or impossible to pin down a precise set of premises in an *ad baculum* appeal, the emotional appeal may not be made up of propositions at all, but other units of speech. For example, a warning may be a proposition – that is, a unit of speech that is, in principle, true or false – but a threat may not be true or false, or meant to be. A warning is a prediction that something will or might happen. It might be true or not. Threats are evaluated differently. A threat is not true or false. A threat may be convincing or it may be hollow. It may be effective or weak, but it is not, strictly speaking, true or false in the same way that a proposition is. So if a speaker's remarks convey threats, these remarks may not be propositions at all. Hence the speaker's remarks may not be an argument, but only part of an accompanying argument.

The *ad baculum* criticism is appropriate where there is a faulty argument, a violation of some procedure of reasonable dialogue, or at least a criticizable failure to engage in reasonable dialogue. A threat, therefore, is not necessarily a fallacy. Because some speech or action should be condemned, it does not necessarily follow that it should be criticized as illogical or fallacious, or that it should be subject to criticism as a bad argument, or failure of reasonable argument. In evaluating *ad baculum* criticisms, one must be careful to examine the justification of an allegation that an appeal to force should be interpreted as a threat. Even if there is good evidence of a threat of force, the second step of analysis is to identify a specific failure or fault in the argument if the threat is to be taken as a fallacy. A threat of force may be rude, vicious, illegal, or immoral, but that does not necessarily mean it is a fallacy or subject to criticism as an erroneous or incorrect argument, or failure of argument.

Another cautionary note is that the use of a threat as an argument can be reasonable in some types of dialogue, even though it is generally fallacious in a persuasion type of dialogue because it is simply irrelevant. The goal of a persuasion dialogue is to resolve a conflict of opinions by determining which side has the stronger argument to support its thesis. Threats are not relevant for this purpose. Indeed, we saw in chapter 1 that the making of a threat to try to make the other party shut up, or to try to distract the other party, is a type of argument that violates one or more of the rules of the dialogue. Since arguments based on threats can sometimes be reasonable in negotiation dialogue, the fallacious use of a threat in persuasion dialogue may be disguised. This kind of illusion or confusion can occur where there has been a dialectical shift from one type of dialogue to another.

How a dialectical shift works in the case of a threat appeal argument can be explained in the common kind of case in which there is a shift from a critical discussion to a negotiation type of dialogue. The making of a threat to influence the other side is in many cases a reasonable kind of argument strategy in negotiation. Threats are risky in negotiation, and can sometimes be inappropriate, but generally they are regarded as a reasonable sort of argumentation in negotiation. For example, in union-management negotiations, threats of various kinds are commonly made by both sides, and are part of the central fabric of the argumentation used in such cases. However, threats are irrelevant and obstructive in a critical discussion. If an argument starts out to be a critical discussion, but then shifts to a negotiation dialogue, the *ad baculum* argument used during the sequence of argumentation could seem to be reasonable. Generally, however, if the dialogue starts out to be a persuasion dialogue and one party shifts unilaterally to a negotiating dialogue in which he tries to get the other party to come to accept her thesis by threatening, this kind of move is not legitimate. In a critical discussion you are supposed to give evidence to support your thesis as acceptable or true. Threatening the other party is not useful for this purpose.

4.6 APPEALS TO PITY

The third type of appeal to emotion is the *ad misericordiam* or appeal to pity. What can be fallacious about the appeal to pity is the same error that we found in relation to the two previous types of emotional appeals – the emotional appeal can be used as a distraction from relevant evidence that should be brought forward to argue for a conclusion. In this respect, the *ad misericordiam* fallacy is just another variant on the *ignoratio elenchi* fallacy except that the special distraction utilized as the modus operandi of the irrelevant appeal is the emotion of pity.

Typical examples of the traditional *ad misericordiam* fallacy are the following. In the first example 4.11, a defense attorney pleads on behalf of his client accused of murder. In example 4.12, a student pleads for a professor to accept her late essay without penalty.

Example 4.11

My client comes from a poor hard-working family in the poorest part of town. As you can see, he is only a young man and his physical disabilities and traumatic emotional scars have made life a cruel struggle out there in the jungle of the crime-ridden streets. He is a victim himself, an individual who has been crushed down by forces beyond his control.

Example 4.12

I know that this essay is six weeks overdue and the final exam is over, but I have many personal problems. I have a part-time job because I need to scrape together enough money to stay in school, and I have been having emotional problems. The person I have been living with has just left me, and my dog just died. Also, my grandmother is very sick. Even so, I would have handed this essay in earlier but my computer was broken and I could not afford to get it fixed. Also, I only need this one course to graduate, but if I fail it I can't stay in this country any longer to complete my degree because I have already booked my flight home.

In example 4.11, what should be questioned is whether the attorney is trying to get the jury to forget about the issue of the guilt or innocence of his client on the charge of murder for robbing and killing a senior citizen, by arousing pity for the defendant's special circumstances. If so, the fallacy is a classical *ignoratio elenchi* that is also an *ad misericordiam* fallacy because the emotion appealed to is that of pity.

Another point about 4.11 is that since the crime was a vicious one, we may feel that the appeal to pity is inappropriate. But if the crime had been less serious, many of us might feel that the appeal to pity may not be completely irrelevant. As Hamblin (1970) has pointed out, more than simple assent to a proposition may be involved where the dialogue is a lawsuit or political speech: "A proposition is presented primarily as a guide to action and, where action is concerned, it is not so clear that pity and other emotions are irrelevant" (p. 43). In example 4.11, we are certainly right to be on our guard lest the powerful appeal to pity distract us from the real issue of whether the defendant is guilty of the crime he is charged with. Having decided that argument, it could be that his pitiable circumstances could be relevant to a decision of whether he should be eligible for leniency in sentencing. On this issue, the appeal to pity might not necessarily be irrelevant in every case.

In example 4.12 the professor must decide whether to accept the late essay. It is an ethical decision which must be made on the following grounds. If the student has a note from a physician certifying a medical reason for the delay, or if there is documentable evidence of some other legitimate reason, e.g., a death in the immediate family, or a traffic accident, then the professor should make, or allow for special arrangements. However, unless he is satisfied that there is a good reason that makes this case a special exception, the cost of his accepting the essay may be to discriminate against the other students in the class who dutifully handed the essay in on time, even though some of them may have had special hardships as well. If the professor accepts this one essay on very weak grounds of pity for this one individual, the word will soon circulate that anyone who has a story of some hardship can expect to be able to hand in his essay late: "After all, you let this other person hand in her essay late, and my case is similar to hers." This pressure to be consistent in treating similar cases alike is a common type of argument, and we will go on to study it in depth in chapter 5.

Example 4.12, then, seems to be similar in some respects to example 4.11. The professor should take special circumstances into account in arriving at a decision, but the appeal to pity should not distract from the primary issue – a certain date for the essay had been announced, and the burden of proof is on the student to show why her case should be treated as a legitimate exception. However, it is the professor's job to grade the student on this particular course, and he should not exempt the student from a reasonable lateness penalty, or give the student a grade she has not academically earned because of her alleged problem with flight bookings. However, this alleged problem could be checked out or verified and perhaps some action could be recommended to help with the problem, if there is one. What this example shows is that good judgment may be needed to reasonably decide the relevance of an appeal to pity in a particular case. While pity may be relevant on arriving at a decision on a course of action in a particular case, one must be careful to see whether the appeal to pity may not be good grounds for accepting the conclusion of an appellant's argument.

4.7 OVERT, PICTORIAL APPEALS TO PITY

Many charitable pleas for aid or assistance use overt appeals to pity. Example 4.13 below is a full-page advertisement that appeared in *Newsweek* (March 4, 1985, p. 75) directing readers to send in money for the relief of famine victims in Ethiopia. Much of the space on the page is taken up by a photograph of a pathetically starved, crying child, squatting on a dirty, torn blanket. The appeal to pity virtually leaps out from the photograph. The text starts with a large headline, reading ETHIOPIA: THE MOST DEVASTATING HUMAN CRISIS OF OUR TIME, and then continues as follows.

Example 4.13

THERE IS SOMETHING
YOU CAN DO ABOUT
THIS TRAGEDY . . .
You've seen the news reports . . .
• Thousands of people a day are starving to death!
• More than 6 million people are threatened by starvation.
• More than 100,000 could die from hunger and its related diseases in the next 60 days.
THE TIME FOR ACTION IS NOW!
HERE'S WHAT YOU CAN DO TO HELP!
Your gift of $15 is all it takes to feed a hungry child for a month! Just $30 can feed two children for a month. And $75 will provide emergency food for an entire family of five for a month!

The page concludes with a coupon that can be used to send in your donation.

Example 4.13 is a direct appeal to the emotion of pity, and yet the emotional appeal in this case seems appropriate and justifiable. There could be plenty of very good evidence that there is a famine in Ethiopia and that many thousands of innocent people are dying from starvation. We should indeed have a sympathetic response to this terrible situation, and it should include pity. Moreover, this emotional, humanitarian, sympathetic response should properly serve as a basis for action. Scarcely anyone would be inclined to deny all this. In other words, the appeal to pity in this case is not fallacious.

The lesson of this is that we must be very careful not to fall into the trap of concluding hastily that any appeal to pity is an *ad misericordiam* fallacy. Pity is a reasonable, legitimate, humane response in some situations, and the emotion of pity can be a sound and intelligent basis for taking action.

Nevertheless, even in the case of example 4.13 or similar cases, we should be careful to specify exactly what the conclusion of the argument is supposed to be. We may all agree that the situation in Ethiopia is pitiable and calls for action, but another issue is precisely what form of action? Getting aid to people in distress is often very difficult, given all the bureaucratic regulations involved in international shipping and transport problems in countries with few roads or vehicles. Whether the particular agency sponsoring this advertisement for aid is the best way to get that aid delivered to the famine victims is an issue that should also be reasonably considered by anyone who wants to help. In this particular ad, pictures of several television celebrities are given as friends of the agency in question, who urge you to "join in this humanitarian effort." If you, as a possible donor, think that the sponsorship of these celebrities is a relatively weak argument for accepting the conclusion that this particular agency will or can deliver the required aid through your funding, then you may have some further reasonable questions to ask. If you feel that this issue has not been given proportionate attention, or backed up strongly enough by the argument of the advertisement, then you may still have a reasonable basis for an *ad misericordiam* criticism of the advertisement.

The classic example of the pictorial appeal to pity is the Nayirah case, summarized briefly as example 4.14.[6]

Example 4.14

After the invasion of Kuwait by Iraq in August of 1990, there was a meeting of the United Nations on whether to respond with military force if Iraq did not pull out. At the meeting a videotape was shown, featuring a fifteen-year-old girl identified as Nayirah, who testified that she had seen Iraqi soldiers take babies out of incubators in a hospital and leave them to die on the cold floor. Tears ran down her face as she told the story. The video of her testimony was widely replayed in the media, and supported by an Amnesty International report documenting the incident. After the U.S. Senate voted to go to war against Iraq, influenced by this video, it was revealed that Nayirah was the daughter of a member of the Kuwaiti royal family. It was also revealed there had been a public relations campaign by the American public relations firm Hill and Knowlton. They had been paid over ten million dollars to persuade the public that the atrocity took place, funded by a group called Citizens for a Free Kuwait. Subsequent investigations also found no evidence that the incubator story was true. It had been a successful use of appeal to pity that was not founded on fact.

The appeal to pity in example 4.14 is interesting because it shows how this form of argument can be extremely powerful when used at the right moment in a developing situation when many of the facts in a case are not yet known. In this case the appeal to pity was a tactic of deception, based on a cleverly crafted falsification of the facts. The appeal had a powerful impact on the deliberations that took place.

6 More detailed descriptions of this case can be found in Walton (1997, ch. 5), and Marlin (2002, pp. 194–200).

4.8 SUMMARY

Although a distrust of emotion is often remarked upon by philosophers, it should be clear that there is nothing fallacious per se about an appeal to emotion. The emotion of fear may have survival value. The emotion of pity can prompt a compassionate response to help someone who is suffering. It is because we are so powerfully moved by our feelings, however, that they can be accorded undue weight in arguments, where specific errors may take place.

The Roman philosopher Seneca felt that reason could be trusted because it considers only the question at issue, whereas the emotions like anger may be moved by "trifling things that lie outside the case" (*De Ira* I, XVII.5–XVIII.2). The basic shortcoming one should look for in any appeal to emotion in argument is that of irrelevance. One must determine what the case or issue of a particular argument is or should be, and then evaluate the relevance of the emotional appeal.

Two types of questionable *ad populum* arguments occur where: (1) speech acts expressing an irrelevant appeal to popular sentiment are offered instead of relevant premises, or (2) where the appeal to popular sentiment could be considered relevant, but is weak, and only masquerades as a serious effort to fulfill an obligation to prove. Another type of *ad populum* argument that is often open to criticism is the fallacy of popularity, which may, as discussed earlier, take the following two forms of argument as valid, or stronger than they really are.

(P1) Everybody accepts that A is true.
Therefore, A is true.
(P2) Nobody accepts that A is true.
Therefore, A is false.

Both (P1) and (P2) are weak but sometimes reasonable forms of argument. For example, if a proposition is widely accepted and you have no evidence against it, then if you have to make a decision, it could be more reasonable to presume that it is true than to presume that it is false. But such a presumption is only a matter of plausibility, not objective proof. If (P1) and (P2) are over-rated, an erroneous *ad populum* appeal may have been put forward, which is being used as a tactic to cover a failure to give adequate argumentation to prove what is on the agenda.

Another aspect of what has gone wrong in many *ad populum* arguments is that the speaker has concentrated too exclusively on the commitments of the particular audience he has addressed. Typically, the *ad populum* argument attempts to forge a common bond between the speaker and his audience. It is as if the speaker is saying: "I am really one of you. We all belong to the same group." The problem with this type of argument is that there may be no serious attempt to give sufficient proof. The speaker, by re-affirming the audience's commitment, may be generating a cosy climate of emotional solidarity. We need to ask in such a case whether the speaker is really arguing seriously for the particular conclusion he is supposed to prove. Or if not, is his affirmation of the audience's commitment even relevant to the conclusion he is supposed to be proving? It could be that he is only trying to plead for the audience to accept that conclusion on purely emotional grounds.

A fifth type of *ad populum* fallacy can occur where a speaker tries to shut off reasonable dialogue by dividing the world into us and them. The fallacy here is the attempt to exclude or prematurely close off reasonable argument. The *ad baculum* fallacy may take this form as well. The threat of force may be used to suggest that any further reasonable argument will be pointless, or even dangerous. However, one must be careful here to remember that not all appeals to force are fallacious arguments, and sometimes it may be hard to clearly distinguish between a threat and a warning as types of speech acts.

An appeal to pity can be the basis of a legitimate excuse or claim for leniency. So in evaluating such appeals, one must be careful to decide what the real issue is. The appeal to pity should not distract from the primary issue, although it may be legitimate to take it into account in deciding on a course of action in a particular case. Here, as in the case of any emotional appeal, one must try to determine what the real issue of the argument is, and evaluate the relevance of the emotional appeal in relation to that issue.

The same kind of approach is needed in relation to arguments where there is a threat of force or an appeal to the emotion of fear. In such a case, we must resist the tendency to automatically pronounce the argument a case of the *ad baculum* fallacy. While it is true that we generally condemn the use of force, and even true that the threat of force may be rightly condemned in a particular case, it by no means follows that anyone who uses the threat of force has committed a logical fallacy. A speaker's utterance may be rude, immoral, illegal, or even brutal, without being a fallacious argument, or a violation of the rules of argumentation appropriate in a particular case. However, the use of emotional appeals to force may be a critical sign of a weak or irrelevant argument, or even an attempt to subvert reasonable dialogue. Thus any such appeal must be carefully examined by the usual steps of analysis. What is the conclusion that the speaker should be proving? And does the appeal to force come down to some specific set of propositions that might be premises? If so, are the premises relevant to the conclusion? If not, is the argument weak, or even entirely lacking in premises? Is the appeal to force being used to convince or persuade the person to whom the argument is directed to accept that conclusion? These are the questions to be asked in approaching a particular case.

The three types of emotional appeals we have examined are, to a significant extent, often basically failures of relevance, as studied in chapter 3. Each of these three types of emotional appeal has certain characteristics that make it worth individual study as a type of move in argument to be cautious about. Where dialogue has become very emotional, and comes down too closely to the personal level, it is generally a bad sign. The objectives of the argument may be closer to the personal quarrel than to those of reasonable dialogue. The problem may be a dialectical shift from one context of dialogue to another.

5

Valid arguments

The basic building blocks of arguments are propositions. Propositions, in contrast to questions, commands, challenges, and other moves made in arguments, are units of language that are true or false. Locating the propositions asserted in an argument can be the first positive step in identifying and evaluating the argument. In practice, real arguments are most often macrostructures made of many smaller arguments or sub-arguments. Often the best way to get a handle on a large and complex network of argumentation is to identify and clearly state one or more of these subarguments.

For this purpose, it is necessary to understand the concept of a deductively valid argument. With this ideal in mind, it will be much easier to organize an argument, and to fairly interpret it prior to considering evaluation. And of course, being able to identify deductively valid arguments is also a useful skill when it comes to evaluating arguments as reasonable or unreasonable.

In this chapter, we will see how once an argument is identified, the form of the argument can be revealed. Certain forms of argument are deductively valid, while others are invalid. Certain characteristic forms of deductive argument are very common in reasoning. To learn to identify these forms of argument is a valuable tool in the business of evaluating arguments reasonably. Another important concept related to validity is that of inconsistency. To allege that someone has adopted a stance in argument that is logically inconsistent can be a serious and damaging type of criticism. So understanding the logical basis of inconsistency is another valuable tool.

After carrying out the task of learning to identify some common deductive arguments, we will turn to examining the properties of some other common arguments that are inherently different from deductive arguments. These arguments are inherently more difficult to analyze and deal with because of their tentative nature. We have to be flexible and open-minded when dealing with such arguments because they are subject to defeat as new evidence enters into a case.

Many arguments we are confronted with in realistic contexts of disputation are lengthy, confusing, incomplete, and seem to be heading in a wandering and unclear direction. Most often, before we can begin to properly evaluate the argument as good or bad, we have a formidable job of trying to determine just what the argument is.

Even though an argument, as a whole, may be very confusing, there are sometimes certain key junctures where a definite conclusion appears to have been reached. A good indicator of such a juncture may be a conclusion indicator like 'therefore,' 'hence,' 'since,' 'accordingly,' or 'because'. When this juncture is indicated, we can single out one proposition in an argument as a conclusion, a proposition maintained or argued for by the person advancing the argument. A conclusion is argued for on the basis of other propositions also maintained by the arguer, called premises. When we find a set of premises and a conclusion in an argument, it means that the arguer has taken a certain stance or position at that point, and may be open to criticism. Before advancing any criticism however, the first requirement is to identify the specific propositions that are the premises and the conclusion.

Suppose that in the middle of an argument on politics, the following sequence of statements is advanced.

Example 5.0

If inflation is receding, the government's economic policies are sound.

Inflation is receding.

Therefore, the government's economic policies are sound.

This part of the argument is made up of three propositions. The first two are premises and the third one is a conclusion. Once we have located this juncture in the argument, we can at least pin something down. These two premises support the conclusion. They give reasons why any-one to whom the argument is directed should accept the conclusion if he accepts the premises. Of course, he may not accept these premises. And there may be other propositions elsewhere in the argument that give reasons to support these premises. But even so, by identifying the two premises and conclusion above, we have definitely pinned some-thing down. We have identified an argument that may be part of a larger argument.

Another thing to notice is that example 5.0 has a general form or structure that is very common in argumentation. Let A stand for the proposition 'Inflation is receding,' and B stand for the proposition 'The government's economic policies are sound.' Then the structure of example 5.0 is revealed as a particular form of argument.

(MP) If A then B
A
Therefore B

This form of argument is so common that it has a traditional name, *modus ponens*, or MP. Is it a valid form of argument? The answer depends on how we interpret the conditional (if . . . then) in the first premise. We could interpret the conditional as meaning that it is not true that the A is true and the B is not true. Under this interpretation MP is a valid form of argument. For if it is not true that A is true and B is false, and if, as the second premise says, A is in fact true, then it must follow that it is not true that B is not true. It follows, by deleting the double negative, that B must be true.

We see then that MP is a valid form of argument, and therefore example 5.0 is a deductively valid argument. What do we mean by *deductively valid argument* here? We mean that in a deductively valid argument, it is logically impossible for all the premises to be true and the conclusion false. In other words, if the premises are true, the conclusion must be true, meaning that the conclusion follows from the premises by deductive validity of the argument.

Recognizing that certain forms of argument are deductively valid is a highly valuable tool in the analysis of argumentation. We can use this knowledge to build up sequences of valid arguments. For if each step in the sequence, each individual argument, is deductively valid, then the whole sequence will never take us from true premises to a false conclusion.

Before going on to study how to evaluate arguments, it will be useful to see how knowledge of the form of an argument can be used to identify the argument that is being advanced.

5.2 IDENTIFYING ARGUMENTS

In example 5.0 above, the conclusion draws our attention to the fact that the arguer has reached a definite stage in his reasoning. The conclusion 'The government's economic policies are sound,' is a proposition that the arguer has thought important enough to single out by concluding to it and offering premises to back it up. Discovering this kind of juncture in an argument is a way to pin down and locate a key part of the argument that can then be used to help you to reconstruct other parts of it.

In the argument above, the indicator word 'so' enabled us to determine which proposition is being designated by the arguer as the conclusion of his argument. But what if there were no indicator word given? Consider the following collections of propositions that might occur as part of an argument.

Example 5.1

Air safety should be given a high priority.

If we must try to prevent disastrous accidents, then air safety should be given a high priority.

We must try to prevent disastrous accidents.

When confronted with these propositions, how should one interpret them as an argument? Which proposition is the conclusion? And which propositions are meant to be premises?

To begin with, it seems likely that the arguer would be linking the middle proposition (the conditional) with one of the other propositions, in order to deduce the conclusion. For consider what the argument would look like otherwise.

Example 5.2

We must try to prevent disastrous accidents.

Air safety should be given a high priority.

Therefore, if we must try to prevent disastrous accidents, then air safety should be given a high priority.

Do you think that this is a plausible candidate for the argument? It seems not. For even if both premises are true, there is no apparent way given to link them together in a way that would justify the conclusion.[1] Could it be that both premises are true, and yet that there might be other ways

---

1 It might be interesting to note that argument 5.2 would come out as having a valid form of argument according to some formal theories of logical inference. That is because, in these theories, no account is taken of the connections between propositions, over and above their individual truth values. In this chapter, the subject of relevance will be taken to include a consideration of such connections between pairs of propositions in arguments.

139

to prevent disastrous accidents, in addition to giving high priority to air safety? If so, the premises of example 5.2 may still leave open the link required to say that the conclusion must be true.

For all we can determine, example 5.2 could be like the following argument: roses are red, Einstein was a genius; therefore if roses are red Einstein was a genius. This argument does not appear to be valid. But even if it is valid, depending on what we mean by 'If . . . then,' it seems to involve a failure of relevance in the conditional conclusion. So let us rule out example 5.2 as a possible candidate, and consider the remaining possibilities.

The remaining possibilities both involve letting the conditional proposition be a premise. But there are two possible arguments of this configuration.

Example 5.3

If we must try to prevent disastrous accidents, then air safety should be given a high priority.

We must try to prevent disastrous accidents.

Therefore, air safety should be given a high priority.

Example 5.4

If we must try to prevent disastrous accidents, then air safety should be given a high priority.

Air safety should be given a high priority.

Therefore, we must try to prevent disastrous accidents.

Which one of these possible interpretations of example 5.1 would most plausibly represent the best choice of conclusion?

Of course, the only foolproof way to determine which choice of conclusion was meant would be to ask the proponent of the argument what he or she really meant to conclude, but suppose this person is not available to answer the question. If, as critics, we must make a choice, the best way is to helpfully interpret the argument so that it seems to make the most sense. In that light, let us turn to a comparative examination of examples 5.3 and 5.4.

Consider example 5.4 first. If we let A stand for 'We must try to prevent disastrous accidents,' and B stand for 'Air safety should be given a high priority,' then example 5.4 has the following form.

If A then B
B
Therefore A

This way of interpreting the argument certainly does not result in a valid argument. If we grant the premises, it does not follow that we have to grant the conclusion, any more than it does in the following parallel argument.

Example 5.5

If I graduate, I have paid my tuition.

I have paid my tuition.

Therefore, I will graduate.

In example 5.5, the premises might well be granted as true, but it does not follow that the conclusion must be true. There may be other requirements than paying one's tuition, in order to graduate. In other words, even if both premises are true, it does not necessarily follow that the conclusion must be true. And therefore example 5.5 is not a valid argument. Even if both premises are true, it may turn out that the conclusion is false.

This leaves us with example 5.3. We can see immediately that it is a valid argument, because it has the form of argument previously designated as MP. Hence we know that example 5.3 is a valid argument.

Our problem was to find the conclusion in example 5.1. The problem was that there was no indicator word like 'therefore' or 'so' to indicate which of the three propositions was meant to be the conclusion. Yet even in the absence of an indicator word, we could arrive at a plausible reconstruction of example 5.1 as an argument. Once we eliminated example 5.2 as a plausible reconstruction on grounds of absence of a relevant connection, the two possibilities represented by examples 5.3 and 5.4 remained.

Why did example 5.4 seem to be the plausible and natural choice? The best explanation is that this interpretation is the one that made the resulting argument valid. This does not mean that this selection was the only possible choice, but that it represents the most plausible interpretation of how the arguer might have meant his argument to be taken.

The problem here is occasioned by the fact that people are sometimes unclear about what their conclusion is in an argument. Even if an arguer doesn't explicitly indicate exactly which proposition is meant to be his conclusion, there may still be some evidence available to enable us to pick the most plausible candidate for the conclusion among the available choices. We can do this by making the assumption that the arguer in question is a constructive participant in reasonable dialogue, and is trying his best to come forward with strong arguments for his side of the issue.

The reason that 5.3 is the most plausible interpretation of example 5.1 is to be sought in the *Principle of Charity*. Where there is doubt or question, other things being equal, the fairest and most reasonable interpretation is to prefer a designation of the conclusion that makes the argument valid (and plausible) to one that makes it invalid (or implausible). It is the Principle of Charity that explains and justifies our inclination to interpret the first proposition in example 5.1 as the conclusion. For 5.3 is the only interpretation that is clearly valid and plausible as an argument.

To sum up, knowing when an argument is valid can be very helpful in identifying arguments. In the next section, the concept of a valid argument is more extensively elaborated.

5.3 VALIDITY AS A SEMANTIC CONCEPT

An *argument* is an interaction between two or more participants which involves a claim by each participant that his contention can be justified. Arguments may involve complex and lengthy sequences of steps, questions, answers, and objections. At any particular stage of an argument, however, we should be able to identify the *semantic core* of the argument. The semantic core is a set of propositions made up of one or more conclusions and some sets of premises.

A *semantic* concept is one that has to do with truth and falsehood. A proposition is said to be a semantic concept because a proposition may be defined as a unit of language that either is true or false. We may not know, in a particular case, whether a proposition is in fact true or false. A proposition is the sort of thing that, in principle, has the property of being true or the property of being false. For example, the proposition 'There is life on another planet in our galaxy' is, in principle, true or false, even if we may not know at present whether it is true or false. That is enough to enable us to identify it as a proposition.

The semantic core of an argument is normally surrounded by pragmatic structures. In the practical analysis of arguments, one often finds that there are missing premises, not clearly stated as propositions by the one who advanced the argument. Filling in these missing or problematic premises is one part of the pragmatics of arguments. An argument is said to be an *enthymeme* if there are premises needed to make the argument valid that are only tacitly, but not explicitly stated or advanced as part of the argument. It may be a difficult job to fairly and reasonably judge whether such enthymematic premises were truly meant to be asserted by the arguer. For example, if someone argued "All men are mortal, therefore Socrates is mortal," it would, in most contexts, be reasonable to presume that the premise "Socrates is a man" is needed to make the argument valid. But if someone argued "All men are mortal, therefore Elizabeth Anscombe is mortal," would it be reasonable to presume that the proposition "Elizabeth Anscombe is a man," is an enthymematic premise? In most contexts, probably not, although adding that proposition would make the argument valid. More plausible, in light of the context, is the suggestion that the proposition "And all women are mortal" should be included as a premise, thereby changing (or extending) the argument.

Determining enthymematic premises is a pragmatic task of argument analysis. Whether a proposition can reasonably be said to be an enthymematic premise in someone's argument depends to a significant extent on that arguer's position, the set of commitments he has previously adopted in the context of the dialogue or dispute. In short, we need to carefully distinguish between the semantic and pragmatic aspects of an argument. The semantic aspect has to do with the truth and falsity of the propositions. The pragmatic aspect has to do with what the arguer may reasonably be taken to be committed to in the context of dialogue. The concept of a valid argument is a semantic notion.

The basic property of something being a valid argument is that it never takes you from true premises to a false conclusion. In other words, a valid argument must be *truth-preserving*, meaning that if the premises are true then the conclusion must be true as well. Validity is one of the most fundamental semantic concepts in the study of argument.

The defining characteristic of a valid argument is that it is absolutely air-tight – there are no loopholes. If the premises are true, then it is absolutely guaranteed that the conclusion must be true. Consider the following argument.

Example 5.6

If Bob goes west, he will arrive at Milan.

If Bob goes east, he will arrive at Venice.

Either Bob goes east or west.

Therefore, Bob will arrive at Milan, or he will arrive at Venice.

This argument is deductively valid, meaning that if the premises are true then the conclusion must be true as well. This is not necessarily to claim that the premises are true, or even that the conclusion is true. It is only to claim that if the premises are true, then the conclusion must be true too. In other words, validity is a conditional concept. It has to do with a certain kind of relationship between the truth or falsity of the premises of an argument, and the truth or falsity of the conclusion.

It may well happen, for example, that there is an argument that is valid but has false premises. Consider the argument below.

Example 5.7

If Plato was born in Chicago, then Aristotle was born in Toronto.

Plato was born in Chicago.

Therefore, Aristotle was born in Toronto.

This argument is valid, meaning that if the premises are true, then so is the conclusion, but the premises are not true, as a matter of fact. And neither is the conclusion, for that matter.

In summary then, a valid argument always takes you from true premises to a true conclusion. Just because the argument is valid is no guarantee the premises are in fact true. To say that an argument is valid is to say something positive about it, but it is not to say that the argument is as good as it could possibly be in all respects.

Another thing to remember is that not all good arguments have to be valid arguments. Inductive arguments can be good or reasonable arguments, but they are not valid – they do not guarantee the truth of a conclusion, but only yield probability. So validity is not the only thing to be worried about when analyzing an argument, although it is very important as a tool for evaluating arguments.

In the practical job of evaluating real argumentation, the first question to be asked is: what are the propositions that make up this argument? Hence identifying the semantic core of an argument is of critical importance for practical logic.

5.4 VALID FORMS OF ARGUMENT

If you want to build up some arguments to support your contention, or to mount arguments to criticize somebody else's contention, there are certain basic building blocks that are useful to know about. These building blocks are basic structures or forms of argument that are always valid. We mean by 'valid' here that if a part of your argument has this structure, then it will never take you from true premises to a false conclusion. A valid argument is fail-safe, meaning that if the premises are true, the conclusion has to be true too, simply in virtue of the structure of the argument. The notion of structure will turn out to be important in understanding the nature of valid arguments.

An example is the following argument.

Example 5.8

premises
=
Pronunciation

If jobholders feel that the workplace rewards extra effort, then they do good work for its own sake.

In fact, jobholders do not do good work for its own sake.

Therefore, jobholders do not feel that the workplace rewards extra effort.

This argument is valid, meaning that if the premises are true then the conclusion must also be true. Now the premises above may or may not be true. Whether they are or not is a question for the sociology of industrial management, one may suppose. But if they are true, then logic tells us that the conclusion must be true too. Why is this so?

The answer is that this particular argument has a form of structure that guarantees its validity. Let A stand for the proposition 'Jobholders feel that the workplace rewards extra effort,' and B stand for 'Jobholders do good work for its own sake.' Then the argument above may be said to have the following structure.

Example 5.9

If A then B.

Not B.

Therefore not A.

The structure above is a valid form of argument, meaning that whatever pair of propositions you put in for A and B, the resulting argument is always valid. You can be sure of it.

Consider this argument.

145

Example 5.10

If Captain Kirk is a Vulcan, he has pointed ears.

Captain Kirk does not have pointed ears.

Therefore, Captain Kirk is not a Vulcan.

This argument clearly has the same form as the jobholders' argument. But in this case, the letter A stands for 'Captain Kirk is a Vulcan,' and the letter B stands for 'Captain Kirk has pointed ears.' Since both arguments have the same (valid) structure, both are valid arguments.[2]

In constructing or evaluating arguments, it is most useful to know what some of the basic valid forms of arguments are. Some of them are displayed below, along with their customary names.

Modus Ponens (MP)	*Modus Tollens (MT)*
If A then B	If A then B
A	Not B
Therefore B	Therefore, not A
Hypothetical Syllogism (HS)	*Disjunctive Syllogism (DS)*
If A then B	Either A or B
If B then C	Not A
Therefore, if A then C	Therefore B

How can we prove that each of these forms of argument is valid? To do this we need to show that if both premises are true, in each case, the conclusion has to be true too. Let us consider each form of argument, one at a time.

Consider DS first. What does the proposition 'A or B' mean? Under what conditions is this form of proposition true or false? Well, one basic fact about a disjunctive proposition 'Either A or B' is that it is true if at least one of the disjuncts is true. In other words, if you have a disjunction

---

2 The only caution here is that you have to be uniform in your use of propositional letters A, B, C, and so forth, to stand for propositions in an argument. For example, once you have used the letter A to stand for the proposition 'Captain Kirk is a Vulcan,' in the first premise of example 5.10, then you must use the same letter, A, again to stand for the same proposition, 'Captain Kirk is a Vulcan,' when it appears in the conclusion of 5.10. In other words, your substitution of propositions for propositional letters in representing the form of an argument must be uniform. You must not switch horses in midstream, as it were. Once you use a letter for a proposition, you must use the same letter each time, when that proposition reappears. This principle of uniform substitution is generally stated in section 5.9.

like 'Either Bob has the measles or chicken pox' then you know that at least one of the following propositions is true.

Example 5.11

Bob has measles.

Bob has chicken pox.

One could be false, but both can't be, if the disjunction 'Either Bob has measles or chicken pox' is really true. So at least one must be true.

In general then, if 'Either A or B' is true, then at least one of the pair, A or B, must be true. But suppose A is not true. Then B must be true. Why? Well, at least one must be true, according to the first premise of DS. But if, according to the second premise, A is not true, then B must be true. B can't be false, if both premises are true. So in general, any argument having the form of DS must always be valid. If its premises are true, its conclusion must be true too.

In effect then, DS is a valid form of argument because of the meaning of either . . . or. In any disjunction, at least one of the disjuncts must be true. If both were false, it couldn't be a true disjunction.

Similar proofs for the validity of the remaining three forms of argument can be given. If a conditional proposition, 'If A then B' is true, then it has to be false that A is true and B is false. For example, let us suppose that the following conditional proposition is true: if Karl drops the egg he is holding, it will break. Now whatever else we might want to say about the truth or falsehood of this conditional, we must say at least this: if the whole conditional is true, then it has to be false that Karl drops the egg but it does not break. Why? Well, because that's what we mean when we say that if Karl drops the egg, it will break. We are denying that we can consistently say both that Karl drops the egg and that it fails to break. So *modus ponens* is valid, and has to always be universally valid as a form of argument, simply in virtue of the meaning of the conditional as a logical connection between the propositions.

By similar reasoning, it can be proved that MT and HS are valid forms of argument as well. The actual proofs that each of these forms of argument is indeed valid, according to the way we have defined 'valid argument', is not so important for the present as your satisfaction and assurance that they are valid. For once you are satisfied that they are valid, you can use them to build up arguments in such a way that you can be confident that the basic parts are valid. These forms of argument then are building blocks for constructing longer arguments. In each case, if you know the premises are true, you can be assured that the conclusion must follow logically, by valid argument.

Proving the validity of HS can be done by looking at the premises of HS and remembering that MP has already been proved valid. Now assume that A is true. By MP and the first premise, B must be true, but if B is true, then by the second premise and MP, C must be true. Hence, if A is true, C must be true too. Therefore, the conclusion of HS follows validly from its premises.

In proving the validity of several valid forms of argument, we have made certain assumptions about the semantics of disjunctions and conditionals. It is useful to summarize these assumptions. First, we define a *disjunctive proposition* as one that presents two or more alternatives in the form 'Either A or B or . . .' In the simplest case, there are just two alternatives, A and B. The rule for disjunction we presumed earlier can be summarized as follows.

> *Rule for Disjunction*: If the disjunction 'Either A or B' is true, then at least one of the pair, A or B, must be true.

This rule implies that if both A and B are false, then the whole disjunction 'A or B' must be false.

We also relied on an assumption about conditionals. Let us define a *conditional proposition* as one that presents one proposition as true on the assumption that another proposition is true. A conditional has the form 'If A then B.' The part that makes the assumption is called the *antecedent*. The part that is presented as true on the assumption made in the antecedent is called the *consequent*. The rule for conditionals reads as follows.

> *Rule for Conditional*: If a conditional 'If A then B' is true, then it is false that the antecedent (A) is true while the consequent (B) is false.

This rule means that for a conditional to be true, it must not have a true antecedent and a false consequent. In this respect, there is a certain parallel between a true conditional and a valid argument, because a valid argument never takes you from true premises to a false conclusion.

Indeed, the rule for conditional above characterizes a type of conditional appropriate only for a context of deductive logic. A conditional appropriate for inductive contexts of reasoning would have a different rule. For example, the inductive conditional, 'If Karl drops this egg, it will probably break,' could still be true, even if there is an instance where Karl dropped the egg, but it did not break. For the conditional could still be true if there were many other instances where Karl dropped similar eggs, and all or most of them broke.

But in the context of deductive reasoning, a conditional is treated as parallel, at least in one respect, to the concept of a valid argument. Any exception to the rule stated by the conditional makes it false. However, because this parallel exists, we must not conclude that a true conditional and a valid argument are the same thing. Truth and falsehood are properties of propositions. Validity and invalidity are properties of arguments. So it makes no sense at all to speak of a "valid proposition" or a "true argument," any more than it would to speak of a valid pair of socks.

Now that we are able to recognize and be familiar with some of the common forms of valid argument, we are in a better position to be able to orient ourselves in sorting out a complex and confusing network of real argumentation. If some parts of it are valid arguments, we can at least identify these parts. If other parts would be valid except for missing premises, we are in a somewhat better position to tackle the job of querying what the arguer may be including or leaving out.

5.5 INVALID ARGUMENTS

A valid form of argument is one where no argument having that form can have true premises and a false conclusion. So the concept of validity has a certain generality – we can say of every argument that has a valid form that if the premises are true, the conclusion must be true. Validity of an argument form guarantees the validity of each and every one of all the countless arguments having that form. For example, any argument that has the form of *modus ponens* must be valid, no matter what particular subject matter the argument is about.

With invalid arguments however, the form of the argument does not have the same guarantee of generality. This asymmetry between validity and invalidity arises because it is possible for a particular argument to have more than one form. Consider the argument below, which obviously has the form of *modus ponens*.

Example 5.12

If computers can reason, they can ask questions.

Computers can reason.

Therefore, computers can ask questions.

This argument has the form *modus ponens*, so it must be a valid argument. So construed the argument has the form: If A then B; A; therefore B. However, *modus ponens* is not the only form that the argument above has. It also has this less specific form: A; B; therefore C. Instead of representing the first premise as a conditional, we could also represent it as a simple proposition, A. Of course, representing it as a conditional would be more specific, but if we did represent it in the less specific form above, that would break no rule of logic we have, so far, required. And that form of argument is invalid. Even if both A and B are true, it is quite possible that C could be false, for all logic tells us.

So we have to be careful here. Even if we know an argument has an invalid form, it need not automatically follow that the argument must be invalid. To be assured of that, we would also have to know that the form presented is the most specific form of the given argument. Even despite this reservation, the criticism that an argument is invalid can be legitimate. However, it is not a decisive refutation of an argument using formal logic, unless the critic can show that the specific form of the argument has been represented.

An argument that is deductively invalid is not necessarily a bad or incorrect argument. Even if it is deductively invalid as presented, it could still be a correct argument by inductive standards. Or it could simply be an incomplete argument. To criticize an argument as deductively invalid is simply to point out that the argument, in the form given, does not meet the standard of deductive validity. Whether the arguer who presented the argument meant it to meet that standard, or should be so required, are other questions.

Despite these limitations, the finding of deductive invalidity can be important in evaluating an argument. If an argument is shown to be invalid as presented, it may mean that the argument could be improved by adding further premises, or by further qualifying the nature or limits of the argument in various ways.

Now let us contrast our four valid forms of argument with some examples of forms of argument that are not valid.

Example 5.13

If A then B

B

Therefore A

150

Example 5.14

If A then B

Not A

Therefore not B

Example 5.15

If A then B

If C then B

If A then C

Example 5.16

Either A or B

A

Therefore B

To see that these forms of argument are not valid, it may suffice to look at some examples of argument having each form. In each case, it is possible for both premises to be true and the conclusion false.

Example 5.17

If it rains, the car will get wet at that time.

The car is wet now.

Therefore, it is raining now.

Example 5.18

If I drop this egg, it will break.

I do not drop this egg.

Therefore, it will not break.

Example 5.19

If I move my knight, John will take it.

If I move my queen, John will take it.

Therefore, if I move my knight, then I move my queen.

Example 5.20

Turku is in Finland or Norway.

Turku is in Finland.

Therefore, Turku is in Norway.

Consider the last argument. Assume both premises are true. Does the conclusion now have to be true? Not at all! In fact, the premises imply that the conclusion is false, if you interpret the disjunction in the first premise as an exclusive one. That is, you might assume that the first premise means that Turku is in one of the countries, Finland or Norway, but not both. Then once you determine that Turku is in Finland, as stated by the second premise, it follows that Turku can't be in Norway. So interpreted, the premises not only fail to imply the conclusion, they actually conflict with it by implying the opposite. No matter whether you interpret the first premise as an exclusive disjunction or not, the argument fails to be valid.

The key to evaluating whether an argument is valid or invalid is to determine the form of the argument. The common argument forms we have encountered are valid or invalid in virtue of the propositional connectives that occur in them. The rules for the connectives very often enable us to determine whether a particular form of argument is valid or not. In a later chapter, certain further theoretical assumptions will be added to define these connectives more fully and thereby yield a mechanical procedure that always proves validity or invalidity. For the present, it is enough that we can recognize certain common argument forms as valid or invalid, and sometimes prove it.

5.6 INCONSISTENCY

The notion of inconsistency is a very important concept in logic and the analysis of arguments. If an arguer is found to be inconsistent, then that is a very strong form of criticism or condemnation of his position. An inconsistent set of propositions is one where a contradiction can be deduced by valid arguments. A contradiction is a proposition that is the opposite, or negation of itself. For example, consider the following set of propositions.

Example 5.21

If courage is a virtue, then courage is an excellence of conduct.

Courage is a virtue.

Courage is not an excellence of conduct.

152

What would we say of someone who maintained all three of these propositions in his argument? We would say that the position he has adopted is inconsistent. Why? Because the three propositions above collectively imply a contradiction.

By modus ponens, the first two propositions above imply 'Courage is an excellence of conduct.' But that proposition is the negation of the third proposition 'Courage is not an excellence of conduct.' We can see, therefore, that the three propositions above imply a contradiction. Hence these three propositions are collectively inconsistent. But what is so wrong with contradictions, you may ask. The answer is that a contradiction can never be a true proposition. Why not? The answer has to do with the concepts of negation and conjunction.

The negation of a proposition is usually indicated by the 'not' particle. For example, 'Paris is not in France' is the negation of the proposition 'Paris is in France.' If a proposition is true, its negation must be false. If a proposition is false, its negation must be true. We can summarize this information in the following rule for negation.

Rule for Negation: If the negation 'Not-A' is true, then A must be false; if the negation 'Not-A' is false, then A must be true.

In other words, the negation of a proposition always has the opposite truth value of that proposition.

The conjunction of two or more propositions is often indicated by the word 'and' in English. For example, if I say 'Paris is in France and Berlin is in Germany' I assert a conjunction of two propositions. For the conjunction to be true, it is required for both the propositions in it to be true. Hence the rule for conjunction.

Rule for Conjunction: For the conjunction 'A and B' to be true, both A and B must be true.

This rule for conjunction means that if either one of the propositions in a conjunction is false, then the whole conjunctive proposition must be false.

Now that we understand conjunction and negation, we can see why a contradiction must be false. A contradiction is a proposition of the form 'A and not-A.' If the A is true, then the not-A must be false, by the rule for negation. But also by the negation rule, if the not-A is true, then the A must be false. Any way you look at it, at least one of the pair, A or not-A must be false. Hence the conjunction, 'A and not-A' can never be true.

Why not? Well, according to the rule for conjunction, if either one of the propositions in a conjunction is false, then the whole conjunction must be false. To sum up then, a contradiction must always be false.

The fact that a contradiction must always be false shows what is open to criticism about an inconsistent set of propositions maintained by an arguer. If an inconsistent set of propositions implies a contradiction, and a contradiction must always be false, then the inconsistent set of propositions can never be all true. At least some of the propositions contained within it have to be false. This means that a position that is inconsistent should be open to criticism or revision. An inconsistent set of propositions may contain some true propositions, but they cannot all be true. At least one must be false, even if we do not know which one it is.

Inconsistency can be very difficult to deal with. Psychologists know that when laboratory animals are subjected to inconsistent treatment, they can start to exhibit frustration and loss of interest in activity. Children who receive inconsistent demands or messages from parents can experience behavior problems as a result. An interesting example studied in Jones (1983) is the case of the double bind situation. A young schizophrenic patient is visited by his mother in hospital. Bateson (see Jones 1983, p. 124) described the patient's reaction to the visit as follows.

Example 5.22

He was glad to see her and impulsively put his arm around her shoulders, whereupon she stiffened. He withdrew his arm and she asked, "Don't you love me any more?" He then blushed, and she said, "Dear, you must not be so easily embarrassed and afraid of your feelings."

After the young man left the room, he assaulted a ward orderly. The nature of the message sent by the mother as an example of inconsistent or double bind communication is studied in detail by Jones (1983). The mother's actions are also a good example of a confusing double message that contains an action that runs contrary to the message that is verbally presented by the mother. She says one thing, but her action of stiffening "says" something distinctly contrary.

But do actions speak as loud as words? Sometimes they do, and the message conveyed by an action needs to be taken account of in the careful analysis of an argument. What about the case where the father who smokes says to his son, "You must not smoke. It's very bad for your health."

154

Is the son justified in feeling that his father's argument is inconsistent? This problem is a complex one, and best studied under the heading of *ad hominem* argument. Suffice it to note here that sometimes arguments may not be outright inconsistent, but an inconsistency can be derived by the addition of further assumptions. If the father is really arguing as represented in example 5.23, then he is inconsistent.

Example 5.23

1. Nobody should smoke, because smoking is bad for health. I smoke.
2. If I smoke, my act is justified. In other words, my action of smoking may be interpreted as meaning that I advocate smoking.
3. Therefore, I should smoke.
4. But, if nobody should smoke, I should not smoke.

If the above is a fair representation of the father's argument, then the argument is inconsistent. For (1) and (4) imply 'I should not smoke,' but (2) and (3) imply 'I should smoke.' But do actions speak as loud as words, in this case? In other words, is premise (2) being asserted by the father? This is the problem of the *ad hominem* fallacy.

The lesson for the moment is that some arguments do contain a contradiction, but only if further assumptions are added. In such a case, one must be careful to inquire whether these additional assumptions are reasonably attributed to the arguer before prematurely claiming that the person's argument is inconsistent. However, in some cases, the attribution of these additional assumptions is fairly uncontroversial.

Consider the two assertions below.

Example 5.24

5. Kevin always tells the truth.
6. Kevin lied about his age on Saturday.

The additional propositions we need here to show that (5) and (6) are an inconsistent set are the following two.

7. If Kevin always tells the truth, Kevin told the truth on Saturday.
8. If Kevin lied about his age on Saturday, then Kevin did not tell the truth on Saturday.

As you can see, the collective set (5), (6), (7), and (8) is one from which a contradiction can be deduced by valid arguments. Now (7) and (8) are probably acceptable assumptions as part of the background of the assertion of (5) and (6) by an arguer in most contexts. If, in the particular context, they are acceptable, then we can say that (5) and (6) amount to an inconsistency.

But you need to be careful. Premature and unfair allegations of inconsistency are often made and accepted uncritically, as chapter 6 will show.

5.7 COMPOSITION AND DIVISION

Other logical constants that determine the validity of arguments are the terms 'all' and 'some.' For example, the following argument is valid on account of the semantics of 'all' and 'some.'

Example 5.25

All rodents are mammals.

Some rodents lurk around docks.

Therefore, some mammals lurk around docks.

By contrast, the following argument has a form that is not generally valid.

Example 5.26

All rodents are mammals.

Some mammals have horns.

Therefore, some rodents have horns.

The reason example 5.26 fails to be a valid argument is that the first premise makes a claim about all rodents, but it does not make a claim about all mammals.

Care is needed, however, in distinguishing between the collective and distributive use of terms. The sentence, 'Rodents are mammals' would normally be rightly interpreted as meaning 'All rodents are mammals.' Here we may say that the term 'rodents' is being used distributively, meaning that a property is being attributed to each individual rodent. However, in the sentence, 'Rodents are widely distributed over the earth,' the term 'rodents' is being used collectively, meaning that a property of the class of rodents as a whole is referred to.

Confusion between the collective and distributive use of terms can result in the fallacy of composition, which argues incorrectly that what may be attributed to a term distributively may also be attributed to it collectively.

156

Example 5.27

In any given day, a bus will use more gas than a car.

Therefore, in any given day, more gas will be used by buses than by cars.

The fallacy implicit in this argument arises from interpreting the conclusion collectively. Because there are many more cars than buses in the world, it is false that buses (collectively) use more gas than cars, even if it may be true that buses (distributively) use more gas than cars.

In other instances, the fallacy of composition can have to do with part-whole relationships.

Example 5.28

All the parts of this machine are light.

Therefore, this machine is light.

Or, this fallacy can have to do with functional relationships.

Example 5.29

All the players on this team are good.

Therefore, this is a good team.

Both these types of argument fail to be generally valid, because the properties of the parts do not necessarily transfer to the properties of the whole made up of those parts.

The fallacy of division is the opposite type of argument, and has variants similar to those of the fallacy of composition.

Example 5.30

This machine is heavy.

Therefore, all the parts of this machine are heavy.

Example 5.31

American Indians have reservations in every state.

The Navaho are American Indians.

Therefore, the Navaho have reservations in every state.

157

Because the first premise is a collective rather than a distributive statement, example 5.28 fails to be a valid argument.

Care is needed in evaluating argumentation that fits the schemes for composition and division. Instances of these argumentation schemes are not all fallacious.

Example 5.32

All the parts of this machine are iron.

Therefore, this machine is made of iron.

This argument is not fallacious, although it appears to have the structure of the argumentation scheme of composition.

The key here is the critical question of whether the property in question is one that composes (or divides) over the type of collection or distribution in the example.[3] In example 5.32, the answer is affirmative, because it is universally true that when all the parts of an entity like a machine are made of a particular substance, then the whole entity is also made of that same substance. Hence there is no fallacy of composition in this case.

The argumentation scheme for example 5.32 is the following.

All the parts of X have property Y.
Therefore, X has property Y.

The critical question for this argumentation scheme is: does the property of Y compose from the parts of X to the whole? In other words, the question is whether the following conditional is warranted in the particular case in question: if all the parts of X have property Y, then X has property Y. The answer to this type of critical question is affirmative in some cases, and negative in other cases.

If the answer to the relevant critical question is affirmative, then the argumentation scheme for composition (or division) can justify a particular argument as correct or reasonable. However, if the answer is negative, then the argument is incorrect, and can be criticized as an error or fallacy of composition or division.

---

3 See Woods and Walton (1977).

5.8 DEFEASIBLE REASONING

We saw in chapter 1, and it has further been shown in this chapter, that the standard set for the deductively valid type of argument is strict. It is impossible for the premises to be true and the conclusion false in a deductively valid argument. Throughout this chapter so far, we've studied deductively valid forms of reasoning of this kind. Deductive arguments are monotonic, meaning that no matter how much new evidence is added to the premises, the conclusion still holds. Such arguments can never fail as new information comes in. Contrasted with this type of argument, in chapter 1 we considered another type of argument called plausible argument that has requirements for success that are less strict. Such plausible arguments are nonmonotonic, meaning that the argument might fail to hold as new information comes in, even though it originally held as a reasonable inference. Because such arguments are tentative in nature, it is very important when accepting them to be aware of the need for being open-minded. Should new evidence come into the case, the argument that was formerly accepted as plausible may need to be rejected as defeated.

To compare different kinds of reasoning, it is necessary to see that there can be different kinds of generalizations. Basically, there are three kinds of generalizations: (1) the universal (absolute) generalization, (2) the inductive (statistical type) generalization, and (3) the presumptive (defeasible) generalization. As an illustration of the universal generalization, let's take the statement 'All birds fly'. If interpreted as a strict universal generalization, this statement is falsified by a single counter-example. A strict universal generalization is one that is subject to no exceptions. For instance, if one example of a bird that does not fly is found, it follows that the strict universal generalization 'All birds fly' is false.

A strict universal generalization can act as a premise in deductively valid logical inference of the following sort.

Example 5.33

All birds (strictly speaking) fly.

Tweety is a bird.

Therefore Tweety flies.

This inference is deductively valid in the sense that it is logically impossible for the premises to be true while the conclusion is false. For example, suppose that all birds fly and that Tweety is a bird. It follows (by valid deductive reasoning) that Tweety flies.

Contrasted with strict generalizations, there are inductive generalizations, like 'Most birds fly,' or '95 per cent of birds fly.' These generalizations support inductive inferences of the kind studied in chapter 8. It is characteristic of this kind of inference that it is logically possible for both premises to be true even while the conclusion is false, but it is improbable (to a greater or lesser degree, measurable in statistical cases by a fraction between zero and one) for both premises to be true while the conclusion is false. The kinds of inference based on these kinds of generalizations are matters of probability and statistics.

There is also a third kind of generalization that may not be so familiar to many, and that is subject to exceptions of a kind that cannot be known or judged by probability in advance. An example of this kind of generalization is the statement that birds generally fly, in the sense that if something is a bird, we would normally expect it to fly. This reasonable expectation is, however, subject to exceptions. So, for example, if Tweety is an ostrich or a penguin, or a bird with a broken wing, then Tweety does not fly, even though Tweety is a bird. The presumptive generalization, like the inductive one, but unlike the deductive one, can hold, even in the face of the existence of a known counter-example. This kind of generalization is said to be defeasible in nature, meaning that if new information comes in, through our learning about exceptional cases, an inference based on the generalization may default or fail.

Example 5.34

Generally, birds fly.

Tweety is a bird.

Therefore Tweety flies.

If the generalization of the first premise is taken as a defeasible one, it is implausible for both the premises to be true while the conclusion is false. A structurally correct plausible inference of this sort has the property that if the premises hold, the conclusion also holds tentatively, in the absence of information to the contrary.

In this case, the original argument was reasonable, but the new evidence made it subject to defeat. Such an argument is called a defeasible one, meaning that even though it holds tentatively in a given situation, it

160

may need to be given up if new evidence goes against it. Horty (2001, p. 337) defines default reasoning as "reasoning that relies on absence of information as well as its presence, often mediated by rules of the general form: given P, conclude Q unless there is information to the contrary." A leading theory of defeasible reasoning (Reiter 1987) is based on the possibility of invoking what is called the closed world assumption, a closure rule that allows us to assume that all relevant positive information has now been collected in a case. Using this rule, it is legitimate to conclude that a positive proposition is false whenever it is not explicitly present in a database (Horty 2001, p. 241).

A defeasible generalization occupies a ground where no contravening evidence, in the form of exceptions to the rule, is known to exist, because it can be assumed to hold as a commitment in a normal situation. As long as there is nothing special about Tweety indicating that he does not fly, then a collaborative respondent is obliged to go along with the inference that Tweety flies. In order to defeat the inference from going forward in a dialogue, the respondent has to disprove it, or to cite special features of the case that show that the generalization does not cover it.

This form of reasoning is closely related to the argument from ignorance cited in section 2.5. Let's reconsider example 2.22, the foreign spy case. We saw in the discussion of this example that the argument from ignorance used as the basis of the reasoning in the case was a plausible but weak form of reasoning, depending on the context. In particular, the context was how thorough the search of the Security Service was. The argument was not conclusive, because it is impossible to be absolutely certain that Mr. X is not a foreign spy. He could be a mole, like Kim Philby, the British intelligence agent who concealed his activities as a spy for the Soviet secret service for most of his working career. But suppose that a thorough search by a competent government security agency turned up no evidence at all of Mr. X's being a foreign spy. This negative evidence would support a defeasible argument for the conclusion that Mr. X is not a foreign spy.

In many cases of reasoning in everyday deliberations, using defeasible reasoning is a matter of striking the right balance between what is known and what is not known. The argumentation scheme for argument from ignorance, or, as it might better be called, reasoning from lack of evidence, can be formulated as follows.

Proposition A is not known to be true (false).
If A were true (false), it would be known to be true (false).
Therefore, A is false (true).

161

Arguments from ignorance presuppose a dialogue structure in which data is being collected in a knowledge base. How strong the argument is depends on how much data has been collected at the given point in the dialogue where the argument was put forward. In the case above, the strength of the argument depends on how much information the FBI collected. If they had undertaken a serious investigation and collected all the knowledge about Mr. X that could be found, so that they could say they knew a lot about Mr. X, then the argument from ignorance about Mr. X could be quite strong. Thus one critical question matching the argument from ignorance is the depth of search question.

CQ1: How complete is the search for knowledge in the investigation?

Another critical question concerns burden of proof:

CQ2: How complete does the knowledge need to be to adequately support the argument?

Suppose, for example, that Mr. X has a job that involves some risk to national security, and Mr. X therefore has to have a certain level of security clearance. The outcome depends on a balance of considerations — the security risk (the bad consequence of losing state secrets), must be weighed against the bad consequence of harming an innocent person who is not a spy. In practical terms then, the lack of knowledge inference about Mr. X above should be evaluated between two alternatives on a balance of considerations basis.

Lack of evidence arguments are defeasible, as shown by the spy case analyzed above. Even if the premises are true, it does not follow necessarily that the conclusion is true. Even so, such an argument could be reasonable provided the premises are substantiated by the evidence in the case, and the proper critical questions are considered. But such an argument could be a fallacious argument from ignorance if the arguer jumps too quickly to the conclusion, failing to satisfy the requirements of depth of search of premise, or even ignoring or suppressing it.

5.9 JUMPING TO A CONCLUSION

When we examine examples of informal fallacies, often a distinctive sign that an argument is fallacious is that it jumps to a conclusion prematurely by not taking contrary evidence into account, or perhaps even not being open to the possibility of contrary evidence. The following argument is a classic case of one kind of failure of reasoning of this type, traditionally called the fallacy of hasty generalization.

Example 5.35

Ten Arab fundamentalists hijacked planes and crashed them into the World Trade Center in New York City. The message is clear: Arabs are nothing but a pack of religious fanatics prone to violence.

In this kind of superficial thinking, the arguer seems to jump too quickly to a conclusion in a less than thoughtful way. He generalizes to a conclusion about all Arabs while ignoring contrary evidence that he might see all around him if he took a closer look, or even thought more deeply about what he already knows. This kind of faulty reasoning is often associated with stereotypes and prejudice.

A common error in reasoning is to fail to take into account that many generalizations of the most common kind are subject to exceptions in circumstances that are not ordinary. Consider the following example.

Example 5.36

Water boils at a temperature of 212 degrees fahrenheit, therefore boiling water is hot enough to cook an egg hard in five minutes. Suppose, however, that we try to use the same reasoning at a high altitude, for example, on a mountain.

Air pressure at different altitudes affects how long it takes an egg to boil. Overlooking this variability of circumstances is to treat the original inference in a strict way that is not justified in light of changing circumstances.

Another example can be used to illustrate more about the nature of this problematic way of thinking and how it arises.

Example 5.37

Generally dogs of the kind I encounter in my neighborhood walks are friendly and pose no threat to people who pat them.

Therefore, it would be safe to pat the dog that is approaching me now.

In this instance, the argument seems somewhat reasonable as it stands. In a normal situation, while walking down the sidewalk and approaching a dog that looks to be friendly, and appears to pose no threat, it might be safe enough to go ahead and pat it. There might be some risk, but on the evidence as known, taking such an action could be judged as reasonably safe. Now suppose the little dog is foaming at the mouth and barking, or suppose it looks like a pit bull, a kind of dog known to be dangerous? In these cases, it would be best to retract the original conclusion that it is safe to pat the little dog.

In such cases, it may be reasonable to draw a tentative conclusion to go ahead in everyday reasoning on a balance of considerations, and conclude to take an action, even though the reasons supporting this conclusion are not conclusive. Of course, this is not to recommend acting rashly or impulsively, but often a balance of considerations is enough of a strong basis of argument to meet an appropriate burden of proof for a reasoned deliberation to (tentatively) go ahead and commit to a conclusion. Recognizing that the reasoning in such a case is tentative, one needs to be open to any counter-evidence that may be available. In many cases, one may have to look around for evidence that goes against a defeasible argument, by collecting more evidence, by more carefully observing the existing data, or even by thinking of possible countervailing considerations. By such means jumping to a hasty conclusion can be avoided.

Consider a different version of example 5.37 by re-expressing the argument as one that could be deductively valid, depending on how the word 'generally' in the first statement is taken.

Example 5.38

Generally dogs of the kind I normally encounter in my neighborhood walks are friendly and pose no threat to people who pat them.

This dog is of the kind I normally encounter in my neighborhood walks.

Therefore, it would be safe to pat the dog that is approaching me now.

If the word 'generally' in the first statement is taken as a strict or absolute universal generalization, this argument is deductively valid. Since deductively valid arguments are monotonic, no new evidence needs to be considered. If both premises are true, the conclusion must be true too. So I can go ahead and pat the dog approaching me.

It may be much wiser to take the generalization in the first premise as subject to exceptions, and take the argument as defeasible. This way of proceeding may be prudent, even if there is no visible evidence that the dog is unfriendly. Even so, it might be wise to reason on the side of caution by thinking of a possible counter-argument. One of the premises in an argument of this sort is based on the principle of tutiorism, or the principle being on the safe side under conditions of uncertainty. As an example, consider the following argument.

164

Example 5.39

Some dogs are not friendly, even though they may appear so.

A dog that is not friendly poses a threat to anyone who pats it.

If a dog is not friendly and poses a threat to anyone who pats it, it is not safe to pat it.

Reason: it may bite.

If a dog bites you, it can have significant negative consequences.

It is not known whether this dog approaching us now is friendly, and poses no threat, or is not friendly, and poses a threat.

Conclusion: it may not be safe to pat this dog.

Principle of Tutiorism: Under conditions of uncertainty and lack of knowledge, if there is a choice between one of two hypotheses, it may be reasonable to accept the less plausible one if (a) accepting the more plausible one may have significant negative consequences that are known, while (b) accepting the less plausible one does not have significant negative consequences that are known. This principle suggests drawing another conclusion: instead of going ahead and patting this dog approaching us now, I will first ask its owner if it is friendly. This conclusion, we should note, is an extension of the conclusion of the last argument set out in example 5.9. It leads to a different action from the one in example 5.37 as the right course to take. In such cases, it is useful to look at not only the arguments supporting a conclusion, but also to consider arguments that might support an opposed conclusion.

In many cases of everyday reasoning, there is too much information to represent all of it explicitly in the premises of the inference. In effect then, the inference has the form of an argument from ignorance that works on a principle of a shifting burden of proof. As long as a proposition has not been disproved, it may be taken to be true, or to hold, in a given case. An understanding of how defeasible reasoning should be evaluated comes out if we see an argument from a pragmatic point of view, as being used in a context of dialogue between two arguers. The proponent puts forward the kind of general claim made in the first premise, and normally, the proponent would incur a burden of proof to back up the claim with evidence, if the claim is challenged by the respondent. In the absence of any known evidence that would challenge the claim, however, the inference goes ahead as tentatively acceptable. But if new information comes in, providing evidence against the claim, the situation is reversed. If the proponent fails to give the evidence required to prove the claim, then he must give up (retract) the claim. This quality of being open-minded, including a willingness to give up an argument one formerly accepted when new evidence comes in that defeats it, is an important characteristic of rational thinking, both in science and in everyday life.

5.10 SUMMARY

A deductively valid argument is one where the premises can never be true while the conclusion is false. The premises and conclusion of an argument are propositions. Propositions are either true or false. The conclusion of an argument is usually marked by an indicator word like 'so' or 'therefore.' If not, the Principle of Charity recommends choosing whichever proposition, as conclusion, makes the argument strongest. The premises are the propositions that back up, or give reasons for the conclusion of an argument.

It is useful to be familiar with the common forms of valid argument studied in this chapter. An argument is determined as valid by certain key terms called *logical constants*, meaning that they can be clearly defined in a fixed or constant way. In this chapter, the constants were the propositional connectives, 'and,' 'not,' 'or,' and 'if-then.' In section 5.7, the constants 'all' and 'some' were also briefly discussed. It is because of the rules that govern the meaning of these constants that argument forms are determined as valid or invalid. If an argument has a valid form, then it must be a valid argument. Therefore, valid forms of argument are useful semantical building blocks both in constructing new arguments and reconstructing old arguments in pragmatic sequences of argumentation.

It is because the validity of the forms of argument MP, MT, HS, and DS are determined by the meanings of the connective words 'not,' 'or,' and 'if-then' that deductive logic is a branch of semantics. Semantics has to do with truth and falsity, and the meanings of these connective words determine which forms of argument are valid by the rules for the connectives which stipulate relationships of truth and falsity. Using these rules, we can generally prove that a particular argument form is valid.

We have learned to recognize several very common valid forms of argument. Familiarity with these forms of argument is very useful for many purposes in constructing and evaluating arguments. However, two of the most important uses we have studied in this chapter are proving that an argument is valid and proving that a set of propositions is inconsistent. Each of these is a valuable capability.

166

Linking arguments together in a deductive chain of argumentation is a way of making proofs absolutely air-tight. Because each step follows from the previous step in the sequence of deductions, it may be rightly said that deductive logic, when correctly applied to arguments, leaves no room for dispute or controversy. Once the premises are postulated or accepted, if an argument is valid the conclusion may be shown to follow with inexorable necessity. Similarly, if a set of propositions is inconsistent, deductive logic can show beyond all shadow of doubt that the set is indeed inconsistent by using a sequence of deductions to deduce a contradiction.

However, sometimes different arguments have the same form. The same argument may also have different forms. Nevertheless, if any form of an argument is valid, then that argument is shown to be valid.

So we have seen that deductive logic has a formal nature. The study of deductive logic involves an ascent to generality because deductive logic, at the theoretical level, involves the study of the forms of argument. In practical logic – often called informal logic – each particular argument must be studied on its own merits. Each case is unique, but in formal logic, if two cases have the same form, then their particular differences may be ignored, at least at the formal level. Even so, applying formal logic to particular arguments is a practical or informal task. This is so because it is usually required by the Principle of Charity that an evaluator of an argument represent the argument by its most specific form, where a choice is possible.

Yet another use of valid argument forms is as an aid to determine which proposition is most plausibly meant to be the conclusion of an argument where no explicit indicator-word is given. When we are given a set of propositions evidently meant to be an argument, but no proposition of the set is clearly designated or meant as the conclusion, what are we to do? Until we determine the conclusion, the method of deduction cannot be brought to bear. Here then is another task of argument analysis. If every designation of a conclusion but one, out of all the possible designations, makes the argument invalid, then the policy of giving an arguer the benefit of the doubt (Principle of Charity) suggests picking the one proposition as conclusion that makes the argument come out valid.

Deductive logic has many uses in the study of reasoned argument. It is in fact an indispensable tool in the study of argument. As a proof of deductive validity of arguments, the method of deduction leaves no room for doubt about the linkage between a conclusion and a set of premises.

Basically, however, we have not given the reader a method (algorithm) of deduction to prove invalidity of arguments. The technique we used to show invalidity was the method of giving a counter-example. A counter-example is an argument that has the same specific form as the argument in question, where the premises of the counter-example are true while the conclusion is false.

Inconsistency is not in itself a fallacy, but if an arguer's set of commitments in a discussion show evidence of being collectively inconsistent, he can (and should) be challenged to defend his position by removing or explaining the apparent inconsistency. The usual way of doing this is to retract one of the commitments. In chapter 6, cases where an arguer is challenged on grounds of apparent inconsistency will be studied.

In evaluating arguments that have the argumentation schemes for composition and division, it is crucial to be aware of the distinction between the collective and distributive uses of terms. Arguments having these schemes are not always fallacious arguments. In order to test for the possibility that they could be fallacious, it is important to ask critical questions about the relationships between wholes and parts.

As stated before, when there is a proof of deductive validity of arguments, the method of deduction leaves no room for doubt about the linkage between a conclusion and a set of premises. If you accept the premises of such an argument, you also have to accept the conclusion. Moreover, deductive arguments are monotonic. No matter how many new premises are added to a deductively valid argument, the argument remains valid. In contrast, with plausible reasoning it is very important to be open-minded. This kind of argument is nonmonotonic. When new premises are added to the argument, the argument may be defeated by the new evidence that is entered into the case. Such arguments need to be seen as subject to retraction as new evidence comes to be known. Thus it is very important with this kind of argumentation to be open to the possibility of defeat, as new evidence comes in.

Strict generalizations of the kind characteristic of deductive reasoning are not open to exceptions. Arguments based on such generalizations are monotonic. However, plausible arguments based on defeasible generalizations are nonmonotonic, and it is vitally important in dealing with such arguments not to jump to the wrong conclusion based on a failure to deal with all the evidence that either might come in or be available now. Such cases of ignoring or suppressing evidence fit the pattern of rigid or stereotypical thinking characteristic of a failure to be open-minded and flexible in taking evidence in the case into account. Although deductive logic is more strict and rigid, and thus more limited in its application to the kinds of arguments we commonly deal with, it is nevertheless simpler and theoretically easier to grasp. In order to study defeasible reasoning, one first of all has to start with deductive logic, as a simpler but nevertheless more mechanical and strict method of evaluating arguments. Having grasped the basic principles and forms of reasoning of deductive logic, one can proceed to the study of defeasible arguments, such as arguments from ignorance, that are comparable to deductive logic in some ways, but depart from it in many other ways.

6

Personal attack in argumentation

The *argumentum ad hominem,* meaning "argument directed to the man," is the kind of argument that criticizes another argument by criticizing the arguer rather than his argument. Basically, this type of argument is the type of personal attack of an arguer that brings the attacked individual's personal circumstances, trustworthiness, or character into question. The *argumentum ad hominem* is not always fallacious, for in some instances questions of personal conduct, character, motives, etc., are legitimate and relevant to the issue. However, personal attack is inherently dangerous and emotional in argument, and is rightly associated with fallacies and deceptive tactics of argumentation. Three basic categories of fallacy have often traditionally been associated with three types of *argumentum ad hominem.*[1]

The abusive *ad hominem* argument is the direct attack on a person in argument, including the questioning or vilification of the character, motives, or trustworthiness of the person. Characteristically, the focus of the personal attack is on bad moral character generally, or bad character for truthfulness.

The *circumstantial ad hominem* argument is the questioning or criticizing of the personal circumstances of an arguer, allegedly revealed, for example, in his actions, affiliations, or previous commitments, by citing an alleged inconsistency between his argument and these circumstances. The charge, "You don't practise what you preach!" characteristically expresses the thrust of the circumstantial *ad hominem* argument against a person.

The third type of *ad hominem* argument is said to occur where the critic questions the sincerity or objectivity of an arguer by suggesting that the arguer has something to gain by supporting the argument he has advocated. This third type of *ad hominem* argument has sometimes been called "poisoning the well," because it suggests that the arguer attacked has a hidden agenda, is supporting his side of the argument for personal gain, or for other private and concealed reasons, and therefore cannot

1 For an account of the traditional categories of *ad hominem* fallacy recognized in the text-books, see Govier (1983).

be trusted as a fair or reasonable exponent of an argument on this, or indeed on any issue. As a reliable source, he has poisoned the well, so to speak, for anything he says is suspect as reflecting his one-sided personal bias.

Sometimes the *ad hominem* argument is associated with the *tu quoque* or "You too!" rejoinder in argumentation. Where a personal attack is initiated by one party, often the response is to fire another personal attack against this first party by replying "You are no better!" The danger here is that excessive indulgence in personal attack can result in a dialectical shift, lowering the level of a critical discussion to that of a personal quarrel, with disastrous results for the logic of the argumentation.

The argument against the person is not always logically unreasonable or fallacious. But when it is wrong, it can be a dangerous and very serious error. Certainly it is not hard to appreciate how personal attack on an individual's character or personal circumstances can be vicious and unwarranted. Such an attack should be severely criticized when it can be shown that it is unwarranted. The argument against the person can be a powerfully convincing or influential form of attack, however, when it is successfully deployed by a clever arguer. The argument against the person is in fact a very common form of argument, for example, in political debates. It could even be said to be the most powerful kind of argument in politics. And it is very important to be on guard against it, and to know how to handle it reasonably. The whole of this chapter will be devoted to the argument against the person. The abusive *ad hominem* will be considered first, then the circumstantial variety, and finally the "poisoning the well" or bias-imputing variant of *ad hominem* attack.

6.1 THE ABUSIVE *AD HOMINEM* ARGUMENT

In the abusive type of personal attack, there can be a range of differing aspects of an arguer's person that may be the focus of the attack. The attack may focus on the personal character or past actions of the arguer in question, or it may focus on the group affiliations of the arguer such as his political, national, or religious beliefs or ethnic background. Very often, personal attacks are directed against the ethics of an arguer, trying to suggest that the arguer is dishonest, unreliable, or lacks integrity. In other cases, the personal attack will question the arguer's credibility, or ability to enter into reasoned argument. For example, it may even be suggested that the arguer is insane or mentally imbalanced, and that therefore no serious attention can be paid to his argument.

171

One has to be careful in defining what constitutes an *ad hominem* argument. Many people who are introduced to this kind of argument tend to classify any kind of attack on a person's character as fitting the *ad hominem* argumentation scheme. However, to qualify as an *ad hominem* argument, several specific requirements have to be met. Not only does there have to be a personal attack made by one party against another, but the personal attack has to be put forward by the first party in such a way that it is meant to refute some argument previously put forward by the second party. To illustrate the point, it is best to offer two examples.

First, consider the following example, in which the character of Bill Clinton was attacked by calling him an "intellectual sociopath" who has no regard for the truth, and who is not only dishonest but "silly" (quoted from George F. Will, *Newsweek*, July 2, 2001).

Example 6.0

Today's bipartisan consensus is that Clinton is neither bad nor dangerous, just silly. Plainly put, almost no one thinks he believes a word he says. Or, more precisely, he believes everything he says at the moment he emphatically says it, and continues to believe it at full throttle right up to the moment he repudiates it. He has the weird sincerity of the intellectual sociopath, convinced that when he speaks, truth is an opinion but convenience is an imperative.

This argument is certainly an extremely aggressive attack on Clinton's character, alleging that he is a hypocrite who continues to believe something he says right up to the moment he repudiates it. This allegation makes Clinton sound not only vacillating and hypocritical, but deeply dishonest. Many, after learning about the *ad hominem* fallacy, might immediately classify it as an *ad hominem* argument against Clinton. But before so classifying it, we need to ask what prior argument put forward by Clinton this argument was designed to refute. If no such argument can be found, we can't really classify the argument as an *ad hominem*. Now it may be, if we were to search through the full text of the original article written by George F. Will, we would find that this attack on Clinton's character was designed to refute some particular argument that Clinton put forward. In the absence of such evidence, we should not classify this personal attack as an *ad hominem* argument.

Now consider another example of an argument typical of one type of abusive personal attack, one that suggests a personal untrustworthiness based on previous (allegedly immoral) conduct of the person.

172

Example 6.1

Richard Nixon's statements on foreign affairs policies in relation to China are untrustworthy because he was forced to resign during the Watergate scandal.

Notice that in this argument it is Nixon's statements on foreign affairs policies in relation to China that are attacked as untrustworthy. Because it is Nixon's statements on these policies that are attacked using the evidence that he was forced to resign during the Watergate scandal, this argument can be classified as *ad hominem*.

This argument against the person is open to critical reply because whatever we might believe about Richard Nixon's personal integrity or honesty in relation to the Watergate affair, it does not follow that his foreign policy statements on China are false or incorrect. From allegations or presumptions about someone's personal character, even if they are justifiable, one is not warranted in drawing the conclusion that certain specific statements they have made are false. In some cases, these statements may turn out to be true, and based on good evidence and reasonable arguments advanced by the arguer, despite his personal shortcomings or misconduct.

The point to be made in this case is that the argument is a weak one. While it may be justified to have some reservations about Mr. Nixon's reliability as an ethical politician in light of the Watergate scandal, these reservations are not very strong grounds for rejecting Nixon's expertise in foreign policy issues in relation to China, an area where he was very strong and where he was widely acknowledged to have a vast fund of experience. In this case, the transference from the premise to the conclusion is (at best) weak. The danger is that the reference to the Watergate scandal is a powerful personal attack that may lead one to whom example 6.1 is directed to dismiss all of Nixon's statements as worthless because they are seen as being based on a source that is either corrupt or inept in all political matters. This closed view of the issue would not allow Nixon or anyone else to try to argue for his statements on any case.

It is not that the abusive type of argument against the person is always totally worthless. It is, however, in this case, a weak kind of argument based on plausible presumptions that cannot be too strongly transferred to another area. So the danger is in over-reacting to it.

In the political arena, an arguer's integrity, personal convictions, and individual conduct can, in many instances, be legitimate subject matter for dialogue. This is because we must place our trust in elected politicians to be our representatives, and we rightly expect them to be honest, and not to give in to corruption. Partly for this reason, the *ad hominem* attack

173

could justifiably be said to be the most common and most powerful form of criticism of an opponent in political arguments. Even so, the prevalence of so-called negative campaigning in recent elections has prompted commentators to remark that the excesses of personal attack as a popular style of argument is a sign of a lack of interest and critical judgment of the issues on the part of the electorate.

In 1986 campaigns for the U.S. Senate, the following instances of negative campaigning were prominent. One candidate accused his opponent of being soft on terrorism and drugs and spent two million dollars on television ads depicting bloody victims of terrorist attacks being carried away on stretchers. His opponent claimed, in return, that this candidate was confused and lacked conviction.[2]

Another candidate accused an opponent of mismanaging union funds. The opponent replied by accusing him of drinking on the job. Yet another candidate labelled her opponent anti-male and a San Francisco Democrat and tried to make her unmarried status an election issue. Commenting on this trend, *Newsweek* remarked that "by historical standards, . . . , today's dirtiest smear jobs look positively polite," but that unfortunately for the level of political debate, ". . . negative campaigning all too often works."[3] Indeed, another comment in *Newsweek* observed that only those candidates who are convinced they have a large lead against their opponents conclude that they do not need to use negative ads.[4] The author's objection is not to "criticizing the public record of public people," which he feels is acceptable in political argument, but the "reckless use" of a candidate's voting record.[5] For example, a candidate whose vote could be interpreted as supporting a "less-than-maximum funding level for a program for the handicapped" can lead to a commercial that makes claims about this person voting "against the handicapped." He concurs that, unfortunately, in recent years these negative ads have worked.[6]

However, it is not only in negative campaign tactics in television commercials that personal attack is found in political argumentation. It is very common in all levels of political debate that politicians strive to find some grounds to accuse their opponents of circumstantial inconsistency, hypocrisy, or lack of personal integrity. Arguing that an opponent is

2 Tom Morganthau and Howard Fineman, 'When in Doubt Go Negative,' *Newsweek*, November 3, 1986, pp. 25–26.
3 Ibid., p. 25.
4 George F. Will, 'So Much Cash, So Few Ideas,' *Newsweek*, November 10, 1986, p. 96.
5 Ibid.   6 Ibid.

possibly guilty of conflict of interest, questionable tax deductions on a personal income tax return, or vulnerable on other questions of personal conduct of this sort, is an important part of current political rhetoric, and can be strikingly dominant when the race for popularity between two parties is close.

Character can be relevant in an argument if the issue of the dialogue is related to the arguer's character. For example, if the issue is alleged defamation of character by one arguer of another, then the character of the arguer allegedly defamed is in fact the main issue on which the argument turns. But when is character relevant in an argument? What matters in answering this question in a specific case is to determine what the issue of the discussion should be, first of all, and then to judge whether the aspect of character in question is relevant to the issue.

In the negative rules of persuasion dialogue outlined in section 1.4, a move in argument can violate these rules if it asks an inappropriate question or is otherwise not relevant to fulfilling the obligation of proving the thesis at issue. Unfortunately, the abusive *ad hominem* argument often violates these rules because, at a particular stage, the discussion should not really be about the arguer's character. Such radical failures of relevance in *ad hominem* arguments have already been illustrated in examples 1.7 and 1.8. In a scientific discussion exclusively about laws of physics and their scientific verification, personal attacks on the character or personal convictions of the arguer have no place. However, in a political debate, questions of personal character and veracity can be highly relevant.

In a news story on the Internet, 'John Edwards Takes Aim at Hillary Clinton Character Issues' (October 30, 2007, http://www.foxnew.com/story/0,2933,306256,00.html), it was reported that Hillary Clinton has often been subject to character attacks.

Example 6.2

A poll conducted earlier this month for CNN found [that] clear majorities of voters see [Hillary] Clinton as a strong and decisive leader; as likable; as able to work well with both parties; and as caring about their needs. But on questions of character, voters were split roughly in half when asked whether she is honest and trustworthy; whether she shares their values; and whether she is a person they admire. [John] Edwards suggested Clinton is mostly running for president out of personal ambition.

Edwards based this character attack on Clinton's statement earlier in her campaign, "I'm in it to win." However, using this statement to support the character attack seems weak, because all the candidates for president in the election campaign supposedly have the aim of trying to win, that is, to be elected president. In this case, even though the attack is weak, it should nevertheless be judged to be relevant because the context is that of an election campaign.

This example raises the question of how far reporters should go in public reporting and examination of personal questions of character in a presidential campaign. The issue raised is whether matters of a candidate's character are relevant to public discussions of his or her suitability as a holder of political office.

One can see in this case how such personal matters can be relevant. If the candidate took a strong stand on family values, for example, it could legitimately be questioned whether his infidelity to his spouse brought the sincerity of his convictions on the family issue into question. Or if he concealed his extra-marital affairs from his spouse, one might reasonably be entitled to question this candidate's veracity or reliability. In other cases, if a candidate shows evidence of lack of good judgment or wisdom in his personal life, there may be legitimate questioning of his ability to guide his country in a difficult and potentially dangerous situation that requires good judgment and an ability to function under pressure. This is all part of the democratic system of representation, where office-holders are elected in the trust that they will show integrity in sticking to their principles in running affairs of state.

Whether personal matters are rightly held to be relevant depends on the issue of the critical discussion or the subject of the inquiry. Ultimately, it is the agenda of the dialogue that is the key factor in evaluating the reasonableness or fallaciousness of an *ad hominem* argument.

Despite all the reservations about personal attacks noted above, sometimes bringing questions of the personal character of an arguer into the argument is reasonable and legitimate. This can occur where the personal characteristics of the arguer are relevant to the issue under discussion.

Example 6.3

A very flattering autobiography of a famous movie star appears in print, written by the actor with the help of a professional writer. The actor is portrayed in the book as a kindly, moral, humanitarian saint, who has often helped people in need and championed charitable causes. In a book review, a critic points out the actor has well-documented criminal connections, has used his paid bodyguards to beat up women and men he took a dislike to, and has committed other vicious and cruel actions. The critic concludes that the autobiography is a one-sided portrait, and that its fairness, objectivity, and accuracy are open to question.

In this case, the critic may have a good argument, depending on the worth of the evidence of personal misconduct he cited, and on the arguments in the book he criticized. Even though the critic has attacked the argument of the actor on the basis of the personal characteristics of the actor, his criticism could still be quite reasonable and justified.

The critic's argument in example 6.3 could be judged as reasonable, even though it is a personal attack on the actor, because the actor's personal characteristics are the real issue in the argument. A personal autobiography quite properly has as its subject matter the character of the writer. Where personal allegations are relevant to the issue, the argument against the person can be reasonable. Hence we must be careful not to condemn every seemingly abusive personal attack as a fallacious *ad hominem* argument.

It should be clear then that the expression *abusive ad hominem* argument refers to the fallacious or illicit use of the direct type of *ad hominem* attack that focuses on personal character, reliability, or veracity. For in some instances, arguments against the person which focus on character, personal reliability, or veracity, can be reasonable arguments. Not all *ad hominem* arguments of the direct, personal attack type are fallacious. When these *ad hominem* arguments are illicit or fallacious, they can fairly be categorized as abusive attacks on the person.

6.2 THE *CIRCUMSTANTIAL AD HOMINEM* ARGUMENT

In contrast to the examples of direct personal attack on an arguer's reliability, veracity, or character, examples of the *circumstantial ad hominem* argument against the person are based on an allegation that the person's circumstances are inconsistent in his own personal advocacy of the position adopted in his argument. This kind of argument is more subtle because it uses the allegation of inconsistency as evidence that the arguer criticized may be a liar or a hypocrite, or even that he may be so logically incompetent that he can't even follow his own argument. This form of attack is extremely powerful in political debate because it suggests that the person attacked does not follow in his own personal conduct, the principles that he advocates for others. The conclusion is that anyone who does not practice what he preaches is not a person worth listening to or taking seriously.

What is characteristic of this second type of argument against the person is the citation of an inconsistency between the argument and the personal circumstances of the arguer. In the examples cited in section 6.1, no allegation of inconsistency was involved as the basis of the personal attack. This new type of argument against the person involves the attempted refutation of an opponent's argument by citing an inconsistency between the propositions advanced by the opponent in his argument and his personal circumstances.

The type of personal criticism characteristic of the circumstantial *ad hominem* is essentially a relative type of argument – the argument against the person alleges that an argument criticized is not consistent with the personal practices, position, or situation of the person who advocates the argument.[7] This sort of criticism can be a reasonable challenge in some instances, but it is easy to be confused about the correct conclusion to be drawn from this relative type of argument.[8] Consider the following dialogue.

Example 6.4

Parent: There is strong evidence of a link between smoking and chronic obstructive lung disease. Smoking is also associated with many other serious disorders. Smoking is unhealthy. So you should not smoke.

Child: But you smoke yourself. So much for your argument against smoking!

Now it might be possible in this case that the parent has a good argument that smoking is linked to lung disease and is therefore unhealthy. Presuming that the child wants to, or should want to be healthy, the parent's conclusion that the child should not smoke could be, in itself, a reasonable argument. The child has not even attempted to disprove or bring reasonable doubt to bear on this argument. Therefore, he may be too hasty in rejecting it.

On the other hand, the child does seem to have a point worth considering. The parent smokes, and admits it. Is it not the case that the parent's advocacy of non-smoking is inconsistent with his own practice of smoking? And is not this personal inconsistency a reasonable basis for criticism, or at least for challenging the parent's personal advocacy of his own argument? It is as if the child were saying: "If your argument is worth anything, why don't you follow it yourself?" So it seems that both the

---

7 The concept of an arguer's position as a systematic network of coherent commitments has been developed very well by Johnstone (1978).

8 This idea that an arguer's position can be revealed through reasonable dialogue is an important part of the analysis of personal attack argumentation given in Walton (1985a).

parent's argument and the child's counter-argument are open to reasonable criticisms. Who then is in the right, or how should we settle the argument?

The first constructive step is to point out a certain ambiguity or confusion in understanding what the conclusion of the argument is. If you take the conclusion in an impersonal way as the proposition 'Smoking is unhealthy' or 'Anyone who wants to be healthy should not smoke,' the argument may be very reasonable. At least, the child does not seem to be challenging this much of the argument. But if you take the conclusion in a personal way, as the parent's saying, 'I am advocating non-smoking as a policy of good personal conduct,' then the argument becomes subject to criticism. Absolutely speaking, the argument is reasonable. Relatively speaking, the argument runs into trouble.

The problem here is to determine how much of the contextual information should count as part of the argument. Should the father's actions of smoking be counted into the propositions that make up the argument? If so, do his actions commit him personally to the practice of smoking? If so, there is an inconsistency, or at least the addition of a plausible assumption leads to inconsistency. For assume that the parent wants to be healthy. Then if anyone who wants to be healthy should not smoke, it follows that the parent should not smoke. But the parent does smoke. And if this practice indicates a commitment to smoking on his part, his practice would suggest that it is all right for him to smoke. But that cannot be consistent with the statement that he should not smoke.

The basic issue is: do actions speak louder than, or as loud as, words? If so, then the child has a point. The parent's words run counter to his action. Granted, sometimes such inconsistencies can be explained, defended, or excused. But surely it is not unreasonable to require that the parent owes the child a defence or explanation of his position. On the other hand, taking the parent's argument in a more impersonal way, the conclusion 'Smoking is unhealthy' could be based on reasonable evidence. Therefore, the child's dismissal of the whole argument is a case of throwing the baby out with the bathwater. It is a hasty and premature dismissal.

To sum up, the basic error in the circumstantial attack in this case is the confusion between two interpretations of the conclusion of the argument. The conclusion can be interpreted in an absolute (impersonal way), or it can be interpreted in a relative (personal) way. Interpreted one way the argument could be strong, while interpreted the other way it could be weak, or open to challenge and criticism. One form of the fallacy of circumstantial argument against the person is the confusion of the two arguments, based on the assumption that both must stand or fall together.

179

This case suggests that it is important to distinguish between a circumstantial argument against the person, and a possible error or weakness in advancing a circumstantial argument against the person. Criticizing a person's argument by challenging his own advocacy of the conclusion of his argument can be a legitimate argument against the person.[9] At least, it is not an unreasonable challenge or criticism to bring forward in some cases. However, to totally reject the argument in itself on the basis of such a relative criticism may be to commit a serious error. At any rate, this is certainly one important type of error that can be committed in arguments against a person.

These distinctions are very reminiscent of some of the components of argument discussed in chapter 1. There, we showed that there are always two participants in an argument, a proponent and a respondent. In the case of arguments against the person the proponent is the original advocate of the argument – for example, the parent in example 6.4. The opponent in arguments against the person is the critic who alleges that there is a circumstantial or personal inconsistency in the proponent's position. In example 6.4, the critic is the child. Therefore we see that in studying weaknesses and errors in personal attack as a type of argument, we must look at the two sides of the argument. In other words, we can't just look at the arguments as a set of propositions, after the fashion of chapter 2. We have to go back to components of argument as two-person dialogue that we studied in chapter 1.

In studying example 6.4, we need to distinguish between several stages of the sequence of dialogue. First there was the original argument. Then there was the circumstantial criticism of this argument by a second party. If that criticism is successful, and there are no good grounds for the original arguer to reply to it, then the original arguer has the burden of proof shifted against his side. However, if the original arguer can successfully reply to the criticism, it could be that the shoe comes to be on the other foot, and it is the critic who is found to have advanced a weak argument, itself open to criticism. In short, it could be either the attacker or defender of an argument against the person who may reasonably be found open to criticism.

Finally, we must be careful to observe another important distinction related to the nature of argument as reasonable dialogue. Taken in an

---

9 The thesis that an argument against the person can be a legitimate form of criticism is defended by Barth and Martens (1977), by appealing to principles of the theory of reasonable dialogue.

impersonal way, the conclusion of an argument is simply a proposition. However, in any reasonable dialogue, a conclusion is designated as being the conclusion of the one arguer who must prove it. Therefore, in criticizing an argument, the critic may not just be claiming that the proposition in question is false or unproven. He may be arguing that the proposition cannot consistently be maintained by his opponent in argument. He may be arguing that his opponent's maintaining that proposition is not consistent with other commitments which can fairly be attributed to the position of his opponent in the argument. Here, the critic is not necessarily challenging the conclusion of his opponent's argument per se. He may be challenging the opponent's own personal advocacy of that conclusion, and questioning his premises.

One basic problem with many cases of personal argumentation is to fairly evaluate whether an arguer's personal actions may reasonably be taken to commit that arguer to certain propositions. From the given context of the argument, it may be required for us to sort out which propositions an arguer may reasonably be said to have committed himself to.

One particular example has been so often cited in logic textbooks as a case of the circumstantial *ad hominem* fallacy that it can justifiably be called the classical example of the argument against the person.

Example 6.5

A hunter is accused of barbarity for his sacrifice of innocent animals to his own amusement or sport in hunting. His reply to his critic: "Why do you feed on the flesh of harmless cattle?"

The sportsman's reply to his critic was traditionally said to commit an *ad hominem* fallacy because it attempts to refute the critic through the critic's own special circumstances. Because the critic is presumably not a vegetarian, the sportsman alleges that the critic is personally inconsistent with his own argument. Why is the sportsman's reply an incorrect argument against the person? The point is the same one made above in relation to example 6.4. The sportsman fails to present good grounds for the impersonal conclusion that hunting is acceptable as a general practice. Instead, he criticizes the critic by arguing against the critic's own special and personal circumstances. The sportsman's personal criticism may be legitimate, but insofar as it fails to refute the general issue raised by the critic, his argument fails to provide grounds for the impersonal conclusion it should address. So far then, example 6.5 seems similar to example 6.4.

181

There is an important new point to be raised in connection with example 6.5. Is the sportsman's personal criticism of his critic's situation a legitimate case of circumstantial inconsistency? To sort this out, let us take a careful look at the propositions that make up the argument. First, what practice is the critic objecting to? He objects to the sportsman's practice of sacrificing innocent animals for his amusement, i.e., hunting. But what practice does the sportsman accuse the critic of engaging in himself? It is the practice of eating meat.

Now is there any inconsistency between eating meat and rejecting the practice of hunting game for amusement? Well, certainly there is no logical inconsistency. If I sit eating a rare filet mignon while criticizing the cruel practices of hunters who take joy in gunning down innocent animals, I am not logically inconsistent. I would be logically inconsistent if I obtained my filet mignon by gunning down an innocent cow and taking joy in it, then making it clear that I advocated this practice as a worthwhile sport. It is quite possible that such activities played no part in my obtaining that particular steak for my dinner table, nor would I advocate them. The lesson so far is that we should be very careful in specifying exactly which are the propositions alleged to be inconsistent when we are advancing an argument against the person.

According to example 6.5 as outlined above, the sportsman claimed that there was a circumstantial inconsistency between the following two propositions.

1. The critic criticizes the killing of innocent animals for amusement or sport.
2. The critic himself eats meat.

There is no logical inconsistency between (1) and (2). And as (1) and (2) are stated above, there is no clear case of a circumstantial inconsistency either. As Augustus DeMorgan (1847, p. 265) neatly observed in connection with this classical example, the parallel will not exist until we substitute a person who turns butcher for amusement for the person who eats meat. What the critic objects to is not eating meat, but taking pleasure in killing animals for amusement or sport.

Therefore, there is an additional dimension to the argument against the person revealed by this case. The sportsman could be on reasonable grounds if he had challenged the critic for himself being a hunter. But that was not his reply. The sportsman fell short of giving solid justification for his suggestion that the critic is circumstantially inconsistent. On initial appearances, the critic could seem open to a charge of personal

inconsistency. By falling far short of establishing this charge, the sportsman commits a second form of error. His argument supports merely a
superficial appearance of inconsistency, rather than a solid justification of
this charge.

This much said, it should also be recognized that there is some connection between the practice of eating meat and the practice of hunting. For
one thing, eating meat as a practice is an economic factor in making the
killing of animals profitable as a source of food. In short, eating meat is
connected to the killing of animals. The practice of eating meat requires
the killing of animals. Of course, the connection between eating meat and
killing animals by hunting is not a direct one. While there is a connection,
it is an oblique one. Moreover, the sportsman's reply is in the form of a
question. That is a point in his favor, because, strictly speaking, he is only
questioning the consistency of his critic.

Now the critic eats meat, and let's say that he concedes this personal
practice. What does that commit him to? What propositions do his actions
reasonably commit him to advocating? Clearly they do not need to commit him to hunting game for amusement as a pastime. But his actions
do connect him indirectly to the slaughter of innocent farm animals,
and might thereby suggest some degree of acceptance of these practices.
Or do they? The best way to find out would be to ask the critic. But
short of that, there could be a reasonable but weak presumption that the
critic's dietary practices do commit him, to some extent, to the acceptability of the slaughter of animals for food. If so, there is some basis, a
fairly weak one perhaps, for the sportsman's rejoinder as an argument
against the person. The problem is to fairly determine in a particular case
what propositions one's acknowledged actions or practices may commit
one to.

This type of problem is related to the ethical problem of "dirty hands."
Does indirect involvement in an activity represent a sponsoring or personal advocacy of all or some aspects or consequences of that activity that
is stronger than passive involvement? Each case must be approached individually in ethics. So too in pragmatic logic, where evidence is derived
from the corpus of argument, so that the issue can be resolved through
reasonable dialogue. Although the sportsman's rejoinder can be criticized
for two kinds of errors as an argument against the person, still it is a persuasive argument because it does rest on a connection that may be not
altogether worthless as a partial basis towards constructing a circumstantial
argument against the person. But by the standards of reasonable dialogue,
it is a weak argument that is very much open to criticism.

One legitimate function of the argument against the person may be to shift the burden of proof in dialogue back onto an attacker. This form of attack and reply, we've seen, is called the *tu quoque* (You too!) rejoinder.

Example 6.6

A student accuses a businessman of selling weapons to countries that use them to kill innocent citizens. The businessman replies: "The university you attend has investments in these very companies that manufacture weapons. Your hands aren't clean either!"

The businessman in effect replies that the student's argument is hypocritical. He is saying, "You too!" He alleges that the student's position is inconsistent. His practices support the very institutions that he condemns. In this case, the response to the personal circumstantial attack is a second personal circumstantial attack.

In analyzing example 6.6, we must remember the lessons of our analysis of 6.5. There is a difference between the proposition 'x sells weapons to countries that use them to kill innocent citizens,' and the proposition 'x attends an institution that has investments in companies that manufacture weapons.' To condemn one activity while engaging in the other is not logically inconsistent. It is not even circumstantially inconsistent, but there is a significant connection between the two propositions.

The businessman's *tu quoque* reply can be criticized as a weak argument on the same two grounds as the sportsman's rejoinder was criticized. Even once we recognize that the businessman's reply is a very weak basis for an argument against the person, perhaps the reply should at least deflect some burden of criticism back onto the student to defend his own position as a critic. If so, then in some cases, the *tu quoque* reply is a not unreasonable form of argument against the person.[10]

Clearly the great danger with arguments against the person is uncritically taking them for much stronger arguments than they really are. Personal attack arguments are so powerful and upsetting that often the mere suggestion of a personal inconsistency can damage an opponent's argument out of all proportion to the impact it should logically be taken to have. While personal criticisms are sometimes not unreasonable, the danger of committing serious errors by over-reacting to them in argument is very real indeed.

10 This example (6.6) is studied in more detail in Walton (1985a, pp. 63–66).

The first step in analyzing any circumstantial argument against the person is to determine and clearly state the pair of propositions that is alleged to be the source of the inconsistency. The next step is to ask whether these propositions are logically inconsistent. If they are not, then the next step is to ask whether they are circumstantially inconsistent. A set of propositions may be said to be *circumstantially inconsistent* for an arguer where that arguer's circumstances or actions clearly indicate that he is committed to a set of propositions in the context of dialogue, and these propositions are collectively inconsistent. To establish a circumstantial inconsistency, we must justify from our reading of the given circumstances that the arguer accused of such an inconsistency indeed has an inconsistent set of propositions in his commitment-store, that is, he has adopted a position that is inconsistent.

The key step in evaluating any such claim of inconsistency is for the evaluator to clearly state each of the individual propositions that are, taken together, supposed to comprise a circumstantial inconsistency in the position of the arguer being criticized. For, as we have seen, it is all too easy, in practice, for a critic to launch a powerful attack by citing a pair of propositions which may superficially seem to be inconsistent, but are really not inconsistent at all, as the argument stands.

6.3 THE ATTACK ON AN ARGUER'S IMPARTIALITY

In some cases, an *ad hominem* argument is designed to attack an arguer's presumed impartiality by imputing a bias to the arguer. In such a case, the criticism alleged is that the arguer in question cannot be trusted to engage in fair argument because he or she has a hidden agenda, a personal motive or bias for pushing one side of the argument and ignoring the other side. The following *ad hominem* attack is a case in point.

Example 6.7

Bob and Wilma are discussing the problem of acid rain. Wilma argues that reports on the extent of the problem are greatly exaggerated and that the costs of action are prohibitive. Bob points out that Wilma is on the board of directors of a U.S. coal company, and that therefore her argument should not be taken at face value.[11]

11 Example 6.7 was derived from a similar case discussed by Robert Binkley during a symposium, 'Walton on Informal Fallacies' at the Canadian Philosophical Association Meeting in Winnipeg, May 26, 1986.

Here Bob's criticism seems to be that Wilma has a hidden motive for pushing for one side of the issue. He is therefore questioning her fairness as an arguer who has looked at all the available arguments on the issue. Is she telling the whole story, or taking a balanced perspective? Bob is suggesting that because she did not tell us at the beginning that she was financially involved with an American coal company, there is some question of her reliability or fairness as an arguer on this issue.

Of course the basic point about all arguments against the person needs to be kept in mind in this case, as in the previous cases. Wilma's arguments could be based on good evidence. Even granted that she is on the board of directors of a coal company, it does not necessarily follow that her arguments must be wrong. So to argue would be a fallacious kind of *ad hominem* argument.

But it could be that Bob's conclusion is the weaker claim, that we should question Wilma's impartiality in emphasizing the points that she stressed. Bob could be saying that we should be careful in taking Wilma's arguments as the whole story. For she has a financial stake in the outcome, and therefore a strong motive for concentrating on the arguments against taking action, and ignoring the arguments for action against industrial polluters of the environment.

What Bob seems to be suggesting is that there is a reason for questioning Wilma's integrity or impartiality as a neutral investigator of the issue. If she had openly told us at the outset that she was taking the side of the industrial companies on the issue, then there would be no need for this type of criticism. For there is nothing wrong with arguing for your own side in a persuasion dialogue, but if the dialogue is supposed to be an impartial investigation (inquiry) rather than a dispute, the situation is different. In this context, if one arguer has a hidden agenda to support one side of the dispute only while appearing to be a neutral investigator, then it can be a reasonable criticism for the other arguer to question the alleged neutrality of the first arguer, if there is a good reason to suspect bias.

In this type of case the basis of the *ad hominem* criticism is the allegation that a dialectical shift has taken place – a change from one context of dialogue to another. As we have seen, one type of reasonable dialogue is the persuasion dialogue, where the thesis of one arguer is the opposite of the thesis of the other. Not every reasonable dialogue, however, is a persuasion dialogue. Sometimes participants in an inquiry can investigate an issue without having definitely made up their minds or taken sides on the issue at the outset. And this inquiry type of argumentation is a different context of dialogue from that of the persuasion dialogue.

The argument against the person in example 6.7 is a challenge to the trustworthiness of an arguer in keeping to the rules and objectives of the game of dialogue that the arguers are supposed to be engaged in. Even more damagingly, Bob could be suggesting that Wilma is engaged in a third type of dialogue, the negotiation, or interest-based bargaining type of argumentation. Bob has indicated that Wilma is on the board of directors of a coal company. Therefore, he claims that she has a financial stake relevant to the issue of acid rain. Bob may be suggesting then that Wilma is even more subject to bias in her argumentation, because she is covertly promoting her own financial interests by trying to convince others that acid rain is not a serious problem.

Although there are elements of both the abusive and circumstantial *ad hominem* types of argumentation tangentially involved in example 6.7, neither personal abuse nor circumstantial inconsistency per se is the main aspect of the attack. Instead, Bob is arguing that Wilma is not really open to impartial inquiry, or perhaps even to two-sided critical discussion of the issue of acid rain, because she is bound by her financial stake in the matter to always press for one side of the argument only, no matter what the real evidence on the question may indicate. Hence this type of case is really more like the "poisoning the well" kind of *ad hominem* attack. It is an imputation of bias, and it essentially involves an allegation that a concealed dialectical shift has taken place within the argument.

Another instance of this "poisoning the well" type of *ad hominem* imputation of bias occurred during a debate on abortion in the House of Commons Debates of Canada (vol. 2, November 30, 1979, p. 1920). During the debate, the Speaker of the House made the following interjection.

Example 6.8

I wish it were possible for men to get really emotionally involved in this question. It is really impossible for the man, for whom it is impossible to be in this situation, to really see it from the woman's point of view. That is why I am concerned that there are not more women in this House available to speak about this from the woman's point of view.

This argument is based on a true premise, namely that a man cannot personally experience unwanted pregnancy or abortion. And therefore, perhaps it is correct to suggest that a man's experience in this area is inherently limited, at least from a personal perspective. But is it right to conclude that it is impossible for any man to see the issue from the woman's

187

point of view? The danger here lies in the suggestion that men have nothing to say on this issue. It is suggested that what they say is not credible because it must always be based on a lack of the required expertise, and therefore on an inability to take part in serious deliberations on the issue.

The problem with this type of argument is that by suggesting an inevitable or inescapable bias on the part of an arguer because of his personal circumstances or characteristics, that person is excluded from any role in any subsequent serious argument on the issue. However, if the critic has the opposite personal characteristic, she too is trapped in an inescapable bias. So what is the use of further dialogue?

This argument suggests that a man can't help having a biased opinion on the issue of abortion, or taking a one-sided view of the subject, simply because he is a man. A criticism of this argument is that the Speaker can't help seeing the issue from the other side, or at least taking a one-sided view of the subject, simply because she is a woman. Such an argument can always be stood on its head in reply, but once the reply is made, the argument has not gone anywhere.

Sometimes the best reply to a personal attack is an opposite personal attack in reply. The danger here is that you may get still another personal attack in reply, and so on, and so on. The resulting personal quarrel may be unproductive and not advance discussion on the issue of the dialogue.

Another problem with this style of argument against the person is that it can create a stalemate that stifles further discussion. For it is implied that neither side can help taking a personal, one-sided stance or position in the argument. So, the message seems to be, what is the point of continuing the argument? Postulating the inescapability of personal bias can be a bad mistake, for it suggests the futility of honestly looking at the evidence and issues on both sides in a reasonable manner. While it can be justified to allege personal bias in some cases, to suggest that one's opponent in argument is totally biased and hopelessly dogmatic is a particularly strong and dangerous form of personal attack. This form of personal attack should be criticized or challenged when it tends to subvert or close our minds to reasonable dialogue. Unfortunately, the argument against the person is often so effective and devastating that it is a conversation-stopper, closing off the possibilities of objective argument and further reasonable discussion of an issue.

In the following case, the leader of a group of black Americans who claim to be the real descendants of Judah living in a country occupied by white devils, is quoted as saying whites are "evil, wicked liars and murderers" whose "tricks must be removed" (*Newsweek*, November 10,

1986, p. 31). This hard line towards disbelievers is reflected in further statements attributed to the leader of this cult.

Example 6.9

The dictionary defines devil as an adversary of God. If you are an opponent of mine, then you would be classified as a devil.

The problem with this point of view is that by classifying all white persons as "evil, wicked liars" and "devils," no room is left for any presumption that further reasonable dialogue can be carried on with any arguer who has the personal characteristic of being white. The reason is that all white people, as "devils" and "liars," cannot be trusted to take part in serious or honest dialogue because they are inherently unreliable and unreasonable. When this point of view is reached, there is no room left for argument, because reasoned argument presupposes an arguer who is, at least to some degree, open-minded, serious, and trustworthy in collaborating in joint dialogue.

The bias type of argument against the person is so effective in undermining argument and discrediting an opponent that it is aptly called "poisoning the well," in many instances. The term is supposed to have been originated by Cardinal Newman, when he was confronted by the argument that, as a Catholic priest, he did not place the highest value on the truth. The allegation was that since Cardinal Newman was personally biased towards the Catholic position, he could not be relied upon as a source of fair or impartial argument. Cardinal Newman's reply was that this accusation made it impossible for him, or any other Catholic, to carry forward any reasonable or successful argument on any subject or issue. In effect then, the presumption was created, by the personal allegation, that any further argument advanced by Cardinal Newman would be automatically discredited. Hence the appropriateness of the term "poisoning the well."

While it may be legitimate in some cases to raise the question of an arguer's commitment to a certain general position or ideology, the problem is that this form of attack can often be so powerful and overwhelming that it stops conversation altogether by so discrediting an arguer that reasonable dialogue is prematurely blocked off altogether. Often, personal attack heightens emotions, leading to rage and frustration, and thence to a desire to hit back at all costs, whether by fair or foul means. Usually this is not a good direction for an argument to take, and it may indicate an underlying dialectical shift.

189

The previous examples have indicated that there are many ways in which criticism directed against the person can go wrong and be fallacious. However, the last examples have suggested that in some cases, and to some extent, a personal attack against an opponent's circumstances or position may be not altogether unreasonable. Does this mean that in some cases arguments against the person could be reasonable? In section 6.1, it has already been suggested that this is indeed the case. And if it is true, it means that we must not reject an argument against the person without giving good reasons.

We saw that example 6.4, from one point of view, could be interpreted as a weak but basically reasonable criticism to raise. Another example will serve to illustrate a reasonable use of the circumstantial argument against the person as a move in argument. Consider the following dialogue.

Example 6.10

George: The notorious problems we have been having with postal strikes means that there is no longer reliable mail service provided by the government. I think we ought to allow private, for-profit mail-delivery companies to compete on an equal footing with the Post Office.

Bob: But George, you are a communist.

Let us suppose that in this case George is an avowed communist, and has based his previous arguments on many standard communist principles and positions. Now in many cases, calling your opponent in an argument a communist could be a fallacious type of *ad hominem* attack. However, in this instance, Bob seems to have a reasonable point. If George is an avowed communist, and communists are for state control and against private enterprise, then how can George consistently argue for a for-profit mail service run by private enterprise? It seems like a legitimate question. Of course, George may be able to resolve the ostensible inconsistency in subsequent dialogue. Surely Bob is justified in challenging the consistency of George's position at this point in the dialogue. If so, then in this case, Bob's circumstantial argument is not fallacious. It is a reasonable use of the *ad hominem* argument to challenge George's position.

If arguments against the person can sometimes be reasonable, we must carefully analyze this type of argument to set out criteria that will enable us to distinguish between the incorrect (fallacious) and reasonable instances of *ad hominem* argumentation. First, let us address the reasonable type of person-directed criticism in argument.

190

A personal attack can be a reasonable criticism of an arguer's position by showing that the concessions or commitments of that arguer are inconsistent with the propositions asserted in his argument. Some might say that such an attack is, or can be, specious because it misses the real point of looking to the external evidence and instead, concentrates on the internal relationships within the arguer's position. For instance, in example 6.10, some commentators might say that Bob would be better off to evaluate George's proposal of private mail service on its own merits, rather than raising the internal question of whether the proposal is internally consistent with George's own political position. What does George's own internal position matter to anyone else, compared with the very important issue of whether mail service should be public or private?

This point of view has some justification. For external evidence should very often have priority, and if we are distracted from that external evidence by purely personal (internal) considerations, that is the very climate in which the personal attack creates the most mischief in argument.

However, internal matters of an arguer's position can sometimes be important too. If George really is inconsistent in his position and confused – a communist who advocates free enterprise – then it is very important to George to sort out his own position. For one thing, if George's position does truly contain a logical inconsistency, then it cannot be right. Second, there may be many other readers or listeners affected by George's argument who may be somewhat sympathetic to some forms of communism, and who may be very irritated and concerned about postal strikes and reliable mail services. For these people, it may be very important to think through the whole issue in much the same way that George is trying to think it through. Even those who strongly reject any communistic political ideals may be concerned to see how a communist could deal with the problems posed by mail strikes. So the internal question of the consistency of George's position on this issue may be very important for George and many others as well.

A third factor is that internal evidence can be enough to swing the balance of acceptance to one side of an argument or the other where external evidence is lacking or cannot be brought to bear on an issue. On a complex and controversial moral or political issue like state control of services, there may be no clear external, factual, or scientific evidence that would definitely resolve the controversy one way or the other. Although internal evidence derived from an arguer's position may always be weaker than external evidence, sometimes, where it is hard to decide on a controversial topic, weak evidence may be enough to shift the burden of proof.

In such a case, if an arguer adopts a position that is open to a criticism of inconsistency, that may be enough to shift the burden of proof against his case. Such an arguer will be put on the defensive, and his credibility as an advocate of his side of the argument may then be questioned.

A fourth factor is that in some cases a successful argument against the person can render an arguer's impartiality, sincerity, or trustworthiness open to question. This may be a weak form of argument, but it may be enough to alter the burden of proof on a controversial issue. And therefore it can be a reasonable criticism.

On controversial issues, hard evidence that can be directly brought to bear on a disputed proposition may be lacking. In such a case, reasonable dialogue may be the only available way of deciding to accept a conclusion or not, short of deciding by random choice, or by following one's dogmatic inclinations. Here, understanding the arguer's positions both pro and con may help one to arrive at a more intelligent or reasoned decision on how to make a commitment, if a decision must be made. If an arguer's position is open to fair criticism of internal inconsistency, that could be a good reason for anyone to withhold acceptance of the arguer's conclusion.

In short, sometimes arguing against an opponent in argument by using his own concessions against his argument can be fair and reasonable, within limits. Such an argument may show that the arguer's position is inconsistent, and may thereby show that the arguer is not a credible advocate of the conclusion he purports to advance. However, an argument against the person does not show that his conclusion is necessarily false, in itself. At best, it shows that the position backing up the argument is open to challenge. In example 6.10, George's conclusion that private companies should be allowed to compete with the Post Office might, for all we know, be true. George may even be able to give some good reasons for it that anyone, even an anti-communist, would wish to take into account. Even so, Bob's criticism is a reasonable argument against the person in reply if it shows that this conclusion does not square with George's own political philosophy. That may be a good criticism, but of course it does not necessarily imply that George's conclusion is false. To so argue would be an incorrect use of the argument against the person. In short then, an argument against the person can sometimes be a reasonable criticism, but only within carefully drawn limits.

Traditionally, the argument against the person, or so-called *ad hominem* argument has been called a fallacy in many textbooks.[12] However, it is

12 See Govier (1983) and Walton (1985b).

more useful to make the following distinctions which allow for the argument against the person to be a reasonable criticism in some cases and an inadequately reasoned or supported criticism in other cases.[13] A *personal attack (personal allegation)* is said to have been advanced in argument where one arguer uses some personal allegations relative to the motives, personal circumstances, personal actions, and so forth, as a basis to criticize an opponent's argument. This form of attack can have three forms, the direct (abusive) personal attack, the circumstantial personal attack, and the attack on an arguer's impartiality. Such an attack becomes a *personal criticism of an argument* where evidence is given by the arguer to back up his personal attack on the argument criticized.

The evidence required for this criticism must fulfill various requirements if the criticism is to be reasonable in a given case. The more subtle and complex type of personal attack is the circumstantial type of instance, where care is needed to identify the nature of the alleged circumstantial inconsistency.

A *circumstantial attack against the person* occurs where an arguer questions the consistency of another arguer's position. A *circumstantial criticism* is advanced where the questioning arguer (1) pins down a specific set of propositions and gives some evidence that the other arguer is committed to these propositions as part of his argument or position, and (2) gives some reason to show that there is a danger of inconsistency, either circumstantial or logical, in these propositions. A *circumstantial refutation* occurs where a circumstantial criticism is successfully backed up by showing that the set of propositions in question is part of the other arguer's set of commitments, and does imply a logical contradiction by valid arguments. Various forms of error occur in a personal attack when the direct personal attack or circumstantial criticism is inadequately supported, and therefore fails either as a reasonable criticism or as a successful refutation of the argument in question. There are several specific types of failures, and we turn to these different types of error and shortcoming in the next section.

As a form of criticism, argument against the person has the effect of challenging an arguer's position and thereby putting that arguer's case on the defensive. All controversial argument is really a dialogue, and there are always two sides to a dialogue. The effect of an *ad hominem* reply in dialogue is to bounce the ball back into your opponent's court. However,

13 A deeply and carefully reasoned defence of the argument against the person as a kind of criticism that can be reasonable in some contexts of dialogue is given by Johnstone (1978).

the ultimate resolution of an argument against the person as a criticism that is successful, or itself open to criticism, is often highly dependent on the subsequent dialogue that takes place between the critic and the defender of the argument. Thus a good personal criticism may be successful if it opens up the channels of dialogue in articulating or exploring two opposed positions on a controversial issue.

Some arguments are more open to personal criticism than others. Consider the following argument.

Example 6.11

Skeptic: All arguments are relative to beliefs that can be challenged. Hence no argument is reliable.

This argument is open to the following personal, circumstantial reply to Skeptic: "What about your own argument (example 6.11) above, Skeptic? Is it reliable?" If Skeptic tries to insist that his argument is reliable, he is clearly in danger of personal inconsistency. For he has just maintained that no argument is reliable. How can he consistently make an exception for his own argument without being illogical? On the other hand, if Skeptic concedes that his own argument in example 6.11 is indeed unreliable, he is also in trouble on grounds of circumstantial inconsistency. For can he really be a sincere and competent participant in reasonable dialogue if he is advocating an argument which he knows to be unreliable? Either way, Skeptic is hoist by his own petard.

So some arguments, like example 6.11, are especially vulnerable to the circumstantial argument against the person as a form of criticism. In such cases, the argument against the person is the most reasonable and appropriate type of criticism to bring forward. In these cases, the argument against the person can successfully refute the argument. However, in many cases the argument against the person is inherently weaker. It is not a refutation in such cases, but nevertheless it can often be a reasonable form of challenge to an argument, and can successfully shift the burden of proof against it.

6.5 REPLYING TO A PERSONAL ATTACK

The argument against the person is not a total refutation in most cases, but a kind of argument that can be replied to by further argument which shifts the burden of proof back onto the attacker. Thus the argument against the person is in most cases a *defeasible criticism*, meaning that it is inherently open to a rejoinder that could defeat, or at least ward off the criticism. One way to reply to an argument against the person is for the respondent to come back, *tu quoque*, with a parallel personal argument against his critic. However, it needs to be realized that such arguments are inherently defeasible because it is always possible that an arguer can claim that his personal circumstances are different enough from those of his critic in some respect to destroy the parallel cited.

In example 6.4, the child's criticism of the parent's inconsistency in smoking while advocating non-smoking turned on the presumption that the parent is not treating himself and the child on the same basis. The parent smokes, but then tells the child he should not smoke. The child, by his allegation of circumstantial inconsistency, is in effect accusing the parent of treating his own personal circumstances, and those of the child he criticizes, on an unequal basis. But notice that it is possible that the parent could cite some relevant difference between his own circumstances and those of the child. Suppose the parent informs the child that he, the parent, is suffering from AIDS, a terminal disease, and that smoking will not significantly affect his prognosis or prospects for health. Whereas, the parent might maintain, smoking in the child's circumstances could radically affect his prospects for a healthy life.

The prospect of new information about the personal circumstances of an arguer entering into the dialogue, in the case of an argument against the person, is made possible because this type of criticism is often more like a questioning than a decisive refutation of an arguer's position. The following case will illustrate how question-reply dialogue is the natural context of the argument against the person, and how this defeasible argument is subject to the reply that the defender's situation is different from that of his attacker.

Example 6.12

Parliamentarian A: Can you assure the public that there will be no increase in interest rates tomorrow?

Parliamentarian B: This is a ludicrous question coming from the Hon. Member who was a minister when his previous Government was pushing interest rates up to 20 and 25 per cent per annum.

B's reply is a circumstantial personal attack. B alleged that during the period when A's party was in power, there was a 20 to 25 per cent increase in interest rates. Given A's personal track record in this regard, B alleged, it is ludicrous for him to request assurance that there will be no rise in interest rates. In other words, B is replying with the classical *tu quoque* circumstantial argument that A does not "practice what he preaches." One reason that this particular example of the use of the argument against the person is novel and interesting however, is that the argument is used in reply to a question. It is a combination of two traditional types of informal fallacies, which shows how the argument against the person can be used in dialogue to powerfully attack a question.

What B is arguing is that A has no right to ask this question, because if A were in B's situation, he couldn't answer the question himself. How reasonable is B's reply? To begin with, there do appear to be good grounds for criticizing B's reply as not conducive to the goals of reasonable dialogue. The reason is that B's clever personal attack effectively avoids the real issue of interest rates by attacking A, and thereby avoiding the necessity of answering the question. By attacking A's question, he has shifted the burden of reply back against A's side of the argument, thereby appearing to make A somehow vulnerable to his own criticism. From this point of view, B's reply can be construed as evasive, or at any rate as a failure to answer the question. But that is not the end of the matter.

If a question is not fair, or contains a loaded presupposition, it is generally reasonable to allow the answerer to reply by questioning the question instead of giving a direct answer. In such a case, a failure to answer the question need not be a wrongful evasion. Now one might observe here that A's question is fairly aggressive. A certain degree of short-term fluctuation in interest rates has become fairly normal in the recent economic climate. Therefore a question requesting assurance that there will be no increase in interest rates on a specific day may not be all that reasonable, relative to the context of this particular dialogue. Moreover, it would probably be politically unwise for parliamentarian B to guarantee that there will be no increase on any particular day in future. For one thing, he most likely has very little or no control over this specific fluctuation or stability. So he dare not answer 'yes,' but if he answers 'no,' he also concedes something that may appear negative, or may be open to further criticism. The question is not as forcefully aggressive as the celebrated spouse-beating question, but it is sufficiently aggressive that one can see the resemblance.

Observing the aggressiveness of the question then, a critic could argue that B's not answering the question should not be judged unduly evasive. By replying with a circumstantial citation of rising interest rates during the questioner's own time in power, B's reply could be interpreted as quite justifiably criticizing the presumptions of the question. And if B

196

feels, with reason, that he can't directly answer the question without being unreasonably forced to damage or undermine his own position or that of his party, then he should have the right to challenge the basis of the question. Indeed, some might say that B is doing the right thing here as a critical reasoner, instead of submitting to a question that has implications that could be misleading.

Since the argument against the person can be a reasonable way of criticizing an arguer's position, B's questioning of A's question can be defended as a reasonable reply. Although B did not answer the question, and although his reply was a personal attack, it does not follow that B has committed an error or given a bad reply in the dialogue.

This case at once illustrates the wisdom of being careful not to give in too easily to the temptation to shout "Fallacy!" without looking at both sides of an argument carefully and the need to look at each case individually on its merits. Now that we have considered how B replied to A, it might be useful to go even further in the dialogue to ask how A might reasonably be able to respond to B's reply. Consider the following hypothetical extension of the dialogue.

> Parliamentarian A: When the previous Government was in power, the world inflationary pressures were at their peak. These high interest rates, at that time, affected all currencies, and were not due to our fiscal policies in particular. At present, the fiscal situation is very different, and it is possible for the Government to keep interest rates down.

By this reply, A is arguing that his initial question was reasonable, and that the parallel drawn by B between his own situation and the previous situation of A's Government is not reasonable.

It is as if B is arguing: "When you were in the same situation you did the very thing you now criticize me for doing, and so you are inconsistent." Whereas A is arguing: "I was not in the same situation – my situation was different from yours – so my criticizing your action is not inconsistent." So the issue of whether the allegation of circumstantial inconsistency can be supported or not depends on the similarity between the two situations, the particular circumstances of A and B.

Ultimately the resolution of the reasonableness of the personal attack as a reply in the dialogue depends on the evidence of whether the personal situation of the one arguer is similar to that of the other in the relevant respect. What our evaluation of example 6.12 has shown is that each individual case of an argument against the person needs to be examined in light of the personal circumstances alleged to be parallel. Thus the

197

argument against the person is defeasible as long as there remains the possibility of the defence that the two sets of circumstances are different in some significant respect.

This is perhaps not too surprising since, as we saw in section 6.2, the resolution of an allegation of circumstantial inconsistency may depend on how an action is to be described. This in turn may depend on the particulars of the situation in which the action was alleged to be carried out.

6.6 CRITICAL QUESTIONS FOR AN
AD HOMINEM ARGUMENT

The *argumentum ad hominem* is essentially a negative kind of argumentation – it is a form of attack or criticism which is applied by one participant in dialogue against the argument of another participant. An *ad hominem* attack can be applied to any kind of argument, but is especially appropriate and effective when external (objective) evidence for the argument is weak or lacking. In such a case, the *ad hominem* criticism attacks the internal, or subjective support of the argument by questioning the reliability, veracity, internal coherence, or impartiality of the arguer himself.

The following is a checklist of critical questions that should be answered in evaluating any argument against the person. In section 6.7, following this checklist, an analysis is given of the four main kinds of error or shortcoming in arguments against the person.

1. Is the argument against the person posed in the form of a question? If so, and the respondent has made a reply to the question, is the reply a relevant answer? Note that even if the attack is made in the form of a question, the respondent may not necessarily be guilty of falla- cious evasion if he fails to give a direct answer to the question. In the sportsman's rejoinder, for example, a better answer is to question the presupposition of the question that the defender's position is inconsis- tent by virtue of his practice of eating meat. In some cases, a defender might also, for example, want to question the presupposition that he does eat meat. More information on the reasonableness or unreason- ableness of questions was given in chapter 2. For the present purpose, it is enough to see that if the question is unreasonable or unfairly aggressive in the dialogue, failure to answer it should not necessarily be evaluated as a fault or error on the part of the respondent.

2. Is the argument against the person a direct or circumstantial attack? If it is a direct attack, check critical questions 3 through 7 below. If it is a circumstantial attack, check points 8 through to the end of the list.

3. What is the critic's conclusion? Is he only questioning the arguer's contention, or is he claiming that it is false? Note that the latter claim is stronger, and requires stronger evidence.

4. Is there a rejection or questioning of the arguer's impartiality? If so, is reasonable evidence given? Are the reasons given strong enough to support the claim?

5. Has the critic rejected the arguer's reliability on one issue where his reliability on another subject has been questioned? If so, are the two topics closely enough relevant to each other to warrant the argument against the person as a strong argument?

6. Does the argument against the person tend to close off further dialogue by "poisoning the well"? If so, can it be "stood on its head" in reply?

7. How relevant are questions about personal character to the issue of the argument, if the attack turns on questions of the personal character of the arguer?

8. In evaluating any circumstantial argument against the person as a reasonable or unreasonable criticism, one must first of all attempt to identify the propositions that are alleged to be inconsistent. Clearly identify them from the given corpus of the argument.

9. Are the given propositions logically inconsistent? Collect together the set of propositions alleged to be inconsistent, and investigate whether they are logically inconsistent or not, as they stand. To show that they are logically inconsistent, you must deduce a contradiction from them by valid arguments. If this can't be done, go on to critical question 10.

10. Are the given propositions circumstantially inconsistent? If there is no logical inconsistency, then evaluate whether there are reasonable grounds for the claim that there is a circumstantial inconsistency in the defender's position. What sort of evidence does the given corpus offer for a claim of circumstantial inconsistency? Is the case strong or weak? Who is alleged to have committed the inconsistency? Often a group is referred to in an *ad hominem* allegation, for example, a profession or a political party. If some members of the group have engaged in certain practices, it need not follow that the defender is one of those members, or accepts all their policies.

11. How well specified is the defender's position? Could further dialogue spell out that position more specifically in relation to the conclusion

at issue? Does the defender's position commit him to certain propositions that could lead to a positional inconsistency, even if he has not explicitly accepted these propositions in his argument?

12. If the allegation of inconsistency is weak, what is the connection between the pair of propositions alleged to be the basis of the conflict in the defender's position? If the parallel is weak, or non-existent, does that mean that the personal attack can be classified as erroneous? See the following four types of shortcoming of the argument against the person.

13. If there is an inconsistency that can be established as part of the defender's position, how serious a flaw is this contradiction? Can the defender explain or resolve it very easily without destroying his position? What could be a plausible reply for the defender?

14. Does the defender have a legitimate opportunity to reply to the personal attack? Most arguments against the person can be answered by further dialogue, so it is important to prevent the criticism from being a conversation-stopper if the accused party can respond. Remember that most arguments against the person are not conclusive refutations, but they can reasonably shift the burden of argument onto the defender to reply.

15. Could the arguer who has been attacked by a circumstantial argument against the person cite a relevant difference in the two sets of personal circumstances alleged to be parallel in the attack?

16. If the defender has in fact replied to an *ad hominem* attack with another *ad hominem* attack, is there enough of a parallel to justify shifting the burden of proof back onto the attacker? In such a case, has a question been evaded or the issue avoided?

17. If a defence against an *ad hominem* attack involves a denial of inconsistency by taking a hard or dogmatic stance on the language used to describe the situations at issue, ask whether the terms used are being defined in a one-sided manner. Is the defender being consistent in his use of terms?

These seventeen critical questions are the main items that need to be considered in evaluating arguments against the person. In any given case, some questions on the list will be more significant than others, but the checklist provides an outline of the main critical guidelines in analyzing arguments against the person. Many violations of rules of persuasion dialogue are possible on both sides in disputed arguments against the person, but certain important errors are listed in the next section.

6.7 IMPORTANT TYPES OF ERROR TO CHECK

There are several distinct types of error or shortcoming that can be made in mounting a personal criticism against an arguer's position. The most basic type of error is to argue that there is a circumstantial inconsistency or questionable impartiality in an arguer's position, and then conclude from that personal criticism that the conclusion of the argument criticized must be false. This was the basic error in the child's argument in example 6.4. The child argued that the parent was circumstantially inconsistent – the parent argued against smoking, but his own practice was to smoke. Then the child concluded from that relative circumstantial inconsistency that the conclusion of the parent's argument could be absolutely dismissed. However, the mistake in this approach is to overlook the possibility that the parent's conclusion might be true. For as we noted, it might be possible that the parent could produce good evidence that smoking is linked to chronic lung disease, and is therefore unhealthy. The child's strong rejection does not leave enough room for this reply.

This first type of error is an extreme form of shortcoming in an argument against the person that may be called the *basic ad hominem fallacy* because it takes the strong stance that the argument criticized is totally refuted, and that its conclusion is absolutely false. However, it is fairly rare that an argument is open to this type of strong refutation as a basic *ad hominem* fallacy. Most arguments against the person are defeasible.

The second important kind of error occurs where the critic questions an argument by citing a plausible appearance of inconsistency in a circumstantial attack, but does not do enough work to make the inconsistency explicit. In this case, the critic may not have claimed to completely refute the argument he has attacked, but nevertheless if he hasn't been explicit in making a good case for a specific inconsistency, his argument may still be much weaker than he considers it to be.

The classic case of this second type of shortcoming, however, is the sportsman's rejoinder, "Why do you feed on the flesh of harmless cattle?" As we saw in studying example 6.5, there is no contradiction in eating meat and decrying the barbarous practice of hunting for sport or amusement. However, because there is a connection between these two actions, one might erroneously be tempted to conclude that the sportsman's rejoinder has strongly challenged the meat-eater's argument position by showing a circumstantial inconsistency in it. If the sportsman purports to have strongly replied to his critic by his circumstantial attack, then he has committed this second type of error. The propositions he cites are in fact not even close to being circumstantially inconsistent. Much more argument would be needed to back up his criticism adequately. In this case the attack is in the form of a question. But the case for circumstantial inconsistency is so weak that the question is open to vigorous challenge, and should not reasonably be taken to shift the burden of proof.

This second kind of shortcoming, while less severe than the first, is still an error to watch for. It is the error of taking a personal attack to be a personal criticism without bridging the gap enough to give reasonably adequate support to shift the burden of proof required for a reasonable criticism. This shortcoming, like the first one, is a case of an argument that is taken to be stronger than its support merits.

The third type of error occurs where the issue of the personal attack is, or becomes, irrelevant to the proper issue of discussion in the dialogue. It is this third type of error that is most often associated with the direct (abusive) personal attack. Where an arguer's personal motives are questioned, it may be difficult for the critic to resist launching into an unwarranted or irrelevant personal attack on the character of his opponent.

The direct personal attack need not always be unreasonable in argument, but the more emotional and abusive it becomes, the more likely it is to become a diversion from the real issue, or even a shift to a different context of dialogue. Such attacks may fail either because they are altogether irrelevant to the issues or because they are too weakly relevant to sustain the strong rejection of an opponent's argument. In example 6.1, there might be some reason to question Nixon's integrity because of his resignation during the Watergate scandal. However, that issue is only weakly relevant to the trustworthiness of Nixon's statements on foreign policy relating to China. To strongly reject Nixon's policy arguments on China could be a mistake because of some doubts about his character, if Nixon's policy arguments were based on long experience and solid evidence.

The fourth type of error is to discount the reliability, integrity, or capability as a reasoned participant in argument of the person so heavily attacked that no room is left for further reply or discussion. The violation here is premature closure of the dialogue by "poisoning the well."

Any circumstantial or direct personal attack raises the question of the integrity or sincerity of the arguer who is attacked, because if someone does not practise what he preaches or has a hidden agenda, it becomes an open question whether he is being a hypocrite, not really saying what he truly believes. And we saw in section 6.3 that in some cases the personal attack even directly criticizes the impartiality, honesty, or reliability of an arguer by citing his questionable personal motives. We saw in several examples that this type of personal criticism can be reasonable, but that it is a weak form of argument that can go wrong if the attack is pushed forward too aggressively. Where this happens because the arguer is too heavily rejected as incompetent or untrustworthy, the fourth type of error has occurred. This type of shortcoming, like the first two, occurs where a criticism, in this case of an arguer's reasonableness or impartiality, is taken for a stronger criticism than the case warrants. For example, we noted that in example 6.7 it would be an error for Bob to conclude that Wilma's arguments on acid rain must be completely worthless despite the evidence she presented for them, because she is on the board of directors of a coal company. Although Bob may be right to question Wilma's impartiality, it does not necessarily follow that her arguments are completely worthless, and should be totally rejected from any further hearing or consideration.

All four types of error are variants of the same kind of fault: taking an argument against the person to be a stronger criticism than the evidence given to back it up really warrants. The argument against the person can be a reasonable argument in some cases. The problem is that it is such a powerful argument in everyday dialogue that there is a strong temptation to be overcome or bullied by it, instead of carefully examining how the attack was mounted. For, more soberly considered, the argument against the person is a form of criticism that requires careful justification, and the filling in of many steps to be properly backed up enough to strongly shift the burden of proof. The critical questioner must not go on the defensive too quickly in the face of this type of attack, and instead be prepared to pose specific critical questions in reply to the *ad hominem* attack.

6.8 SOME CASES FOR FURTHER DISCUSSION

Three further examples will illustrate some additional problems and dimensions of difficulty for discussion that concern the distinction between personal morality and expressed political policies of a person in political argumentation. Each example of these three cases poses a specific problem for the reader to reflect on.

Example 6.13

A Minister of Parliament admitted saving a large amount of money through a "quick-flip" tax shelter. However, his own political party had long been vociferously critical of the "tax dodges for the wealthy" allegedly favored by their conservative opposition. This Minister belonged to a socialist party that had been very critical of the wealthy who take advantages of tax loopholes.

Indeed, the Minister explicitly said that he had been long opposed to tax breaks like the one he personally took advantage of.

The Conservative Leader of the Opposition called this behavior hypocritical, because it was a case of preaching one thing and doing another. He argued that this tax "scam" was undertaken by a member of a government that claimed to be the "champion of the little guy," yet who was "first at the trough" to take advantage of a tax loophole.

The socialist Minister defended his position, however, that his actions and principles were not inconsistent. By taking advantage of tax breaks, he claimed, he was "operating within the system," and at the same time, he maintained, he was being consistent all along and was still arguing that the system should be changed. His position was that he was operating within the law, and therefore need have no qualms about taking advantage of the tax laws, even though he was against those laws. He cited the difference between legality and personal morality as vindicating his consistency of position.

The Leader of the Opposition disagreed, insisting that the Minister has damaged his own credibility and integrity, and the credibility of his party as well. He expressed the view that a Government Minister must personally maintain his expressed standards of ethical conduct, and not contravene them by his own personal actions, or else suffer a loss of credibility as a political spokesman.

The basic problem with this example is that although the Leader of the Opposition would appear to have a strong case for a criticism of circumstantial inconsistency by the previous guidelines of this chapter, still the Minister criticized has some grounds for rebuttal. In effect, he is accusing his critic of a confusion, an equivocation between matters of public policy and private morality. Does he have a way out?

He might have argued that legal rules or political policies are forged through compromise and majority pressures. And therefore, he might argue, in a pluralistic democracy with freedom of thought and religion, questions of personal morality and conscience are private matters, and therefore may be different from public policies one adheres to. This distinction has been persuasively cited in politics, as the next example illustrates.

As background to the following case, the reader might like to consult Kenneth L. Woodward, 'Politics and Abortion' (*Newsweek*, August 20, 1984, pp. 66–67), and Mario M. Cuomo, 'Religious Belief and Public Morality' (*New York Review of Books*, October 25, 1984, pp. 32–37).

Example 6.14

A Catholic politician running for a high federal office declared that she supported freedom of choice on the abortion issue, even though, as a Catholic, she personally opposed abortion. She argued that her personal views were not in conflict with her position on public policy. A Catholic Bishop criticized this stance as illogical, replying that he did not see how a good Catholic, who should be against the taking of human life, can vote for a politician who supports abortion. She replied that as a Catholic she does not personally support abortion, but that she feels she has no right to impose that view on others, who may have different religious viewpoints. She stated that her political support of reproductive freedom of choice is logically consistent with her personal opposition to abortion because of the separation of church and state.

This type of case poses a kind of paradox. For if one is committed to deeply held moral principles concerning ethical conduct or religious belief, that personal conviction cannot be completely irrelevant to one's political stances on matters of public policy. Yet if public policies are matters of group agreement and concessions that may have to involve some degree of tolerance and compromise, there may be room for explanation of apparent practical inconsistencies between personal commitments and political commitments to social policies.

Questioning the arguer's motives can be a weak but reasonable form of criticism of an argument in some cases. However, this form of challenge can be carried to excess, and it is in just such a case that an irrelevant attack constitutes an incorrect type of argument against the person. An example cited by Brinton (1985, p. 56) provides a case for how an initially reasonable *ad hominem* criticism can go wrong. Such cases often degenerate into direct personal abuse, indicating a dialectical shift.

Example 6.15

The subject of debate in the U.S. Congress in 1813 was the New Army Bill, a proposal to raise more troops for the war against England. The majority, led by Speaker of the House Henry Clay, argued that an invasion of Canada with these additional troops would help to win the conflict. Josiah Quincy, speaking for the opposition on January 5, 1813, argued that the additional troops would be insufficient, that an invasion of Canada would be unsuccessful and immoral, that a conquest of Canada would not force England to negotiate, and finally that the bill was politically motivated, "as a means for the advancement of objects of personal or local ambition of the members of the American Cabinet." (Annals of the Congress of the United States, Comprising the Period from November 2, 1812, to March 3, 1818, Inclusive [Washington, D.C.: Gales and Seaton, 1853], pp. 540–570)

In his speech, Quincy backed up his last argument that the advocates of the bill were not to be trusted because of their hidden motives. He cited facts

205

to support his allegation that the most outspoken supporters of the bill were motivated by personal ambition. This last argument then is clearly a personal attack on the motives of the bill's supporters. Could it be a reasonable argument against the person?

The answer is that it is a weak form of argument. But even if the other arguments advanced by Quincy could be stronger, this personal argument also has some legitimate weight, if Quincy has given good reasons to support his contention that the advocates of the bill are behind it, to a significant extent, because it favors their personal interests. For when a country is at war, the interests of the country should be foremost in the deliberations of Congress. If personal interests play a role in somebody's argument, then that arguer may not be taking a balanced and impartial approach to the issue of the larger fate of the nation. Thus the arguer's impartial judgment may reasonably be questioned in such a case. Quincy's conclusion is not that the bill should be defeated exclusively because of his personal criticism, but that the opinions of the other party should carry less weight than they would apart from his criticism of his opponent's personal position on the issue.

However, when Quincy went on in his speech, he is reported to have called his opponents "toads, or reptiles, which spread their *slime on the drawing room floor*" (p. 599). Here he has gone too far, and resorted to direct personal abuse. In short then, criticism of an arguer's motives can be a reasonable if weak argument in some cases. But when it is carried too far, the argument can cease to be a relevant one, and it can become an abusive personal attack that is not justifiable in reasonable dialogue.

The last example is based on an article that appeared in the *National Post* (October 14, 2005, p. A10). It would be better to read the whole article, but here only a brief summary of the main argument is presented.

Example 6.16

Rocco DiSpirito, a New York chef and best-selling food author, made famous as the star of the NBC reality show *The Restaurant*, wrote a public letter supporting a campaign by the U.S. Humane Society to end the Canadian seal hunt. The article quoted Mr. DiSpirito as saying, "Most of the seal clubbers [in Canada] are also snow crabbers. By refusing to use Canadian or Canadian-sourced snow crab in our restaurants, we can make a very vocal statement against the seal hunt." The Humane Society had been lobbying for an American boycott of Canadian seafood, especially snow crab from Atlantic Canada, advocating the boycott as an economic tactic to stop the seal hunt. Many American restaurants and seafood wholesalers had joined the boycott, pledging not to buy Canadian seafood. Newfoundland fishermen in the sealing industry replied by arguing that DiSpirito was a hypocrite for calling the seal hunt inhumane while serving *foie gras* made from the engorged livers of force-fed geese in his restaurant. This practice was officially banned in some European countries and California, where the humane society condemned it. Frank Pinhorn, managing director of the Newfoundland-based Canadian Sealers Association, was quoted as saying, "He's an absolute hypocrite, a man of double standards." Earl McCurdy, president of the Fish, Food and Allied Workers Union in St. John's was quoted as saying, "I think somebody who lives in a glass house shouldn't throw stones. It shows the hypocrisy of these celebrities, who know nothing about the seal hunt . . . if he wants to serve *foie gras* in his restaurants, that's fine with me, but he shouldn't pass judgment on us." John Grandy, senior vice-president of the Humane Society, defended the chef. He was quoted as saying, "Absolutely the society is opposed to *foie gras*, but this issue is about seals, and a man of his distinction and abilities, who is simply appalled at the brutal destruction of these seals, well, *if* we can use him on the seals issue, we're happy to do so."

It is not hard to identify the *ad hominem* argument in this case. The chef put forward an argument for refusing to use Canadian or Canadian-sourced snow crab in restaurants in order to make a vocal statement against the Canadian seal hunt. His reasoning was that the seal hunt is inhumane, and that taking this action about the importation of Canadian seafood would make a statement against the importation of this seafood that would help to stop the seal hunt. The argument in example 6.16 attacks the chef's argument using the following circumstantial *ad hominem* argument.

Premise 1: The chef advocates the proposition that inhumane treatment of animals should be stopped.
Premise 2: The chef is personally committed to the opposite of this proposition, as shown by commitments expressed in his personal actions or circumstances of serving *foie gras* made from the livers of force-fed geese (something generally accepted as an inhumane practice).
Premise 3: The chef's credibility as a sincere person who believes in his own argument has been put into question (by premises 1 and 2).
Conclusion: The plausibility of the chef's argument has been put into doubt.

This circumstantial *ad hominem* argument uses premises 1 and 2 to support the interim conclusion that the chef is a hypocrite. Since a hypocrite is someone of bad ethical character, by *ad hominem* argument it can be concluded that the chef's argument is not plausible. For the chef is advocating the ethical proposition that the inhumane treatment of animals should be stopped, but he himself engages in the inhumane treatment of animals by serving *foie gras* in his restaurants. How can he plausibly argue for this conclusion when he himself has been shown to be an unethical person by his hypocrisy? Not only is he doing something that is wrong, and which has been widely condemned, but he has the temerity to pose as an ethical person while condemning a practice that he himself engages in.

This example is a good one for discussion because not only is it put forward strongly, but there is so much in it to discuss and analyze. One aspect for discussion is that several individuals actively put forward the *ad hominem* argument used to attack the chef's previous argument. This shows that even though several individuals are involved, there are basically two sides to the dialogue. First, there is the argument put forward by the chef, and then there is the *ad hominem* attack used to criticize his argument and to try to undermine its plausibility.

7

Appeals to authority

The *ad hominem* attack is the negative use of personal argumentation to undermine or destroy the credibility of a person in a critical discussion. An opposite type of tactic is the argument from expert opinion,[1] which uses the opinion of a respected authority or expert on a subject as positive personal argumentation to support one's own side of an argument. The *ad hominem* criticism attacks a person as an untrustworthy source, while the argument from expert opinion cites an expert who is presumably reliable and authoritative as a source of advice. In certain respects however, these two types of argumentation are similar. Both are appeals to personal sources of opinion that center on the internal position or credibility of a particular individual as a reliable source of knowledge. Both types of argumentation can be contrasted with the appeal to external or objective knowledge, which comes from scientific evidence such as experimental observations, the kind of knowledge that comes from nature, not from a personal source.

In general, the use of argument from expert opinion is a reasonable, if inherently defeasible, type of argument. Appeals to expert opinion can be a legitimate form of obtaining advice or guidance for drawing tentative conclusions on an issue or problem where objective knowledge is unavailable or inconclusive. It is well recognized in law, for example, where expert testimony is treated as an important kind of evidence in a trial, even though it often leads to conflicting testimony, in a "battle of the experts." And argument from expert opinion is now highly familiar in computer science through uses of expert systems. This technology has applications to all kinds of domains of expert knowledge. So there is nothing wrong, in principle, with backing up your argument by appealing to an expert opinion.

Such an argument is so powerful, in many cases however, that it can be very tempting to deploy it too crudely or aggressively in order to stifle disagreement unfairly. Authority-based arguments can become questionable or fallacious when they are misused as tactics to try to beat an opponent

---

1 Argument from expert opinion is also often called appeal to expert opinion in the logic textbooks. We will treat them as equivalent names for the same kind of argument.

into submission or silence by appealing to an inflated respect or reverence for authority. The famous Milgram experiments in psychology (Milgram 1974) showed how experimental subjects deferred to a scientific expert, even carrying out actions that would cause pain or injury to persons said to be experimental subjects, if ordered to do so by an experimenter thought to be a scientific authority.[2]

The phrase *argumentum ad verecundiam* literally means "the argument from modesty," and it was John Locke who evidently first used this phrase to refer to a kind of error or deceptive tactic that can be used by one person in discussion with another.[3] In the chapter 'Of Wrong Assent, or Error' of his *An Essay Concerning Human Understanding* (1690), Locke described the *argumentum ad verecundiam* as a sort of argument that a person can use, in reasoning with another person, to "prevail on the assent" of that other person, or to "silence his opposition." This way of prevailing is to allege the opinion of a third person who has "gained a name" and settled his reputation in the "common esteem" with some kind of authority. According to Locke, "When men are established in any kind of dignity, it is thought a breach of modesty for others to derogate any way from it, and question the authority of men who are in possession of it."[4] Thus anyone who does not "readily yield to the determination of approved authors" may be portrayed as impudent or insolent by the arguer who is using the *argumentum ad verecundiam* to prevail on his assent in an argument.

Locke does not claim that all appeals to authority in argumentation are fallacious, however.[5] The fallacy he describes is the misuse of an appeal to an authoritative source to try to prevail unfairly, or to "silence the opposition" in a discussion. Locke's approach will be supported by the conclusions of this chapter. There can be legitimate appeals to a third-party authoritative source when two people reason together in a critical discussion, but fallacies can occur when one party presses too hard in deploying authority to try to suppress the critical questioning of the other party.

---

2 In this classic experiment the subject is told he is going to participate in an experiment to test learning behavior. He is asked to administer electrical shocks to a learner each time the learner makes a mistake, and to increase the severity of the shock each time. The learner is really an actor who fakes discomfort, and even considerable pain, as the severity of the shocks increases. In Milgram's early experiment, 60 percent of subjects administered a final 450 volt shock, and these results were later replicated by other psychologists.
3 Hamblin (1970, p. 159).
4 This passage from Locke's *Essay* is quoted in full in Hamblin (1970, p. 159f.).
5 Ibid., pp. 159–160.

7.1 REASONABLE APPEALS TO AUTHORITY

Although appeals to authority can be erroneous, it must also be recognized that some appeals to authority can be reasonable and legitimate in argument. For example, suppose you have a toothache, and you go to your dentist for advice. He replies as follows.

Example 7.0

This tooth is badly decayed, but not beyond repair. I propose to replace the decayed portion with a filling immediately.

Your dentist's advice in example 7.0 is the judgment of a suitably qualified expert in his field. In asking for his or her advice, therefore, you have appealed to an expert authority. However, it by no means follows that by acquiescing to his proposal you have committed a fallacy. It could be that your dentist's advice is eminently reasonable, and you would be wise to take it, and act on it soon. That does not mean that if you have any reason to question his judgment, his advice, his competence, or his qualifications, you should not get a second opinion. For any appeal to authority is best treated as fallible, a form of plausible argument. However, it does remain that some arguments based on the say-so of authorities can be highly reasonable, even excellent arguments. The point is then that appeals to expertise are not intrinsically fallacious, even if they can be erroneous in some cases, when misinterpreted, taken too seriously, or taken uncritically.

It is important to realize that the term 'authority' contains an important ambiguity. One meaning is that of *administrative authority*, which is a kind of right to exercise command over others or make rulings binding on others through an invested or recognized position or office of power. A second meaning of authority refers to expertise in a domain of knowledge or skill, and expertise may be very different from administrative authority in many instances. Wilson (1983, p. 13) calls the authority of expertise *cognitive authority*, a relationship between two individuals where what the one says carries weight or plausibility, within a certain domain or field of expertise, for the other individual.

The two kinds of authority are very different in nature, even though in some instances the same individual may possess or convey both kinds of authority. Take the example of a physician who certifies a person as fit to possess a driver's license according to the legally required standards as determined by a physician's examination. In making such a judgment, the doctor is arriving at a conclusion based on medical expertise. His pronouncement is therefore based on his cognitive authority as a medical expert. However, his ruling is also an instance of the exercise of administrative authority, for it is his being a licensed physician that confers on him the right, and perhaps also the obligation, to make this official and binding pronouncement.

It is important to make this distinction because there is often an immediate feeling of resentment or hostility to the idea of authority. By confusing the two meanings of 'authority,' we may be led to exaggerate our feeling that all authority, of any sort, is somehow fallacious or contrary to reasoned argument and scientific investigation.

Good scientific method is based on the idea of reproducible evidence. In other words, it is better to do an experiment yourself than rely on the say-so of someone else who has done it and claimed certain results. But does that mean we should always mistrust and reject the say-so of an authority as fallacious? It need not, if our reliance on cognitive authority is only regarded as a means of supplementing experimental investigation in those cases where an immediate decision is required and independent experimental investigation is not possible or practical.

Example 7.1

The captain of a ship surveying for wrecks in the South China Sea discovers a heap of antique porcelain in a submerged wreck, and has it hauled aboard. It is blue and white Chinese porcelain that might be old and valuable. There is only one way to be sure. The captain calls in an expert, an authority on Chinese ceramics. The expert surveys the find and pronounces his opinion: "Definitely eighteenth century. Probably late Ming and Traditional Period Chinese porcelain." On this advice, the captain continues to probe the wreck for further treasure.[6]

In this case, subsequent study of the porcelain will determine whether the expert was right or wrong. But at the moment, the captain must make a decision whether to continue his search. So if he has chosen a well-qualified and reliable expert on porcelain, his reliance on this cognitive authority as a source of advice could be a reasonable conclusion in making a decision on how to proceed.

Of course, later scientific investigation of the findings will bear out the expert's judgment or not. In the absence of this scientific confirmation,

6 This example is loosely based on content of an article by John Dyson, 'Captain Hatcher's Fabulous Sunken Treasure,' *Reader's Digest*, November 1986, 63–67.

the captain may be making a good decision by acting on the presumption that the expert is right.

In contrasting the uses of subjective versus objective sources of evidence in reasoning, it is well to be clear that in some cases, testing an appeal to expertise by experiment may not be practically feasible or wise.

Example 7.2

On a very cold day in Northern Canada, a mother runs outside when she is told that her daughter has her tongue stuck to a metal flagpole.

Mother: I've told you a hundred times not to put your fingers or your tongue on very cold metal. I told you that if you did, you would get stuck to it. Why did you put your tongue on the flagpole?

Daughter: I wanted to see if it was true.[7]

In this case, the desire to test the logic of the mother's argument by experiment might indicate a laudable interest in scientific investigation. At the same time, it suggests the wisdom of paying attention to a subjective source of advice if it is based on valuable experience, where experiment may not be practical in the given situation.

This case also illustrates that not all reasonable appeals to authority are based on expertise in a narrow, well-defined domain of professional experience. Some appeals of this sort can be based on a claim to a special position to know about a particular situation or set of facts. For example, if foreign policy requires making a decision about political conditions in a certain foreign country, it may be a good idea to consult with persons who have had the experience of recently living in that country. Such persons may not be experts in the sense of being political scientists, but they may be in a special position to know about current political conditions in that country at present. Because they are in a special position to know, from the point of view of those attempting to formulate foreign policy relative to these conditions, the advice of these consultations could reasonably be given a special status akin to expert judgment. Again, their opinions should not be treated as the absolute truth, and they may be questioned in many cases. Yet in dialogue, some judgments of those who are in a special position to know, by virtue of their experience in relevant matters, may be taken as more plausible than the judgments of those without the requisite experience.

7 This example is a paraphrase of some of the dialogue in a cartoon strip by Lynn Johnston, "For Better or Worse," *Winnipeg Free Press*, January 3, 1987, p. 15.

In this chapter, we are primarily concerned with cognitive authority. Cognitive authority is always relative to a domain of knowledge or experience in which the expert's judgment can be given greater weight or burden in argument than the layperson who lacks equivalent experience or knowledge in this particular domain. However, the asymmetry that gives rise to the expert-layperson relationship is defined not only by the expertise of the expert, but also by the ignorance of the one who uses expert advice. The general practitioner who consults the specialist is taking the advice of an expert, but his relationship to the specialist may be quite different from that of the medical layman who consults the same specialist on the same question.

The reason that appeals to authority have been traditionally mistrusted in science as a source of argument is that such appeals are inherently subjective. The expert bases his judgment on rules of thumb and accepted methods for carrying out procedures that he and other experts have found to be useful in their practical experience of working in their special area. It may be difficult, or in some cases even impossible, for the expert to translate his practical experience or judgment into hard evidence that can be explicitly and completely described to a layperson. Since the expert's judgment is really based on his professional training, long experience, and practical know-how, his conclusion is, in an important respect, an individual and subjective judgment, from the point of view of the layman who acts on his advice.

However, science has traditionally questioned such a supposedly subjective appeal as good evidence or hard evidence in confirmation of hypotheses. This is because it is important for scientific hypotheses to be confirmed by experimental verification that is reproducible and that can be confirmed objectively by empirical evidence or mathematical calculations. Hence appeals to expertise, being essentially subjective and judgmental, have often been systematically rejected as a reliable source of knowledge.

There are good reasons for a certain mistrust of evidence obtained by appeal to authority. The strongest form of argument is the deductively valid argument. The acme of scientific knowledge is the axiomatic system, in which the only proof of a hypothesis is the deduction of that hypothesis by valid arguments from clear or well-established propositions called axioms. A weaker form of argument is inductive confirmation. A hypothesis is said to be inductively confirmed if it is based on evidence that is highly probable. Both types of evidence are objective, but the appeal to expertise fits neither of these patterns and, as we have seen, is inherently subjective. Therefore, an argument based on the appeal to expert judgment should be rejected or discarded if deductive proof or inductive confirmation of the proposition in question can be given.

Moreover, because appeals to expertise are based on plausible reasoning, in practice they should be generally treated as arguments that can shift a burden of proof, but are inherently weak and subject to questioning. Experts can be subject to the same kinds of bias and prejudice that were studied in connection with arguments against the person in chapter 6. If an expert has something to gain by taking one side of an argument, or is even being paid to argue for one side – as frequently happens in courtroom disputes – then pointing out this potential for bias may be a legitimate criticism.

The law allows that expert testimony (e.g., that of a ballistics expert) can be a reasonable form of evidence to be considered in a trial. Thus legal standards of evidence accept appeals to scientific expertise as necessary and reasonable in many cases. However, there do remain many questions about how expert opinion arguments should be evaluated. And as we will see, there are many problems here, and some dramatic cases in which arguments from expertise have gone quite wrong in courtroom decision making.

Another area that has increased acceptance of the concept of expert reasoning as a distinctive and intrinsically reasonable form of argument is the development of expert systems in the field of artificial intelligence. Expert systems are computer programs that duplicate the skills of an expert in a well-defined area of expertise. Expert systems are widely used in medical diagnosis, geology, electrical troubleshooting, and many other industries. For example, expert systems that incorporate the knowledge of senior automotive engineers who have helped design, or are familiar with, particular vehicles are used to advise mechanics who work on that type of vehicle. It is a way one expert (the mechanic) can take advantage of the specialized skill and experience of experts by asking questions and receiving programmed answers from a computer terminal. These developments have tended to counteract the older ideas that appeal to expertise is inherently erroneous or fallacious, now that the practical usefulness of expert systems has been well established.

7.2 ARGUMENTATION SCHEME FOR APPEAL TO EXPERT OPINION

Because it is a defeasible, and therefore often a weak form of argument, appeal to expertise has, in the past, often been mistrusted as a fallacious form of argument. And to be sure, if the appeal to authority ignores better evidence for a conclusion based on harder evidence, it can be fallacious. Nonetheless, in many cases, appeal to the expertise of a legitimate authority can be a reasonable argument.

The expert consultation dialogue is a subspecies of the knowledge elicitation type of dialogue, and is different from the type of dialogue called the inquiry. The inquiry is proof-seeking and both (or all) parties to the inquiry are (relatively) ignorant. In the expert consultation one party is ignorant, called the layperson, and the other party is an expert in a certain discipline or topic area. The goal is for the non-expert party to get pertinent advice from the expert. The initial situation is a need for expert advice, and informed (intelligent) action is a benefit or potential outcome of the expert consultation.

However, the most characteristic, primary context of argumentation where the *argumentum ad verecundiam* is a problem is the persuasion dialogue. In this type of dialogue, the goal of the proponent is to persuade a respondent that the proponent's thesis (point of view) is true (right), but when the proponent appeals to the opinion of an expert, he brings in a third party to the context of the argument.

Typically, two participants – let us call them Black and White – are engaged in persuasion dialogue, when one of them attempts to back up his side of the argument by citing the opinion of an expert authority. Let us say that White backs up his argument by claiming that an expert, Green, has vouched for the proposition that White is maintaining. This move in the persuasion dialogue (between Black and White) has been advanced by White with the objective of persuading Black. Or let's say that White's strategy is evidently to put forward his argument strongly and forcibly so that it will be overwhelming against Black's side.

Once such a move has been made, it implies the existence of a secondary knowledge-elicitation dialogue interchange between White and the expert Green, whose advice or opinion has been used in argument by White. The existence of this secondary context of dialogue can be inferred, because every *ad verecundiam* type of argument from expert authority involves a secondary dialogue between the expert and the user of the expert's opinion. The critical questions appropriate for this secondary dialogue are given in section 7.3.

The internal type of reasoning built into an expert system is *knowledge-based reasoning*, meaning that it draws its premises from a set of facts and rules (or frames) called a *knowledge base*. There is nothing inherently illicit or fallacious in this type of reasoning. Neither is there anything fallacious or illicit per se in the use of conclusions drawn by an expert (or expert system) in order to solve a problem, answer a question, or back up an opinion in argumentation. Argumentation based on solicitation of an opinion from knowledge-based expert sources is a species of plausible reasoning which has a legitimate function of shifting a burden of proof in interactive argumentation (dialogue).

Whether the appeal to expert opinion is used reasonably or fallaciously by a proponent, it is based on the respondent's commitment to expert opinion as representing a kind of knowledge-based premise that can be used as evidence in a dialogue as a form of argumentation. In Walton (1997, p. 258), it is shown how an appeal to expert opinion can be a reasonable argument that has the following form, where A is a proposition, E is an expert, and D is a domain of knowledge.

E is an expert in domain D
E asserts that A is known to be true
A is within D
Therefore, A may plausibly be taken to be true

The three premises in the scheme represent assumptions that, if made in a given case, warrant the drawing of a presumptive inference to the conclusion indicated. When a proponent of the proposition A in a dialogue uses an argument fitting the scheme for argument from expert opinion to support her claim, a weight of presumption in favor of A is placed on the commitment set of the respondent to whom the argument was directed. Seen in this presumptive and dialectical way, the appeal to expert opinion is evaluated as a defeasible kind of argument that can put a weight of presumption behind a contention in a dialogue, but is subject to rebuttal and defeat by critical questioning.

7.3 CRITICAL QUESTIONS FOR THE APPEAL TO EXPERT OPINION

Like other fallacies we have studied, the problem is to sort out the fallacious or questionable instances from the more reasonable instances of the appeal to expert opinion. The following six critical questions must be kept in mind when evaluating any appeal to authority. A reasonable appeal to authority must satisfy all the requirements cited in these six questions. If a particular requirement is violated by an appeal to authority, then the appeal should be criticized or questioned in this regard. To shift this weight of presumption back to the other side, the respondent must ask at least one of the following six critical questions (Walton 1997, p. 25).

1. *Expertise Question*: How credible is E as an expert source?
2. *Field Question*: Is E an expert in the field that A is in?
3. *Opinion Question*: What did E assert that implies A?
4. *Trustworthiness Question*: Is E personally reliable as a source?
5. *Consistency Question*: Is A consistent with what other experts assert?
6. *Backup Evidence Question*: Is E's assertion based on evidence?

If the respondent asks any one of these critical questions, the burden of proof is shifted back onto the proponent to answer the question. If the proponent fails to give an adequate answer, then by default, the appeal to expert opinion loses whatever weight of support it had. However, if the proponent manages to give an adequate answer to the question asked by the respondent, the appeal to expert opinion once again has a weight of presumption in its favor, so that it supports the claim that A is (plausibly) true.

The problem is to get the right kind of balance between the two sides, so that no legitimate moves of argument or attempts to raise appropriate critical question are stifled. The best method for making such a determination in a given case is the profiles of dialogue method. The fallacious type of case is one where the proponent of the appeal to expert opinion has pressed ahead too aggressively in the dialogue exchange, and not allowed the respondent enough room for raising appropriate critical questions at the right junctures in the dialogue sequence. Thus argumentation in a case can be evaluated by comparing an ideal sequence of questions and replies with the real sequence in the case. If the real sequence is in an incorrect order, or if the moves are of such a kind that the respondent's ability to ask critical questions is continually hemmed in and thwarted, this is the kind of case we should judge to be an instance of the *ad verecundiam* fallacy.

To say that E is credible as an expert source means that E has mastery of a domain of knowledge or skill. The first requirement of any appeal to authority is that the cited expert must actually be an expert, and not merely someone quoted because of their prestige, popularity, or celebrity status. There are five critical subquestions that are relevant to establishing whether someone can reasonably be called a legitimate expert in a particular field.

1. What degrees, professional qualifications, or certifications by licensing agencies does this person hold?

2. Can testimony and evaluations of colleagues or other experts be given to support his status?
3. Does the expert cited have a record of experience in the field or particular technique being discussed?
4. What is this individual's previous record of predictions or successful accomplishments in this field of expertise?
5. Can evidence be given of publications or other projects that have been evaluated, refereed, or reviewed by other authorities?

By responding to these five critical subquestions, the proponent should be able to give some reasons why the authority cited actually has the special competence to qualify as a legitimate expert. Many of the more superficial appeals to authority that are so commonplace in everyday reasoning simply fail to pass this test. Instead, the would-be authority is often cited more for reasons of celebrity status or personal popularity. In this type of case, the individual cited may not be an expert at all.

Another consideration relating to the first critical question is just how authoritative a particular expert is. Even if the individual cited is a legitimate expert in the field in which the question lies, there still remains the question of how strongly the appeal should be taken as a plausible argument. Because someone is quoted as an expert on some controversy or problem by the media, that should not mean that the final word has been said, even if this person is truly an expert. An appeal to authority can be reasonable (non-fallacious) yet weak, as arguments go.

The second question is whether the judgment put forward by the authority actually falls within the field of competence in which that individual is an expert. Some cases are clear violations here. If the expert is a physicist and the judgment is about religion, and has nothing to do with physics, then such an appeal should be rejected as of questionable value or relevance. In some cases, the appeal is so vague that the name of the would-be expert is not even given. This type of case should be criticized by asking for more documentation of its claim to expert authority.

In other cases, the relevance of a field of experience to a particular issue may be harder to judge. For example, suppose the issue is the health value of taking vitamin C. The views of a famous biochemist may lay some claim to expert value. But perhaps the judgment of a medical doctor who has done research on this topic would be more authoritative. Here, each case must be judged on its own merits from the information given. But one must be careful to question the credentials of an expert authority in relation to the specific issue. If the expert's field is only indirectly related to the issue, that could be grounds for caution, and critical questioning of the claim.

The third critical question arises from a legitimate concern whether the expert's quoted or reported opinion has been correctly interpreted. It must be in a form that is clear and intelligible, yet it must not be merely a simplistic re-wording of what the expert said, overlooking necessary qualifications or exceptions. Preferably, the expert should be quoted directly. If not, it could be reasonable to question whether his view has been presented fairly and accurately.

The fourth critical question concerns the ethical reliability of the source. For example, if this expert is untrustworthy and has been known to lie in the past, that would bring his ethical reliability into question. Or suppose an expert is employed by an agency that has something to gain financially by putting forward a particular opinion. In such a case we may correctly judge that the expert is biased and therefore we might think less of his opinion than otherwise we might have. It has been shown in Walton (1997, p. 217) that there are three critical subquestions that fall under the trustworthiness critical question.

Subquestion 1: Is E biased?
Subquestion 2: Is E honest?
Subquestion 3: Is E conscientious?

Bias, meaning failure to represent both sides of an issue in a balanced way, is an important factor in evaluating appeals to expert opinion. Bias is normal in argumentation. It is not always a bad thing. But an expert who gives advice, is supposed to try to avoid bias. If bias is found in what she says, her advice will be discounted and will be thought to be less likely to be right. Honesty is a matter of telling the truth, as the expert sees it. If an expert who gives advice is found to have lied, this finding can quite seriously detract from the worth of what she says. Conscientiousness is different from honesty, and refers to care in collecting sufficient information. If an expert has been shown to be sloppy or hasty in collecting data, that too can be quite a serious criticism.

Asking any of these critical questions in an examination dialogue can lead to argumentation of a kind that seems more like that typical in a persuasion dialogue. For example, asking any one of the three critical subquestions above can easily lead into an *ad hominem* attack on the expert. This sort of shift is quite common in trials during examination of expert testimony. The examining defense lawyer, for example, may ask the expert witness if she is being paid to testify by the prosecution. If the witness admits she has received a fee, the examiner may then suggest to the jury that the witness is biased to one side in presenting her testimony. The rules of evidence allow this kind of *ad hominem* attack on a witness because the trustworthiness of a witness is regarded as relevant, although many kinds of character attack are barred by the rules of evidence as inadmissible.

The fifth critical question concerns the issue of whether there may be disagreement among several qualified authorities who have been consulted. Here there are several methods that may be used to resolve the disagreement. Usually, further dialogue among the experts is the best method, where this is possible or feasible. If there is inconsistency among the well-qualified experts whose advice has been appealed to, then the *ad verecundiam* is certainly open to question. However, such a case of inconsistency need not always be an indication of fallacy. For sometimes the inconsistency can be dealt with by further critical discussion or clarifications. However, it is in general a requirement of a successful appeal to authority that known pronouncements of other qualified authorities be consistent with the proposition cited as advocated by the expert appealed to. If not, the inconsistency must be resolved, or further questions raised.

The sixth critical question is whether objective evidence on the opinion cited is presently available, and whether the expert's opinion is based on it. First, we noted that the appeal to authority is no substitute for objective evidence in the form of experimental or direct scientific confirmation of the proposition at issue. If this sort of evidence is available, it should be given preference to the say-so of an authority, because inductive confirmation is generally a stronger form of argument than plausible reasoning. Second, we also noted that where experts disagree, they should be able to defend their position by citing objective evidence in their field.

If a respondent asks any of the six basic critical questions (Walton 1997, p. 223) appropriate for the appeal to expert opinion, the proponent must either give a satisfactory answer to the question asked, or else she must give up the appeal to expert opinion argument. The argumentation scheme and its set of matching critical questions are the tools that should be used to analyze and evaluate any given case in which appeal to expert opinion has been used as an argument. The scheme identified the form of the argument and its premises. For the argument to be of this type, it must have the premises represented in this argumentation scheme. How strong the argument is taken to be in a given case depends on how well it stands up to critical questioning in the dialogue. There is a difference, however, between an argument that is merely weak, or poorly supported, and an argument that is fallacious.

The first step towards understanding the structure of this type of dialogue is realizing that the critical questions matching the argumentation scheme for appeal to expert opinion are the gateway through which the dialogue is filtered. To see how this works, let's once again consider the set of basic critical questions to see how they might apply to the kinds of expert dialogue we are so familiar with in everyday life. When someone like you or me is confronted with the task of questioning an expert, the task can be highly intimidating. For example, suppose your doctor recommends some kind of treatment like surgery that has serious side effects and will affect your health very significantly. It is hard to question the doctor. He is the expert, and you are dependent on his care. Or suppose your dentist recommends that you have a root canal, an expensive kind of procedure that you have heard is often unnecessary. The dentist may even tell you that this procedure represents "optimal" care, suggesting perhaps that you may be able to get by without it. You know very little about dentistry. What should you do? It is easy to just go along with what the dentist says, and harder to question what he says, or try to find out more about why he recommends that course of action. If you go to another dentist for a second opinion, your original dentist may not be very pleased. He may feel that it shows that you don't really trust his judgment. In short, questioning an expert is not too easy, but in the end, you will be much more likely to get better health care if you make the effort to do it.

The first step is to accept that it can be useful to question experts, even though you respect the expert, and treat what he says as having standing and authority. The problem is often to know where to start. The six basic critical questions give an entry point to begin the dialogue. You need to pick which question is most appropriate to the case, or most useful to pursue, and then go from there. Critical question 6 is often the best starting point for an examination dialogue. You need to ask the expert basically why he makes the recommendation delivered to you. What is the evidence supporting this claim or piece of advice? That is the question to ask. Often it is a fairly harmless question, and invites the expert to go into his reasons and knowledge. Notice, though, that this particular question is inherently argumentative. It asks for a reason to support a claim that was made. It asks for evidence to back up some assertion made by the expert. Of course, the questioner is typically not himself an expert, so he can't argue with the expert on an equal footing. Still, reasons have been asked for. The why-question asks for an argument, or reasons to support a view, and not just an explanation, even though the expert may treat the process as an explanation.

7.4 THREE COMMON ERRORS IN CITING
EXPERT OPINIONS

If the appeal to authority is on an issue that is outside the field of the expert cited, then the appeal can be criticized as an erroneous argument on the ground that the field question has a negative answer. The topic of the following argument is economics.

Example 7.3

This alarming defence spending will lead to economic disaster. According to Einstein, heavy defence spending in a country is a sign of political instability that is not consistent with sound fiscal policies that can yield lasting financial recovery from a recession.

Einstein was a great physicist, but using the prestige of his name in an appeal to settle an argument on economics is highly questionable. Because some individual is an acknowledged expert in field A does not necessarily imply that his pronouncement in field B should also be treated as a highly plausible or authoritative proposition. Einstein was often consulted by the media on issues in religion and politics after he had achieved celebrity status as a scientist. Like a lot of academic specialists, he tended to be somewhat naive and idealistic in moral and political matters outside his field of expertise. The fact that his opinions were taken so seriously, and often printed as headlines, was often a source of puzzlement, difficulty, and embarrassment for him.[8]

The problem here is that there is a sort of halo effect with experts. If someone is acknowledged to be a prestigious expert in one particular field of specialization, then that halo of authority often carries over into any pronouncement made by that expert, even if it is in a totally unrelated field.

Here then is one type of common error in appeals to expertise in argument. If the expert's field is A, but the issue he is cited as pronouncing upon is in another field B, then the argument from authority should be questioned. The problem here is that many fields of expertise are extremely specialized. To achieve eminence, a specialist may have to restrict his concentration on research and learning to a narrow area. Therefore, the expert may have even less time or resources than the layman to accumulate knowledge about areas of controversy or opinion outside his field of expertise.

8 Ronald W. Clark, *Einstein: The Life and Times* (New York: Avon Books, 1971).

Appeals to expert opinion are highly subject-matter sensitive, because of the narrowness of specialization. Hence they can be highly fragile outside a narrow domain.

Sometimes the appeal to expertise is so vague that the name of the expert is not even cited, or the relevant field of expertise identified.

According to the experts, corporal punishment has a traumatic effect on a child's later development. So parents should never spank a child under any circumstances.

The problem here is a severe lack of documentation of the argument from expertise. When the cited say-so of experts is left this vague, it would be a serious error to accord it much weight in the argument. The appropriate reply is to ask who the experts are, and what is their field (or fields) of specialization. However, because of the power of any appeal to expertise in argument, such questions often go unasked. Often the mere phrase "according to the experts" is enough to silence opposition and end the argument. The fact is that we may be so intimidated by the authority of technical or specialized fields of expertise, that the mere phrase "according to experts" may inhibit reasonable dialogue or further questioning. This failure can be very bad because it prevents us from even asking the expert a critical question.

A third kind of error of appeal to expert opinion in argument occurs where the names of the so-called experts are identified, but the person cited is no real authority at all. This failure clearly violates the requirement stated by the first premise of the scheme for argument from expert opinion. Often the person cited is a powerful opinion leader simply because of personal popularity or prestige. We are all familiar with advertising testimonials where a famous actor or baseball star endorses some product like a particular brand of car or chocolate bar. These appeals are sometimes not appeals to authority at all, but are more simply just appeals to popularity. But where they are appeals to authority, one may well question whether the person appealed to is a legitimate expert at all.

Example 7.5

A famous comedian recommends a particular brand of soft drink on the basis that it contains no sugar and is therefore a good way to maintain a healthy diet and take off weight.

In this instance, the comedian may have no expert credentials in any field related to nutrition, health, or weight loss. Nevertheless, his recommendations on choosing this soft drink over some other type of drink may carelessly be given credibility on the basis that he is a trend-setter who seems to know what he is talking about. However, if you really want reliable advice about your health, a comedian might not be the best place to go. The danger here is that of being unduly influenced by the advice of a person who is no expert at all.

7.5 EVALUATING APPEALS TO EXPERT OPINION IN WRITTEN SOURCES

In studying examples of appeal to expert opinion in courses on critical thinking, many of the examples tend to be from media sources such as newspaper or magazine articles. No questioning of the expert source is realistically possible, and the only evidence one has to go by is the text of discourse given in the case. Thus there are limits to the kind of examination of an appeal to expert opinion that can take place in this kind of case. Even so, it is often quite valuable to use the devices of the argumentation scheme with its matching set of critical questions as applied to the case. By analyzing the structure of the argument and finding critical gaps and weaknesses in it, one can reach a more objective and judicious decision about how strong or weak the argument is, and how much weight should be placed on it as evidence. Even though one cannot actually question the source, still, by asking critical questions, one can get a more realistic assessment of the argument's worth. Thus one may not be so impressed by such arguments, or even overwhelmed by them, if one lacks the resources to put them in a critical perspective.

It is very common to find articles on health and medical issues in the media that are based on reporting of expert scientific opinions of one kind or another. In an article in *Newsweek* on hepatitis C,[9] a viral blood infection that is probably four times more widespread than AIDS in the United States, the issue was raised of how the virus is spread. One question posed was whether one way the hepatitis C virus is spreading is through the needles used in tattooing. The article cited the opinions of two expert sources on this question. The first source, quoted below

9 Geoffrey Cowley, 'Hepatitis C: Insidious Spread of a Killer Virus,' *Newsweek*, April 22, 2002, pp. 46–53.

(p. 51), is a physician named in the article, who has published research on the subject.

Example 7.6

Dr. Robert Haley, an internist and epidemiologist at the University of Texas Southwestern Medical Center, believes the risk is substantial. In a study published last year, he and a colleague tested 626 people for hepatitis C, then questioned them about different possible risk factors. Drug use was the strongest predictor, but tattoos were in the same league, causing a sixfold increase in risk. And because tattooing was more prevalent than drug use, the researchers concluded that it actually accounts for more cases.

Then the *Newsweek* article went on to quote (p. 52) epidemiologist Dr. Miriam Alter of the U.S. Center for Disease Control (CDC) in Atlanta, whose opinions "supported the opposite conclusion." Dr. Alter's opinion was based on other studies, summed up by the article in the quotation below.

In one CDC survey, researchers questioned patients with acute (newly acquired) hepatitis C and found that they were no more likely than other people to sport fresh tattoos. In another study, researchers surveyed 8,000 Texas college kids and found no link between dyed skin and HCV-positive blood tests.

From these results, Dr. Alter concluded that there was no reason to think that anyone with a tattoo should get his or her blood tested. In this case, the comment in the *Newsweek* article that the two experts have come to opposite conclusions looks to be right. They disagree about the link between tattooing and hepatitis C, based on their different statistical findings. In this case, there is a difference of opinion between the two expert sources on whether hepatitis C is caused by tattooing. The reason for the disagreement is that each group of experts has different statistical data they use to support their claim. This sort of disagreement in citing expert opinion is common. It is "my statistics against your statistics."

In this case, no fallacy is committed by the appeal to expert opinion in the *Newsweek* article. The article merely reports a difference of opinion between the groups of experts. The reader can then look at the evidence on both sides, and make up her own mind on how to proceed. In this case, the critical questioning has already been carried out in the article itself. The conflict of expert opinions has been noted. Thus the consistency critical question has been asked, and then answered by the experts. Also,

226

the backup evidence question has been asked by the article and then answered on both sides by the expert sources. When you examine appeals to expert opinion in newspapers, magazines, and other media reports, it is more usual to find appeals that don't raise these critical questions, and leave them up to the reader.

When it comes to looking at interesting cases of appeal to expert opinion in argumentation, there are many kinds of examples that can be studied. Many of these cases are not fallacious *ad verecundiam* arguments, but are weak arguments based on appeal to expert opinion. They can be weak for many reasons. For example, articles in newspapers, magazines, and other media outlets are very often based on quoting expert sources of one kind or another. Sometimes the expert is not even named. The article will simply preface the claim by a phrase like "according to the experts." Of course, just because the expert has not been named, still, she may be a genuine expert and may have given exactly the opinion attributed to her. The problem is, if the expert was not named in the article, how can the reader judge whether the opinion claimed is really worthy of rational acceptance. If the expert is not named, that avenue of trying to verify or even investigate the worth of the claim is closed off. In this kind of case then, calling the failure to cite an expert source an instance of the *ad verecundiam* fallacy can be justified. In contrast however, in many cases, the appeal to expert opinion is not so bad that it should be called fallacious. It should be called a weak appeal if the documentation of the claim is lacking in enough of the right kind of detail to give it much support.

Between the fallacious cases and the perfectly reasonable cases lies a vast range of real cases where critical questions need to be asked, but where the argument is not so deficient that it should be judged to be fallacious. For example, consider the following advertisement for Becel margarine found in *Reader's Digest* (October 1996, p. 42).

Example 7.7

Many doctors and dieticians agree that important qualities of margarines are that they are low in saturated fat and are non-hydrogenated. These are essential qualities you'll find in Becel. And that's important to know. Because Becel believes that with sufficient information and encouragement, you can make sensible dietary choices. So ask your doctor or dietician about Becel. If you choose by listening to that little voice inside yourself that's always right, you'll be reassured to know that many doctors and dieticians feel the same way.

The argument in this ad is based on an appeal to expert opinion of "doctors and dieticians," which is questionable, because these doctors and dieticians are not named. Also, their professional qualifications and specific subfields of expertise are not mentioned. In addition, the category of "dietician" is somewhat vague and ambiguous. Because specific experts are not even named, or quoted directly, it is hard to apply the six critical questions to this specific appeal to expert opinion. On the other hand, the argument is not entirely unreasonable. It could be quite true that many doctors and dieticians agree about these qualities of margarines, and it could be quite true that *Becel* has these qualities. In fact, there seems to be no really strong reason to doubt these claims. After all, the argument is part of an ad, which the reader knows was paid for by the manufacturer of Becel. Thus there is no good reason to suppose that the burden of proof required to make the argument sufficient for its purposes should be quite high. So although other commentators might find things about this ad they don't like, in my opinion it would not be justified to say that the appeal to expert opinion used in the ad is a fallacious *ad verecundiam* argument.

The argument used in the ad above is typical of many examples of appeal to expert opinion found in the media. These arguments fall into the middle range between the appeals to expert opinion that are highly plausible and well supported, and those that are deceptive, obstructive, and fallacious. Such appeals to unnamed sources are often questionable, and certainly not much weight of presumption should be placed on their claims, given the lack of documentation. On the other hand, they do not have the characteristic profile of dialogue that would justify categorizing them as fallacious. In the fallacious cases, it is the respondent's commitment to expertise as a source of knowledge in argumentation that is the basis of his undoing.

A major problem with appeal to expert opinion in written argumentation of the kind typically found in the news media is that the reader can't access the expert source directly in order to examine her views by questioning her. All the critical reader can do is to judge the worth of the appeal to expert opinion by what is written, and by the information that is given in the article. This kind of case can be contrasted with the appeal to expert opinion typically used in court when an expert witness is brought forward to testify. In this kind of case, the expert can be questioned by both sides, and then the so-called trier of fact, the judge or jury, can judge the worth of the appeal to expert opinion based on the expert's having been examined and cross-examined. The rules of evidence regard it as important that expert testimony should be open to scrutiny by both sides in a trial. In many legal cases, a battle of the experts can even occur, where experts on both sides testify to opposite opinions.

The use of expert testimony in the courts has grown to the extent that nowadays most major trials involve some kind of expert testimony. Medical specialists, psychologists, ballistics experts, statisticians, and scientists of all sorts may be called in to a trial to give evidence on all sorts of questions. One of the most notable cases in the United States concerning evidence introduced by scientific experts is the Wayne Williams case, where Mr. Williams was convicted of child murders in Atlanta in 1982. A main factor in the conviction was scientific evidence based on microscopic analysis that matched fibres from the carpet in Mr. Williams' bedroom with fibres found on the bodies of the victims. The statistical odds of the match presented by the scientific experts was thought to be convincing evidence by the jury, and it led to the conviction of Mr. Williams.

Appeal to expert testimony is generally accepted as a form of legal evidence, but there are many questions about what the standards and limits of this kind of evidence ought to be. Until recently, the standard in the United States, based on the case of *Frye v. United States* (1923), was that any technique or theory to be used as legal evidence must be "sufficiently established to have gained general acceptance in the particular field in which it belongs."[10] However, this ruling, by keeping to demonstrable evidence, has been criticized for excluding newly developed scientific techniques. This pressure to include new and promising scientific developments, however, has led to a liberalization of standards of expert testimony which seems to give too much power to the expert in some cases.

According to Imwinkelried (1986, p. 22), expert testimony based on theories or techniques that are not generally accepted in a field is now admissible in many states.

Example 7.8

When trying accused child molesters, for example, many courts now permit psychiatrists to testify that the psychological problems of an alleged victim are evidence that abuse has in fact occurred. The notion that abused children develop characteristic "syndromes" can be useful to clinicians making diagnoses or prescribing treatment; as care-givers, they are concerned primarily with the patient's current state of mind.[11]

Under the *Frye* ruling, such evidence might not have been admissible because a "syndrome" is not used by a scientist to make factual

---

10 *Frye v. United States*, 293 F. 1013, D. C. Circ., 1923.   11 Imwinkelried (1986, p. 22).

determinations. It is only used by psychologists to guide therapy. Now, however, this type of testimony could be brought in.

The U.S. Supreme Court first provided new guidelines called the Daubert factors (Godden and Walton 2006, p. 270):

1. Testability: whether it [the evidence, theory or technique] can be (and has been) tested.
2. Error Rate: the known or potential rate of error.
3. Peer Review: whether the theory or technique has been subjected to peer review and publication.
4. General Acceptance: the "explicit identification of a relevant scientific community and an express determination of a particular degree of acceptance within that community."[12]

In 2000, the courts made several amendments to the Federal Rules of Evidence concerning the admissibility of expert testimony (Godden and Walton 2006, p. 273). One ruled that a qualified expert may testify if (1) the testimony is based upon sufficient facts or data, (2) the testimony is a product of reliable principles and methods, and (3) the witness has applied the principles and methods reliably to the facts of the case.

In addition to the Daubert factors, notes to the Federal Rules of Evidence[13] amendment of rule 702 set out the following criteria (Godden and Walton 2006, p. 274).

1. Whether experts are "proposing to testify about matters growing naturally and directly out of research they have conducted independent to the litigation, or whether they have developed their opinions expressly for the purposes of testifying."
2. Whether the expert has unjustifiably extrapolated from an accepted premise to an unfounded conclusion.
3. Whether the expert has adequately accounted for obvious alternative explanations.
4. Whether the expert is being as careful as he would be in his regular professional work outside his paid litigation consulting.
5. Whether the field of expertise claimed by the expert is known to reach reliable results for the type of opinion the expert would give.

---

12 *Daubert v. Merrell Dow Pharmaceuticals*, 509 U.S. 579, 1993 (p. 594).
13 Federal Rules of Evidence, December 1, 2005: available at this site (February 9, 2007): http://judiciary.house.gov/media/pdfs/printers/109th/evid2005.pdf.

According to Imwinkelried (1986), because of these new more liberal rules, there has been a gradual lowering of standards concerning the introduction of expert testimony in the courts, and a worry is that experts are freely allowed to draw conclusions without being challenged. One problem is that under the newer, liberalized standards, lawyers, judges, and juries are put in the position of having to try to assess the merit of a scientific theory, even though they are not experts in the field. Imwinkelried (p. 23f.) cites the case of the technique of voiceprint analysis produced by the sound spectrograph. At first, this technique seemed a reliable way to identify a ransom caller from a telephone tape, but as criminals learned to disguise their voices over the phone, the technique became less reliable. Yet according to Imwinkelried (p. 24), few lawyers tended to question the reliability of the technique, and if the general acceptance of the technique could not be challenged, the testimony was typically allowed to stand as evidence.

A typical response to use of expert testimony as evidence in law is for the opposing lawyer to bring in another expert who will oppose the evidence of the first expert. The result is what has been called the battle of the experts in court. In some areas of psychiatry for example, where theories are not exact or universally accepted, it may not be difficult for a lawyer to find an expert who will take an opposite conclusion on an argument from the opposing side's experts.

In fact, expert witnesses are chosen by an attorney in a partisan manner. That is, the attorney typically pays the expert a fee to testify, and the attorney chooses an expert who – he thinks or hopes – will give testimony that will support the attorney's side of the case. The expert is not obliged to appear in court, like the lay witness or bystander, for example. The opinion of the expert witness is his private property, and he or she is free to sell it or give it away.

According to Younger (1982, p. 8), the expert used by an attorney in court is usually a so-called house expert, often used previously by the law firm. Younger notes that many law firms have a stable of experts, ten or fifteen doctors, who are often used as witnesses.

These are doctors who prefer to be in court. They are very good at it; they enjoy it. They all look like Spencer Tracy; they make an infallible impression upon the jury and each side then produces somebody drawn from that group of experts. In the normal situation, you just call up somebody, you work things out financially, and the expert appears in court.

Hence it may be an over-simplification to think that the expert witness who testifies in a court of law is entirely neutral. The selection of such witnesses by the lawyer reflects the realities of the adversary system of legal argumentation.

On the other hand, there are checks and balances in the adversary system of the law, because the opposing lawyer is free to attack the testimony of an expert, and to introduce his own expert witnesses. When this happens, it is up to the judge or jury to decide which side's expert testimony is the more credible or stronger. However, the lawyer can do much to aid this decision by questioning the other side's experts.

Weber (1981) has set out advice on how a lawyer can attack the other side's expert testimony in a trial. According to Weber (p. 303) such a cross-examination should require careful preparation and study of the expert's qualifications and, if possible, advance study of any reports or documents submitted as evidence by the expert. Then the lawyer must carefully devise a plan of attack. Weber (p. 303) even refers to checklists for cross-examination of an expert appropriate to the type of case and expert. For example, he gives a checklist for cross-examination of an economist (p. 312). This is a list of questions that can be used to question the expert's track record, qualifications, sources of information, and the fallibility of judgments in his field.

Cross-examination of an opposing witness by an attorney in court is a practical art of question-answer dialogue that lawyers learn through practice, and many lawyers can become very skilled at the art. Much of this skill involves attacking the weak points of the expert's argument, and exposing them to a jury. For example, Weber (1981, p. 305) advocates that the questioner try to expose bias by showing whether critical information came from a potentially biased source like the plaintiff, his wife, friend, attorney, or boss. Or if the expert is projecting into the future, the lawyer could ask whether it is true that nobody can guarantee the future. The skills involved in carrying out these techniques of cross-examination clearly involve using the kinds of complex questions and arguments against the person outlined in previous chapters. That, of course, does not mean that the lawyer using these techniques is necessarily resorting to bad or deceptive argumentation. But it does show the adversarial nature of the use of expert opinion in legal argumentation in the trial setting.

7.7 HOW EXPERT IS THE AUTHORITY?

Clearly some experts are more authoritative on a particular topic or issue than others. Let us say that I want to get an expert opinion on whether I ought to have gallbladder surgery. Dr. Smith has had twenty years experience as a gallbladder surgeon, and has published a book and numerous articles on the subject. His work is highly regarded by other gallbladder specialists, and often cited by them in articles on this subject in the leading medical journals. Dr. Jones is a psychiatrist who is an expert on bulimia, and is director of a weight-control clinic.

Now both Dr. Smith and Dr. Jones are medical doctors. Both are therefore experts in medical matters. But in making up my mind about whether or not to have gallbladder surgery, clearly I would be well advised to attach more weight to Dr. Smith's recommendation than to Dr. Jones'.

Another question to be raised is whether the claimed area of specialized expertise is a recognized area of specialization within the field, or just a particular topic of interest for the scientist or practitioner in that field. This question has arisen in connection with the issue of whether doctors should be allowed to advertise their services, for example, in the yellow pages of the telephone directory, by advertising their interest in a special disease or particular type of medical problem. Should a psychiatrist with a special interest in adolescent mental health, for example, be allowed to advertise this interest in the yellow pages?

According to the current standards of the College of Physicians and Surgeons in Manitoba, Canada, for example, this form of advertisement would not be allowed, because adolescent mental health is not presently a recognized area of medicine. According to the Registrar of the College, even though a practitioner with a predominantly adolescent clientele might have more working experience with the special problems of adolescents, "it is an interest, as opposed to a qualification."[14] In other words, a physician would not have to pass a special qualifying examination to be licensed in this area of specialization, as he would, for example, to become a specialist in anesthesiology or internal medicine. It is a good question, therefore, to ask whether a claim to specialized expertise within a field is based on a recognized area of subspecialization with special qualifications, or is only an area of special interest. A familiarity with an area of special interest may make an expert's advice more valuable than that of another expert who lacks such a familiarity. Even so, an important distinction can be made between an interest and a qualification.

Generally speaking then, some experts are much more expert than others on a specific problem or issue. So even if an opinion is correctly

14 Anonymous article, 'Medical Advertising Views Sought,' *Winnipeg Free Press*, January 27, 1986, p. 3.

233

quoted as the say-so of a qualified expert, it is a separate question how seriously the opinion may be taken as an authoritative statement.

One problem here is that someone cited as an authority may look to an outsider like an impressively credentialed expert – a senior scientist who is head of an established institution – but to those in the know his reputation may be less than glorious. This person may be an expert, but not the best expert on the question.

Shepherd and Goode (1977) conducted a study to question whether scientists cited as experts by the press are in fact the scientists who have done the research on the subject in question. The particular scientific controversy they investigated was the issue of whether marijuana causes brain damage. They found that of the ten marijuana researchers most frequently cited in the scientific literature, only one was included in the ten authorities most publicized in the press. Of these ten press authorities, seven were found not to have published anything at all in the scientific literature.

What Shepherd and Goode's findings suggest is that the press tends to seek out the administrative head of an institute or faculty as an authoritative spokesperson, rather than obtaining the views of the working researchers. In other words, why quote a mere working scientist when you can quote the head of the organization?

The problem here is that for those of us who are ourselves not familiar with a field, any expert may sound good, because we are not in a position to know who are the real authorities in a specific area of research. It may be hard to question an expert's credentials or authority, or to ask for a second opinion, but in some cases you may be well advised to persist in a quest to find the best expert advice you can. The fact that an expert has spoken may not be the final word.

A researcher who is busy contributing to the leading edge of scholarship in his field does not want or need publicity in the popular media, and probably does not have time for television bookings or talking to journalists. Instead it is the quote-meister we most often hear from, that most-quoted authority whose name is already familiar to the public. According to Alter (1985, p. 69), the news media has developed a habit of heavy reliance on a few sources who are often quoted as experts.

Example 7.9

"Round up the usual suspects," the editor or producer snarls as deadlines loom. Reflexively, a story involving feminism becomes a story quoting Gloria Steinem or Susan Brownmiller. Starved for a cogent quote on science (any science)? Get astronomer Carl Sagan on the line. None of this is necessarily a reflection on the Usual Suspects themselves; they are usually genuine resources in their fields. Still, the impression conveyed is of a world that contains only a handful of knowledgeable people.[15]

Alter mentions several celebrities who are usual media favorites. Alan Greenspan was often quoted on economic issues, Alan Dershowitz on legal affairs, and Gloria Steinem on anything to do with women's issues, for example.

Now the various quote-meisters so heavily relied upon by the media are, in most cases, genuine experts in their various fields. That is not the problem. The problem, according to Alter, is that there are good reasons to believe, in many instances, that these people are not the best or most informative experts that could be consulted on a specific problem or controversy. The quoted person so favored by the press is more likely to be chosen because he or she is provocative and co-operative, rather than because he or she is the best expert. And the problem with provocative authors or personalities is that they are popular precisely because they are animated and trenchant. They are the people who tend to avoid making scholarly qualifications or reservations, and are therefore more colorful and quotable because they shoot from the hip. In other words, they become quotable precisely because they show a style that is contrary to the more careful qualifications of sound scholarship. In short then, there are grounds for suspecting that these much-quoted experts may be far from the most genuinely authoritative experts on a particular issue. They are popular to reporters more because of media deadlines and their quotability. They are accessible, colorful, already known to the public, and willing to volunteer to be quoted.

Consequently, many appeals to expertise utilized by the media on topics of popular controversy should be carefully evaluated. They may be reasonable appeals to expertise, but on the other hand they may also be very weak arguments because the authorities cited are not the best experts that could be cited on this particular question.

A good way to check or verify expert advice is to get a second opinion. But in some cases experts disagree, or contradict one another. Particularly on controversial issues, experts may strenuously disagree. Many famous cases of the battle of the experts have occurred in criminal trials, where so-called expert witnesses are called in by both sides to give expert testimony on matters of evidence. Ballistics experts give evidence on weapons.

15 Alter (1985, p. 69).

Pathologists may be called in to give expert testimony on questions of the cause of death or wounds. Psychiatric experts may be called in by both sides to testify that the defendant was insane, or was in control of his actions. Since each side can call forth experts that support his side of the argument, conflicts of expert testimony are notorious in criminal trials.

In one famous case (*Regina v. Roberts*: Canadian Criminal Cases, 34, 1977, pp. 177–183), a man was convicted of murder mainly on the basis of physical evidence found at the scene of a woman's murder. The basis of the conviction was expert testimony that hair found on the scene matched samples of the defendant's hair. Mr. Dieter von Gemmingen, an analyst from the Center of Forensic Scientists, was the expert who testified that the hair samples were similar, based on his experience of over five hundred investigations involving hair analysis. The testimony of Mr. von Gemmingen concluded that the hair of the defendant was similar to the hairs found on the victim. A summary of the nature of the evidence presented by Mr. von Gemmingen's testimony is presented in the example below.[16]

Example 7.10

On the basis of scientific intuition developed over thirteen years of experience, an expert can use the comparison microscope to compare pigmentation granules from two hairs, and determine with overwhelming probability that the two hairs came from the same person. Hence one can arrive at a scientific conclusion that it is very unlikely the two hairs are not from the same person, even though the expert cannot put a probability number on it.

On the basis of this expert testimony, the defendant was found guilty. After spending several years in prison, the defendant was finally able to get a hearing for an appeal for re-trial on the basis of new evidence.

The new evidence was the testimony of another expert. Dr. Robert Jervis, a professor of nuclear physics and radiochemistry, who had done research in radiochemical techniques for twenty-six years. Dr. Jervis had developed a new radioactive technique to detect and measure trace elements in hair samples. Dr. Jervis presented evidence summarized below.

Example 7.11

Irradiation and measurement of isotopes found in hair samples can be used to run computer tests to determine amounts of trace elements in the hair. On the basis of these tests it was concluded that it was very unlikely that the hair

16 A more complete analysis of this case is given in Walton (1984, pp. 198–214).

samples found at the scene of the crime matched those taken from the head of the accused man.

On the basis of this new expert testimony, the defendant's appeal was granted, and he was released from prison.

One interesting aspect this case illustrates is how dramatically experts' conclusions can conflict. In this case, the second expert's argument was found to be the stronger, no doubt largely because it was based on a more up-to-date scientific technique that had been developed, established, and recognized by scientific experts in the field. The defendant's attorney brought in a third expert who supported the method of neutron activation analysis of hair, and the judge indicated in his remarks that he found it plausible that neutron activation is a more reliable method of analysis than microscopic examination. The plausible conclusion to draw then, is that the new evidence introduced by the advent of the more reliable method is enough to overturn the presumption that the defendant was guilty beyond reasonable doubt. And that in fact was the conclusion drawn by the judge.

This case illustrates the danger of relying on an authority whose techniques may be out-of-date. It also illustrates the problem of attempting to deal with the appeal to several authorities who contradict each other. Matching of hair samples has now been widely discredited as a form of expert testimony that carries weight as evidence in the courts. Since the advent of DNA evidence, the DNA found in hair samples is a much more accurate and reliable kind of evidence than probabilistic reasoning based on examining hair samples.

7.8 INTERPRETING WHAT THE EXPERT SAID

Another whole area of concern in judging arguments from authority is the question of correctly interpreting what the authority has said. It is always better if the expert cited can be quoted directly. Most often, however, experts are not quoted, and instead their opinion is reported. However, there are several problems with this. For one thing, experts characteristically use technical, specialized terms (jargon) that may be difficult to adequately translate into non-misleading layman's language. Second, real experts often make qualifications and special exceptions. Their advice may be based on certain contingencies relative to a particular situation or problem queried. Overlooking these subtleties can lead to many errors or oversimplifications.

237

Some of these potential errors are indicated by the following list of critical questions.[17]

1. Is the expert's pronouncement directly quoted? If not, is a reference to the original source given? Can it be checked?
2. If the expert advice is not quoted, does it look like important information or qualifications may have been left out?
3. If more than one expert source has been cited, is each authority quoted separately? Could there be disagreements among the cited authorities?
4. Is what the authority said clear? Are there technical terms used that are not explained clearly? If the advice is in layman's terms, could this be an indication that it has been translated from some other form of expression given by the expert?

Even if we are sure that we have gotten right what the expert has said – for example, if the expert has been quoted directly – there may still be further room for questioning an appeal to authority.

In legal cases, lawyers have to learn how to question experts effectively. Although the lawyer may not be a trained physician, nevertheless he must actively cross-examine expert witnesses giving medical testimony. This means that the able attorney must become somewhat acquainted with the medical facts relevant to a case, and use this knowledge effectively. In other words, the expert's say-so cannot be altogether accepted at face value in every case. Sometimes the layman must persist with intelligent questioning of the expert in dialogue.

An example is the following specimen of dialogue where a lawyer cross-examined a medical expert during the course of a murder prosecution.

Example 7.12

Q: Dr. Exe, in the study of psychiatry isn't it more beneficial in formulating an opinion as to a person's state of mind on a particular or a given day to conduct an examination of him as soon thereafter as possible?

A: That is true.

Q: So that if a person committed an act on a particular day, an examination conducted of him three days later or two weeks later would be more beneficial to the psychiatrist in evaluating and forming an opinion than an examination conducted fourteen months later?

17 The points in this checklist are given in a more inclusive list of errors in the citing of sources warned of by DeMorgan (1847, pp. 281–285).

238

A: It doesn't necessarily follow. No. It depends on the situation, the type of reaction and the type of patient we are dealing with.

Q: Well, as a psychiatrist, you yourself, would you not prefer to examine a patient closer in point of time to the incident than fourteen months later?

A: I'd like to examine him five minutes after the crime.

Q: So then you do agree that it is better to examine closer in point of time than at a remote period of time?

A: I would agree that it would probably be better.

Q: And is it not true that mental diseases and their manifestations are subject to change?

A: Very much so.

Q: And a person may display symptoms of a particular disease or mental condition of an active psychosis one day or one week and then the next week or the next month that sickness may be in remission?

A: May be either way, yes.

Q: Right?

A: Yes.

Q: Now, are you aware of the fact that Dr. Zee examined John Small three days after the incident?

A: Yes, sir, I am aware of that.

Q: And do you concede, Doctor, that John Small's mental condition three days after the incident would not necessarily be the same condition as it was on the day that you examined him?

A: That is true.

Q: If he had a mental condition such as schizophrenia and if he received medication, if he received therapy and he had consultation and it was over a ten-month or twelve-month period, in your opinion, would that condition change?

A: Again, it depends on the condition and the type of condition. Not all people improve under treatment and not all people stay static without treatment. (Cohen 1973, p. 543f.)

In this dialogue, the defence attorney has shown that the psychiatrist who has testified for the prosecution has a weak case for an accurate diagnosis of the defendant. For as the attorney's questioning showed, the psychiatrist did not examine the defendant until fourteen months after the time of the crime. This line of questioning opens up the possibility that the defendant's condition may have improved during these fourteen months. The jury then can be left with this implication.

Notice how the lawyer's questioning works. He is not an expert, but by asking intelligent and relevant questions, he can pin the expert down to making commitments. Once the expert has made a statement, he is then committed to it. It is part of his position, and he cannot then retract it or go against it, on pain of contradiction. The lawyer knows this, and uses it effectively by organizing his questions in a well-planned order so that the dialogue moves towards a conclusion favorable to the defence argument. Therefore, experts can be questioned, and if the appeal to authority is to be a valuable part of reasonable dialogue, the word of an expert must sometimes be questioned. In a trial, this form of questioning is called examination, and when a lawyer is questioning a witness of the opposing side, it is called cross-examination.

An expert examination dialogue is basically an information-seeking dialogue. The questioner is trying to get information from the expert. Often this information is in the form of advice on what the questioner should do in some sort of situation he is in. For example, Bob may need to invest his savings for retirement. He does not want to lose it all in taxes or the stock market, but he does not know very much about financial matters and he does not have time to research them very thoroughly. Thus Bob will have to take the advice of an expert on what to do. He needs someone he can trust, who is ethical, but also someone who is well informed and knows about taxes and investments. Bob will have to have some conversations with this expert, and he will have to ask questions to try to understand what the expert is telling him and what the implications of that are for his investment actions. The best way Bob can do well as an investor is to not only understand what the expert is saying, but to probe into it somewhat critically, and come to his own decision on the right thing to do, based on all the information he can collect. This information will include not only what this expert is telling him, but also independent facts that Bob has collected, and what other experts say. In short, for Bob's decision to be the best it can be, there needs to be a shift from the information-seeking dialogue to an interval in which Bob critically examines and probes into what the expert is telling him. Both Bob and the expert need to take part in this conversation interval.

The problem for Bob is to figure out how to do this in a useful or efficient way. Bob will already know instinctively how to do it, based on his experience and practical knowledge. He may have to probe into the parts of what the expert said that he does not understand, because of his lack of knowledge of financial matters, or because of technical terminology that he does not understand. He will also have to question things the expert said that don't make sense, meaning that they appear to be illogical or even contradictory, or that appear to be inconsistent with other known facts. The problem for us is to reconstruct the logical structure that overlays Bob's ability to carry out this task in collaboration with the expert source. Bob may know how to go about it, but that is because he has certain practical skills, based on similar tasks he has carried out in the past. These practical skills have structures, and are based on routines or common ways of doing things that Bob is familiar with.

One thing Bob will have to do is to probe into and test out what the experts say by drawing inferences from it, based on common forms of inference. The role of argumentation schemes is quite important, because it shows how the examination interlude is more than just information-seeking, and involves elements that we normally associate with persuasion dialogue. It looks as if the questioner is trying to persuade the expert to change his opinion, and aspects of persuasion dialogue are involved. The questioner is not really trying to persuade. He is merely trying to probe into what the expert is saying both to understand it better by seeing the reasons behind it, and to test it out and judge its plausibility. This sort of dialogue is complex, because it blends information-seeking with persuasion dialogue, and it also typically combines argumentation with explanation. Thus examination dialogue of this sort is not a basic type of dialogue. It is a mixed type of dialogue that is part information-seeking and part persuasion dialogue. Although its main goal is to get information or advice, it uses argumentation to help to achieve this goal.

7.9 A BALANCED VIEW OF ARGUMENT FROM EXPERT OPINION

Because appeals to expertise are based on defeasible reasoning, in practice, they should be generally treated as arguments that can shift a burden of proof, but are inherently weak and subject to questioning. Experts can be subject to the same kinds of bias and prejudice that were studied in connection with arguments against the person in chapter 6. If an expert has something to gain by taking one side of an argument, or is even being paid to argue for one side – as frequently happens in courtroom disputes – then pointing out this potential for bias may be a legitimate criticism. The role of critical subquestions is important because they indicate that argumentation schemes are inherently defeasible and open-ended in a way that deductive arguments are not. A critical question can lead to other critical subquestions, thus prolonging a dialogue. This possibility suggests that presumptive argumentation schemes have a certain characteristic kind of incompleteness or open-endedness. You might think that if the proponent has successfully answered all of the basic critical questions matching a scheme that the argument is then closed. The term 'closed' means that the proponent has proved his conclusion and the respondent now has to accept it, but what we've shown is that the respondent could still go on, by asking critical subquestions. Thus presumptive argumentation schemes are incomplete, in an important dialectical sense of the term.

Some people might throw up their hands once this incompleteness has been recognized and say, "See, I told you that these arguments never prove anything!" But that is not the point. The point is that these kinds of argument can only be judged in a dialogue setting, and they are only closed off once the dialogue itself has reached the closing stage. At any prior point, further critical questions can be asked as an argument is questioned or criticized in more and more depth. That does not mean that the argument never proves anything, or is altogether closed to new evidence, in the way a deductively valid argument is. It just means that what counts as proving or disproving, in relation to presumptive argumentation scheme, is dependent on the context of dialogue. It depends on the type of dialogue. It depends on the stage of the dialogue the argumentation is in. It depends on the burden of proof appropriate for that type of dialogue. The argument cannot be evaluated in a context-free manner, like a deductively valid argument. Its worth or weight as an argument needs to be seen in light of how it shifts a burden of proof or questioning back and forth, from one side to the other, during the course of a dialogue.

Just as the critical questions matching an argumentation scheme form a gateway or filter through which the argumentation proceeds, the critical subquestions function as even finer filters that direct the flow of a discussion. In a given case, the discussion can go one way or another. It might start out with a critical question asked in response to an argument that was put forward. If that question is answered successfully, the dialogue may then go on by the respondent's asking a critical subquestion. But it could go a different way. The respondent could ask a different critical question instead. Or he could just accept the argument and not ask any critical questions. In a given case, we are never sure which way the dialogue will go. Whether one critical question is more appropriate, or more pressing than another, depends on the subject matter of the dialogue.

What we can and should judge is how the question is answered, or indeed whether it is even answered at all. If the proponent tries to evade the question, say, by switching to a different topic, or attacking the respondent personally instead of answering the question, these are faults that can be detected. They are argumentation tactics associated with informal fallacies.

A most graphic case (Walton 1997, pp. 135–136) used to illustrate how this analysis of the *ad verecundiam* fallacy works is the Lorenzo's oil case, based on a sequence of dialogue transcribed from the movie *Lorenzo's Oil*.

Example 7.13

In this case, the five-year-old son of Augusto and Michaela Odone had been diagnosed with a rare and incurable disease called ALD (adrenoleukodystrophy). The disease is caused by the body's inability to eliminate certain very long chain fatty acids (VLCFAs) that eventually destroy myelin sheaths that cover nerves in the brain. Physicians could not cure Lorenzo, and the movie depicts the struggles of the Odones (not themselves physicians) to try to do something about the deteriorating condition of their son. Eventually, the Odones discovered that a kind of oil – hence the title of the movie – did help their son, but the medical experts consistently refused to even seriously discuss the possibility that this treatment was beneficial. Their argument was that since clinical trials had not been run to prove the worth of the oil as a medical treatment, any evidence appearing to be in its favor should be dismissed as merely "anecdotal."

The part of the case quoted in Walton (1997, pp. 135–136) is a sequence of dialogue in a meeting of a support group for parents of children with ALD. The parents try to have a show of hands to indicate whether the oil is working to help their children. The chairperson of the meeting argues that this would not be real evidence because it is not a clinical trial based on proper statistical samples and a control group. This is just one short sample of dialogue, but the whole movie illustrates the frustration of the Odones in trying to help their son in the face of the resistance of the medical experts to even consider the possibility that someone who is not a doctor could question the accepted medical treatments or investigate possible alternatives.

What is shown by many cases of this sort is that the argumentation scheme for appeal to expert opinion is defeasible, meaning that it only holds tentatively in a dialogue, and can later be defeated as new evidence comes in. Such an argument is open to defeat when an appropriate critical question is asked by the respondent, and is defeated (undercut) if the critical question is not properly answered by the proponent. Thus the critical questions are an important part of the evaluation of this kind of argumentation. How the proponent of the argument handles the critical questions is an important part of the evidence that should be used in judging the worth of the argument. The fallacy is not a mere failure to answer a specific critical question, although that may be part of it. The fallacy is committed in the type of response that wards off asking critical questions altogether by suggesting that even asking them is inappropriate. The failure is treating the appeal to expert opinion as a conclusive type of argumentation instead of acknowledging that it is defeasible. The failure is one of not continuing the dialogue in a manner consistent with the recognition of the legitimacy of critical questioning.

An appeal to expert opinion in argumentation commits the *ad verecundiam* fallacy if the context of dialogue shows that it is an instance of Locke's type of strategy of being overly aggressive in trying to prevail on the assent of the respondent to prevent that respondent from advancing critical questions. This fallacy is a violation of the negative rules of persuasion dialogue given in chapter 1. It is a failure of the proponent to defend his point of view by argument – a type of systematic (and often very clever) tactic to evade the obligation of presenting proof for a contention. Instead, this type of arguer is trying to close off the dialogue prematurely in his own favor by browbeating the respondent to yield to the authority of revered experts, approved authors, or others who are held high as opinion-setters in common esteem. This tactic is a kind of suppression of argument that deceptively aims to close off the process of legitimate dialogue prematurely, and to defeat the respondent by a short cut to persuasion.

Reasoned use of expert opinion can be a legitimate and helpful way of introducing external evidence into a critical discussion to shift a burden of proof, where direct access to technical or specialized knowledge is not available for practical purposes. The many errors encountered in this chapter have shown that the appeal to authority is an inherently weak type of plausible argumentation that can go badly wrong. It can be weak and undocumented. When pressed too hard in a persuasion dialogue, it can even commit the *ad verecundiam* fallacy. The fallacious aspect of *ad verecundiam* relates to the use of expert opinion by one party to unfairly put pressure on the other party by saying, in effect, "Well look, you're not an expert, so nothing you can say about the matter is anything less than presumptuous." The implication is that the second party does not have sufficient respect for the opinion of an expert. What is exploited is the proponent's commitment to expert opinion as something that should command respect in argumentation. The fallacy tries to prevent the respondent from asking critical questions. It is an attempt to fix commitment. The tactic is to awe the opposition into silence. So the fallacy is the abuse of appeal to expert opinion by pressing ahead too aggressively and not leaving the other party enough room to challenge or critically question the expert opinion that has been used against him in a dispute.

8

Inductive errors, bias, and fallacies

In a deductively valid argument, if the premises are true, the conclusion must be true. Deductive validity is a very strict standard of argument. If an argument is deductively valid, it is impossible for the premises to be true while the conclusion is false. In an inductively strong argument, if the premises are true, it is probable or likely that the conclusion is true. If an argument is inductively strong and the premises are true, it is logically possible that the conclusion could be false. So inductive strength is a less strict standard of argument than deductive validity. Inductive strength is a matter of probability.

Probability and statistics have an acknowledged place in scientific reasoning and experimental methods, but even outside these specialized contexts, the use of inductive argument is an important part of most reasonable dialogue. For example, the use of statistical arguments seems to play an increasingly significant role in political decision making on virtually any subject of discussion.

Of the many different kinds of inductive arguments, we will single out three for discussion in this chapter. An *inductive generalization* is an argument from premises about a specific group or collection of individual persons or things to a more general conclusion, about a larger group or collection. Traditional logic textbooks have often stressed the perils of hasty generalizations, for it has been rightly perceived that inductive generalization is associated with significant and common fallacies. To give an example of an inductive generalization, suppose I have looked around at books shelved in various parts of the reference room of the library, and I have observed that each book I have looked at has a call number beginning with an R. I might then conclude by an inductive generalization that most or all the books shelved and catalogued in the reference room have numbers beginning with an R. My premises were based on my observation of a few books, a specific set of books. My conclusion generalized to the larger group of books in the reference room.

A second type of inductive argument singled out for discussion in this chapter is the statistical argument. A *statistical argument* is an inductive argument where the degree of probability of the strength of the argument is either given as a specific percentage (number) or where a non-numerical statistical term is used. These statistical terms include expressions like: most, many, nearly all, a few, rarely, almost, least, at least, never, and so forth. To determine whether an inductive argument is a statistical argument, you must examine the conclusion to see whether the claim is statistical. Such a judgment is relative to the context of dialogue, but normally the presence of a statistical term in the conclusion is the best indicator. The inductive generalization above about the call numbers of books in the reference room is a statistical argument because the conclusion uses the term 'most.'

The third type of inductive argument we will be concerned with in this chapter is the *causal argument*. Judgments of causality are of basic importance both in scientific and also less structured contexts of reasoning about the world. However, exactly what it means to say clearly that a causal relationship exists between two events is a question that has proved notoriously difficult to answer. Indeed, the concept of causality is so elusive that scientists often try to avoid the language of cause and effect altogether. Such attempts have largely proved unsuccessful however, most notably in the applied sciences, for disciplines like medicine and engineering are essentially practical in nature. In these contexts, the practical language of cause and effect is altogether unavoidable, because the whole intent and nature of the subject is to manipulate causal variables.

We will not try to offer an analysis of the causal relation in this chapter, any more than we will try to offer an analysis of probability or induction. Our goal will be the more modest one of understanding some basic and useful criticisms of inductive and causal arguments. When statistical claims are the basis of conclusions arrived at by causal or inductive argumentation, it is useful to ask certain basic types of critical questions about how these conclusions were arrived at. For statistical evidence is nowadays a very common basis of argument in so many contexts of everyday reasoned dialogue.

8.1 MEANINGLESS AND UNKNOWABLE STATISTICS

The *error of meaningless statistics* occurs where a statistical claim uses a vague term that is so imprecisely defined that the use of a precise statistical figure in the claim is meaningless. The error of meaningless statistics has to do with vague language, and is therefore a linguistic problem, even though it is of course also a problem in inductive reasoning and statistics. A classic illustration is the following statement, made by then Attorney General Robert F. Kennedy, in a speech in Athens, Georgia in 1960.[1]

Example 8.0

Ninety percent of the major racketeers would be out of business by the end of the year if the ordinary citizen, the businessman, the union official, and the public authority stood up to be counted and refused to be corrupted.

One can appreciate the sense and good intent behind this statement, but unfortunately, the exact figure of ninety percent is misleadingly precise. The use of this number gives punch to the statement, but if we stop to think about it, how could such a figure be reasonably arrived at? You might try to devise a precise cut-off point in terms of a criminal's income, say fifty thousand dollars. But even if that cut-off point could be justified, finding out a particular criminal's income could be difficult, even dangerous. The term major racketeer is extremely vague. One could well imagine that there would be considerable controversy, in a particular case, whether some person should reasonably be described as a racketeer, major racketeer, or even a minor racketeer. Moreover, the use of this term might vary with different contexts. A major racketeer in Sioux City, Iowa might be described as a minor racketeer in New York City.

The *error of unknowable statistics* occurs where a statistical claim requires evidence that is practically or logically impossible to verify. In this type of fallacious claim, the terms used by the arguer may be sufficiently clear or precise, but the problem is that it is implausible that evidence could be available to support such a precise statistical and numerical hypothesis as the one given. A classical illustration is the claim attributed to Dr. Joyce Brothers (*This Week*, October 1958).[2]

Example 8.1

The American girl kisses an average of seventy-nine men before getting married.

The critical question to ask in relation to this sort of statistical claim is how anyone could possibly compile this sort of information. It would be extremely dubious that any girl would keep an exact tally of the number of men she kissed before she got married. Even if anyone did try to keep track, there are good possibilities of remembering wrongly. And even so,

1 Reported in Seligman (1961, p. 146).   2 Ibid., p. 147.

what reason would we have for thinking that respondents to a question or poll on this subject would answer correctly or truthfully? Many women would be insulted by such a question, and no doubt refuse to answer it at all. Once you think of it, the claim is absurd because it would be practically impossible to get enough reliable data to support or refute the claim with anything like enough confidence to yield an exact statistical figure.

With any statistical claim, one should ask how the data were collected. Sometimes just asking this question can point to problems, especially where a precise number is given in the claim. Suppose you are presented with the statement that 33.87 per cent of all forest fires are intentionally set by a person. Initially, this statement may seem a lot more plausible than if it only said that some, or a few forest fires are intentionally set by a person. But if you reflect on it, how could one obtain reliable data to support the precise figure of 33.87 per cent? By the nature of occurrences of this sort, it has to be that the cause of many forest fires must remain unknown. And once again, if you think about it, even if the cause is known, for example, somebody's cigarette, there must be many cases where there would be no way to know whether the burning cigarette was tossed somewhere to start a fire intentionally or not. Here the difficulties of determining an exact ratio of types of causes, juxtaposed with the exact figure of 33.87 per cent, strongly indicates the practical impossibility of verifying the statistical claim, as stated. This is the type of case where we can reasonably question whether the argument commits the error of unknowable statistics.

A famous example of unknowable statistics comes from the claims often given in newspapers concerning the rat population of New York City.

Example 8.2

According to Seligman (1961), newspaper feature writers have claimed for years that there are eight million rats in New York City. This sounds impressive, but how would you know that this figure is correct? Seligman interviewed the Rodent and Insect Consultant for New York City, and was referred to two studies. The investigators counted rats in certain areas, and then extrapolated from these findings to figures for the whole city. But how could one be confident that even the original counts could be accurate or representative of the rat population of an area? The problem is that the rats do not tend to be too co-operative. They tend to stick to inaccessible places, like sewers, and they are not too willing to stand around and be counted. According to the Insect and Rodent Consultant, "You can count a rat on the eighth floor of a building and then another on the seventh floor, and then another when you get to the sixth – but after all, you may just be seeing the same rat three times."

249

The problem here is one of spurious accuracy. An exact statistical figure makes the claim look impressive, but the practical difficulties in the way of getting the evidence required to support such an exact figure make it clear that the use of an exact figure is spurious. Even if rats in buildings could be counted by using some form of electronic surveillance, there is no plausible reason for thinking that it would be practical to devise or use such a technique. And the account given by the newspaper feature writers yield no reason to believe that the collection of such evidence is possible.

Unknowable and meaningless statistics have traditionally been called statistical fallacies, but the term 'fallacy' only seems appropriate if the statistical argument is so badly flawed in its underlying pattern of reasoning that it is beyond recovery. However, the real error with the kinds of statistical argument studied in this chapter is the failure to indicate proper doubts, critical questions, and reservations. The error is presenting a weak argument made out to be stronger than the evidence warrants.

For example, the statistician who made the claim that there were eight million rats in New York City could have made a valid statistical extrapolation from rats in a specific area that he really did observe. But the fault lies in reporting the estimate without adding a confidence factor or estimate of reliability to indicate that the figure given is, at best, a rough estimate. Too often the media fail to put in estimates of confidence, or fail to even indicate in any way how the specific figure was arrived at. Given this lack of information, the use of a specific figure conveys a false and unwarranted sense of accuracy that should be questioned as a serious error.

The error of unknowable statistics has to do with the lack or impossibility of access to data for certain claims, whereas the error of meaningless statistics has to do with the vagueness of definitions of terms used in some statistical claims. Both errors involve the use of exact figures where such precise claims are impossible to reasonably support without important qualifications.

The fact that it is not easy to eliminate important biases in statistical polls about significant political or economic matters can be appreciated if you ask yourself how you would determine the current rate of unemployment in your country at the moment. The obvious answer would be to phone a number of homes and ask how many people are in the household, and how many of these are currently unemployed. What could be simpler? However, a statistician would know that there are many biases that could be built into your procedure. It is known, for example, that more women would be respondents to your phone call than men. So gender might be a bias in your results. Other known forms of bias in this type of sampling would include income, age, education, and rural versus urban respondents. So a statistician would have to build in a procedure for adjusting for all these kinds of bias in the poll.

Another problem you would have to solve is how to define 'unemployed person.' Does an actor who is between jobs count as unemployed? Does a mother who has not seriously considered going back to work count as unemployed? Let's say you define unemployed person as an individual who is presently not working but who is seriously trying to find work. Then you have partly solved your problem of definition, and the mother not seriously considering going back to work is not defined as an unemployed person, but you still have the problem of applying your definition to a particular person. Suppose the actor between jobs has tried to find more work to fill in, but will only take on assignments that he finds artistically satisfying. Should we classify him as a person who is "seriously trying to find work" or not? This is a problem of interpretation that may significantly affect the unemployment figure arrived at.

Statisticians who have the job of taking sample surveys of the labor force to give official unemployment figures have devised careful guidelines to define their terms and eliminate biases. But it is not the simple job it may appear to be, and when making a decision based on a figure of current unemployment, to know what the figure really means it may be helpful to know, or to ask about, the assumptions and definitions on which the figure was based.

If a vague term is used in a statistical claim, then the critical questions to ask are how the claimant defines the vague term, and whether the definition offered is a reasonable one that can be justified. But if reasons can be given to show that the term in question is vague to the extent that its use in the claim makes the exact statistical figure given in the claim impossible to justify, then the error of meaningless statistics has been committed. If reasons can be given why statistical verification of a statistical claim is impossible, then the error of unknowable statistics has been committed. In each case, the burden of proof is on the critic to show why the claim is fallacious.

8.2 SAMPLING PROCEDURES

The conclusions derived from polls, surveys, and many other common kinds of statistical generalizations are based on the reasonableness of a process called a sampling procedure. A sampling procedure is a way of drawing things from a certain population having a certain property and then generalizing from the properties of the things in the sample to the properties of the things in the whole population.

For example, suppose you want to estimate what proportion of the Canadian people are in favor of a bilingual Canada. It would be impractical to try to poll all Canadians, so the usual approach would be to select a sample of Canadians and then ask them whether they are in favor of a bilingual Canada. The reasonableness of sampling as a way of making generalizations depends on the presumption that the sample selected is representative of the population in the distribution of the property in question.

To understand what is at stake in a sampling procedure, think of a large urn full of black and white marbles, where the problem is to determine the proportion of each color marble in the urn. Let's say that we don't have the time nor resources to take all the marbles out and count them, and we can't see into the urn. However, when we take out a handful of the marbles from the top of the urn, we can easily see that half the marbles in the handful are black and half are white. Using the handful as our sample, we could conjecture that half the marbles in the urn are black and half are white. The marbles remaining in the urn taken together with the marbles in the sample would constitute the population we are making our generalization about.

In this instance, the basic assumption underlying the reasonableness of our sampling procedure is that the proportion of black and white marbles in the sample represents the proportion of black to white in the whole population. In other words, we are working on the assumption that the marbles in the urn are mixed up so that the proportion of black to white marbles is uniform throughout the whole urn. For example, if we have good reason to believe that most of the black marbles are concentrated towards the bottom of the urn, our sampling procedure would be highly questionable.

The basic type of sample is called a simple random sample, or simply a random sample. A *simple random sample* is defined as one where each sample of the same size has an equal chance of being selected. For example, if the urn contained five marbles, and the sample is to contain two marbles, then there are ten different possible pairs of marbles which constitute samples. Now suppose that more of the black marbles are known to be concentrated at the bottom of the urn. Then if a sample did not have an equal chance of being selected from the bottom, it would not be a random sample.

Sampling can be a reasonable way of estimating that a property is likely to be distributed throughout a population in a certain proportion of instances provided a certain basic assumption is met. We could say that the *assumption of representativeness* is met where the sample selected is representative of the whole population in relation to the distribution of the relevant property or properties throughout that whole population. However, the problem for statisticians is that in practical terms it may not be easy to have reasonable assurance that the assumption of representativeness is adequately met in particular cases. In realistic cases, the possibilities of bias are very real, because real populations can be less homogeneous and more variegated than one might initially think. It seems that simple random samples are not always appropriate, and that more complex types of sampling procedures must be devised to make representative generalizations.

For example, suppose we want to find the average weight of an elephant in a herd of elephants, but we can only weigh a few elephants. But suppose the herd is composed of adult elephants and baby elephants. In this case, there are two *strata* in the population, adults and babies. Therefore, the sample must fairly represent both strata. Here statisticians would speak of a *stratified random sample*, in which independent random samples are drawn from each *stratum* or level in the population. Once again, the sample must meet the assumption of being representative of the variations in the whole population.

It is important to remember that sampling is basically an inductive form of reasoning. If the sample is representative, then the population will be likely to have the same proportion of relevant properties. But by the very nature of sampling, we never know for sure what relevant properties the population has as a whole. Our conclusion is based on reasonable probability. According to Campbell (1974, p. 142), the single, most important basic concept of sampling is this: "If sample items are chosen at random from the total population, the sample will tend to have the same characteristics, in approximately the same proportion, as the entire population." But Campbell warns us that in order to be able to have confidence in this basic assumption, we must have proper respect for the word "tend." Sampling is a way of making a reasonable estimate based on probabilities. It is not meant to be a substitute for direct observation of the properties of a whole population. In evaluating any generalization based on a sampling procedure, it is important to know how the sample was selected.

We now turn to some problematic cases where the sample for a statistical claim was inadequate or poorly chosen.

8.3 INSUFFICIENT AND BIASED STATISTICS

The *criticism of insufficient statistics* should be raised where the sample selected is so small that the generalization to the whole population may be virtually worthless. For a generalization to be seriously worth consideration, the sample must be sufficiently large.

One problem here is that claims may be made on the basis of a sample where no information at all is given on sample size. We may be told, for example, that a test group of children who brushed with Brand X had sixty per cent fewer cavities than those who brushed with Brand Y. This claim might be quite true, but if the two groups each consisted of five children, any generalization based on this claim would be meaningless. There is just too much chance of error. Perhaps the five children who brushed with Brand X just happened to have good teeth and were generally healthy, whereas the other five subsisted largely on chocolate bars and soft drinks during the test period. With such a small sample, there is no way to rule out the many possibilities of chance or coincidence that might affect these particular two groups of children. The use of the words "test group" or "controlled study" may sound impressive, but a little reflection about the size of the sample should lead us to question this sort of generalization. Until we know the size of the sample, we should not be prepared to place any confidence in this sort of claim.

In general, how large should a sample be? It is difficult for a statistician to answer this question in general terms, for it depends on several detailed factors in a particular case. One such factor is that where there is more variation in a population, a larger sample size is required. According to Campbell (1974, p. 148), the more variable the population, the larger the sample size should be, other things being equal. For example, a small blood sample is normally acceptable as a good sample because the chemical composition of blood throughout a person's body does not normally vary too much in relevant respects. However, to cite another example given by Campbell (p. 148), polling eight men in a bar would not be an adequate sample to determine the political leanings of a whole country. Of course, it would be a non-random sample as well.

To avoid the problem of inadequate statistics, two critical questions should always be considered. The first question to ask is whether information is given, or can be produced, on the size of the sample. In many cases, such information is simply not given. But second, if the information is given, we need to question whether the size of the sample is adequate to sustain the generalization that has been made. If the sample is very small, the question should be raised whether it may be so small as to be worthless.

The *criticism of biased statistics* should be raised where the assumption of representativeness may fail to be met, not because the sample is too small, but because the distribution of the property in the generalization may not match the distribution of the property in the sample. In our previous illustration of the marbles in the urn, suppose that all the black marbles happen to be located near the bottom of the urn. Now suppose the handful of marbles chosen as a sample is scooped up from the top of the urn. Such a sample would not be representative of the distribution of colors of marbles in the whole urn. It would be a biased sample.

Example 8.3

In 1936, the Literary Digest mailed out ten million ballots in a political poll to try to predict whether Franklin Roosevelt or Alfred Landon would win the upcoming election. According to the two million three hundred thousand ballots returned, it was predicted that Landon would win by a clear majority. The names for the poll were randomly selected from the telephone book, lists of the magazine's own subscribers, and lists of automobile owners.[3]

In this famous case, it turned out that Roosevelt won by a 60 per cent majority. What had gone wrong with the poll? The problem was that the sample selected tended to be from higher-income groups. People in the lower income brackets tended to be people who did not own a telephone or a car. This biased sample went wrong because, in the particular election, there was a strong link between income bracket and party preference. So despite the enormous size of the sample, it turned out not to be representative of the population of voters in the relevant respects.

It is very common for statistical claims and generalizations to be used as evidence for a causal conclusion. Some of the most important statistical errors and weaknesses in argument arise in connection with causal

3 This classic case is outlined in Campbell (1974, p. 148) and Giere (1979, p. 214). A more detailed analysis is given in Freedman, Pisani, and Purves (1978, pp. 302–304). In their account, Roosevelt won by a landslide of 62% to 38%. According to their analysis, the names and addresses for the survey came from sources such as telephone books and club membership lists, which tended to screen out the poor. They note that in 1936, there were eleven million residential telephones and nine million unemployed. Freedman, Pisani, and Purves conclude (p. 303) that there was a strong selection bias against the poor in the *Digest* survey. They add that in 1936 the political split followed economic lines, and the poor voted overwhelmingly for Roosevelt.

conclusions drawn from statistical premises. In the next sections, we turn to a study of these arguments.

8.4 QUESTIONABLE QUESTIONS AND DEFINITIONS

Where data are collected by polls or surveys that direct questions to the respondents, the exact wording of the questions may be significant. According to Moore (1979, p. 20), it is surprisingly difficult to word questions so that they are entirely clear to the respondents. Moore cites the case of a survey asking about "ownership of stock" that found most Texas ranchers owned stock. However, for all one can know, the kind of stock they were referring to was probably not the kind traded on the stock exchange. This particular question ran a large risk of committing the fallacy of equivocation (outlined in chapter 9), in the case where the respondents were ranchers.

All statistical claims are based on assumptions about the meanings of the terms used in the claim. What numerical figure results from a poll or other statistical study can be highly influenced by exactly how a term is defined. For example, statistical claims are often made about the poverty level in a country. How "poverty" is defined can be very crucial in determining what figure is arrived at, representing the number of poor persons at a particular time.

The usual way of defining "poverty" is by specifying a cut-off income level. If this type of definition of "poverty" is used, one should ask whether it takes into account inheritances, insurance payments, gifts, or money from sale of property. A retired couple living comfortably in their owned home with a modest income from investments could be classified as a poverty family, by some definitions.

One could more carefully set a definition of "poverty" by setting some minimal standards of nutritional adequacy on diet, and then calculating the cost of minimally adequate nutrition at current food prices. From the assumption that a low-income family should spend a third of its income on food, one could then arrive at an income figure to determine the poverty level. One can see, however, that such a definition makes some basic assumptions that could be open to reasonable argument.

We can see then that in the course of argument, statistical claims are open to the use of loaded definitions of the kind we studied in the previous chapter. Indeed, in connection with the example of defining "poverty," Campbell (1974, p. 16) reports grim amusement at the "numbers game" played on the poverty issue by political economists. To play the game,

Campbell observes, all one needs is a friendly definition of poverty – friendly to one's own side of the political argument.

Another problem is that what qualifies as meeting the definition or criterion of an object of study in a sample of a population may change in a different time, place, or situation. This may occur even if there is no good ground for disputing the definition itself. Although the definition of the type of individual to be studied may be clear and reasonable, figures may be biased by the way these individuals are selected. Two research statisticians, Dr. Alan Fisher and Dr. Wendy North, have suggested that apparent improvements in survival rates for lung and breast cancer cases may be an illusion resulting from improved techniques of earlier detection.[4] The problem stems from the practice of reporting survival rates in terms of the percentage of cancer victims who live for at least five years after they have been diagnosed. As techniques for earlier diagnosis have improved, a bias is introduced into the survival rate statistics that makes the patients appear to live longer. Thus as time goes on, the figures for survival of cancer keep improving. The optimistic interpretation of these figures so often given is that a cancer patient's chances for survival are now much better because of improved diagnosis and treatment over the years. Critics claim that these statistics can be deceiving, because the sample identified as meeting the criteria for a cancer patient has also changed over the years.

If this type of criticism is justified, what sort of error does it reveal? The problem is not so much with the definition of the terms used by doctors to describe or identify the types of cancer. It is that improvements in screening programs for cancer have meant that the populations selected as having a diagnosis of a particular type of cancer have changed significantly over the years. How the sample population is picked has varied at different times. The shift is in picking out the individuals that meet the definition.

Moore (1979, p. 20) notes that bias can be introduced into a sample survey by slanting the questions in the direction of the conclusion the survey taker wants to prove. For example, the question "Do you favor banning private ownership of handguns in order to reduce the rate of violent crime?" would be a loaded question because it would tend to draw positive responses from those respondents worried about violent crime. This question is comparable to the question in example 2.28: "Do you favor cracking down against illegal gun sales?," also designed to get a particular response. These types of cases are called statistical errors in reasoning

4 Fisher and North (1986, p. 6).

257

because they relate to polls and other statistical methods of collecting information. Clearly the dangers implicit in them are types of weaknesses and faults we are already familiar with under the headings of loaded questions and question-asking problems (chapter 2).

Sometimes surveys can be very controversial because the questions asked must be reasonably simple. For if the questions are too complicated, they will undoubtedly confuse many respondents, who are then likely to respond in a misleading way. But if the questions are too simple, they may also be open to criticism for that very reason.

In a forty-one-question survey for the Prayer Book Society conducted by Gallup, the following questions were asked of a sampling of Episcopalian clergy and laity.[5]

Do you believe that the gospel miracles are mostly historical facts, mostly the gospel writers' interpretation or mostly legends? (Choose one.)

Would you approve or disapprove of a merger of the Episcopal (Anglican) Church and the Roman Catholic Church?

In general, do you think the Episcopal Church is too "trendy" or "too old-fashioned"?

Episcopal Church leaders were described as "seething" over these questions because "they reduce complex theological and sociological issues to simplistic yes or no answers." Church leaders took the position that the questions were phrased in such a way to produce answers that would support the agenda of the Prayer Book Society. Although Gallup conceded that he was receiving a great deal of criticism of the questions in the returned questionnaires, he felt that he was "not uncomfortable" about the poll.[6]

In this particular case, whether or not the questions can fairly be criticized as unreasonable depends on the theological position of those church leaders who were supposed to respond to them. The reasonableness of this first question, for example, depends on the Episcopalian doctrine of the gospel miracles, and how central that doctrine is to the Episcopalian theology. For example, suppose that most Episcopalians accept the position that the gospel miracles were writers' interpretations based on historical facts as transmitted through legends and other oral traditions and sources. Then the instruction "Choose one" appended to the first question certainly

5 Marjorie Hyer, 'Episcopal Wrath Quick to Descend on Gallup Poll,' *Winnipeg Free Press*, June 22, 1985, p. 74 (originally from the *Washington* Post).
6 Ibid.

forces the respondent to choose an answer that must fail to reasonably represent the full spectrum of his beliefs as an Episcopalian. From the position of that respondent then, the question may fairly be criticized as an instance of the unreasonably dichotomous black and white question.

Commenting on the second question, Reverend John R. Frizzell, Jr. of St. Alban's Episcopal Church in Annandale, Va., replied, "Clearly, anyone who takes seriously the words of our Lord that 'there shall be one flock and one Shepherd' is committed to the reunion of the church . . . yet the questions do not even recognize the complexities of reunion."[7] What Reverend Frizzell's comments suggest is that the second question may be introducing bias into the survey by slanting the question. The question could then be criticized as a loaded question because it would tend to draw positive responses from Episcopalians. For all Episcopalians would, at least in principle, be committed to the proposition that there should be a church reunion in virtue of the biblical injunction that there shall be one flock. The bias imposed on the question by this general commitment might tend to produce affirmative answers without due consideration of all the complexities inherent in the particular question of a merger with another specific denomination like the Catholic Church.

Finally, the third question is a good example of a faulty black and white question (the fallacy of unreasonable dichotomy studied in chapter 2) presuming, as seems reasonable, that many of the respondents would want the option of answering that the church is "old-fashioned" in some respects but "too trendy" in others.

To sum up then, we can see that many of the same kinds of error and criticism studied in the chapter on question-asking are also relevant in the context of the statistics drawn from polls, surveys, and opinion sampling. Generally speaking, with any generalization based on collecting data from a sample, it is always a good idea to inquire into the precise wording of the question or questions that were used. The questions may not be clear, but even if they are clear and exact, they may still be open to serious critical questions or reasonable objections.

8.5 THE *POST HOC* ARGUMENT

The traditional *post hoc* fallacy was said to be the unjustified argument that concludes that one event causes another event simply because there is a

---

7 Ibid.

positive correlation between the two events. Let A and B stand for events, or states of affairs that may obtain at a certain time.[8] Then the *post hoc* fallacy was said to occur where it is concluded that A causes B simply because one or more occurrences of A are correlated with one or more occurrences of B. The full Latin name for this traditional fallacy is *post hoc, ergo propter hoc,* meaning "after this, therefore because of this."

Example 8.4

Every time I wash the car, it starts to rain shortly afterwards. Therefore my car-washing activities are causing outbursts of precipitation in the clouds.

The reason why this kind of causal inference has been viewed as a fallacy is that an association or correlation between repeated occurrences of two events can, in some cases, turn out to be a coincidence. Therefore, to leap too quickly to infer a causal connection between two events on the basis of their single or repeated correlation, could turn out to be an unfounded conclusion.

The initial problem with the *post hoc* fallacy, like the other so-called fallacies we have studied, is that the argument from a correlation to a causal relationship is sometimes a reasonable type of argument. In fact, if there is a positive correlation between two events, this can be very good positive evidence that there is a causal relationship between them. Even so, errors in *post hoc* reasoning can occur where an arguer leaps too quickly to conclude that one variable A causes another variable B where the only evidence given is that there has been a positive correlation between occurrences of A and occurrences of B. It seems then that positive correlation is not enough, by itself, to conclusively establish a causal relationship. The errors implicit in *post hoc* reasoning, therefore, may be in overlooking other factors, in addition to positive correlation, that may be important in evaluating a causal relationship between two events.

There are so many different kinds of errors implicit in the hazardous process of arguing from correlation to causation – as we will see in the next two sections – that it is difficult to avoid them. Certainly we can see why tradition has labelled *post hoc* argumentation as fallacious.

8 In other chapters, we have used the letters A, B, C, . . . , to denote propositions. However, in this chapter, we depart from that practice and let the same letters stand for states of affairs (sometimes also called events). Just as propositions are true or false, states of affairs have as their defining property that they obtain or do not obtain at a particular time.

If it is basically reasonable to argue from correlation to causation, why is this form of reasoning so heavily subject to bias and error? Is there some underlying reason for our propensity to commit the *post hoc* type of fallacy? The reason may be ultimately connected to the Kantian thesis that causality is based on a selective interpretation of external events as filtered through the perceiver's framework of logical reasoning, which fills gaps in the multitude of signals it receives. An individual's causal expectations can serve to fill gaps in a perceived sequence of events by imposing a logical completion on the sequence, based on causal patterns and routines familiar to the individual. Because such causal orderings are based upon a selection of events, and then upon a combination or sequential ordering of them based on familiar expectations drawn from similar cases in past experience, they are subject to occasional mistakes, that is, perceptions of apparent causal connections subject to correction, when seen from a different point of view.

This type of error has been studied by Trankell (1972) who suggests that our causal judgments are inevitably based on a personal interpretation of data because the logical completion mechanism that fills in causal gaps is based on patterns of earlier experiences. The following case from Trankell (p. 18) illustrates the seriousness of the kind of mistake that can be made in reasoning based on plausible completion of a series of real events.

Example 8.5

A taxi carrying a lawyer through a busy city street was forced to come to a fast stop behind another taxi which had also stopped quickly. Through the car window, the lawyer saw the back door of the taxi in front had swung open, and at the same time, he noticed an older man fall through the open door and lay unconscious on the street. The next day, reading about the accident in the newspaper, he found that his observations had been wrong. What had really happened was that the old man had crossed the street without looking, and the car in front braked to avoid hitting him, resulting in a collision that knocked him down.

In this case, what the lawyer had actually perceived was the open door of the car and the man lying on the ground. However, he made sense of these perceptions by combining them into a natural causal sequence. Evidence from other sources subsequently made it clear that the lawyer's plausible completion of what he saw was based on an erroneous interpretation of the real sequence of events. Because of this natural psychological tendency to fill in a "logical completion" of causal links between events as we see

261

them, the urge to fall into *post hoc* errors is powerful. Even so, it is an exaggeration to suggest that all reasoning from observed correlations to causal conclusions is inherently fallacious.

In some cases a correlation can appear to strongly suggest a conclusion, but there may be many countervailing indications that caution against jumping too quickly to acceptance of that conclusion. Prozac is one of a family of drugs known as selective serotonin reuptake inhibitors (SSRIs). According to *Newsweek* (July 16, 2007, p. 48) a strong correlation was found between a drop in pediatric SSRI prescriptions and an increase in teen suicides during the same (overlapping) time frame.

Example 8.6

According to a new study in the *Journal of American* Psychiatry, the number of SSRI prescriptions for pediatric depression (ages 5 to 18) tumbled more than 50 percent between 2003 and 2005. In a troubling parallel development, the number of teen suicides jumped a record 18% between 2003 and 2004, the most recent year for which data exist.[9]

What should one conclude from this striking correlation? Should it be concluded that the drop in SSRI prescriptions caused the increase in teen suicides? According to the *Newsweek* article, one expert, Dr. Kelly Posner, a Columbia University child psychiatrist, claimed that the two trends are connected. She said that the Food and Drug Administration (FDA) may have scared parents and doctors away from SSRIs when they issued a health advisory warning of a potential link between these drugs and teen suicide. This kind of health advisory warning is called a black box warning. Another expert, Dr. Robert Gibson of the University of Illinois Center for Health Statistics, said that the FDA had made a serious mistake, and should lift its warning against teens taking these drugs. The article also cited other experts who had reservations about the black box warning.

In this case the impressive correlation between the drop in pediatric prescriptions for these drugs and the increase in teen suicides during the same time frame appears to strongly suggest the conclusion that there is a causal connection. However, the disagreement between the experts shows that it would be premature to accept the conclusion that the drop in prescriptions is indeed the cause of the increase in teen suicides, without further study and deliberation, or at least without taking the evidence on

9 Tony Dokoupil, 'Trouble in a Black Box: Did an Effort to Reduce Teen Suicides Backfire?,' *Newsweek*, July 16, 2007, p. 48.

the other side of the issue into account. On the other hand, it would be misleading and inappropriate to say that the argument that the drop in prescriptions is the cause of the increase in teen suicides commits the *post hoc* fallacy. There is a difference between hesitating to accept a conclusion because further questions need to be asked, and dismissing it as based on fallacious reasoning. In a case like this, the experts do genuinely disagree, for reasons that could be quite valid. As new data comes in, a pendulum seems to swing back and forth between supporting this conclusion and rejecting it.

It is misleading and simplistic to look at *post hoc* as a fallacy, for four basic reasons. First, arguing from a correlation to a causal conclusion is not inherently incorrect or fallacious. Sometimes it can be a reasonable type of argument. Second, when this type of argument should be subject to critical questioning, it is not because of a single fault. Rather, there are several distinct types of gaps or weak points that can be implicit in arguing from evidence of correlation to a causal conclusion. Third, when one of these gaps is pinpointed, it is characteristically not a kind of fault that refutes or destroys the argument as "fallacious." More typically, it calls for a critical question that points up a need for more study, or further support of the claim, in order to clarify the nature of the relationship between the two factors in question. Fourth, when one of these specific questions is raised, it typically points up a weakness in the argument that can be remedied. So the criticism is that the evidence for a causal link is not as strong as it may have initially seemed. Thus the argument is not necessarily a "fallacious" argument. Most often it is better seen as an argument that is weak but not worthless, an argument that needs further backing in order to fulfill its burden of proof in the discussion. Or as in case 8.6, it may be an argument in which further evidence needs to be collected, or at least one in which critical questions need to be asked and opposed views considered, before jumping to a conclusion.

8.6 SIX KINDS OF *POST HOC* ERRORS

There are several different kinds of factors to be taken into account in causal reasoning, and consequently there are several different and distinctive kinds of *post hoc* weaknesses, shortcomings, or errors that are important to recognize.

The first type of *post hoc* error can occur where the number of positive correlations between the events in question is too small to rule out coincidence. A classic example is given by Fischer (1970, p. 166).

263

Example 8.7

On the fatal night of the Doria's collision with the Swedish ship, Grisholm, off Nantucket in 1956, the lady retired to her cabin and flicked the light switch. Suddenly there was a great crash and the sound of grinding metal. Passengers and crew ran screaming through the passageways. The lady burst from her cabin and explained to the first person in sight that she must have set the ship's emergency brake.

In this type of case, event B, the sinking, followed event A, the flicking of the switch, but this correlation would be extremely weak evidence at best that there may be a causal relationship between A and B. In fact, in this situation, there is plenty of evidence to show that the real cause of B is not connected to A at all. To conclude a causal relationship from a single instance of one event occurring with another is a weak type of argument that runs great risk of error.

A second type of error concerns the possibility of getting the causal relationship backwards. Sometimes we know that there may be some sort of causal relationship between events A and B, but we are not sure which way the relationship should go. For example, there is definitely a positive correlation between personal wealth and ownership of stocks and bonds. But is it the stocks and bonds that cause the wealth, or is it that the acquisition of wealth leads to the investment of it in stocks and bonds? Probably both factors are at work to some extent in many cases. So in this case, we know that there is a correlation between A and B, but it is not clear whether it is better to conclude that A causes B or that B causes A.

A classical example of this second type of instance is given by Huff (1954, p. 98).

Example 8.8

The people of a certain island had observed, perfectly accurately, over the centuries, that people in good health have body lice and people in poor health do not. They had traditionally concluded that lice make a man healthy.

What happened here is that when a person became ill with fever, they came to have a higher body temperature. The lice did not find this comfortable, and departed. Observing this, the people of the island concluded that lice make a person healthy. But they could, more correctly, have concluded that being healthy is a causal factor in providing suitable conditions for body lice.

This second type of error can occur because correlation is always symmetrical, meaning that if A is correlated with B, then B is always correlated with A. Causation is different, however. Sometimes if A causes B, then B may also cause A, but the causal relationship does not always go both ways.

Consider the following example from Damer (1980, p. 69): "It's no wonder that Phillip makes such good grades and always does what the teacher asks. He's the teacher's pet." Damer notes that it is more likely the case that Phillip is the teacher's pet because he does what the teacher asks. In other words, the causal relationship is just the other way around from what is stated in the argument.

However, in this particular case, it is quite plausible that the causal relationship goes both ways. Because Phillip is a co-operative student and a hard worker, the teacher gives him special attention and respect. But the converse causal relationship is also likely to be at work. Because Phillip gets special attention and respect from this teacher, he may tend to be especially co-operative and hard working as a student in this teacher's class.

Therefore, given that there is a correlation between A and B, it may not be established whether it is better to conclude that A causes B or that B causes A. And the two conclusions are not mutually exclusive in every case. There may be a reciprocal, or feedback (circular) type of mutual causal relationship between A and B in some cases.

A third type of causal error occurs where it is overlooked that two states of affairs, A and B, are correlated because there is some third factor C that is the cause of both A and B.

Figure 8.1.

Here there may be a genuine correlation between A and B, yet it may be quite incorrect to conclude that A causes B. For it may be, in reality, that C causes A and C causes B. Thus C, which may account for the association between A and B, may also make it clear that there need be no causal relation between A and B. The following example from Zeisel (1968, ch. 9) illustrates this type of case.

265

Example 8.9

It was found that married persons ate less candy than single persons. A second look at the data showed that if married and single individuals of equal age were compared, the correlation vanished. Hence it would be misleading to conclude that getting married causes less candy consumption in an individual. Age is the operative factor in both increased likelihood of marriage and decreased candy consumption.

This example also illustrates the practical nature of causal relationships. Suppose the candy manufacturers were able to prevent people from getting married. Would that result in a massive increase in candy consumption? No; to increase candy consumption they would have to keep people from getting older. And preventing them from getting married would not keep them from getting older. Thus causation is a practical matter. To say that A causes B means that if you can change or manipulate A, then you can change the occurrence of B as well. Correlation between A and B does not always mean that there is a genuine causal relationship between them.

In some cases, it is not too clear how the causal relationship works, but the particular form of the relationship concluded in an argument can and should be questioned. Observing that a college student is both severely obese and severely depressed, an observer might conclude that the obesity is causing the depression. However, it may well be that there is a reciprocal causal relationship, and that the depression is a causal factor contributing to the student's tendency to overeat. But then again, as Damer (1980, p. 70) observes, in this type of case a more plausible conclusion is that there may be an underlying physical or psychological problem that is a common cause of both these effects.

This type of case shows that if there is a positive correlation between two states of affairs A and B, it may be hasty and premature to conclude that A causes B, and it may be equally erroneous to conclude that B is the sole cause of A. It could be both A and B are caused by some third factor, a common cause where failure to recognize the possibility or plausibility of this third factor could be a serious bias or misrepresentation of the case.

A fourth type of error is to overlook the complex chain of linkages in a causal sequence. It may be that A causes C, but that the causal relationship between them is more clearly brought out by observing that there is a third causal factor, B, intervening between A and C.

Figure 8.2.

In a case like this, C may more correctly said to be *indirectly* caused by A. The causal relationship between A and C may be said to be *complex* (*recursive*).

Example 8.10

A motorist observes that whenever he applies the brakes, his defroster fan starts to squeak. He concludes that the brakes must somehow be connected to the fan mechanism.

The real explanation of what has happened here is that the braking caused deceleration of the car, which in turn caused the loose fan motor to tilt and squeak. So while it was correct to say that the braking caused the squeaking, it was fallacious to conclude that the braking directly caused the squeaking.

Sometimes the sequences of causal linkages between two states of affairs can be quite complex. In the example 8.10, the sequence could be described as a relationship between four states.

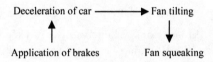

Figure 8.3.

So in some cases, there may be a number of intervening causal variables between two states of affairs. Failure to appreciate these intervening factors is a kind of fallacy of oversimplification.

The following case illustrates that sequences of states of affairs taken as causal variables are often more complex than a situation initially suggests.

Example 8.11

It was found by a study of admissions data that rejection rates were much higher for women than for men at the University of California at Berkeley. This statistical finding seemed to indicate the conclusion that being a woman causes one to be rejected at Berkeley. Consequently, Berkeley was accused of discriminating against women. However, Bickel, Hammel, and O'Connel (1977) showed that if you looked at the figures for each of the eighty-five departments individually, you could see that the probability of admission was just about the same for both sexes, or even somewhat higher for women. What had been overlooked is that women tended to apply for admission to the more popular departments, which also happened to be the departments with the higher rejection rates.

What initially seemed to be the conclusion to be derived from the data was a causal relationship between being a woman and being rejected at Berkeley.

Being a woman ————————➤ Being rejected at Berkeley

Figure 8.4.

But then a closer look at the situation seemed to indicate that the real causal relationship was between a third variable (applying to a popular department) and the outcome of being rejected at Berkeley. Yet, as it happened, being a woman was associated with the variable of applying to a popular department.

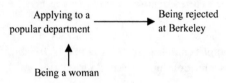

Figure 8.5.

The error here was to overlook the intermediate variable. Instead of there being a direct causal relationship between two variables A and C, as it initially appeared, there was a more complex sequence of relationships. It just happened that A was correlated with B, and it was really B that caused C. But by overlooking the intervening step, the situation seemed to indicate a causal link between A and C. Now if being a woman were to be causally related to applying to a popular department then there would be a causal sequence of the form A → B → C. But to conclude that A directly caused C without mentioning or taking into account the middle variable B would be a serious error of causal reasoning.

We must be careful not to mix up the last two types of causal error. In the third type of error, the initial two states that seemed to be causally related were not causally related at all, in the sense that one caused the other. The third factor C, caused both A and B, but it turned out to be false, in that type of case, to say that A caused B (or that B caused A). The fourth type of error was quite different however. The two initial states were not directly causally related. But it did truly turn out that the one variable (indirectly) caused the other. Hence the two types of fallacy are distinctively different. The third error involves getting the attribution of causality wrong, whereas the fourth error only involves oversimplifying the nature of the causal relationship.

Considerable care is needed here because in some more complex cases, both types of error can be involved. The following case is related by Croxton and Cowden (1955, pp. 9–10).

Example 8.12

A meteorologist discovered that the fall in the price of corn is inversely correlated with the severity of hay fever cases. Should we conclude that there is a causal relationship between severe cases of hay fever and a drop in the price of corn? Two other factors suggest some second thoughts. First, the price of corn tends to be low when the crop is large. Second, where weather conditions favor a bumper crop of corn, they also favor a bumper crop of ragweed. It seems fair to conclude that the price of corn and the suffering of hay fever victims are related, but they are not directly causally dependent on each other.

To get a grasp of this example, we have to look over the sequence of causal linkages between all the pairs of causal variables, below. Basically, this example is a case of the third type of error. The favorable weather is a common causal variable behind the initial variables of the drop in the price of corn and the rise in severe hay fever cases. It would be false to say that either one of these initial variables causes the other (see figure).

Figure 8.6.

However, the fourth type of error is involved here as well. For the favorable weather is indirectly causally related, by two intervening variables, to the drop in the price of corn. Also, the favorable weather is indirectly related to the severity of hay fever cases, once we realize that the favorable weather causes an increase in ragweed growth.

269

In this case both the third and fourth types of error are combined. To properly analyze the case, we need to sort out the involvement of each type of error.

A fifth type of causal error involves extrapolation beyond a given range of cases. Sometimes there is a positive relationship between two variables A and B within a certain range of cases, but then the relationship falls outside that range.

Example 8.13

It is often observed that rain is good for the crops. Within a certain range of conditions, this causal relationship holds – the more rain, the better the crops. But if there is too much rain, it can have a negative effect on crop yields.

In this type of case, it is correct to say that in some circumstances, a positive correlation between A and B means that A causes B. The problem is that in other circumstances, it may come about that A does not cause B, or even that A is counterproductive for B. The relationship, in this case, is nonlinear.

8.7 BIAS DUE TO DEFINING VARIABLES

A sixth kind of error in arguing from a statistical correlation to a causal conclusion has to do with how the events or items studied in the correlation are classified and defined. For in some cases, an apparent trend or causal link may turn out to be merely a statistical artifact, created by a shift in the way the variables are defined or identified. The classic case of this type of problem concerns criticisms of media reporting of cancer survival rates.

The message given out by the media is that we are winning the battle against cancer, because early detection and new methods of treatment have resulted in increased survival rates. Statistical presentations of these results show significant increases in survival rates for many types of cancer – including lung, colon, prostate, and breast cancers – from the initial period of 1950–1954 to the period of 1977–1981. However, numerous respected researchers have criticized the validity of these statistics. This criticism is based on the contention that the real survival rates may not have changed at all, and that the apparent improvement may only be due to a shift in how 'cancer patient' is defined, over the years.

Fisher and North (1986) identify six types of bias in reporting cancer survival rates.

270

1. *Lead Time Bias.* Advances in cancer detection have led to increasingly earlier diagnosis. Lead time (p. 6) is the extra time added on to a patient's survival due solely to earlier detection, and not to a later time of death. Critics claim that lead time biases cancer statistics because compilation of current survival rates contains greater lead time than cases compiled in the past.

2. *Length Bias.* Newer methods of detection now identify greater numbers of cancer patients with slower growing types of cancer than before. Patients with slower growing cancers tend to have a more positive prognosis, and tend to live longer, even over and above the factor of lead time. Length bias (p. 6) is like comparing two different diseases – a slow-growing disease with *a positive prognosis versus a fast-growing disease with a negative prognosis.*

3. *Overdiagnosis.* The newer detection methods identify cancer patients with small, harmless tumors, or tumors that get smaller on their own. Using the older methods of detection, these individuals were not even identified as cancer patients. Today's practice of counting these patients introduces a favorable bias into cancer statistics.

4. *Patient Self-Selection.* People who often volunteer to be tested for cancer by the latest detection methods tend to have better results of treatment, for several reasons. These people tend to be more health-conscious, better educated, more compliant with physicians' orders, and with higher incomes. These people may be able to obtain better quality treatment, and therefore have better prospects for survival.

5. *Stage Migration.* Better detection of the spread of cancer (metastasis) means that cancer patients are classified differently at different stages of the development of cancer.

6. *Increased Reporting of Non-Fatal Cases.* Better reporting of non-fatal cases by physicians in recent times may make for a false improvement of survival rates because the recording of cancer deaths has changed over the years.

Some of these criticisms of bias relate to a kind of *post hoc* error. Others are similar to the general kinds of problems with defining terms in inductive reasoning already encountered in section 8.4. In discussing the six types of bias in cancer statistics reporting, it is important to separate two questions: (1) Is there a real improvement in survival rates? (2) Is the improvement in survival rates due to the improved medical treatment of cancer? Question (2) presumes an affirmative answer to question (1). And question (2) relates to *post hoc* reasoning, and singles out a special kind of new *post hoc* error.

Question (1) relates to a combination of (a) biased statistics, and (b) how the term 'cancer patient' is defined. Thus question (1) combines the problem of biased statistics and the problem of loaded definition in the same criticism. The claim is that the shifting definition has introduced a bias into the way the sample for study has been selected.

Probably the basic worry about the presentation of cancer statistics that seems to suggest an improved survival rate is the concern that the apparent improvement may not be due to improved treatment methods in recent times. Thus the basic problem is one of *post hoc* argument. All six forms of bias point to a generally reasonable requirement of any argument from correlation to causation – the change in the variable alleged to be caused should not be solely due to the way the variable is defined or classified. For the problem that can arise is that changing standards of the variable as defined or classified can change over a period of time, thereby introducing a possibly hidden bias into the statistical correlation. Terms can change their meanings over the years, as procedures for identifying an item, or determining a condition change as scientific procedures of identification and classification improve. An apparent causal link may only be due to such a shift in terminology.

One can easily see how this type of unduly optimistic interpretation of statistics can be tempting where research support is needed, or where the media may overlook subtleties in reporting statistical findings. Yet to document the precise extent of the bias may itself require a scientific study.

8.8 *POST HOC* CRITICISMS AS RAISING CRITICAL QUESTIONS IN AN INQUIRY

As a study becomes more advanced, and more data is processed, initial correlations that suggested a causal relationship may become subject to criticisms, as knowledge of other operative variables may begin to appear. Thus the initially postulated relationship may emerge as not as simple as the earlier knowledge of the situation made it seem. Instead of being a simple two-place causal relationship between two variables, the newer data may suggest that there are other factors, which were previously in the background, that are causally related to A and B. Therefore a fuller description of the causal network of events may require dropping the original, simple causal relationship as a hypothesis, and moving towards a more complex set of linkages of several events.

This need not mean that the original postulation of a simple two-place causal relationship between A and B was necessarily a fallacy or a blameworthy error. In light of the available evidence at that time, it may have been a reasonable presumption. Although it was a good place to start, the initial presumption may have to be given up in light of the new information, and overcome in favor of a new hypothesis.

Of course, the dogmatic course of insisting on sticking to the original, simple presumption even in the face of, or despite the new information, could be a fallacy. That is because there is a failure to allow further discussion, or change one's argument, even in the face of new evidence or critical questioning.

Instead of putting down an argument by condescendingly claiming that it commits a *post hoc* fallacy, it is more constructive to raise specific questions about the strength of the argument from the correlation to the causal conclusion. Such a criticism is more constructive because it may suggest specific critical questions. Answering these critical questions could strengthen or weaken the causal argument through subsequent critical discussion that introduces new evidence.

A study published in the journal *Nature* on May 13, 1999, found that babies who slept with a night-light on had an increased chance of developing myopia (nearsightedness) later in life. A subsequent study, co-authored by Professor Karla Zadnik of the College of Optometry at Ohio State University, found other factors that explained the correlation between babies sleeping with a night-light on and later myopia. These other factors are cited in example 8.14 (http://www.sciencedaily.com/releases/2000/03/000309074442.htm).

Example 8.14

The previous study, conducted by researchers at the University of Pennsylvania, found that "ambient light exposure during sleep at night in the first two years" of a child's life greatly increase that child's chances of developing myopia. This earlier study showed that nearly half of the children who had slept in a fully lit room had become myopic later in childhood. But the same study did not take into consideration whether or not parents were nearsighted, according to Zadnik. Her study took into account parental myopia. The researchers noticed that nearsighted parents were more likely to use a night-light in their child's room. "We think this may be due to the parents' own poor eyesight," Zadnik said. Also Zadnik said her study found that genetics plays a significant role in causing myopia.

In this case, the earlier study showed an impressive correlation between children who had slept in a fully lit room and those who became myopic later in life. As the later study showed, other factors were at work. Parents

273

who were more likely to use a night-light were also more likely to be myopic, and parents who are myopic are more likely, for genetic reason, to have children that also tend to be myopic.

To deal with this kind of case, we need to recognize that the initial correlation between night-lights and myopia sets up a causal hypothesis between these two factors that needs to be explored further by asking critical questions. Could there be other factors, for example, linked to both myopia and the use of night-lights with babies? Further studies needed to be made, and in this case were made, to answer this critical question.

What cases like this one bring out is that a dialogue or inquiry can proceed by asking questions, or suggesting possible causal relationships at the opening stages of the inquiry. Later on, as the inquiry proceeds, and more evidence comes in, these relationships may be firmed up, repudiated, questioned further, or even made more complex by the discovery of other factors that had not previously been identified. To leap ahead, and ignore or pre-empt the natural and reasonable order of dialogue by drawing a causal conclusion too firmly or too quickly could be a *post hoc* error. On the other hand, it may be natural and reasonable, at the early stages of the investigation, to advance causal connections as hypotheses that may later on turn out to be refuted. This in itself is not inherently fallacious or incorrect, provided the hypothesis is corrected once further evidence contradicts it.

The following case also illustrates how initial observation of a plausible connection often suggests a causal link between two variables, and how further studies may raise questions and criticisms, thereby opening the way to study other possibly related factors.

Example 8.15

At a conference on the bond between humans and pets in Boston in 1986, researchers reported that pets can lower blood pressure in humans, can improve the survival odds of heart patients, and can even penetrate the isolation of autistic children. According to a report in *Newsweek* Sharon Begley and Karen Fitzgerald, ('Freud Should Have Tried Barking,' September 1, 1986, pp. 65–66), researchers at the conference reported on the beneficial effects of pet companionship. Studies showed that women who had owned dogs as children scored higher on self-reliance, sociability, and tolerance tests than petless women. Men who had owned a dog "felt a greater sense of personal worth and of belonging and had better social skills" (p. 66). Children with pets also showed greater empathy.

These correlations cited by the studies reported could be based on good research, but questions remain what causal conclusions should be drawn from them. How confident can we be that the loving interaction with the

274

pet is actually the cause of the improvement in the health or well-being of the human companion?

Animal ecologist Alan Beck of the University of Pennsylvania is quoted by the *Newsweek* article (p. 66) as saying that while early work assumed a positive relationship between people and pets, later studies have raised some criticisms. One critical question cited is whether it is the pet that is producing the empathy in the child, or whether it may be the case that parents who tend to buy pets for their children are the kind of parents who would foster empathy in a child.

Another question is whether any kind of change in a nursing home, not specifically the arrival of a pet, may have a cheering effect on elderly patients. In other words, the effects on health could be due to other variables which are associated with the introduction of pets into a situation. Perhaps elderly patients in a nursing home can tend to be bored and have very little in common to talk about. The introduction of a pet is a visible change that affects everyone and provides much in the way of interesting common events that affect everyone in the institution. But is the affectionate interaction with the pet here the specific cause of everyone perking up, or would any change in routine that provides common material for interaction among the patients have an equally positive effect on morale? One could only address this question by studying the effects of further variables in the situation.

Post hoc criticisms of causal arguments are therefore often reasonable and constructive questions to ask. They are often better viewed as questions that invite replies by the other participant in a critical discussion rather than as refutations of an argument, or indications that the argument is fallacious. Indeed, these critical questions are usually very helpful ones to ask, because any causal conclusion or hypothesis runs the risk of turning out to be a correctable *post hoc* argument, if not properly qualified.

8.9 STRENGTHENING CAUSAL ARGUMENTS BY ANSWERING CRITICAL QUESTIONS

To understand the logic of causal reasoning in relation to the *post hoc* fallacy, we need to appreciate how most attributions of a causal relationship in controversies about causal claims have a highly practical nature. Characteristically, when it is alleged that one event or state of affairs A causes another one B, it is meant that *in these particular circumstances* A was accompanied by and produced B. Such a claim need not imply that whenever you have A, you always get B, or even that most times when you have A, you will

275

probably also have B. For example, suppose it is claimed that Bob's lighting a match burned down a warehouse. What is meant is that the lighting of the match in the particular circumstances, at the time, caused the burning down of the warehouse. The particular circumstances may have included the facts that the warehouse was full of dry lumber on that day, and that it was a hot day, and so forth.

Causality is always a practical kind of relationship between two variables A and B, because it states that if A is introduced into a stable or normal situation where, by assumption, no interfering new variables are introduced, then B will result. Thus a causal relationship always obtains relative to a *field*, a stable environment which can be presumed to be constant, or at least similar, from one case to another. When it is said that A causes B relative to a given field, it can never be ruled out absolutely and for certain, that the change B has been affected or partly caused by some other intervening factor I, which is contained in the field, but not known by the observer. This field-dependent property of causation is what makes causation practically useful in fields like medicine and engineering where individual cases must be dealt with causally at the singular level.

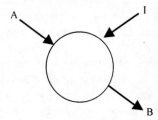

Figure 8.7. Causation as a field-dependent relation.

This field-dependent characteristic shows why particular arguments based on causal inference, in most causal claims and arguments on controversial issues, are instances of plausible reasoning. Causal arguments of these kinds often have to do with probability and induction, but they may be based more fundamentally on a judgment of plausibility than probability. To see why, let us look at the basic argumentation scheme in which *post hoc* controversies occur.

The elementary argumentation scheme for arguments from correlation to causation (C) is very simply given below.

(C) There is a positive correlation between A and B.
      Therefore, A causes B.

In the simplest cases, the premise may only amount to the claim that B followed A in time, in one particular case. Now what are we to say about (C) as an argumentation scheme? Is it correct or erroneous?

The first observation, as we have already indicated, is that an argument that fits the scheme (C) can be a reasonable argument. For in many instances, a positive correlation, even a weak one that has only one instance, is a perfectly good and reliable indication that there may be a causal connection between two states of affairs. The problem – as we saw when we examined instances of erroneous *post hoc* reasoning – is that there are too many ways that use of scheme (C) can go wrong. An instance of (C) can be erroneous where some other factor accounts for the correlation, showing that the apparent causal relationship between A and B is really spurious or misleading. Here we get the various different types of *post hoc* errors.

However, we must resist the thesis that (C) is itself an incorrect type of argumentation. As a plausible inference, in some situations, an argument which fits the scheme (C) can be a quite reasonable kind of argument. The erroneousness comes in when further information is brought in that may tend to undermine the plausibility of the use of (C) by suggesting gaps, and thereby throw the burden of proof back onto the proponent of (C) to account for other factors relevant to the argument. This leads to several different types of critical questions.

What we should conclude then is that (C) can be a reasonable form of argument in some cases, but it is a form of argument that can be open to several different kinds of critical question. And in this chapter we saw seven different types of critical question that can be used to show that an argument of scheme (C) is weak or erroneous. A critic may respond to any causal argument of scheme (C) by indicating that failure to reply adequately to any of these seven critical questions brings out the weakness and vulnerability of the argument.

How can an argument from correlation to causation be made stronger? The proponent of the argument can strengthen it by responding to, or taking account of these seven types of critical question. Each of these seven critical questions covers one of the characteristic errors previously studied.

1. Is there is a positive correlation between A and B?
2. Are there are a significant number of instances of the positive correlation between A and B?
3. Is there good evidence that the causal relationship goes from A to B, and not just from B to A?

4. Can it be ruled out that the correlation between A and B is accounted for by some third factor (a common cause) that causes both A and B?
5. If there are intervening variables, then can it be shown that the causal relationship between A and B is indirect (mediated through other causes)?
6. If the correlation fails to hold outside a certain range of causes, then can the limits of this range be clearly indicated?
7. Can it be shown that the increase or change in B is not solely due to the way B is defined, the way entities are classified as belonging to the class of Bs, or changing standards, over time, of the way Bs are defined or classified?

Our confidence in any causal conclusion is always likely to be somewhat shaky, because there are so many other practical factors in any situation that might be involved. In the basic argument (C), a critic can always suggest that there might be some other factor at work that might throw doubt on the causal relationship between A and B. As each of the above seven critical questions is adequately answered in the discussion or inquiry, however, the causal claim is strengthened. The respondent must specify which of these factors has not been established, or why the claim made for it is weak. By this means, the burden of proof is thrown directly on to the proponent. He must substantiate his causal argument by showing that some other factor is not also at work, like an intervening cause, a common cause, or simply coincidence.

When starting out with a correlation between two variables A and B, one may have a strong suspicion that there is a causal link between A and B that accounts for the correlation. As each of the seven critical questions of the argument from correlation to causation is adequately answered, that initial suspicion can become more and more highly strengthened as an argument that fulfills its obligation in the discussion or inquiry. It is not easy to establish conclusively that there is a causal link between two states of affairs. To establish conclusively that A causes B, an investigator must arrive at a clear theoretical understanding of the mechanism whereby A is causally related to B. Understanding this mechanism typically involves an understanding of the chemistry or physics, the underlying structural linkage between A and B as physical or causal processes. This means shifting the context of dialogue to that of a scientific inquiry.

8.10 EXAMPLES OF DRAWING CAUSAL CONCLUSIONS
FROM SCIENTIFIC STUDIES

If all seven critical questions are answered, then an investigator may be able to say in practical terms that, in all plausibility, A is the cause of B. But the causal hypothesis cannot be conclusively confirmed, with scientific precision, until more is known about the underlying theory of the linkage between A and B. It is for this reason that the strengthened form of argument from correlation to causation remains a relatively weak (plausible) type of argument in many instances, even if all seven critical questions are answered.

Example 8.16

In 1925, pernicious anemia was a fatal disease that caused affected people to die because their bones mysteriously failed to produce red blood cells. By 1926, Dr. George R. Minot had found through clinical experience that feeding large quantities of liver to forty-five of his patients with pernicious anemia was followed by a great increase in red corpuscle count in each one. Moreover, each of these patients stated feeling better and, when kept on a diet of liver, survived to continue a healthy life.

With these results, anyone might conjecture reasonably that there could be a causal link between the consumption of liver and the recovery from anemia. But as de Kruif (1932) tells us in his account of the story of Minot's work, many more steps were taken before a causal relationship was established.

Minot's first reaction, according to de Kruif (p. 107f.) was that a scientific doctor might suspect that this group of recovering patients could be a coincidence: "Minot was too cagy to trust such embryo statistics [and] knew the illness always had its ups and downs before killing its victims." Minot's reservations here relate to the kind of factor described by the sixth premise of the strengthened causal argument form. It could be that the recovery persisted only temporarily, and did not continue for a more prolonged period. Subsequent study of these patients eventually put these doubts to rest.

Another concern was the worry expressed by the first premise. It could still possibly have turned out that with the limited number of patients studied, the apparent connection could be a coincidence. Subsequent studies of larger numbers of patients soon brought further evidence against this reservation as well. Eating liver worked on every pernicious anemic patient except those who had gone so far that they couldn't eat any solid food at all. But when pulped liver was poured into the stomachs of these patients through a tube, they began to recover, and after a week, were greatly recovered.

At this point, it became more and more plausible that there was a causal connection between ingestion of liver and recovery from pernicious anemia. However, the precise nature of the causal connection was not fully established until laboratory studies set out on the trail of tracking down the mysterious X factor in liver that went through the blood to start the bone marrow producing new red blood cells. Now we know that it was the vitamin B_{12} in the liver that enabled this process to take place and cause the patients to recover.

In scientific inquiry, the technique used to study correlations between two variables where there is a suspected causal connection is the method of the controlled experiment. If there is an interesting correlation between two variables A and B, scientific experiments can tend to confirm the existence of a causal relationship by studying A and B in different circumstances. If A always tends to be followed by B, even in different circumstances after many trials, the claim that A causes B is made stronger. If B fails to obtain in circumstances where A is not present, the claim may be even stronger. As common causes for the correlation of A and B are ruled out, the claim becomes even stronger, and so forth, for all the seven types of critical questions answered. If all the questions are adequately answered, the claim for a causal relationship may be very plausible, and a critic is then put on the defensive to find counter-evidence to criticize the plausibility of a causal conclusion. The burden is now shifted to the critic.

The next example graphically illustrates how questions about whether a causal inference can be derived from a correlation are closely related to arguments from expert opinion. Statistical findings of a correlation that concern a questionable causal inference are typically based on experimental findings by scientific experts. Discussions with these experts and their colleagues who are knowledgeable on the same subject are frequently very important as evidence in judging the link between correlation and causation. In this example, medical researchers found a correlation between regular drinking of sweet soda pop, whether it is the regular or diet type, and serious health problems.[10]

10 Thomas S. Maugh II, 'Diet and Regular Pop Increase the Risk of Disease,' *The Vancouver Sun*, July 24, 2007, p. A9. The article was widely reprinted in major news sources, but originally appeared in the *Los Angeles Times*, July 24, 2007.

Example 8.17

Researchers reported in the *Circulation Journal of the American Heart Association* that drinking as little as one can of soda pop per day, whether it is regular or diet, is associated with a 48 per cent increased risk of a predecessor of heart disease and diabetes called metabolic syndrome. Metabolic syndrome is a cluster of symptoms including excessive abdominal fat, high blood pressure, high blood sugar level, and lower levels of good cholesterol. The study found that those who had consumed more than one such drink per day, whether the diet soda or regular kind, had a 48 per cent higher risk of having metabolic syndrome than those who did not. The findings of the study suggested the conclusion that drinking as little as one can of regular or diet soda per day is a cause of metabolic syndrome, a syndrome known to be associated with heart disease and diabetes.

It certainly seems plausible, given these findings, that there could be a causal relation between drinking soda regularly and health problems, including heart disease and diabetes. The findings are so dramatic that one wonders what other experts would say about it, and what the investigators who wrote the paper think.

Another researcher, Dr. Meir Stampfer of Harvard Medical School, who had previously reported that drinking diet soda increases the risk of obesity and high blood pressure, but who was not involved in this study, said that he was not surprised by the finding, but was surprised by its magnitude. He had previously reported that the drinking of diet soda and beverages increases the risk of obesity and high blood pressure. This additional evidence provides a supporting argument to back up the original argument that regular drinking of diet or regular soda increases factors associated with heart disease and diabetes. For those of us who are worried about such health risks, the finding itself, along with its support by other experts who have studied the subject, makes the conclusion that drinking soda beverages is a cause of diabetes and heart problems quite plausible. Still, there is a danger of committing the *post hoc* fallacy when interpreting such experimental findings and trying to express them in causal terms.

The author of the study, Dr. Ramachandran S. Vasan of Boston University School of Medicine, said that it is unlikely that an ingredient in soda causes the effect. He added that it is more likely that consuming these drinks is "simply a marker for the poor eating habits of the participants." This remark suggests that those who drink soda beverages regularly also consume other foods of poor nutritional value, and it is all their diet choices as a whole that cause conditions, such as being overweight and having high blood pressure, that are known to have adverse consequences for diabetes and heart problems. To jump to the conclusion that drinking soda causes metabolic syndrome would be an instance of incorrect *post hoc* reasoning. To single out drinking soda regularly as the cause of these unhealthy outcomes, there would need to be an additional experimental investigation that studied whether people with otherwise healthy diets, but who regularly consume diet or regular soda, also have metabolic syndrome.

We might ask which of the seven critical questions should be asked in this case before jumping to a causal conclusion. It could be question 6, because if the correlation between drinking soda and metabolic syndrome fails to hold outside the range of people who drink soda and also eat and drink a lot of other questionably healthy foods, drinking of soda is not itself the causal factor. The cause could be poor eating habits generally and the drinking of soda may be just one indicator of a larger pattern of eating habits. Certainly there needs to be a strong reservation in this case between drawing a causal conclusion on the basis of the evidence found so far. Still, even though critical questions need to be asked, and some reservations about drawing a causal conclusion should be expressed, the finding is very interesting from a point of view of health and nutrition. In this case, the statistical correlation found between drinking these beverages and a condition associated with serious health problems suggests the causal conclusion strongly enough to make those interested in nutrition and health sit up and pay attention.

The plausibility of drawing a causal inference in example 8.17 also suggests that further collection of scientific data on the question would be interesting. The conclusion that A causes B in such a case should be treated as a practical hypothesis or presumption that should be studied further and that those deliberating about what to do should pay attention to it. It should be treated in this provisional way as a hypothesis worth considering, or perhaps even tentatively worth acceptance, rather than as a scientifically established fact. The only way that the hypothesis that A causes B should be taken to be a certified scientific finding is by means of the theoretical clarification of the precise causal connection between A and B according to established scientific laws, in a rigorous scientific inquiry. Only then can we be confident of the existence of a definitely confirmed causal link between A and B. In this case, what needs to be established is a causal linkage between some ingredient in the soda pop and the outcome of metabolic syndrome.

It is interesting to contrast example 8.17 with another case, where it is highly dubious whether a strong inductive argument can be made out for a causal conclusion despite impressive statistical evidence of the correlation between two factors.

Example 8.18

In an article in the *Lancet* (June 15, 1985, pp. 1375–1378), Steffie Woolhandler and David Himmelstein found from examining data from 141 countries that infant mortality rates in 1979 were correlated with increases in military spending. From these statistical findings, they derived the conclusion that arms spending is causally related to infant mortality. Their conclusion is that "It seems that bombs, both nuclear and conventional, may kill before they explode" (p. 1377). They argued that even after allowance for other relevant factors, their analysis confirms a significant correlation: "While correlation does not prove causation, we think it highly plausible that such a causal link does exist" (p. 1377). However, Dr. John Bailar, a biostatistician at the Harvard School of Public Health has criticized the conclusion of these two authors saying, "The methods they've used are adequate for some kinds of description but simply are not up to the job of telling what causes what. It may be high infant mortality that causes military spending" (*Winnipeg Free Press*, Associated Press; June 15, 1985, p. 70). Dr. Bailar also indicated that the approach of Woolhandler and Himmelstein could be used to show a link between infant mortality and the consumption of bananas: "Bananas are a greater staple of diet in a good many poor parts of the world, but that doesn't mean that bananas cause infant deaths."

Could the statistical findings of Woolhandler and Himmelstein indicate that arms spending causes infant mortality? Their argument is of the form (C) which, as noted, can be a reasonable type of argument. However, (C) can be open to several different types of critical questions, and therefore requires considerable strengthening to be substantiated, as a scientific conclusion.

Has the argument been sufficiently strengthened in this case? We do not know, without studying the Woolhandler and Himmelstein article more thoroughly, except to note that they claim that they have allowed for "other relevant factors." But observe also that Dr. Bailar's criticism that it may be the high infant mortality that causes the military spending, is a query of the form of critical question 3 as it applies to the argumentation scheme from correlation to causation. Thus our confidence in the plausibility of the conclusion suggested by Woolhandler and Himmelstein should be reserved until we are assured that they can provide adequate evidence that the causal relationship is not the reverse of what they conclude. Dr. Bailar's parting remark about the bananas also suggests that we should not be too quick to interpret the correlation between arms spending and infant mortality as anything more than coincidence until we can be satisfied that other critical questions can be answered.

Further developments in this controversy will turn on the various factors we have studied in relation to the seven types of critical questions above. The statisticians have sophisticated methods for arguing out the degrees of probability we can reasonably attach to the correlations involved. These arguments cannot, however, at this point in the inquiry, conclusively establish the existence of a causal connection between the two variables. At best the causal conclusion must remain an argument based on plausible reasoning, and therefore subject to further criticisms and replies, until some underlying physical or causal link is found between the two variables.

Some cases are highly controversial and those personally caught up in the situation find it very hard to be flexible, and to bend from the viewpoint that they're so convinced is reasonable to them. Scientific evidence, of the sort delivered by experts and that is technical and specialized, can be in a process of change as new experimental evidence comes in. In such cases, it may be very difficult for someone personally involved in such a distressful matter to agree with what the experts are saying, especially when what one expert says appears to conflict with what another says. Example 8.19 is a brief summary of a report in a newspaper article (Arthur Allen, 'Don't Blame the Needle,' *National Post*, July 24, 2007, p. A9).

Example 8.19

A woman who was convinced that her son became autistic after receiving a vaccination for measles and mumps and rubella (MMR) took her case to court, alleging that the vaccination caused her son's autism. Scientific opinion seemed to be divided on the issue, and to be in a process of change. The theory of a causal link between vaccine and autism was initially reported in 1998 by a London gastroenterologist, Andrew Wakefield. His study was later criticized as flawed, and subsequent scientific studies raised doubts about whether the small amounts of mercury used in the early vaccines was large enough to cause autism. This evidence did not convince the mother who went to court, who said, "I know what happened to my son after he got his MMR shot. I have no doubt. There's no way they'll convince me that all these kids were not damaged by vaccines."

In this case the mother sees what she takes to be the effect of the vaccination, based on her personal experience of raising her child. Since the expert scientific evidence is technical, and seems to be conflicting, to her it seems better to judge on the basis of her personal opinion of what she knows of the facts of the case. Also, some of the scientific opinions, and

284

also some books that have been written on the subject of autism and vaccination, appear to corroborate her belief that the vaccination caused the autism. However, there has been a growing body of scientific evidence put forward by experts raising critical questions about a causal link between vaccination and autism. The more recent body of expert opinion provides abundant grounds for doubting that such a causal link exists.

8.11 SUMMARY

Many common generalizations and causal claims are based on inductive and statistical arguments. If these arguments are carefully constructed using scientific methods of experimental verification, it may take specialized statistical knowledge to properly evaluate them.[11] However, many of the most common generalizations and causal claims can be very effectively questioned and criticized without any specialized knowledge of statistical techniques, or at least any more than is given in this chapter. The first question to ask is "What is the evidence?" If the evidence given is based on a sample, then it can be questioned whether the sample is inadequate or biased. If there are vague terms used, or there is evident lack of access to data, questions relating to the fallacies of meaningless and unknowable statistics can be raised. If the survey that provided the evidence for a claim was based on a question asked of a sample of respondents, it may be reasonable to inquire into the precise wording of the question.

In general, any vague terms used in a precise statistical claim should be questioned. The burden of proof should be on the arguer who advanced the statistical claim to offer a definition that gives clear cut-off points. Some terms, however, are so vague, and so open to interpretation and controversy that, if they are used in a statistical claim, they must be very carefully defined and these definitions must be defended as reasonable. If such definitions or defenses are not forthcoming, the statistical argument must be regarded as weak, or open to criticism.

Whether a failure to offer clear enough definitions is so hopeless that it can justifiably be said to commit the error of meaningless statistics is a question of judgment for the context of dialogue in each particular

---

11 I would like to thank Hatem Howlader, Jan Kmenta, and Günter Weiss for reading this chapter and suggesting many improvements of formulation to more accurately represent or be consistent with correct developments in the field of statistics. These friendly statisticians also pointed out several books and articles that turned out to be very useful.

case. The two hallmarks of this error are (1) the use of an extremely vague term, subject to broad interpretation, and (2) no attempt to define the term clearly, or to justify a definition. When these failures are so bad in a particular argument that it is highly implausible that any precise, justifiable definition could possibly be given that would be consistent with the exact statistical precision of the type of figure given, then a critic is justified in alleging that a case of the error of meaningless statistics has occurred. Similarly, the error of unknowable statistics takes place where the practical impossibility of gathering evidence to support a statistical claim is so extreme that no defense of the claim could be plausibly made.

Finally, if the argument is one that goes from correlation to causation, it may be reasonable to ask many kinds of questions. How many instances of the correlation were determined? Can we be assured that the causal relation goes in the direction indicated? Is there some third factor, a common cause that might account for the correlation? Could the causal relationship be indirect – mediated through other causal variables? Could the causal relationship be limited to a certain range of cases only? As each criticism is dealt with successfully in the particular case at issue, the plausibility of the argument from correlation to causation is strengthened.

Generally speaking, correlation and causation are two different kinds of relationships. Correlation is a symmetrical relationship, meaning that whenever A is correlated with B, B will always be correlated with A. However, causation is not generally a symmetrical relation, for there are many cases where A causes B but B does not cause A. Yet causation is not totally asymmetrical either, for there are some instances where A causes B and B causes A. This can happen in the type of feedback relationship between two variables that we encountered in our analysis of arguing in a circle. For example, in a particular case it might be that emigration of families from an area causes a slump in the building trade in that area, while at the same time it may also be true to say that the slump in the building trade is causing emigration of families. Here the two variables are not causally independent of each other, so there is a circular relationship between them.

Generally then, correlation and causation are different types of relationships, and you cannot argue directly or conclusively from correlation to causation. Correlation is established by observation of instances of one type of event and how often it occurs or does not occur when another type of event occurs or does not occur. Once instances of correlations are observed and reported, the statistician can draw inferences about them. Causality, by contrast, is a relationship that links two events, or types of events in a practical way such that the occurrence of the one event is affected by the occurrence of the other in a particular situation. Even though causation and correlation are fundamentally different, you can argue, in a suitably careful and circumspect manner, from one to the other. The problem of dealing with *post hoc* argumentation is to know how to construct and evaluate such arguments without committing specific basic errors or lapses in your argument.

In evaluating a particular case where a causal conclusion is advanced by a proponent, it may be difficult to know, or to conclusively establish that any or all of the relevant critical questions have been satisfactorily answered, according to the obligation of proof appropriate for the context of dialogue. However, if there seems to be plausible doubt that any of them is met in a particular case, an initial burden of proof is on the respondent to ask the right critical questions, and to thereby challenge the causal conclusion put forward by the proponent. If the question is reasonable, according to the given evidence and knowledge of the case is in dispute, the burden of proof is thereby shifted onto the proponent to give reasons why each premise challenged can reasonably be accommodated by evidence. Only in the more extreme kinds of cases however, may it be justifiably said that a *post hoc* fallacy has been committed when no adequate response has been given or is forthcoming, and the arguer dogmatically insists that his causal conclusion cannot be challenged or questioned in the discussion. Such a refusal to meet the obligations of answering reasonable questions, and to give arguments for one's claim, violates the negative rules of persuasion dialogue given in chapter 1.

In this chapter it has been shown how characteristic types of gaps can occur in statistical and causal arguments that should invite relevant questions to be asked by the reasonable respondent to the argument. Where a clear gap is left open, then the respondent's question may indicate that an error or bias has occurred. However, errors can be rectified, and the reasonable respondent should not leap too quickly to accuse one who has left such a gap of having committed a fallacy. For, as we have often emphasized, an allegation of fallacy is a very serious type of criticism of an argument. Only where the critic can show that the gap cannot plausibly be filled should the arguer be reasonably accused of having committed a fallacy in his argument from correlation to causation or statistical argument. Only if an argument is so weak or bad that any possible defense of it appears hopeless, and no response to relevant critical questions is given, should the argument be condemned as fallacious.

The basic problem with arguing from correlation to causation is that it may be possible that the correlation is simply due to coincidence, or to some link other than a causal relationship. Hence in a scientific inquiry, a serious effort must be made to answer each of the critical questions 1 through 7, using careful experimental methods of investigation. To work to rule out error, tests may have to be repeated. Study of a control group is another important step to work towards ruling out error. Careful use of random procedures for selecting test subjects may also help to rule out bias.

In this chapter we have not tried to set out complete criteria for good scientific method in gathering data. Our goal has been the more modest one of giving a critical reasoner some basic tools for reasonably questioning the evidential basis of common statistical claims and generalizations that play such an important role in everyday arguments.

9

Natural language argumentation

All the arguments and disputes we have been concerned with have been conducted and evaluated in the medium of natural language. But in natural language, words are vague and ambiguous. Words are most often not defined very precisely, and are therefore subject to the interpretation of the disputants in an argument. And since words in an argument may be interpreted in different ways, or according to different standards of precision, they can be used in a fashion that is friendly to the case of the arguer, and unfriendly to the case of the person to whom the argument is directed. Words can be used as weapons in argument.

When an Israeli border town is bombed, the newspapers in Israel describe the event as a terrorist attack, but Arab sources describe the same event as an action taken by freedom fighters in defence of their rights. However, when an Arab city is bombed, its inhabitants describe the event as a terrorist attack, unlike the Israelis, who describe it as a defensive strike against terrorists. The same group of individuals, in each instance, are described as "terrorists" by one side and "freedom fighters" by the other side. Now neither of these contentious terms has been defined, so they are subject to wide and various interpretations in a particular situation. For this reason, it is appropriate to question whether the two terms are being used in such a way that any action by the other side is routinely classified as that of "terrorists," and any action by one's own side is classified as that of "freedom fighters." In effect, the words are used as weapons, like guns and bombs.

This aggressive and one-sided use of words in argument is not consistent with the aims of reasonable dialogue. It is a form of pre-empting or stifling reasonable dialogue. The program of this chapter is to study the most important problems and strategies in argument related to the sophistical deployment of vague and ambiguous terms in natural language.

A term is said to be ambiguous if it has more than one meaning. For example, the term 'bank' is ambiguous. It could mean 'savings bank' in one context, but it could also mean 'river bank' in another context. Sometimes a whole sentence can be ambiguous. Amusing examples of sentence ambiguity sort are often found in newspaper headlines that have an unintended interpretation.

Example 9.0

Astronaut Takes Blame for Gas in Spacecraft

Apparently there was a leak in a gas line somewhere in the spacecraft, but when you first read the sentence, it seems to have another meaning. Such cases may seem fairly trivial. In many arguments we may get into no trouble even if a word or sentence is ambiguous, for the context of the dialogue may make it clear which meaning is meant. For example, the sentence, 'Kills mosquitoes for up to five hours' was displayed prominently on the box of a mosquito coil, a product designed to create smoke that kills mosquitoes. When you first read the sentence, it looks like it claims that the product kills mosquitoes for up to five hours, at which point they come alive again, and are no longer dead. This interpretation makes no sense. If you kill a mosquito, it follows that it is dead, and it follows that it cannot come alive again. Clearly, what the sentence really claims is that the coil goes on burning, and killing mosquitoes, for a period of up to five hours. The confusion seems to arise because, at first glance, it looks as if the sentence is saying that the product kills each individual mosquito for up to five hours. What it is really saying, of course, is that the product kills any mosquitoes that come into contact with the smoke, for a period of up to five hours. It would be clear to any reader of the sentence on the box who is looking at it in a store that this is what is meant.

It is where the context does not clearly disambiguate that we can get into trouble with ambiguous terms or sentences. If Smith tells his wife to meet him at the bank at three o'clock, there might be doubt in some contexts whether he meant the river bank or the savings bank. In such a case, Smith might be taken to task for not being sufficiently clear. Ambiguity resulting in miscommunication can be a very serious matter, in some cases leading to loss of money, property, health, or human lives, as the following case (Cushing 1994, p. 10) shows.

Example 9.1

The pilot of a plane taking off from Los Rodeos airport in the Canary Islands radioed the message, "We are now at takeoff," to the tower. The pilot meant the message to say that the plane was now in the process of taking off, but the air controller took it to mean, 'We are now at the takeoff point' – that is, getting ready to start taking off. The result of this failure of communication was a collision with another aircraft, in which 583 lives were lost.

It is useful to mention this kind of case because of the widespread belief that finding ambiguity and defining terms precisely are trivial matters, mere hair-splitting. However, billions of dollars are often at stake in lawsuits that turn on the meanings of terms like 'contract' or 'wetlands.' Many fallacious arguments are widely accepted because most people are generally disinclined to take communication problems arising from ambiguity, vagueness, and obscure language seriously.

A term is said to be *vague* if there exist borderline cases where it is not clear whether the term correctly applies to the case. For example, the term 'rich' is vague. If a man has eight hundred thousand dollars as his total assets, some would say he is rich. But if the conversation were among a group of billionaires during a meeting of the Oil Magnates' Club, such a man would not be called rich.

There is no clear or exact cut-off point at which a person may definitely be said to pass from being not rich to rich. Of course, one could stipulate an exact point by saying, for example, that any person who has a million dollars or more is rich and nobody with less than that amount is rich. However, such a precise definition could be open to reasonable dispute or question. Why? Because the term rich is vague.

In some contexts of dialogue, it can be useful to give a precise definition of a vague term. Unless a good reason can be given for selecting a particular cut-off point, the precise definition may be of no use for the purposes of reasonable argument. Vagueness is all-pervasive in natural language, and it is neither possible nor useful to eliminate all vague terms from every argument.

Because we are continually discovering or inventing new things, terms that were not vague or ambiguous can become vague or ambiguous. For example, the meaning of the term 'death' used to be clear enough. Death was defined as irreversible cessation of breathing and blood circulation. But with the advent of technology to artificially continue breathing and blood circulation even after the irreversible destruction of the brain, a new definition of 'death' had to be considered. Or at any rate, new standards for the determination of death in borderline cases had to be considered. The problem was posed by the fact that these borderline cases were not previously known to exist. So the term 'death of a person' had to be made more precise, in order to deal with the developments in medicine.

This continual increase in the clarification of terms is true of the sciences, as well as in the law and in non-scientific language. In plant taxonomy in biology, for example, a taxon classification category may later be split up into several taxa, so plants that were many years ago considered to be the same may now be classified as different. For example, according to Jeffrey (1982, p. 70), the family Saxifragaceae, as circumscribed by Hooker in 1865, is now considered to represent eleven different families of plants.

In short, vagueness and ambiguity can never be totally and entirely eliminated. Vagueness and ambiguity are not completely intolerable, or always destructive of reasonable argument. They can, however, lead to failure of communication and other problems in some contexts of argument. Terms need to be defined precisely enough in relation to the specific context of dialogue.

It is the mark of the pedant to use unnecessarily precise definitions of terms in contexts where this extra precision is not practically useful. In fact, the use of spurious precision can itself be a positive obstacle to good argument. If you see a claim that seventy-five to eighty per cent of all convicted criminals are products of broken homes, you should be careful that these figures may reflect a spurious precision. For whether the claim is plausible very much depends on how you define 'broken home.' If no definition is offered, the numerical claim is meaningless. Even if a more precise definition of broken home were attempted, the definition itself might well be open to dispute or questioning in the context of the issue being argued. In a case like this, the use of precise figures or cut-off points may not necessarily be a sign of justifiable or reasonable argument.

The degree of precision that best serves good argument must be relative to the context of dialogue. The nature of a particular controversy must set a reasonable standard for precision of the definitions of the terms that occur in an argument.

You may be inclined to think that deciding upon the definition of a word is a matter of harmless quibbling, of no serious consequence. In fact, an adoption of a definition of a term like 'poverty' or 'unemployment' by an organization or government agency can have serious economic consequences for large numbers of people.

292

Consider the vague term 'farmer.' A hobby farmer who has a few acres which he does not regularly cultivate or depend upon for a living may call himself a farmer, but his neighbors, who have huge grain farms, may not call him a farmer. However, if he wants to call himself a farmer, nobody may care to dispute it. If the context of argument is a government benefit or income tax exemption that applies only to farmers, his claim may now become subject to considerable dispute. To make the new regulation workable, the government will have to offer some more precise definition of farmer that will clearly rule whether this man is eligible for the benefit. Such definitions are often tied in closely to statistical arguments, as chapter 8 showed. Governments often base their policies and regulations on statistical findings that are, in turn, based on definitions of key words and concepts. However, in many cases, arguments about these policies may conceal the controversial nature of an underlying definition of a vague term.

Even more curiously, in some cases one side to a dispute or controversy may declare a definition, and the other side may even challenge the first side's right to advance the definition. According to a note in the In Brief column of the Hastings Center Report of August 1986 ('For Access to Health Care, Who Is an Indian and Who Decides?,' by C.L.), the U.S. Public Health Service published a rule which specified who would qualify as an Indian, and therefore be eligible for Indian Health Service benefits. The definition of 'Indian' required that the individual must have one half or more Indian or Native Alaska ancestry, or have one quarter or more Indian or Native Alaska ancestry if they reside in a designated health service delivery area. The reaction of the director of the National Indian Health Board, Mr. Jake Whitecrow, was to declare that the Government was "infringing on the rights of individual tribes to determine who is eligible to be called a member." The problem here is who should have the right to decide how the term 'Indian' is to be defined in this context.

In some contexts of argument, terms can be ambiguous or vague, and no problems may result. In other cases however, we can get into terrible trouble with vague and ambiguous terms in an argument. Since many words in natural language tend to be vague or ambiguous, there is often room for argument on how a term should best be defined. Indeed, words and phrases are often used, defined, or invented by one party in a dispute in such a manner to defeat or undermine the other party's side of the dispute. Here the term in question is being used, in effect, as an argument. Therefore the other side should have a right to reply to, or even to reject the controversial term.

An argument contains a *loaded term* (*argumentatively loaded term*) when a term in the argument is defined or used in such a way as to defeat or undermine the position of the participant(s) in a dialogue to whom the argument is directed. The word term is meant here in a broad sense, to include both words and phrases. As noted in part one, the use of loaded terms in argument often takes the form of defining two parallel terms, one of which has connotations of being good or right, and the other having connotations of being bad or wrong. Then the latter term is applied to the opponent's side of the argument and the former term reserved for the proponent's side.

Indeed, in some extreme cases, the opponent himself is defined as coming under the heading of the bad term. Where this happens, the use of loaded terms is combined with an *ad hominem* attack. We have already seen a case of this sort. In example 6.9, the leader of a religious group, in effect, defined all his opponents as "devils" by the following sweeping proclamation.

Example 6.9

The dictionary defines devil as an adversary of God. If you are an opponent of mine, then you would be classified as a devil.

This appears to leave the opponent little room for maneuver. He may accept the dictionary definition, but if he accepts the application of the term to himself, he has lost the argument.

There are really two kinds of problems with the use of loaded definitions in argument, from the point of view of the respondent who has to try to deal with them. One is the reasonableness of the definition itself. The other is the reasonableness of the application of the term in question to one's own side of the argument, or to the proponent's side. In example 6.9, it is the second problem that appears paramount. Somehow it appears that the opponent against whom the argument is directed has been classified onto the devil's side whether he likes it or not.

A slightly more subtle case of the same type of strategy occurs in the example below.

Example 9.2

A psychologist, commenting on the case of a pair of parents who encourage their little girl to play with dolls and their little boy to play with a model construction set, describes the parents' behavior as "gender-prejudiced." He concludes that the parents should try harder to make their behavior gender-neutral. The parents object to this term as applied to them because they say that they feel there are genuine and important differences between boys and girls, and according to their view, respecting these differences may be justifiable rather than "prejudiced" behavior.

In this case, the parents are certainly objecting to the psychologist's argument on the ground that it contains a loaded term that stacks the argument unfairly against their point of view. They evidently do not see the description of their behavior as "prejudiced" as being reasonable in the case in question. For the use of the term "prejudiced" implies that their behavior is wrong, and that their position in the argument is biased and unreasonable.

What is going on in this type of case seems fairly clear. Terms may be defined or applied in a way that is not neutral with respect to an argument. And how a term is to be defined may itself be an issue subject to argument. Hence to define or use a term in a one-sided, argumentative way can be objectionable.

Words and definitions often have persuasive force in an argument. So you must be careful in argument to watch that the terms are not defined or applied in a way that stacks the argument against your case at the outset. When this happens in reasonable dialogue, it can be appropriate to challenge your opponent's argument on the ground that it contains a loaded term or definition.

So far, things are relatively clear. However, a complication arises, because the term 'begging the question' is often used to describe the kind of objection made by the parents in example 9.2. The parents might have objected that the psychologist's use of the phrase "gender-prejudiced" begs the question. What could this objection mean, over and above the objection already lodged above? According to section 2.7, begging the question is arguing in a circle. But where is the circle in the psychologist's argument in example 9.2? It seems hard to say, and hence the use of the phrase 'begging the question' has introduced a puzzle.

According to Hamblin (1970, p. 32), the origin of the term 'begging the question' is through translation of Aristotle's original Greek phrase τὸ ἐν ἀρχῇ αἰτεῖσθαι, in turn translated into Latin as *petitio principii*, which means "beg for that which is first [in the question at issue]." The meaning of this curious phrase becomes clearer in the context of persuasion dialogue as based on a conflict of opinion between two parties. In persuasion dialogue, one party may *ask to be granted* certain premises he needs to build up his case to persuade the other party of his thesis (his conclusion to be established in the dispute). The thesis (conclusion) is the *question* which is to be answered by this party through his argument. Hence to include this conclusion within the premises asked to be granted is to *beg the question*, i.e., to "beg for" the question (conclusion) which is supposed to be proved. In other words the fault is that of "begging for" something which should be earned through the work of argument.

According to the account given in section 2.7, begging the question is essentially the same fault in argument as arguing in a circle. However, unfortunately, the phrase 'begging the question' seems to be used in popular tradition, and even in logic textbooks, in various other ways. In some cases, the alleged fault of "begging the question" is taken to mean simple lack of evidence in argument. Similarly, the fallacy of question-begging epithet (question-begging appellative, question-begging term) is often used to refer to cases where a loaded term has been used in argument. This can be a misnomer, because the use of a loaded term in an argument does not necessarily imply that the argument is circular.

This tendency may have been historically encouraged by the treatment of Bentham who interpreted the fallacy of begging the question very broadly. Bentham (1962, p. 437) was concerned with appellatives (terms) that can be used in a laudatory (positive), neutral, or vituperative (negative) way in argument. He linked the use of such terms to the fallacy of begging the question by observing that in a certain type of example, the use of a loaded term can be used to disguise an absence of proof for a conclusion.

Example 9.3

This doctrine is heresy.

Therefore, this doctrine must be condemned.

According to Bentham (p. 436f.) this type of use of a loaded (vituperative) term to classify something can be an instance of the fallacy of begging the question because (a) the conclusion requires to be proved, and (b) the use of the loaded term is meant to cause it to be taken to be true that the conclusion has been true, but (c) the conclusion in fact has not been proved.

Now we can see that example 9.3 could indeed represent an interesting kind of failure that can occur in argument. But is it an instance of begging the question? The problem is that it is not necessarily a case of begging the question, if we mean circular argument by this phrase, as proposed above.

Consider the point of view of an arguer who has championed the doctrine in question, and then is confronted with the argument in example 9.3.

What is he to say? Well, of course, he could agree that if the doctrine is heresy, it should be condemned, and accept the validity of the argument. Even so, he might reject the classification of his doctrine as "heresy," and would be likely to do so if he had championed it. And therefore, he could reject the argument as an instance of the use of a loaded term. So far, there is no problem. The critic may have every right to make this objection.

What if he claims that the argument begs the question? How could he support this criticism? He might say that he doesn't accept the conclusion that the doctrine must be condemned. Therefore he doesn't accept the premise that the doctrine is heresy either, because the proponent of the argument has not proved it. This too is a reasonable objection, but it does not show that the argument is circular. It only shows that the argument is weak – that it lacks sufficient evidence to support the premise.

How could the critic support a contention that the argument is an instance of begging the question? One possibility is the following. He could argue that the premise could only be plausible on the prior presumption that the doctrine must be condemned, because 'heresy' is a vituperative (loaded) term for something bad. The problem is that the proponent of the argument could reasonably reject this contention, arguing that 'heresy' means 'contrary to the accepted teachings of the Church' and that he can offer independent evidence that this particular doctrine is contrary to the teachings of the Church. He might, for example, cite an official Church council that declared that this doctrine is contrary to Church teachings. He might also concede that heresy is something bad, and that therefore 'heresy' is a loaded term. Yet he could argue that the proposition 'This doctrine is heresy,' neither requires the prior presumption of, nor is equivalent to the proposition 'This doctrine must be condemned.'

In short, the argument in example 9.3 is not necessarily a case of begging the question. It may be an instance of a loaded definition. Yet it does not necessarily follow from the latter that it is an instance of begging the question. The problem is that the term 'begging the question' is somewhat confusing because of its unfamiliar and curious etymology, and this phrase has become widely used in popular speech for many faults or objections in argument other than circular argumentation. Indeed, according to D. D. Todd (1987), the phrase "to beg the question" has been commonly used in newspaper articles to refer to the practice of earnestly requesting or demanding that a certain question be raised or answered. This extreme of misusage suggests that the phrase is often incorrectly used to refer to something other than arguing in a circle.

In some cases, the problem is a *loaded definition* rather than a loaded term. In this type of case, a definition that tends to pre-empt or exclude an opponent's side of the case is advanced.

What Black has done here is to define 'murder' as unjustified killing. This move appears to win the argument by proving White's thesis false, and by ruling out White's argument based on his counter-example of the case of the hypothetical murder of Hitler. For if murder is unjustified killing, then if White is right that the killing of Hitler would have been justified, it would follow that the killing of Hitler would not have been murder. Hence White's counter-example no longer counts against Black's thesis that murder is always wrong.

How could White reply to Black's strategy? There are two options. He could dispute Black's definition of murder as unjustified killing. Or he could insist that the case of the killing of Hitler would have been murder, no matter how you reasonably define 'murder.' Either way, White would be criticizing Black's argument for its use of a loaded and unacceptable definition.

Could White accuse Black of having used a question-begging definition? To do this he would have to take an additional step. One way he might try to do this is as follows. White might argue that to prove something is unjustified requires the prior presumption that it is morally wrong. He might argue, for example, that 'unjustified' simply means 'morally wrong,' and that therefore Black's argument is circular. Note however, that Black could dispute this contention. He could argue that 'unjustified' means 'not justified' which means that a justification has not been given. He could argue that this does not necessarily require that the act in question be morally wrong. So once again, care is needed. Black's definition of murder as unjustified killing can be objected to by White as a loaded definition, but that does not necessarily mean that the definition begs the question.

Why is it that the term 'question-begging' is so tempting to apply to cases of a loaded definition in argumentation? The explanation could be that any use of a term or definition that seems to be contrary to one's own side of an argument, or could be contrary to it, is often a source of worry that the term in question could be somehow used to beg the question without anyone being clearly aware of what has transpired. A scientific case study may illustrate this kind of concern.

Disputes can arise among scientists on how terms in an area of science should be defined. Recently there have been heated debates about the Darwinian theory of evolution as a clear and verifiable scientific theory. New evolutionists have offered criticisms and improvements of the traditional theory of evolution, based on new scientific findings in other areas of science like genetics. These critics are now beginning to question whether the familiar way of classifying animals into mammals, reptiles, amphibians, and so forth, is defensible. A new school of classification called *cladistics* (from the Greek term for branch, *clade*) insist on classifying groups of animals without making prior assumptions about evolutionary descent of the groups so classified. According to the account of Begley (1985, p. 81), cladists are agnostic about evolution. The Hennig Society is named after the East German entomologist Willi Hennig, who founded cladistics in the 1950s.

Example 9.5

Unlike evolutionists, they do not take into account which animals might share a common ancestor – something that can be inferred from fossils but never proved. "Fossils are just a bunch of bones at different time levels. [Ancestry is] something you fill in with your mind," says biologist Steve Farris of the State University of New York at Stony Brook, who is also president of the three-year-old Hennig Society. Because cladists care about how many traits various groups of animals share today, not how they got that way, they are agnostic about evolution. Says Farris, "You don't have to presuppose evolution to do cladistics." (Begley 1985, p. 81)

The cladistic approach to classification results in some differences between their definitions and those of the more traditional evolutionists. For example, crocodiles are grouped with birds instead of lizards because their ankle joints and hearts resemble those of birds more than those of lizards. The traditional evolutionist would link crocodiles and lizards, but separate birds as a different class. However the cladist would regard birds and crocodiles as the more natural grouping because of the characteristics that they share.

299

According to Bowler (1984, p. 330) it is the more radical exponents of cladism that maintain that relationships between forms can be established without reference to evolution. These so-called transformed cladists are outspoken critics of Darwinism who argue that the traditional arguments for natural selection are unscientific.

As the quotation from Begley above suggests, the worry of the cladists about the traditional approach to taxonomy is that the traditional classifications may beg the question. By allowing assumptions about common descent of groups of animals into the very definitions of the groups, one may be begging the question of which animals share a common ancestor. Why? Because the question of which animals share a common ancestor is inferred from the fossil evidence, once the fossils are grouped into certain taxonomic categories. However, the prior act of grouping the organisms into these taxonomic categories may, in the traditional approach, be done partly on the basis of which ones are thought to share a common ancestor. Clearly, this procedure presents a real danger of having adopted question-begging language. However, in this case, the issue of potential circularity is related to the definitions of terms used by biologists. The cladists are not necessarily claiming that the traditional classifications and definitions beg specific conclusions about evolution. Because they are worried about the potential danger of circular reasoning, they try to choose terms that make no specific assumptions about lines of evolutionary descent.

Thus it is not necessarily fallacious to use vague terms, ambiguous terms, or even loaded terms in argument. However, such use of terms can lead in some cases towards the possibility of question-begging language. That is not the only problem that can arise from argumentative language however. Other important problems arising from the use of vague and ambiguous terms are the subject of the remainder of this chapter.

9.3 EQUIVOCATION AND AMPHIBOLY

The traditional fallacy of equivocation is said to occur in an argument when a word or phrase is used ambiguously, and shifts into different meanings during the course of the argument. The danger of equivocation is that if the ambiguous term is taken in one way in one occurrence in the argument, and in another way in the other occurrence, the argument could seem to be valid without really being valid. The resulting deception is the source of the fallacy.

A simple example may serve to illustrate how equivocation works.

300

Example 9.6

All stars are in orbit in outer space.

Sarah Flamingo is a star.

Therefore, Sarah Flamingo is in orbit in outer space.

This argument would be said to be an equivocation because the term 'star' is used ambiguously. In the first premise, 'star' is most plausibly taken to mean 'distant, luminous celestial body.' Then there is a shift of meaning. In the second premise, 'star' would most plausibly be taken to mean 'entertainment celebrity.' Because of this meaning shift, the argument could be taken to be valid when in fact it may not be valid.

If you look at example 9.6, it has the form of a valid argument: every x has property F; y is an x; therefore, y has property F. This form of argument is deductively valid. But is example 9.6 a valid argument? No, it is not, if the two occurrences of 'star' are disambiguated according to the most plausible interpretations of the premises.

Example 9.7

All celestial bodies are in orbit in outer space.

Sarah Flamingo is an entertainment celebrity.

Therefore, Sarah Flamingo is in orbit in outer space.

This argument is not valid. According to the most plausible interpretation we have in mind, the premises are true and the conclusion is false.

So now we see how equivocation can work as a fallacy. Example 9.7 is clearly invalid, and would not fool anybody. But example 9.6 has a valid form of argument, and might therefore convince somebody to accept its conclusion because they had accepted both premises, not realizing the ambiguity. An equivocal argument is one that may appear valid, but is not valid when disambiguated.

What makes an equivocation work is the contextual shift. We are tugged to interpret 'star' one way in order to make one premise plausibly come out true, but tugged another way in the different context of the other premise. By being tugged both ways, we equivocate.

The problem with an equivocal argument is that it is not really a single argument at all. In reality it is a bundle of arguments. The person to whom the argument is offered is presented with too many arguments, and is thereby invited to confusingly accept what appears to be a single

301

argument that is both valid and has true premises. In example 9.6, the person to whom the argument is directed is really offered four arguments. Only one of the four, namely example 9.7, has two plausibly true premises. But example 9.7 is an invalid argument. If you interpret 'star' consistently in both premises as meaning the same thing, then you will get an argument that is valid, but one of the premises will be false. In short, once you disambiguate, no matter how you do it, you can never get a valid argument with two plausible premises. So example 9.6 is really a cheat. It is not what it purports to be. It looks like you are getting one good argument. But in reality, you are getting four bad arguments.

With some of the previous fallacies, the problem was that an emotional appeal masked the very lack of argument. There, what seemed to be an argument was no argument. Here, what seems to be an argument is, in reality, too many arguments – a bundle of worthless arguments dressed up to look like one good one.

In some cases equivocation can be associated with the shift of meaning of a relative term as it occurs in different contexts. For example, 'tall' and 'short' are relative terms that shift their meanings in different contexts. A short basketball player may not be a short man. And a tall jockey may not be a tall woman. When such a shift in the meaning of a relative term occurs in two or more different propositions in an argument, an equivocation may occur.

Example 9.8

An elephant is an animal.

A grey elephant is a grey animal.

Therefore, a small elephant is a small animal.

Both premises are true in this argument, but the conclusion is false. A small elephant is plausibly taken in most contexts to be a relatively large animal – for example, if you had to transport it from one zoo to another.

The fact that words can shift in meaning as the context of argument changes, means that in longer arguments the process of shifting can be more gradual. Changing standards of comparison can be less easily detected where several steps are involved. A simple case is the classic example 9.9. In this case, each individual premise is plausible. But when you put all three premises together, a shift of meaning seems to gradually take place.

302

Example 9.9

The more you study, the more you know.

The more you know, the more you forget.

The more you forget, the less you know.

So why study?

Each of the three premises of this argument can plausibly be interpreted as being true, but if you look at the second and third premises together, you can see a problem. If you learn more, and consequently forget more, it doesn't follow that you know less. Your total increment of knowledge might be greater than before. As you learn more, you may forget more, but it does not follow that, on the whole, you must know less. The type of gradual equivocation in example 9.9 is developed through a series of gradual steps towards a conclusion, and therefore it could be a shift that could slip by unnoticed. A gradual shifting of meanings or standards of precision over several steps in argument could be an error that is harder to catch. In section 9.9 below, we will encounter a more subtle example of this phenomenon, and consequently gain a deeper understanding of equivocation.

Some sentences have more than one meaning because of the structural ambiguity of the sentence as a whole, rather than because of the ambiguity of any single word or phrase in the sentence. In some instances, as in the case of the following newspaper headline, this kind of ambiguity is fairly harmless.

Example 9.10

Juvenile Court to Try Shooting Defendant

These sentences suffer from grammatical ambiguity, because the grammatical structure of the sentence admits of two or more possible interpretations. Commercial ads sometimes use grammatical ambiguity as a deceptive sales tactic.

Example 9.11

A large ad in a newspaper stated "Two pizzas for one special price". Because pizza outlets had been offering a special "two pizzas for the regular price of one" in the past, readers of the ad got the impression that if you buy one pizza

303

at the regular price, then you get another pizza of the same size free. When pizza outlets who ran the ad were contacted however, the price they quoted for the two pizzas was higher than the regular price of one. A pizza outlet owner denied that the ad was misleading, saying, "The bottom line is that our menu says two pizzas for one great price." (Walton 1996, pp. 117–118)

The grammatical ambiguity in this case arises from the possibility that the sentence 'Two pizzas for one special price' can be taken in either of two ways. It could mean 'Two pizzas for one (special price)' or it could mean 'Two pizzas (for one special price).' The pizza outlet owners claimed that the second meaning was their intended message, but they knew that their buyers would take it in the first way. Their real meaning was indicated by the excuse they offered, saying that "with all the other places selling two-for-one," we "didn't have much choice" (Walton 1996, pp. 117–118). In this case, the grammatical ambiguity was used as marketing device, sometimes called the bait-and-switch technique.

In legal cases of contracts, wills, and other written agreements, the grammatical ambiguity of a sentence frequently leads to serious legal disputes. In the following case (*Gorgichuk v. American Home Assurance Co.*, CCHDRS 43–004 I.L.R., Ontario S.C., April 19, 1985) the disputed issue was whether a man's accidental death was covered by his insurance policy, according to the contract.

Example 9.12

The plaintiff's husband died as a result of a motor vehicle accident that occurred in Barbados. The bus in which the man died was transporting him, the plaintiff, and others from their hotel in Barbados to the airport at the end of their fourteen-day vacation. The couple had purchased the vacation package through an agent. As part of the package they purchased accident insurance under a group policy. The policy provided $45,000 in coverage for death occurring in consequence of riding in: (1) any aircraft . . .; or (2) 'any airport limousine or bus or surface vehicle substituted by the airline.' The policy provided $15,000 in coverage for death arising out of the use of other public conveyances. The plaintiff argued that the words 'substituted by the airline' in (2) above referred only to the words 'surface vehicle.'

The issue at trial was how clause (2) was to be interpreted, depending on its grammatical structure. Two interpretations are possible. It could be taken to mean 'any airport limousine, or bus or service vehicle substituted for an aircraft by the airline.' Or it could be taken to mean 'any airport limousine or bus, or service vehicle substituted for an aircraft by the airline.'

The insurance company argued for the first meaning. The bus had not been "substituted" for an aircraft by the airline. It was the normal mode of transport from the hotel to the terminal. So the insurance company argued that they did not have to pay the $45,000 death benefit. However the plaintiff argued that clause (2) should be interpreted as having the second meaning. On this interpretation, the bus did not have to be "substituted" for an aircraft. On this interpretation, the insurance company would have to pay out the $45,000 death benefit for the fatal bus accident. The court ruled that the phrase 'substituted by the airline' referred to all the modes of transport mentioned in clause (2), because the first meaning was the correct interpretation. The court ruled that the plaintiff was not entitled to collect the death benefit of $45,000.

9.4 ARGUMENTS BASED ON ANALOGY

Often, comparison to a similar situation can be forcefully used as an argument to press for consistency. This type of argument is based on the presumption that practical inconsistency, once alleged in argument, shifts a burden of reply onto the arguer who is accused of failing to be consistent. In this regard, the mechanism of burden of proof is similar to that of the circumstantial argument against the person.

Example 9.13

A lawyer for three prison inmates claimed that the law denying all sentenced prisoners the right to vote is irrational. The lawyer argued that the present law does not make sense because it excludes those who are in jail from voting, but allows those who are out on parole or awaiting sentence to vote. He also argued that the law makes no distinction between prisoners convicted for serious crimes and those in prison for minor infractions of the law. The lawyer argued that if lawmakers want to exclude prisoners from the democratic process, they must ensure that the reason is sufficiently important to override the constitutional right to vote. He concluded that the burden of proof must be on the state to show why prisoners should be denied this fundamental civil right.[1]

In this example, the lawyer's argument uses two comparisons between classes of prisoners to argue that the law is inconsistent, and thereby tries to shift the burden of proof onto the state to defend the current law.

1 This example is based on information in the article by Paul Moloney, 'Voting Right Denial Called Unfair to Prisoners,' *Winnipeg Free Press*, March 5, 1986, p. 3.

The first comparison is between those on parole or awaiting sentence, on the one hand, and the remainder of prisoners not in either of these categories. The one group is allowed to vote and the other is not. The argument is that this practice is not consistent because there is no relevant difference, with regard to the right to vote, between the two groups. The second comparison is between those who have committed serious crimes and those who are in prison for minor infractions. Here there is a relevant difference, according to the lawyer's argument, but the law does not recognize this difference with regard to voting, and is therefore once again inconsistent. The lawyer concludes that the present law, excluding all prisoners from voting, is irrational.

The lawyer is using these allegations of inconsistency to argue for changing the present law. Normally, the burden of proof would be on the arguer who argues for changing an existing practice. However, in this case the lawyer argues that the burden of proof should be on the state to defend the present law because, he argues, all persons have a constitutional right to vote. The kind of argument used here is the basis of the wedge argument studied in connection with slippery slope reasoning in section 9.7. The lawyer is arguing that we already allow convicted persons who are on parole or awaiting sentence the right to vote. To be consistent then, we should allow other convicted persons, who do not happen to be in either of these two situations, the right to vote as well. The argument is that we should treat the two similar cases alike.

The principle of treating similar cases similarly is a kind of argument that underlies many of the different kinds of arguments and criticisms studied in previous chapters. In the case of the *ad hominem* argument in example 6.4, the child's criticism of the parent's inconsistency in smoking while advocating non-smoking turned on the presumption that the parent is not treating himself and the child on the same basis. The parent smokes, but then tells the child he should not smoke. The child, by his allegation of circumstantial inconsistency, is in effect accusing the parent of treating similar cases differently.

The requirement of practical consistency means that similar cases should be treated alike, but it allows for a case to be treated differently if a good argument can be given that two cases are different in a relevant respect. Thus case-by-case consistency is different from logical consistency as defined in chapter 5. If two propositions are logically inconsistent, then if one is true the other has to be false. But if two cases are not treated consistently with each other, then this means that they are not similar in some respects, but they may be similar in other respects.

Sometimes the best way to argue against an argument based on comparison to another case is to produce yet another case that is also similar, but leads to the opposite conclusion. In example 9.13, the comparison between groups of individuals led the lawyer to the conclusion that convicts should be given the right to vote. However during the controversy on this issue, another argument from a parallel case was used to question whether convicts should be given the right to vote, in a letter to the Reader's Forum of the *Winnipeg Free Press*.

Example 9.14

In mock elections held in high schools, teenagers have shown themselves politically aware and capable of expressing their views in a civilized fashion. On this evidence, it is reasonable to have more confidence in the ability to reason and sense of honesty and fair play of many seventeen-year-olds, and less cause to be vigilant of their motives or integrity than you could say for many of those adults convicted of crimes. "In our haste to create a fair and equitable society for all, does it really make sense to extend the right to vote to criminals and degenerates in our jails but not to our young people? Why should anyone whose birthday falls one day too late be any less entitled to vote than someone else who has been found guilty of committing a crime and has been exiled out of society behind bars?"[2]

The conclusion of this argument seems to be a questioning of the wisdom of allowing convicted persons the right to vote. The argument contends that if we allow convicted prisoners the right to vote in elections, then in all consistency, how can we fail to recognize the right of our young people to vote as well?

By raising this question, the argument of example 9.14 suggests that we should not give convicted prisoners the right to vote, at least so long as we have the practice of not allowing minors the right to vote. Here the use of the comparison to the case of minors leads towards a conclusion opposed to the conclusion of the previous argument based on comparison of the cases used in example 9.13.

An argument that proceeds on the basis of a comparison of two similar cases is called an *argument from analogy*. Arguments from analogy are often extremely powerful forms of persuasion to a particular audience because they can compare an issue to something the audience is very familiar with or has very positive feelings about. Arguments based on analogies are a

2 Roger Young, 'No Vote for Convicts,' Reader's Forum, *Winnipeg Free Press*, March 22, 1986, p. 7.

form of plausible reasoning. Two situations may be similar or dissimilar in indefinitely many respects that could be cited. If a relevant similarity is cited, it may be used to shift the burden of proof in an argument. Arguments which press for consistency by means of a comparison between two cases alleged to be similar are arguments from analogy. It is therefore useful for us to study the argument from analogy.

9.5 ARGUMENTATIVE USE OF ANALOGY

The following example shows the use of analogy in a dispute, a type of dialogue where the conclusion of the one arguer is opposed to the conclusion of the other.

Example 9.15

President Reagan, in a speech advocating congressional funds to aid the Contra rebels in Nicaragua, compares the Contras to the American patriots who fought in the War of Independence. A speaker in Congress opposed to sending aid to the Contras compares the situation in Nicaragua to the war in Vietnam.

This example shows an argumentative use of analogy. Reagan's argument operates on the presumption that the patriots in the War of Independence must be accepted as having fought for a good cause that Congress must support. By his analogy then, Congress should likewise support the cause of the rebels in Nicaragua. The conclusion that Reagan would appear to be arguing for, one may presume, is that Congress should therefore grant funds to aid the Contra rebels.

The opposing speaker is evidently arguing for the opposite conclusion. His conclusion is that Congress should not get involved in the situation in Nicaragua, i.e., that Congress should not grant funds to support the Contras. The basis of his argument is the comparison between Nicaragua and Vietnam. U.S. intervention in Vietnam was disastrous. That is the presumption that the opposing speaker's argument operates on, because the present climate of opinion is that U.S. involvement in the Vietnam War led to an expensive, protracted war that the United States lost, with politically divisive results. It is not a situation that any country would want to repeat. Therefore, since the situation in Nicaragua is like that of Vietnam, by the speaker's analogy, the conclusion is that Congress should not get involved in aiding the rebel forces in Nicaragua.

Both speakers have advanced powerful analogies in this debate. Whether one argument is more persuasive than the other will depend on the continuation of the debate. Each can try to support his own analogy by bringing out relevant similarities, and to refute his opponent's analogy by citing relevant differences between the two cases.

The argumentation scheme for each side can be represented as follows, where S_0 represents the situation of the Vietnam War, S_1 represents the situation at the time of the American War of Independence, and S_2 represents the situation in Nicaragua. Also, let A represent the course of action that support be given to the forces fighting against the larger regime. The first argumentation scheme (F_1) represents the form of Reagan's argument, and the second scheme (F_2) is that of the opposing argumentation.

(F_1) The right thing to do in S_1 was to carry out A.
S_2 is similar to S_1.
Therefore, the right thing to do in S_2 is to carry out A.
(F_2) The wrong thing to do in S_0 was to carry out A.
S_2 is similar to S_0.
Therefore, the wrong thing to do in S_2 is to carry out A.

Notice that in this dialogue, each of the two analogies is being used argumentatively. This means that the analogy in the premises is used to derive a conclusion to the argument that is based on the analogy in the premises. The first premise says that something applies in one situation. The second premise says that another situation is similar to the first situation. The conclusion is that the same thing mentioned in the first premise also applies to the second situation.

An argument from analogy is not necessarily limited to two situations. If several situations can be shown to all share a particular characteristic, then it can be concluded that a new situation also shares that characteristic. Many texts – for example, Copi (1982, p. 389) – notice that analogies may be based on similarities among multiple cases, and conclude that all arguments from analogy are essentially inductive in nature. Their thesis is that an argument from analogy starts from a premise that one thing has a certain property, and that a second and third thing, and so forth, all have the property, to the conclusion that some other thing will also *probably* have the same property. However, the thesis that all arguments from analogy are inductive arguments is open to question.

The following example is cited by Copi (p. 390) as an everyday inference by analogy.

Example 9.16

I infer that a new pair of shoes will wear well on the grounds that I got good wear from other shoes previously purchased from the same store.

However, if example 9.16 is treated as an inductive argument, we would have to evaluate it by the standards of inductive argument as a bad argument. For one thing, it should be criticized as an instance of the fallacy of insufficient statistics, for no information is given on the size of the sample. How many pairs of shoes did I previously buy from this store? Perhaps not enough to justify an inductive generalization. Second, it could be a case of biased statistics. It could well be that the shoes I previously bought from this store were not representative of the new pair of shoes I just bought. For example, it could be that all the other shoes I previously bought there had thick soles, whereas this new pair of shoes has thin soles.

Many arguments from analogy that could be reasonable arguments, unfortunately, turn out to have to be evaluated as weak, questionable, or even fallacious if treated as inductive arguments. Why is this so? It is so because many powerful arguments from analogy are plausible arguments rather than inductive arguments.

To see why, look back to argumentation schemes (F_1) and (F_2). The first premise in each of these arguments was based on the presumption that the audience to whom the argument was directed must accept this proposition as basically plausible, given their basic position. The second premise is based upon a perceived similarity between two situations, again an assumption that essentially rests on plausible rather than inductive grounds.

Consider the following everyday type of inference based on analogy.

Example 9.17

Bob has a certain type of car and his brakes needed important repair work after he had driven it for thirty thousand miles. We have just driven our new car of the same type for almost thirty thousand miles. The next time we take it in for servicing, we should have the brakes checked.

Here again, if we treat the argument as essentially inductive, it is a weak argument at best, because it could be a case of insufficient or biased statistics. However, it does seem to be a good argument from analogy, for there is some reason to believe that my car and Bob's might be similar in the relevant respect.

You could say with justification that example 9.17 is a sort of *ad ignorantiam* argument. It is like example 2.23, where there was reason to be cautious about a rifle because we did not know that it was not loaded. Here again, we do not know that the car is unsafe, but because there are reasonable grounds for caution, it is better to assume that the car might be unsafe. It is reasonable, in other words, to stack the burden of proof against the presumption that the car is safe high enough to justify checking the brakes. So if it is an *ad ignorantiam* argument, it is a reasonable and not fallacious instance of it. In this case then the argument from analogy does support its conclusion because it is a plausible argument, not because it is an inductively strong argument.

Generally speaking then, the argumentative use of analogy shifts the burden of proof against an opponent's contention and towards one's own argument in controversial disputes where inductive evidence is not available and plausible reasoning is the moving force in shifting opinion one way or the other. It is exactly in this context of dialogue that analogy is a powerful basis for argument for a conclusion.

Analogies are often used nonargumentatively, for example, as similes and metaphors to create vivid mental pictures in literature, or to explain something unfamiliar by comparing it to something more familiar.

Example 9.18

The name of the baleen whale is derived from the long flexible plates which hang down from the roof of the whale's mouth, known as baleen or whalebone. The margin of each plate is frayed into a hairlike fringe, and the action of these fringed plates serves as a food strainer.[3]

Most of us have not observed the inside of a whale's mouth and it is not easy to visualize how the baleen functions or what it is like. Describing the margin of the baleen as a "hairlike fringe" is an analogy that helps the reader to picture the mouth and to get an idea of how it functions in straining out marine organisms when the whale is feeding. So there we have an analogy, but its use is not argumentative. The author is not using the analogy to shift the burden of proof to his side in an issue of controversy. We cannot pick out a conclusion that he is using the analogy to establish

3 Robert T. Orr, *Marine Mammals of California* (Berkeley: University of California Press, 1972), p. 11.

311

in his argument. Rather, the more reasonable interpretation of example 9.18 is that the author is using the simile of hair to help the reader to visualize an unfamiliar object so the whale can be described to the reader. When approaching any corpus, a first question is always to ask what is the conclusion, or if there is a conclusion to be established by the arguer. So in this instance too, it is well at the first point of examining a corpus containing an analogy to carefully distinguish whether there is an argument from analogy or whether it is an instance of the nonargumentative use of analogy.

9.6 CRITICIZING ARGUMENTS FROM ANALOGY

Arguments from analogy are common in law. In cases of alleged copyright infringement, both access to the material and copying of it must be proved. Similarity, for example, a similarity between two melodies in a pair of songs, can also be part of the evidence. In some cases however, such a similarity seems so striking that it can overwhelm any need to prove the other two elements of the evidence, being sufficient to convince a judge or jury all by itself. For example, if there is a striking similarity between two songs in which the melodies and note structure show what appears to be an almost complete identity during certain bars, the analogy could cause a jury to be strongly persuaded that there must have been a copyright violation. An interesting comment on this kind of case was made by Judge Alex Kozinski in a paper called 'How I Narrowly Escaped Insanity' (2001).

Example 9.19

Judge Kozinski related that around 1980 he wrote a science fiction novel about extracting a person's mind and implanting it into another person's head. When the movie Total Recall came out in 1990, he found the similarities between the movie and his unpublished novel uncanny. He found the story lines appeared to him to be identical, but the clincher was near the end of the movie, where there's a scene where the villain kicks over a fish tank and the camera shows the fish squirming on the floor. The identical scene had appeared in his novel. Therefore he was convinced there could be no doubt that his novel had been pirated. Later he started to have second thoughts. He had never finished the novel, nor had he ever sent it to any one to read. Nevertheless, he found that the striking similarity was so plausible and so seductive it made it very hard to resist the feeling that his ideas had been stolen. After much reflection he concluded, however, that despite the similarities, it was just a coincidence, and his strong impression that his idea must have been stolen was a persuasive illusion.

312

Arguments from analogy are persuasive because they compare two situations, at least one of which is familiar to the audience, and because there is a plausible basis of similarity between the two situations. Exactly what set of propositions comprise a familiar situation? Exactly when are two situations plausibly similar? In a particular case, these may be hard questions to answer very firmly. Arguments based on analogy may be slippery to either decisively confirm or refute. Yet, as we will see, there are critical questions for the argument based on analogy.

Any two situations can go on being compared in a dispute in a potentially unlimited number of ways pro and con. Therefore the use of an analogy characteristically leaves the dispute open to further argument. What a powerful analogy does, however, is to shift the burden of proof to one side, thereby requiring a response from the other side. When an analogy is challenged by pointing out a dissimilarity, the burden of proof is placed on the defender to respond. If the defender can successfully respond, the burden of proof is once again on the critic to argue for a relevant dissimilarity. In many cases, this pattern of challenge and response can go on for several moves in a sequence of reasonable dialogue.

After the disastrous fires in southern California in 2007, some 10,000 evacuees were housed in San Diego's Qualcomm stadium. This event drew comparisons with the use of the Superdome that was used as a shelter of last resort after hurricane Katrina struck New Orleans in 2005. The Superdome was flooded, leading to a deterioration of sanitary conditions. There were three deaths, and there were reports of vandalism, drug abuse, and gang activity. Inevitably, there were comparisons between the two events, as shown by an analogy cited in *Newsweek*.

Example 9.20

The Superdome had death and mayhem; Qualcomm had Starbucks and free massages.[4]

The insinuation drawn from this comparison was that affluent, white San Diego behaved better than poor, black New Orleans. Thus the comparison sets up an argument from analogy with the implicit conclusion that white San Diego behaved better than poor, black New Orleans. On the surface, the argument seems plausible, because the basic facts of the two situations

4 Jonathan Darman, 'A Tale of Two Cities, and Two Stadiums,' *Newsweek*, November 5, 2007, p. 12.

313

are similar. There was a huge natural disaster in both cases, and the citizens in the area had to be housed in a stadium. The argument also seems plausible because the two situations contrast in how they were handled and in what the outcomes were. In New Orleans it was assumed that the citizens would rather flee the area than stay in the stadium, and hence the long-term planning for housing them in the stadium was not properly carried out. In San Diego, in contrast, there was much better planning. The evacuees had ample space and plenty of food was provided. So one can see several reasons why the argument from analogy appears plausible on the surface.

However, it was also shown in the *Newsweek* article that the comparison was highly misleading, for the following reasons.

The Superdome offered no escape. Surrounded by water, evacuees could not leave for days, even after electricity, food, and water supplies dwindled. The storm blew part of the roof off the Superdome itself. Qualcomm was never in fire danger. Most shelter seekers arrived in their own cars and could leave at any time.

These differences between the cases show why the analogy is weak and highly questionable in certain respects. By asking critical questions about the similarities between the two situations, one can see there are important differences that need to be taken into account. Once these differences are considered, the original argument from analogy is shown to be weak and implausible.

There are three basic critical questions for the argument from analogy. One criticism is to question whether the comparison between the two situations is plausible or right. In this case, such a criticism would be easy to argue persuasively, because it is highly plausible that the two situations initially appear to be similar. The second criticism would be to argue that the analogy premise fails. This means questioning whether the analogy is faulty because the two situations compared are not similar in the relevant respect. This is the reason the argument from analogy fails in example 9.20.

A third way of raising a critical question would be to propose a counter-analogy. A good example of this type of strategy would be to try to question Reagan's argument from example 9.15 by offering the counter-analogy that the situation in Nicaragua is like the situation in Vietnam. In the present case, for example, a critic might argue that gun control has worked in Britain to significantly reduce armed robberies and other violent crimes where firearms are used; therefore banning ownership of firearms would also work in North America. Here the critic draws a parallel between one situation and another, thus deploying one analogy against another, in order to criticize the original analogy set out in example 9.20. By using a possibly better counter-analogy, the critic shifts the burden of proof back onto the original arguer to defend the plausibility of his analogy if he can.

Once an analogy between two cases is conceded, in some cases this concession can be exploited even further by an aggressive arguer by pressing for consistency with yet another case. When such a chain of arguments is set into motion, it is called a slippery slope argument.

9.7 SLIPPERY SLOPE ARGUMENTS

A slippery slope argument gets started when you are led to acknowledge that a difference between two things is not really significant. Once having acknowledged this first step, it may be difficult to deny that the same difference between the second thing and some other third thing is likewise not really significant. Once this sort of argument gets started, it can be too late to decisively stop it. You're on the slippery slope. It can be applied over and over, driving you to concede a conclusion that is absurd.

Example 9.21

A man is clocked at fifty-six miles per hour by a radar detection unit of the highway patrol in a fifty-five mile per hour speed limit zone. He argues to the patrolman that he should not get a ticket because the difference of one mile per hour in speed is insignificant: "After all it's really arbitrary that the agreed-upon speed limit is fifty-five rather than fifty-six isn't it? It's just because fifty-five is a round number that it is chosen as the limit."

What happens if the police officer accepts this argument? Then the next speeder, who is clocked at fifty-seven miles per hour, will argue: "Well, you let Smith off when he was clocked at fifty-six miles per hour. You conceded that one mile per hour doesn't really make a significant difference. By the same criterion, you must let me off without a ticket as well. If you don't, I am going to complain that you are not fair in doing your job. You did a special favor for Smith in letting him off. If you don't do the same for me, then that is favoritism and special treatment." Now the police officer is really in trouble. For the next motorist who is clocked at fifty-eight miles an hour can use the same argument over again: "I hear you let Jones off when he was clocked at fifty-seven. Since you admitted that one mile an hour doesn't make any difference, you have to let me off too." And so on, and so on. Ultimately, the poor police officer will have to let any speeder go without a ticket, no matter how fast he was going. Once the word spreads, everyone can demand "equal treatment."

A slippery slope argumentation scheme is a sequence of steps, a chain-argument of the following form. First it is conceded that there is no significant difference between two things A_0 and A_1. And since A_0 is acceptable, A_1 must be acceptable too. Then, since there is the very same relationship between A_1 and yet another thing A_2 as there was between A_0 and A_1, it must be conceded that A_2 is acceptable as well. Each time, the difference is not significant, it is argued, until by a sequence A_0, A_1, . . ., A_k, we eventually arrive at some absurd or disastrous result A_k. The inevitable conclusion is that A_k must be acceptable too. In the example above, we might eventually reach the point where a driver clocked at one hundred miles per hour could argue that he should not receive a speeding ticket.

How should the traffic patrolman have critically replied to the first speeder's argument? He could have replied that although the speed limit of fifty-five might be arbitrary to some degree, that is the exact limit set as uniform policy. And that uniform policy must be applied equally and fairly to all motorists. If a motorist is speeding to the hospital to save a badly injured passenger, then that could be fairly judged as a significant difference to exempt this driver from the policy in a particular case. So there may be exceptions in exceptional cases. The claim that a motorist is only exceeding the limit by a small amount may not be a significant difference between his case and that of the motorist who is driving within the limit. By this type of reply then, the patrolman could resist the slippery slope argument of the speeder.

In many cases of slippery slope argumentation there is some legitimate room for attack and defense. The reason is that with any organizational, legal, or social rules and policies, we rightly demand fair policies that apply equally to all persons who come under the rule. We also require that rules should not be rigidly applied by a thoughtless bureaucracy. If an exception is reasonably judged to be a relevantly different enough case to fairly qualify as an exceptional case, then we require that the rule should be broken. It is a question of how much one case resembles another.

In realistic argumentation, judging whether one case is relevantly similar enough to another case may require considerable judgment. This kind of judgment is based on an analogy between the cases. No doubt each case must be judged on its own merits, but the slippery slope enters the picture once an initial judgment is made that two cases are similar. Then if a third case has no less similarity to the last one, consistency requires that the next step be made to accepting that third case as well. And once on the slippery slope, there may be no way off.

The slippery slope is a particularly inviting trap where the first steps are the easiest to take. Some steps can be easier to take than others because vague terms can apply more easily in some situations than others. A traditional type of argument exemplifying this variability of different steps in the sequence is called the *sorites* argument. The sorites argument in example 9.22, like all sorites arguments, has two premises: a base premise (B_0), and an inductive premise (I).

Example 9.22

(B_0) Every man who is four feet in height is short.

If you add one tenth of an inch to a short man's height, he still remains short.

Therefore, every man is short.

In this instance, the base premise is highly plausible. If you apply the inductive premise to the base premise, the result, B_1, is also highly plausible.

(B_1) Every man who is four feet and one tenth of an inch in height is short.

But the sorites is a species of slippery slope argumentation because, each time you apply the inductive step (I) to the next new premise, B_2, B_3, . . ., B_k, you have to accept the next premise after that. It is typical of slippery slope argumentation that once you have conceded the first step, then consistency requires that you concede each succeeding step. And you must keep going as long as the purveyor of the slippery slope argument keeps leading you along. If you keep going indefinitely, you must concede an absurd conclusion. In example 9.22, you must eventually concede that every man is short.

The sorites is a puzzling argument and has often been thought to be a fallacy or sophistical argument because the premises seem true, the argument seems valid, and yet the conclusion is clearly false. That appears to be a contradiction, for if the premises of a valid argument are true, then the conclusion must be true. The sorites argument has traditionally been called the "heap," or "bald man" argument. If you have a heap of sand, and you take one grain away, it is still a heap of sand. You can continue to apply the process however and eventually, there will no longer be a heap. Or similarly, if you remove one hair from a man's head he is not bald. But if you keep doing it, then eventually he will cease being not bald. The sorites argument works because terms like 'short,' 'heap,' and 'bald' are vague. There is not a single precise point x, for example, where we can say that a man is bald if he has less than x hairs on his head, and not bald if he has x or more hairs on his head. Because of this lack of an exact cut-off point, there is no clear step of the slippery slope argument where the defender can resist applying the inductive step.

The reason the sorites argument is so effective as a tactic of argumentation is that there is a variation in the degree of plausibility with which a vague concept can be applied in different situations. For example, it is very highly plausible to claim that a man who is four feet in height is short. It is still highly plausible to say that a man who is five feet in height is short, in most contexts, even though in some contexts – for example, if we are talking about jockeys – the plausibility of the claim may be less. Although it may still be fairly plausible to say that a man who is five foot six is short, this claim has become less plausible than the two earlier ones.

Recognizing this variability, we can see how the sorites argument starts out strong, but then gets weaker in plausibility. When you apply (I) and (B_0) at the first step, the next conclusion (B_1) follows by the deductively valid form of argument *modus ponens*. Since both (B_0) and (I) are very highly plausible, (B_1) must be just as plausible. But in reality, (B_1) may be a little less plausible than (B_0). For in a plausible argument, the conclusion is only as plausible as the least plausible premise. Hence, the inductive step (I) must be less plausible than (B_0). And as we go along each step in the chain of *modus ponens* steps, (I) must become less and less plausible.[5]

What this shows is that the conditional (I) is not absolutely true, but rather has a practical legitimacy that can vary in plausibility value at different stages of application to men of different heights. As this conditional is applied over and over each time, its plausibility value tends to decrease somewhat. And eventually it reaches a range of cases where its plausibility has become marginal. Hence the sorites argument fails to prove that its conclusion (C) is true. You cannot conclude from it that every man must be short. So we can see that the sorites argument can involve a kind of fallacy or sophism, when applied to a particular case.

Why the sorites argument is a particularly powerful scheme of slippery slope argumentation is precisely because of the variability of the inductive premise in different contexts. Applied to the first step (B_0), the inductive step (I) is very highly plausible. It is virtually impossible to resist accepting

5 This analysis of the sorites is based on a solution to the sorites paradox similar to one offered in King (1979).

it as a plausible argument from a practical point of view. Then, it seems, to maintain consistency, the arguer to whom the slippery slope is directed, must continue to accept (I) at each succeeding step. If he refuses, he can be accused of inconsistency. His problem is that there is no particular, clear point in the sequence at which he can refuse to accept (I). For with vague terms, there is no precise cut-off point where the term clearly fails to begin to apply. So the slippery slope is like the processes of temptation and seduction. Once it is begun and then set into motion, it becomes progressively harder and harder to stop from going along with it.

The *domino effect argument* is the counteractive use of the possibility or threat of a slippery slope argument to counsel against taking a first step. It is often used as a conservative argument against any new policy or proposal that is untried. For example, it might be argued that if terminally ill patients are allowed to refuse heroic medical treatment, this might lead to elimination of the unfit. And this then eventually might lead to concentration camps and Nazi genocide squads. The domino effect argument is not a positive use of the slippery slope argument, but is a kind of defensive argument tactic or critical reply against a potential slippery slope that might develop. When dealing with the domino argument it is important to distinguish between the claim that certain consequences might develop and the claim that they *will* develop. The suggestion that they might develop is often used as a scare tactic, or strategy of intimidation to try to silence the opposition and prematurely close off the argument.

The slippery slope argument is often premised on exploiting the vagueness of a term in natural language. There is nothing wrong or fallacious about vagueness, in itself. However, just as ambiguity is exploited by an equivocation, vagueness is exploited by the slippery slope argument. For when the term deployed in a slippery slope attack is vague, there is no precise cut-off point at which the defender can start to resist deployment of the inductive step by the attacker. To successfully defend against the use of a slippery slope argument then, one must be careful not to commit oneself to the application of the inductive step right at the base premise, until it is seen where the argument is going, and what its ultimate conclusion might be.

The domino effect argument is a mirror image of the sorites argument, and it also involves a series of steps or stages, $S_0, S_1, \ldots, S_k$. Both the sorites argument and slippery slope argument generally have to do with vagueness of a term, but both of them can also typically involve causal links between the various stages of a sequence. The domino effect argument, for example, is often based on the premise that there is a causal link between

S_0 and S_1, and between S_1 and S_2, and so forth until some "horrible" outcome S_n is reached.

Sometimes the causal domino effect argument is reasonable. For example, if a row of dominos is set up so that each one is close enough to its neighbor, then if the first domino is pushed, the last one in the row will ultimately fall over as well. Where the causal domino effect argument becomes a fallacy is in the context where the premise that each step *might* cause the next is used to frighten an arguer to conclude that the last "horrible" step *will* happen unless he refuses to do anything that might cause the first step to happen. This type of argument can be criticized as inadequate if not enough additional proof or evidence is given to show that what might happen really will happen, or is likely to happen.

Whether a causal type of domino effect argument is reasonable or not depends on the strength or plausibility of the evidence given to support the causal linkages proposed at each step. The classical case of the domino effect argument was its use during the Vietnam War era to argue that if Vietnam fell to the Communists then neighboring countries like Cambodia would also fall. Then other adjacent countries would fall until the whole of east Asia would be in Communist hands. This argument was often used as a kind of scare tactic by its exponents, and because not much evidence seemed available to back it up very firmly, it came to be thought of as a fallacious type of argument, in this particular instance.

However, the domino effect argument can be a reasonable argument in a particular case if enough evidence can be given to make its premises plausible. Only when such evidence has not been given can we say that an instance of the domino effect argument is erroneous, incorrect, or unpersuasive.

In any slippery slope argument, there is an attacker and a defender. In example 9.21 the attacker is the motorist who tries to argue that his case should be the exception to the rule. The police officer tries to defend the applicability of the rule. In this instance, it was the attacker who used the argument incorrectly because his argument did not justify that his case should be treated as an exception. Sometimes the attacker's side of the argument is called the wedge argument, because it has the effect that once the defender makes the first exception, he will not be able to resist making more and more exceptions, until the rule is overwhelmed and destroyed. So the wedge argument as a tactic of argumentation is opposed to the domino effect argument, its counter-tactic (rebuttal).

To counter a slippery slope argument, the defender can use the domino effect response incorrectly or badly if he sticks dogmatically to requiring adherence to the rule in a particular case, even where a reasonably well-justified argument for admitting an exception has been made by the attacker. A case in point here is the use of the domino effect argument where the defender tries to use scare tactics instead of plausible evidence to keep the wedge from being driven in. This illicit use of the domino effect argument could also be called the *all hell will break loose* argument, and it has also been called the argument from *rigorism*.

Very often slippery slope arguments turn on the use of a vague term in natural language, but sometimes they have to do with questions of exceptions to a rule where the issue is not necessarily related to a vague term in the rule, or with causal sequences. In some cases, all three of these aspects are mixed together.

9.8 SUBTLE EQUIVOCATIONS

The examples of equivocation examined in section 9.3 were simple cases that would not be likely to seriously deceive alert and thoughtful participants in realistic arguments. Once the ambiguity is realized, these simple examples can easily be perceived as equivocal and dismissed as fallacious. However, in a context of discussion, there can be some complicating factors to make equivocation less easy to detect and criticize.

One problem is that in arguments in natural language, the meanings of the words or phrases that occur in the argument may themselves be subject to dispute. Consider the following argument, advanced in the context of a dialogue on the morality of law.

Example 9.23

Following the law is obligatory.

Failing to do something obligatory is morally wrong.

Therefore, failing to follow the law is morally wrong.

Anyone to whom this argument is directed might criticize it as committing the fallacy of equivocation, on the following grounds. In the first premise, 'obligatory' means legally obligatory. That is, the first premise means that a citizen has no choice but to follow the letter of the law – laws apply to everyone alike, and anyone who breaks a law may be subject to penalty. In the second premise, 'obligatory' means morally obligatory. Since 'obligatory' has shifted its meaning from the one premise to the other, example 9.23 is an equivocation. The only way both premises can plausibly be taken as true is to equivocate.

This criticism seems very reasonable, but what if the proponent of example 9.23 replies to the criticism as follows: "My argument is not an equivocation. It is a perfectly convincing and sound argument. For in the argument, I have identified the class of morally obligatory acts and the class of acts prescribed by law as perfectly equivalent in meaning. In fact, I am stipulating that, for the purposes of this argument 'morally obligatory acts' and 'acts prescribed by law' shall mean the same thing." Now according to this reply, example 9.23 cannot any longer be fairly considered an instance of the fallacy of equivocation. Or so it seems, for there is no longer any ambiguity on which to base an equivocation. For this arguer, there is no double meaning. Hence there can be no shift of meaning from the one premise to the other.

Of course we might question this arguer's right to impose his own definition unilaterally upon the dispute, or even criticize his definition as loaded or prejudicial. But apart from these possible objections, his reply to the charge of equivocation seems very reasonable. What are we to say now? Is example 9.23 a fallacy of equivocation or not? To resolve this dilemma we need to probe a little more deeply into the context of the dialogue.

We need to ask what the issue of the dialogue is supposed to be. Let us suppose that the issue is the moral basis of the law. Black, the proponent of example 9.23, is a legal positivist. That is, Black's position is that black-letter law (the statement of the law in "black and white" as it occurs in the current codes or law books) is identical to what the law should be taken to be, at any given time. White has a different position. He feels that the law as written is not always right, and that it can and should be subject to improvements. According to White then, real law is not the same as black-letter law.

Let us presume then that the context of dialogue is that Black and White are opposed in a dispute. Black is set to prove his thesis that failing to follow the law is always morally wrong. White is set to argue for his thesis that failing to follow the law can, in some cases, be morally acceptable. In this context then, Black has put forward example 9.23 as an argument. Is it a fallacy of equivocation or not? To answer this question we have to ask what the purpose of Black's argument should be in the context of the persuasion dialogue on morality of law. Since the dialogue is a dispute, Black's objective should be to argue from premises that White is committed to, in order to derive the conclusion that his own (Black's) thesis is true.

Black must try to show by valid arguments that his conclusion follows from propositions that White will accept as plausible. Now the problem with Black's use of example 9.23 for this purpose is White will only accept the two premises as plausible if 'obligatory' is disambiguated differently in each one.

So the problem with example 9.23, as an argument put forward in the context of reasonable dialogue with White on the issue of the dispute, is that the argument is not practically useful as a means of persuading White. True, from Black's point of view, there may be no ambiguity. From the viewpoint of Black's position as a legal positivist, the argument may be valid and both premises may be acceptable (to Black). That is not, however, necessarily a completely successful defence against White's objection that the argument is an equivocation.

For White, there is a very real and important distinction to be made between 'morally obligatory' and 'legally obligatory.' Any argument that denies the moral significance of this distinction would beg the question against White's case. Therefore, once White recognizes the ambiguity in the premises of example 9.23, this argument is worthless against his case in reasonable dialogue. Or at any rate, the burden of proof is on Black to show that his definition of the disputed term can be justified. If the premises are interpreted ambiguously, they could both be plausible, but the argument would then be invalid. If the premises are interpreted consistently, then the argument would be valid, but one premise or the other would not be plausible from White's point of view. Either way then, the argument is worthless as a means for Black to carry forward his case against White's position. Therefore, White is justified in criticizing the argument as an equivocation.

However, Black is also justified in his defence against White's charge of equivocation, to some extent. For from the viewpoint of Black's argued position, there is no ambiguity. Who then has the strongest argument? It depends on what the term 'obligatory' really means. In other words, the argument between Black and White has become a verbal dispute about the meaning of a term. In this regard, it is similar to example 9.4.

Sometimes, in a dispute about the meaning of a term in natural language, one side can be shown by appeal to linguistic evidence to have the stronger claim. In this case, both disputants have some claim to being justified in their usage of 'obligatory,' since this term does appear to be open to different interpretations. However, it seems fair to judge that a heavier burden of proof should be placed on Black's side of the argument, because most of us would be reasonably prepared to concede that there are some acts that are legally obligatory but not morally obligatory and vice versa. The plausibility of White's distinction shifts the burden towards Black.

In this case, equivocation has turned out to be similar, in an important respect, to question-begging epithet. By aggressively insisting on a meaning of the term 'obligatory' that is friendly to his own side of the argument, Black attempts to block White's side of the argument by refusing to countenance a distinction between the terms 'morally obligatory' and 'legally obligatory.'

Our discussion of example 9.23 shows that a charge of equivocation can reveal serious problems in realistic arguments. Moreover, by filling in a plausible context of dialogue for the argument, it has been possible to see how a realistic criticism of equivocation could be much harder to nail down than you might initially have thought. Definitions of key words in an argument are often open to dispute. Hence the burden of proof is initially on the critic who alleges an equivocation to show that there is an ambiguity used in an illicit way in the argument claimed to be fallacious. If the charge is substantiated, however, the burden is then on the defender to reply if he can.

Equivocation can be harder to detect when the shift of meaning takes place gradually over several steps in a longer argument. Standards of precision for vague terms, we have seen, may vary from proposition to proposition. When this sort of shift is more subtle and gradual, then the danger of sliding gradually into a fallacious argument is an even more serious threat to reasonable dialogue. The equivocation by Black in example 9.23 is like the question-begging language studied in section 9.2. It aggressively defines a term from the point of view of one side of the argument in an attempt to block the opponent's argument. In such a case the defender against the charge of equivocation may be open to a further criticism of using a loaded definition.

We could say then that equivocation is a kind of use of ambiguity of a term or terms in argument. Sometimes simply revealing the ambiguity is enough critical questioning to refute the argument as a fallacy of equivocation. However, in other cases, the defender of the argument may stick to his guns more resolutely and deny any ambiguity, from the point of view of his position in the argument. When this happens, the situation is very much like that of the case of a loaded definition, where the arguer may insist on defining a contentious term in a way that supports his own side of the argument and undermines his opponent's side. Or it may even be a case of question-begging language. In such cases, the argument has degenerated into a terminological dispute. This frequently happens in hotly contested arguments on controversial issues, and it can be a bad sign that reasoning is degenerating into a quarrel.

Some terminological disputes can be moderated by appealing to the dictionary, common usage, or plausible interpretations of a term, in order to judge where the burden of proof should lie. In other cases, a terminological dispute can be just as subject to reasonable argument as any other subject of reasonable dialogue. In such a case, it may be no trivial job to get a charge of equivocation to stick. So it is always a good idea when you are criticizing an argument as an instance of equivocation to ask how the argument could be defended against the charge by a determined defender.

9.9 VARIABILITY OF STRICTNESS OF STANDARDS

If vague terms are used in a consistent manner throughout an argument, there may be no logical difficulties or fallacies in the use of these vague terms in the argument. A problem can arise, however, where a vague term occurs more than once in different propositions in an argument, and differing standards of precision are required at each occurrence to make the propositions plausible. The problem that arises in such a case is a special kind of equivocation that is posed through the vagueness of terms in an argument. This is different from the slippery slope type of problem, but exhibits some of the same features.

The context of dialogue for the following example is the question of whether one should get married. Frank takes the traditional view that marriage is an excellent institution or practice that couples should enter into in good faith, and seek to preserve by serious efforts. Larry takes the progressive thesis that marriage is no longer practical or relevant in the 1980's and that couples should no longer enter into it or take it seriously. At one point in the dispute, Larry advances the following argument.

Example 9.24

Getting married involves promising to live with a person for the rest of your life, but nobody can safely predict compatibility with another person for life.[6]

Frank then asks: "Don't we often make promises that we don't keep?" And Larry replies: "Yes, but the point is that one should not make a promise

6 This example is derived from a similar example in Cederblom and Paulsen (1982, p. 59)

unless one can safely predict that one will keep it." Finally, Frank replies: "So you mean that if two people aren't compatible, they can't live together. So they shouldn't promise to do something they can't do." Larry concedes that this is exactly what he means, adding, "I conclude that nobody should ever get married."

Larry seems to have a logical argument worked out here. How should Frank criticize it? For the premises seem plausible and the argument seems valid. As a first step of analysis, let us set out Larry's argument more explicitly, listing the premises and conclusion.

Example 9.25

1. Getting married involves promising to live with a person for the rest of your life.
2. Nobody can safely predict compatibility with another person for life.
3. One should not make a promise unless one can safely predict that one will keep it.
4. If two people aren't compatible, they can't live together.
5. One should not promise to do something one can't do.
6. Therefore, nobody should ever get married.

Now if you look at each of premises (1) to (5) separately, each seems fairly plausible, or at least arguably plausible, but when you put them together, they imply (6) by valid arguments. (2) and (4) together imply that nobody can safely predict that two people can live together for life. Together with (3) and (5), this implies that one should not make a promise to live together with someone for life. This conclusion, however, taken together with (1), implies that nobody should ever get married. In short then, Larry appears to have a valid argument for his conclusion, with plausible premises as well. Poor Frank seems to be getting the worst of the argument.

Let us look at the argument more closely. The term 'compatible' occurs both in premise (2) and premise (4). 'Compatible' is a vague term. It could be hard to say exactly when two persons have reached the point of being incompatible. Should we say that two people are incompatible if they have occasional disputes or differences of opinion, or do not have much in common? Or should we reserve the term incompatible for cases where there is a deep hatred or bitterness between them, or constant fighting. It seems hard to say. Some couples can tolerate differences and disagreements better than others. We can have higher standards of what qualifies as compatibility, but then in other contexts we could equally well adopt more relaxed standards.

326

High standard
Really getting along smoothly
(great harmony, love, and respect)

Compatibility

Low standard
Functioning as a couple
(coexisting with tolerable friction)

Figure 9.1.

We sum up the two extreme possibilities of different sets of strictness in our standards of compatibility in figure 9.1. Now let us look at (4), which states that if two people can live together, they must be compatible. If we demanded the high standard of compatibility, (4) could plausibly come out false. To make (4) plausible, we have to drop to the low standard of 'compatible.' For some couples can manage to live together, even during bad periods when you could not really call them 'compatible,' according to the high standard.

Now let us look at (2), a premise that also contains the term 'compatible.' Here, the lower your standard of compatibility, the more couples are going to qualify as compatible. So if you predict compatibility with the lower standard in mind, the more likely you are to be right that a couple will remain compatible for a longer period. In this case, going for the lower standard makes for more danger that the proposition (2) will come out false. The higher your standard of compatibility, the harder it will be to predict that couples will remain compatible for life. To make (2) plausible, we tend to opt for the high standard of 'compatible.'

The same sort of ambiguity of strictness of standards affects the term 'safely predict' in premises (2) and (3) (see figure). Premise (3) states that you should not make a promise unless you can safely predict that you will keep it. But only if you interpret 'safely predict' by lower standards,

High standard
Predict without chance of error

Compatibility

Low standard
Be reasonably assured, but
exceptions could arise

Figure 9.2.

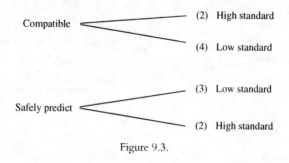

Figure 9.3.

does (3) come out as plausible, because promises cannot always be kept in every situation. Perhaps I couldn't have predicted that I couldn't keep my promise of being present on my father's birthday. I had no way of knowing, when I made the promise, that my wife would be ill on the same day as my father's birthday.

On the other hand, if you interpret (2) by the same low standard of 'safely predict,' it could most plausibly be interpreted as false. For if your standards of safe prediction are low, then someone who predicts compatibility for life in a reasonable number of cases is much more likely to be right. The low standard for 'safely predict' that makes (3) come out as plausible tends to make (2) come out as implausible, and consistent interpretation of (2) and (3) using the high standard would have the opposite result.

With respect to the two vague terms 'compatible' and 'safely predict' in the argument of example 9.25, what is the most plausible interpretation of the standard of precision appealed to in one premise is the least plausible interpretation in another premise. The most plausible interpretation of each term at each occurrence is summarized in figure 9.3. What has gone wrong with the argument of example 9.25 is that the vague terms appeal to different standards of precision in different premises during the course of an extended argument. The result is a kind of ambiguity imposed on the person to whom the argument is directed when he tries to interpret each individual premise as a plausible proposition. So it is a classical case of equivocation, yet one that occurs in a subtle pragmatic context of shifting standards over the course of an argument as it develops in dialogue.

9.10 CONCLUSIONS

In a relatively simple case of equivocation, where there are only two premises and one ambiguous term that occurs in each, the problem is usually easy to detect. Why? Because once you look at the two premises together, you may perceive that to make both of them plausible, you must interpret one premise one way, and the other in another way. If the argument is longer, however, with several different premises and several ambiguous or vague terms, the shift in meaning may be harder to detect. Why? Because you may not see the two premises next to each other when there is an equivocation between them. There may be several other premises between each of these two premises. In the meantime, you may well have forgotten that a particular word occurred before, in a previous plausible premise, and that you now need to interpret the same word in a different way than before to make the new premise plausible. The longer the argument, and the more vague and ambiguous words it contains, the more likely it is that the equivocation may slip by unnoticed.

The trick of an equivocation is that each premise appears individually plausible. It is only when you put two premises together, and compare the terms that have occurred in each, that the suspicion of equivocation may arise. Thus to deal with realistic cases of equivocation in practical argument, it is necessary to take a global perspective. The critic must scan the whole argument and see if there has been a shift of context that might affect any pair of premises that have been used in the argument.

With all the fallacies of language we have looked at in this chapter, the important thing is to study the whole argument in the context of the dialogue. If there has been a contextual shift, then we may have gotten into trouble with vagueness or ambiguity. Example 9.25 showed how a careful analysis of realistic cases of equivocation may require attention to subtle shifts of standards of accuracy that take place over a longer sequence of argumentation.

Here, as elsewhere in the study of fallacies, a fundamental axiom of reasonable criticism is once again borne out, as remarked upon by Whately (1836, p. 162): ". . . a very long discussion is one of the most effective veils of Fallacy; . . . a Fallacy which when stated barely . . . would not deceive a child, may deceive half the world if diluted in a quarto volume." In any analysis of an argument, therefore, an important step prior to criticizing the argument is to reconstruct the context of dialogue in order to see what its purpose can reasonably be presumed to be. Otherwise, the evidence to support the claim that the argument contains a fallacy may be incomplete. As J. L. Mackie (1967, p. 179) put it: "When we suspect a fallacy, our aim must be to discover exactly what the argument is". Mackie added that the first step in carrying out a reasoned evaluation of an argument is to pick out the main outlines, and then go on to examine the more subtle aspects or qualifications of the argument.

Since arguers are often vague, wandering, and inconsistent in what they assert over the course of a discussion, the first important step of analysis is always to determine what the type and goal of the argument is. Precisely in those cases where the argument is long and a "mass of verbiage," this process of deleting the unimportant details and sorting out and fairly interpreting the main stages can be crucial, and constitutes an important prerequisite of criticism.

Operating on the basis of the principle of charity, where a proposition contains vague or ambiguous terms, we naturally want to interpret the proposition in such a way that it comes out as most plausible. That is reasonable and correct. But if we do this in relation to two different propositions in the same argument, we may get into trouble. With the slippery slope argument, we want to accept the first step, and we are invited to, because it is a plausible proposition. As each step proceeds down the slippery slope, the propositions we are required to accept become less and less plausible. Once we are committed however, it becomes more difficult to turn back. We are sliding down the slippery slope.

The slippery slope argument becomes a problem in those middle regions of the application of the vague term where the inductive step becomes less and less plausible. The slippery slope argument is such an insidious attack on an arguer's position because once the defender accepts the first steps, which are highly plausible premises, he appears to become more and more heavily committed to accepting each succeeding step along the way. Hence if he stops, and tries to resist the attack in these middle ranges, the attacker may accuse him of being inconsistent.

However, each case must be studied on its own merits, because it is possible for the defender to commit a fallacy if the attacker has plausible arguments for overturning a rule or definition of a term in a particular case, and the defender tries to enforce the rule or definition against a stronger argument. Thus the context of each defense and attack depends on the burden of proof in the context of dialogue. If there is a strong burden of proof behind retaining an established rule or meaning of a term, those who argue that their case is a justifiable exception must meet high standards to meet the burden of proof.

The cleverness of the slippery slope attack, however, is that it starts out with a highly plausible first premise, and then attacks the defender's position by small degrees. Similarly with equivocation. We generously interpret an ambiguous term in such a way to make the proposition in which it occurs plausible. Then at the next step, we can make the next proposition plausible only by accepting a shift of context. It is at this point that the danger of equivocation is present.

The concept of a loaded definition is reminiscent of the concept of a loaded question that we have already encountered in the context of question-asking fallacies. And indeed there are some common aspects here. A presupposition of a question is said to be loaded if it automatically prejudices the position of the answerer as soon as he gives any direct answer to the question. Similarly here, a definition in a proposition in somebody's argument may be said to be loaded if assenting to the definition by accepting the proposition in the argument automatically prejudices the position of the person to whom the argument was directed. Loaded definitions are an unduly aggressive way of trying to force an arguer to accept some proposition, whereas in a critical discussion the arguer should be given the option of accepting the proposition or not. These tactics are violations of the negative rules of persuasion dialogue given in chapter 1. They are tactics to evade the obligation of proof by trying to bully a respondent into prematurely closing off argumentation. However, an argument that contains a loaded definition is not necessarily a fallacious argument. Similarly, you recall, a loaded question is not necessarily fallacious in every instance.

In general, the concept of a loaded definition and the concept of a question-begging epithet are two distinct types of criticisms. The latter is a stronger type of criticism. As we saw in the case of the loaded term in example 9.2, it does not necessarily follow that the parents are claiming that the psychologist's argument is fallacious or contains a question-begging epithet. For it could be possible that the psychologist might have various independent arguments based on evidence from psychology for viewing the parents' behavior in this case as an instance of "gender-prejudiced behavior." And it could well be, for all the parents know or have claimed so far, that the psychologist's arguments for this view do not depend on or are equivalent to his conclusion that the parents should try harder to make their behavior more gender-neutral. If this is possible then it shows that the parents can object to the psychologist's argument on the grounds that it contains a loaded definition without necessarily claiming that the psychologist's argument must contain a question-begging epithet. Of course, the parents could conceivably go on to claim that the psychologist's argument does contain a question-begging epithet, by building up a more extensive analysis and refutation of the psychologist's argument, but they need not do so in order to criticize or question the loaded definition.

To say that an argument contains a loaded definition is to say that a term in the argument is defined or used in such a way as to tend to be prejudicial against the position of the person to whom the argument is directed. However, an argument containing a question-begging epithet is so strongly loaded against the position of the person against whom it is directed that it can be shown to have required presumptions that exclude or negate that person's possibility of proving his thesis in the issue under contention. To prove that an argument is an instance of the unfair use of question-begging language then, a critic has to do more than to show that the definition is loaded. He has to show that the argument is viciously circular. He has to show that the premise containing the term or clause in question is so tightly connected to the conclusion of the argument to be proven by the one who advances the argument that there is a vicious circle in the argument.

Arguments and criticisms arising out of vagueness and ambiguity of terms in natural language can be difficult and frustrating at times. A precise definition may not be agreed upon because a term is inherently controversial, and even if a precise definition is advanced by one side, the other side may think that such a definition is prejudicial to their point of view. Similarly with analogies, two cases may be similar or dissimilar in one respect or another, but whether the feature cited is a relevant respect may be open to dispute. Hence, in many cases, the best one can hope for is a criticism that will reasonably shift the burden of proof. Often, plausible reasoning is the best standard one can reasonably hope to achieve in natural language argumentation. That is usually a high enough standard to conclude a successful argument in a critical discussion, inquiry, or negotiation.

Bibliography

Adler, Jerry. 1994. 'The Numbers Game.' *Newsweek*, July 25, pp. 56–58.

Alter, Jonathan. 1985. 'Round Up the Usual Suspects.' *Newsweek*, March 25, p. 69.

Apostel, L. 1982. 'Towards a General Theory of Argumentation.' In *Argumentation: Approaches to Theory Formation*, ed. E. M. Barth and J. L. Martens. Amsterdam: Benjamins, 93–122.

Aqvist, Lennart. 1965. *A New Approach to the Logical Theory of Interrogatives*. Uppsala: Filosofiska Studier.

Aristotle. 1958. *Topica et Sophistici Elenchi*, trans. W. A. Pickard-Cambridge, ed. W. D. Ross. New York: Oxford University Press.

Bailey, F. G. 1983. *The Tactical Uses of Passion*. Ithaca, N.Y.: Cornell University Press.

Barth, E. M., and E. C. W. Krabbe. 1982. *From Axiom to Dialogue; A Philosophical Study of Logics and Argumentation*. Berlin: de Gruyter.

Barth, E. M., and J. L. Martens. 1977. '*Argumentum ad Hominem*: From Chaos to Formal Dialectic.' *Logique et Analyse* 77–8: 76–96.

Bateson, L. 'The Message "This is Play."' 1956. In *Group Processes: Transactions, of the Second Conference*, ed. B. Schaffner (New York: Josiah Macy Jr. Foundation), 145–242.

Begley, Sharon. 1985. 'Science Contra Darwin.' *Newsweek*, April 8, pp. 80–81.

Belnap, Nuel D., and Thomas B. Steel, Jr. 1976. *The Logic of Questions and Answers*. New Haven, Conn.: Yale University Press.

Bentham, Jeremy. 1962. *The Book of Fallacies*, vol. 2 of *The Works of Jeremy Bentham*, ed. John Bowring. New York: Russell & Russell (originally published in 1838).

Best, Joel. 2001. *Damned Lies and Statistics: Untangling Numbers from the Media, Politicians and Activists*. Berkeley: University of California Press.

Bickel, Peter J., Eugene A. Hammel, and William J. O'Connell. 1977. 'Sex Bias in Graduate Admissions: Data from Berkeley.' In *Statistics and Public Policy*, ed. William B. Fairley and Frederick Mosteller (Reading, Mass.: Addison-Wesley). First printed in *Science* 187 (1975: 398–404).

Bowler, Peter. 1984. *Evolution: The History of an Idea*. Berkeley and Los Angeles: University of California Press.

Brinton, Alan. 1985. 'A Rhetorical View of the Ad Hominem.' *Australasian Journal of Philosophy* 63: 50–63.

Campbell, Stephen K. 1974. *Flaws and Fallacies in Statistical Thinking*. Englewood Cliffs, N.J.: Prentice Hall.

Cederblom, Jerry, and David W. Paulsen. 1982. *Critical Reasoning*. Belmont, Calif.: Wadsworth.

Clements, Colleen D., and Richard Ciccone. 1984. 'Ethics and Expert Witnesses.' *Bulletin of the American Academy of Psychiatry and Law* 12: 127–36.

Cohen, David. 1973. *The Crucial 10% That Really Counts for Trial Victories*. Englewood Cliffs, N.J.: Executive Reports.

Copi, Irving M. 1982. *Introduction to Logic*, 6th ed. New York: Macmillan.

Crossen, Cynthia. 1994. *Tainted Truth: The Manipulation of Fact in America*. New York: Simon & Schuster.

Croxton, Frederick E., and Dudley J. Cowden. 1955. *Applied General Statistics*, 2nd ed. Englewood Cliffs, N.J.: Prentice Hall.

Cushing, S. 1994. *Fatal Words: Communication Clashes and Aircraft Crashes*. Chicago: University of Chicago Press.

Damer, T. Edward. 1980. *Attacking Faulty Reasoning*. Belmont, Calif.: Wadsworth.

de Kruif, Paul. 1932. *Men against Death*. New York: Harcourt Brace.

DeMorgan, Augustus. 1847. *Formal Logic*. London: Taylor and Walton.

Dunne, Paul E., and Trevor J. M. Bench-Capon, eds. 2006. *Computational Models of Argument: Proceedings of COMMA 2006*. Amsterdam: IOS Press.

Epstein, Richard L. 1979. 'Relatedness and Implication.' *Philosophical Studies* 36: 137–173.

Fischer, David Hackett. 1970. *Historians' Fallacies*. New York: Harper & Row.

Fisher, Alan C., and Wendy North. 1986. 'Cancer Survival Rates: What the Media Haven't Told You.' *American Council on Science and Health News & Views* 7: 1–7.

Freedman, David, Robert, Pisani, and Roger Purves. 1978. *Statistics*. New York: Norton.

Freeman, James B. 1988. *Thinking Logically*. Englewood Cliffs, N.J.: Prentice Hall.

Froman, Lewis A., Jr. 1967. *The Congressional Process*. Boston: Little, Brown.

Gevarter, William B. 1983. *An Overview of Artificial Intelligence and Robotics*, NASA Technical Memorandum 855838. Houston: NASA Headquarters, Scientific and Technical Information Branch.

Giere, Ronald N. 1979. *Understanding Scientific Reasoning*. New York: Holt, Rinehart & Winston.

Godden, David M., and Douglas Walton. 2006. 'Argument from Expert Opinion as Legal Evidence: Critical Questions and Admissibility Criteria of Expert Testimony in the American Legal System.' *Ratio Juris* 19: 261–286.

Govier, Trudy. 1983. 'Ad Hominem: Revising the Textbooks.' *Teaching Philosophy* 6: 13–24.

Govier, Trudy. 1985. *A Practical Study of Argument*. Belmont, Calif.: Wadsworth.

Govier, Trudy. 1987. *Problems in Argument Analysis and Evaluation*. Dordrecht: Foris.

Graham, Michael H. 1977. 'Impeaching the Professional Expert Witness by a Showing of Financial Interest.' *Indiana Law Journal* 53: 35–53.

Grice, H. Paul. 1975. 'Logic and Conversation.' In *The Logic of Grammar*, ed. Donald Davidson and Gilbert Harman (Encino, Calif.: Dickenson), 64–75.

Hamblin, C. L. 1970. *Fallacies*. London: Methuen.

Harrah, David. 1984. 'The Logic of Questions.' In *Handbook of Philosophical Logic*, vol. 2, ed. D. Gabbay and F. Guenther (Dordrecht: Reidel), 715–764.

Hinman, Lawrence M. 1982. 'The Case for *Ad Hominem* Arguments.' *Australasian Journal of Philosophy* 60: 338–345.

Hintikka, Jaakko. 1976. *The Semantics of Questions and the Questions of Semantics*, Acta Philosophica Fennica, vol. 28. Amsterdam: North-Holland.

Hintikka, Jaakko. 1981. 'The Logic of Information-Seeking Dialogues: A Model.' In *Konzepte der Dialektik*, ed. Werner Becker and Wilhelm K. Essler (Frankfurt am Main: Klostermann), 212–231.

Hintikka, Jaakko. 1988. 'What is the Logic of Experimental Inquiry?' *Synthese* 74: 173–190.

Hooke, Robert. 1983. *How to Tell the Liars from the Statisticians*. New York: Dekker.

Horty, John. 2001. 'Nonmonotonic Logic.' In *The Blackwell Guide to Philosophical Logic*, ed. L. Goble (Oxford: Blackwell), 336–361.

Huff, Darrel. 1954. *How to Lie with Statistics*. New York: Norton.

Hurley, Patrick J. 2003. *A Concise Introduction to Logic*. Belmont, Calif.: Wadsworth.

Imwinkelried, Edward J. 1981. *Scientific and Expert Evidence*. New York: Practicing Law Institute.

Imwinkelried, Edward J. 1986. 'Science Takes the Stand: The Growing Misuse of Expert Testimony.' *The Sciences* 26: 20–25.

Jeffrey, C. 1982. *An Introduction to Plant Taxonomy*, 2nd ed. New York: Cambridge University Press.

Johnson, Ralph H., and J. Anthony Blair. 1983. *Logical Self-Defense*. Toronto: McGraw-Hill Ryerson.

Johnstone, Henry W., Jr. 1978. *Validity and Rhetoric in Philosophical Argument*. University Park, Pa.: Dialogue Press of Man and World.

Jones, Andrew, J. I. 1983. *Communication and Meaning*. Dordrecht: Reidel.

Kesterton, Michael. 1995. 'Social Studies.' *The Globe and Mail* June 8, p. A24.

Kielkopf, Charles. 1980. 'Relevant Appeals to Force, Pity and Popular Pieties.' *Informal Logic Newsletter* 2: 2–5.

King, John L. 1979. 'Bivalence and the Law of Excluded Middle.' *American Philosophical Quarterly* 16: 17–25.

Kozinski, Alex. 2001. 'How I Narrowly Escaped Insanity.' *U.C.L.A. Law Review* 48: 1293–1304.

Krabbe, Erik C. W. 1985. 'Formal Systems of Dialogue Rules.' *Synthese* 63: 295–328.

Levinson, Stephen C. 1983. *Pragmatics*. Cambridge: Cambridge University Press.

Locke, John. 1961. *An Essay Concerning Human Understanding*, ed. John W. Yolton, 2 vols. London: Dent (originally published in 1690).

Lorenzen, Paul. 1969. *Normative Logic and Ethics*. Mannheim: Hochschultaschenbücher.

Mackie, J. L. 1967. 'Fallacies.' In *The Encyclopedia of Philosophy*, vol. 3, ed. Paul Edwards. New York: Macmillan, 169–179.

Mann, William C. 1988. 'Dialogue Games: Conventions of Human Interaction.' *Argumentation* 2: 511–532.

Manor, Ruth. 1979. 'A Language for Questions and Answers.' *Theoretical Linguistics*, 6: 1–21.

Manor, Ruth. 1981. 'Dialogues and the Logics of Questions and Answers.' *Linguistische Berichte* 73: 1–28.

Marlin, Randal. 2002. *Propaganda and the Ethics of Persuasion*. Peterborough, Ontario: Broadview Press.

Milgram, Stanley. 1974. *Obedience to Authority: An Experimental View*. New York: Harper & Row.

Moore, Christopher W. 1986. *The Mediation Process*. San Francisco: Jossey-Bass.

Moore, David S. 1979. *Statistics: Concepts and Controversies*. San Francisco: Freeman.

Moore, David W. 1992. *The Superpollsters*. New York: Four Walls Eight Windows.

Newton-Smith, W. H. 1985. *Logic: An Introductory Course*. London: Routledge & Kegan Paul.

Nicoloff, Franck. 1989. 'Threats and Illocutions.' *Journal of Pragmatics* 13: 501–522.

Payne, Stanley L. 1951. *The Art of Asking Questions*. Princeton, N.J.: Princeton University Press.

Prakken, Henry. 2006. 'Formal Systems for Persuasion Dialogue.' *The Knowledge Engineering Review* 21: 163–188.

Reed, Chris, and Glenn Rowe. 2002. 'Araucaria: Software for Puzzles in Argument Diagramming and XML.' *Technical Report*, Department of Applied Computing, University of Dundee. Http://www.computing.dundee.ac.uk/staff/creed/araucaria.

Reed, Chris, and Glenn Rowe. 2006. *Araucaria, Version 3_1, User Manual*. Http://www.computing.dundee.ac.uk/staff/creed/araucaria.

Reiter, Raymond. 1987. 'Nonmonotonic Reasoning.' *Annual Review of Computer Science* 2: 147–186.

Rescher, Nicholas. 1964. *Introduction to Logic*. New York: St. Martin's Press.

Rescher, Nicholas. 1976. *Plausible Reasoning*. Assen: Van Gorcum.

Rescher, Nicholas. 1977. *Dialectics*. Albany: State University of New York Press.

Sanders, Robert S. 1987. *Cognitive Foundations of Calculated Speech*. Albany: State University of New York Press.

Schuman, Howard, and Stanley Presser. 1981. *Questions and Answers in Attitude Surveys*. New York: Academic Press.

Seligman, Daniel. 1961. 'We're Drowning in Phony Statistics.' *Fortune*, November, 146–171.

Sell, Peter S. 1985. *Expert Systems: A Practical Introduction*. London: Macmillan Press.

Shepherd, Robert Gordon, and Erich Goode. 1977. 'Scientists in the Popular Press.' *New Scientist* 76: 482–484.

Simon, H. A. 1954. 'Spurious Correlation: A Causal Interpretation.' *Journal of the American Statistical Association* 49: 467–492.

Sperber, Dan, and Deirdre Wilson. 1986. *Relevance*. Cambridge, Mass.: Harvard University Press.

Stebbing, L. Susan. 1939. *Thinking to Some Purpose*. Harmondsworth: Penguin.

Tindale, Christopher W. 2007. *Fallacies and Argument Appraisal*. Cambridge: Cambridge University Press.

Todd, D. D. 1987. 'Begging the Question.' *Globe and Mail* (Letters to the Editor), February 24, p. 6.

Trankell, Arne. 1972. *Reliability of Evidence*. Stockholm: Beckmans.

van der Meij, Hans. 1986. *Questioning*. The Hague: Selecta Reeks.

van Eemeren, Frans H. 1986. 'Dialectical Analysis as a Normative Reconstruction of Argumentative Discourse.' *Text* 6: 1–16.

van Eemeren, Frans H., and Rob Grootendorst. 1984. *Speech Acts in Argumentative Discussions*. Dordrecht: Foris.

van Eemeren, Frans H., Rob Grootendorst, and Tjark Kruiger. 1987. *Handbook of Argumentation Theory*. Dordrecht: Foris.

van Eemeren, Frans H., Rob Grootendorst, J. Anthony Blair, and Charles A. Willard. eds. 1987. *Argumentation: Across the Lines of Discipline*. Dordrecht: Foris.

van Eemeren, Frans H., and Peter Houtlosser. 2002. 'Strategic Maneuvering with the Burden of Proof.' In *Advances in Pragma-Dialectics*, ed. Frans H. van Eemeren (Amsterdam: Sic Sat), 13–28.

van Eemeren, Frans H., and Peter Houtlosser. 2006. 'Strategic Maneuvering: a Synthetic Recapitulation.' *Argumentation* 20: 381–392.

Verheij, Bart. 2003. 'Dialectical Argumentation with Argumentation Schemes.' *Artificial Intelligence and Law* 11: 167–195.

Walton, Douglas. 1980. 'Why Is the Ad Populum a Fallacy?' *Philosophy and Rhetoric* 13: 264–278.

Walton, Douglas. 1981. 'The Fallacy of Many Questions.' *Logique et Analyse* 95–96: 291–313.

Walton, Douglas. 1982. *Topical Relevance in Argumentation*. Amsterdam: Benjamins.

Walton, Douglas. 1984. *Logical Dialogue-Games and Fallacies*. Lanham, Md.: University Press of America.

Walton, Douglas. 1985a. *Arguer's Position: A Pragmatic Study of Ad Hominem Attack, Criticism, Refutation, and Fallacy*. Westport, Conn.: Greenwood.

Walton, Douglas. 1985b. 'New Directions in the Logic of Dialogue.' *Synthese* 63: 259–274.

Walton, Douglas. 1987. *Informal Fallacies*. Philadelphia: Benjamins.

Walton, Douglas. 1988. 'Burden of Proof.' *Argumentation* 2: 81–102.

Walton, Douglas. 1996. *Argumentation Schemes for Presumptive Reasoning*. Mahwah, N.J.: Erlbaum.

Walton, Douglas. 1997. *Appeal to Expert Opinion*. University Park, Pa.: Penn State University Press.

Walton, Douglas. 1998a. *Ad Hominem Arguments*. Tuscaloosa: University of Alabama Press.

Walton, Douglas. 1998b. *The New Dialectic: Conversational Contexts of Argument*. Toronto: University of Toronto Press.

Walton, Douglas. 2000. *Scare Tactics: Arguments that Appeal to Fear and Threats*. Dordrecht: Kluwer.

Walton, Douglas. 2004. 'Classification of Fallacies of Relevance.' *Informal Logic* 24: 71–103.

Walton, Douglas. 2005. *Argumentation Methods for Artificial Intelligence in Law* (Lecture Notes in Artificial Intelligence Series). Berlin: Springer.

Walton, Douglas. 2006. *Fundamentals of Critical Argumentation*. New York: Cambridge University Press.

Walton, Douglas, and Erik C. W. Krabbe. 1995. *Commitment in Dialogue*. Albany: State University of New York Press.

Walton, Douglas, and Chris Reed. 2005. 'Argumentation Schemes and Enthymemes.' *Synthese* 145: 339–370.

Weber, O. J. 1981. 'Attacking the Expert Witness.' *Federation of Insurance Counsel Quarterly* 31: 299–313.

Whately, Richard. 1826. *Elements of Logic*, 9th ed. London: Longmans Green.

Whately, Richard. 1836. *Elements of Logic*. New York: Jackson.

Whately, Richard. 1846. *Elements of Rhetoric*, 7th ed. Douglas Ehninger. Rpt. Carbondale: Southern Illinois University Press.

Wheeler, Michael. 1990. 'How to Read the Polls.' In *The Classics of Polling*, ed. Michael L. Young (Methuchen, N.J.: Scarecrow Press), 191–209.

Wilson, Patrick. 1983. *Second-Hand Knowledge: An Inquiry into Cognitive Authority*. Westport, Conn.: Greenwood.

Woods, John, and Douglas Walton. 1974. '*Argumentum Ad Verecundiam*.' *Philosophy and Rhetoric* 7: 135–153.

Woods, John, and Douglas Walton. 1976. 'Ad Baculum.' *Grazer Philosophische Studien* 2: 133–140.

Woods, John, and Douglas Walton. 1977. 'Post Hoc, Ergo Propter Hoc.' *Review of Metaphysics* 30: 569–593.

Woods, John, and Douglas Walton. 1978. 'The Fallacy of *Ad Ignorantiam*.' *Dialectica* 32: 87–99.

Woods, John, and Douglas Walton. 1979. 'Equivocation and Practical Logic.' *Ratio* 21: 31–43.

Wright, Richard A., and Ken Tohinaka. 1984. *Logical Thinking*. Englewood Cliffs, N.J.: Prentice Hall.

Younger, Irving. 1982. 'A Practical Approach to the Use of Expert Testimony.' *Cleveland State Law Review* 31: 1–42.

Zeide, Janet S., and Jay Leibowitz. 1987. 'Using Expert Systems: The Legal Perspective.' *IEEE Expert* 2(Spring): 19–21.

Zeisel, Hans. 1968. *Say It with Figures*, 5th ed. New York: Harper & Row.

Index

D'Sousa, Dinesh, 30
Dynagrip example (2.14), 52

educational dialogue, 8
egg will break example (5.18), 151
Einstein example (7.3), 223
either A or B example (5.15), 151
elephant animal example (9.8), 302
emotional appeal, 107
emotions, 19; pity, 133
enthymeme, 143
equivocal argument, 301
error of meaningless statistics, 247,
    285, 286
error of unknowable statistics, 248–50
Ethiopia crisis example (4.13), 130–1
evasiveness, 50
evidence: Daubert factors, 230;
    empirical, 214; external, 191;
    Federal Rules of Evidence, 230,
    702; *Frye v. United States*, 229; hard,
    192; internal, 191; putative, 61;
    rules of, 228; scientific, 284
existence of God example (1.1), (1.2),
    (2.21), (2.26), 11–12, 57, 64–5
expert: commitments of, 240; critical
    questions about, 238; medical, 238
expert consultation dialogue, 216
expert systems, 214
extra-sensory perception example
    (2.24), 61

fair hiring practices example (2.9), 46
fallacy, 244. *See also specific fallacies*
fallacy of arguing in a circle, 65
fallacy of arguing from consequences,
    27
fallacy of arguing from ignorance, 56
fallacy of the *argumentum ad
    ignorantiam*, 21
fallacy of begging the question, 296
fallacy of composition, 22, 157, 158
fallacy of equivocation, 21, 256,
    300–301, 321–2, 324
fallacy of hasty generalization, 163
fallacy of *ignoratio elenchi*, 79, 128, 129
fallacy of irrelevance, 18

fallacy of irrelevant conclusion, 101
fallacy of language, 329
fallacy of many (complex) questions,
    18, 40
fallacy of oversimplification, 267
fallacy of popularity, 133
fallacy of question-begging epithet,
    296, 324
fallacy of relevance, 19, 93–4
fallacy of unreasonable dichotomy, 259
fallacy of wrong conclusion, 92, 94,
    97, 102
feedback, 265
Fermat's last theorem, 56–7, 58
Fischer, David Hackett, 263, 270
foreign spy example (2.22), 57–8,
    161–2
forensic debate, 3–4
fourteen-year-old-son example (1.0),
    2
fear appeal argument, 119–20,
    120–21 (argumentation scheme)
Freeman, James B., 23
Froman, Lewis A., Jr., 53
Frum example (3.4), 87–9

game of dialogue, 187
gender-prejudice example (9.2),
    294–5, 331
generalization: common, 285;
    defeasible, 161; hasty, 246;
    inductive, 159–60, 246–7, 310;
    presumptive, 159; statistical, 251;
    universal, 159, 164; worthless,
    254
George's position example (6.10),
    190–2
ghosts example (2.20), 56–7
Goode, Erich, 234
Gore's internet example (1.10), 23–4
government health care example
    (2.15), 52
graduation example (5.5), 141
Grunberger example (4.5), 117–19

Hamblin, C. L., 13, 129
Hammel, Eugene A., 267

342

married for life example (9.24), (9.25), 325–9
married person's candy (8.9), 266
Martens, J. L., 180n9
measles/chicken pox example (5.11), 147
medical expert example (7.12), 238–9
metal flagpole example (7.2), 213
Mexican War example (1.14), 27–31, 35
Milan and Venice example (5.6), 143–4
Milgram experiments, 210
misdirected argumentation, 94
mock elections example (9.14), 307
modus ponens (MP), 138, 146, 148, 153, 318
modus tollens (MT), 146
Moore, Christopher W., 91, 256, 257
murder is a horrible crime example (3.1), 84, 92, 95–6, 98

natural language, 323–4; aggressive, 289; ambiguity, 20, 124, 211, 228, 290, 291; cause and effect, 247; collective terms, 156; conjunction, 153; connectives, 166; contentious terms, 289; controversial terms, 293; defining terms, 251, 257, 291–4, 297–8, 324, 331–2; disjunction, 148; distributive terms, 156; equivocation, 324, 329; indicator words, 12, 137, 139, 141, 167; loaded question, 331; loaded terms, 294, 300; meanings of terms, 256, 321; miscommunication, 290; negation, 153; negative connotations, 67; one-sided use of, 289; question-begging language, 300, 324, 332; question wording effect, 67; specialized terms, 237; strength of terms, 58; terminological disputes, 324–5; vagueness, 20, 228, 251, 285, 289, 291, 319, 325, 326
Navasky, Victor, 19
Nayirah example (4.14), 132

negation, 92, 153
negotiation dialogue, 6, 128, 187
new shoes example (9.16), 310
Newman, Cardinal, 189
night light example (8.14), 273
Nixon example (6.1), 172–3, 202
North, Wendy, 270

O'Connell, William J., 267

pacifism example (2.12), (2.19), 51, 54–5
Parliamentarian example (6.12), 195–8
participant: goal of, 7; obligation of, 9, 12; preconceptions of, 91
patient's reaction example (5.22), 154
Payne, Stanley L., 69
pediatric depression example (8.6), 262–3
peer pressure, 114
pernicious anemia example (8.16), 279
personal attack, 19, 106, 170, 188; circumstantial, 193; direct, 193, 202; excessive, 171; on impartiality, 193
persuasion dialogue: described, 4; faults in, 66; goal of, 4–5, 6, 64, 127, 216; negative rules of, 15, 16–18, 35, 106, 107, 109, 117, 125–6, 175, 244, 331; positive rules of, 15; stages of, 16, 17, 20, 35; symmetrical, 11–12. *See also* critical discussion;
petitio principii, 295
pizza advertisement example (9.11), 303–4
pizza outlet threat example (4.9), 125
plaintiff's husband's death example (9.12), 304–5
Plato/Aristotle example (5.7), 144
plausible argument: function of, 15; nonmonotonic, 159; weak, 14, 58
players on the team example (5.29), 157
poisoning the well, or bias-imputing, 171, 187, 189, 199, 202
politics, 173–4

344